ARABIC THOUGHT IN THE LIBERAL AGE
1798-1939

ALBERT HOURANI

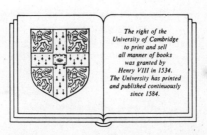

*The right of the
University of Cambridge
to print and sell
all manner of books
was granted by
Henry VIII in 1534.
The University has printed
and published continuously
since 1584.*

CAMBRIDGE UNIVERSITY PRESS

CAMBRIDGE

NEW YORK   PORT CHESTER

MELBOURNE   SYDNEY

TO THE PRESIDENT AND SCHOLARS
OF THE COLLEGE OF ST MARY MAGDALEN
IN THE UNIVERSITY OF OXFORD

Published by the Press Syndicate of the University of Cambridge
The Pitt Building, Trumpington Street, Cambridge CB2 1RP
40 West 20th Street, New York, NY 10011, USA
10 Stamford Road, Oakleigh, Melbourne 3166, Australia

First published by Oxford University Press 1962
Reissued, with a new preface, by Cambridge University Press 1983
Reprinted 1984, 1986, 1987, 1988, 1989

Printed in Great Britain at the
University Press, Cambridge

Library of Congress catalogue card number: 83-1788

British Library Cataloguing in Publication Data
Hourani, Albert
Arabic thought in the liberal age, 1798–1939.
1. Arab countries—Intellectual life
I. Title
181′.9 DS36.88

ISBN 0 521 25837 5 hard covers
ISBN 0 521 27423 0 paperback

CONTENTS

PREFACE TO THE 1983 REISSUE

MY purpose in writing this book was not to give a general history of all kinds of thought expressed by Arabs, or in the Arabic language, during the nineteenth and earlier twentieth centuries. I was concerned with thought about politics and society within a certain context: that created by the growth of European influence and power in the Middle East and North Africa. In the course of the period which the book covers, the Arabic-speaking peoples were drawn, in different ways, into the new world-order which sprang from the technical and industrial revolutions. It was an order which expressed itself in the growth of European trade of a new kind, the consequent changes in production and consumption, the spread of European diplomatic influence, the imposition in some places of European control or rule, the creation of schools on a new model, and the spread of new ideas about how men and women should live in society. It is to such ideas that I refer rather loosely when I use the word 'liberal' in the title; this was not the first title I chose for the book, and I am not quite satisfied with it, for the ideas which had influence were not only ideas about democratic institutions or individual rights, but also about national strength and unity and the power of governments.

As the century went on, it became more and more difficult to ignore the processes of change and not to react to them in some way. More than one kind of reaction was possible, and my book deals with only one of them: that of those who saw the growth of European power and the spread of new ideas as a challenge to which they had to respond by changing their own societies, and the systems of beliefs and values which gave them legitimacy, in a certain direction, through acceptance of some of the ideas and institutions of modern Europe. This of course raised problems of different kinds. What should they accept? If they accepted it, could they also remain true to their inherited beliefs and values? In what sense, if any, would they still remain Muslims and Arabs? A debate which began on the level of political institutions or laws might in the end raise questions about how men and women identified themselves and what they could believe about human life.

Such questions were first raised, and the debates about them were carried on most continuously and at the highest level of knowledge of the new world of Europe, in two places, Cairo and Beirut, and my main concern was therefore with what was thought, written and published there. It seemed to me all the more appropriate to give most attention to these two places because they were closely linked with each other, in various ways, and in particular through the migration of Lebanese and Syrian writers to Egypt, and also because in both places there were not just one or two scattered writers, but groups interacting with each other and with those who came before and after them, so that it was possible to trace continuities of thought. There was yet another reason why the links between Cairo and Beirut were important. Most of the prominent writers in Beirut belonged to the Christian communities of Lebanon and Syria, who played a part in the assimilation of European thought which was disproportionate to their numbers. As Christians they reacted to western culture in ways rather different from those of Muslim thinkers, and the interaction between the two groups helps to illustrate some of the problems facing those who tried to come to terms with the power and thought of the west.

To write a history of thought demands certain choices. It is possible to deal in a general way with 'schools' of thought, but to do so may blur the differences between individual thinkers, and impose a false unity upon their work. The other way is to lay the main emphasis on a number of individuals, chosen because they are broadly representative of certain tendencies or generations, and to explain as fully as possible the influences, the circumstances, and the traits of personality which may have led them to think about certain matters in a certain way. This method also has its dangers. Most of the writers I have discussed in the book scattered their writings in articles for newspapers and periodicals, written for a particular purpose; some wrote over a long period, during which circumstances changed and they too may have changed. There is a risk therefore of imposing an artificial unity on their thought, of making it seem more systematic and consistent than in fact it was, and also of giving the impression that they were more important and original than they really were; most of them (although not quite all) were derivative thinkers of the second or third rank of importance.

For all its dangers, I chose the second method, because it made it possible for me to do what most interested me at the time. First, I wanted to catch, by close attention to what they wrote, echoes of the European thinkers whose books they had read or heard about, and so to discover, if I could, the point at which certain ideas entered into intellectual discourse in Arabic. Secondly, I wished to try to relate different thinkers with each other, and to construct a chronological framework within which they could be placed. Scattered work, some of high quality, had been done on certain persons or movements: on 'Islamic modernism' and Arab nationalism in particular. My book, however, represents one of the first attempts to see how they were related to each other.

The book tries therefore to trace the line of descent of four generations of writers. The first phase, which stretches roughly from 1830 to 1870, is that in which a small group of officials and writers became aware of the new Europe of industry, swift communications, and political institutions, not as a menace so much as offering a path to be followed. What they wrote was linked with the attempts being made by the governments in Istanbul, Cairo and Tunis to adopt some of the laws and institutions of modern Europe in order to increase their strength; and they wrote primarily for readers still living within an older world of thought, in order to convince them that they could adopt institutions and laws from outside without being untrue to themselves.

The second generation, stretching roughly from 1870 to 1900, faced a situation which had changed in some important ways. Europe had become the adversary as well as the model: its armies were present in Egypt, Algeria and Tunisia, and its political influence was growing throughout the Ottoman Empire; its schools were forming students whose processes of thought and view of the world were far from those of their parents; the cities were being re-made on a European model, and the familiar signs of urban life were being replaced by others. In such circumstances, change had become unavoidable, and the writers considered were not trying to persuade those rooted in their own traditions that they must accept change, but to convince those formed in a new mould that they could still hold on to something from their own past. The main task of thinkers in this generation was to reinterpret Islam so as to make it compatible with living in the modern world, and even a source of strength in it. The representative figure of this phase was Muhammad 'Abduh. His work was carried on by the periodical *al-Manar*, and this is significant, for it was during this period that newspapers and periodicals became important.

In the third period, stretching roughly from 1900 to 1939, the two strands of thought which 'Abduh and others had tried to hold together moved further apart from each other. On the one hand were those who stood fast on the Islamic bases of society, and in doing so moved closer to a kind of Muslim fundamentalism. On the other were those who continued to accept Islam as a body of principles or at the very least of sentiments, but held that life in society should be regulated by secular norms, of individual welfare or collective strength. This was a line of thought already indicated by some Lebanese Christians in the previous generation, but now carried further by some Egyptian Muslim writers, and it reached its logical end in the work of Taha Husayn, conscious as he was of the need to preserve the Islamic past in the imagination and heart, but to become part of the modern culture which had first shown itself in western Europe. For most of the writers of this generation, the secular principle for the remaking of society was that of nationalism, whether defined in Ottoman, Egyptian or Arab terms. With the growth of new classes of educated officials and officers, the emergence of students as a political force, and the imposition of foreign rule on more Arab countries, nationalism became a motive to action as well as a principle of thought.

A fourth phase opens with the Second World War, and in the Epilogue I tried to define some of its features. The War ended the period of European ascendancy and opened the way to that of the United States and Russia, expressing itself not in direct political control but in a final military and economic power. The unrest generated by war, the spread of education, the growth of cities and industry, and the use of the new mass media brought about a change in the scale of political life: there was a broader field of political action, and a larger public for ideas and rhetoric. I tried to indicate some of the new ways of thought and action, although when I wrote the Epilogue they could not be seen so clearly as now: the movement for a revival of Islam as the only valid basis for society, exemplified by the Muslim Brothers; the movement by which nationalism began to acquire a content of social reform, expressed often in the language of socialism; and the broadening of the idea of Arab nationalism, to include all Arabic-speaking countries. It was to make this last point that I included a brief treatment of the movement of ideas in North Africa; but the centre of gravity still lay further east, and 'Abd al-Nasir can be taken as the representative figure of this period.

2

A book can tell us something not only about its explicit subject but about the time when it was written. Reading this work for the first time after twenty years, I can see clearly that it reflects a certain way in which I and perhaps others looked at Middle Eastern history during the 1950's and 1960's. The underlying assumption of the book is that a small group of writers, who were set apart from those among whom they were living by education and experience, nevertheless could express the needs of their society, and to some extent at least their ideas served as forces in the process of change. Without making such an assumption, it would scarcely have been worthwhile to write at such lengths about thinkers some of whose ideas had a certain intrinsic interest, but none of whom were of the highest calibre.

I do not think this was a false assumption, and if I were to write a book on the same subject today I think I should write about these thinkers, and perhaps a few others, in much the same way. I would try to give it another dimension, however, by asking how and why the ideas of my writers had an influence on the minds of others. To answer such questions would involve a fuller and more precise study of changes in the structure of society from one generation to another, with careful distinctions between what was happening in different Arab countries, and also some attempt to study the process of communication, both direct and indirect. The ideas I was concerned with did not spread only through the writings of those whose work I studied, but were mediated to a larger public in writings of another kind, and above all in poetry.

I am aware that there might be a completely different way of looking at these writers, by regarding their ideas not as expressing what they really believed, but as half-revealing, half-hiding their pursuit of their own interests. Such a view has been expressed with force and elegance by Elie Kedourie. Writing of Afghani and 'Abduh, he describes them as men 'involved in complicated and obscure transactions' and asks whether it would not be better to 'assume that what is done has no necessary connection with what is said, and that what is said in public, may be quite different from what is believed in private'.[1]

I am not convinced by this argument. About Afghani there is indeed a mystery, and I am not sure I have unravelled it, although I still think Professor Kedourie is wrong to describe his attitude as one of 'religious unbelief', and Professor Keddie is right in trying to place him somewhere within the wide spectrum of Shi'i thought.[2] About later thinkers, from 'Abduh onwards, there seems to me to be nothing mysterious. They were writing for the most part within a Sunni tradition where writers said what they believed, in however cautious a way; and the range of what could be published, certainly in Egypt and even in late Ottoman Syria, was fairly wide. Even if they were insincere, there was a certain consistency in what they said, and it is therefore possible to articulate the logical structure of their thought, and it is useful, because if they did have a certain influence on the readers of their own or later generations, it was not because of their 'obscure transactions' but because of their ideas. I agree on this with Hamid Enayat: 'ideas seem to have a life of their own: people, especially those of generations subsequent to the authors', often tend to perceive ideas with little or no regard for the authors' insidious designs, unless they are endowed with a capacity for mordant cynicism'.[3]

What really troubles me is not this, but the thought that perhaps I should have written a book of a different kind. When I wrote it I was mainly concerned to note the breaks with the past: new ways of thought, new words or old ones used in a new way. To some extent I may have distorted the thought of the writers I studied, at least those of the first

---

[1] E. Kedourie, *Afghani and 'Abduh: an essay on religious unbelief and political activism in modern Islam* (London, 1966), p. 2.
[2] N. R. Keddie, *Sayyid Jamal ad-Din 'al-Afghani': a political biography* (Berkeley, 1972).
[3] H. Enayat, *Modern Islamic Political Thought* (London, 1982), p. ix.

and second generations: the 'modern' element in their thought may have been smaller than I implied, and it would have been possible to write about them in a way which emphasized continuity rather than a break with the past. A book by Christian Troll on Sayyid Ahmad Khan[4] seems to me to provide the kind of analysis which I now think to be necessary; it shows the 'traditional' bases of his thought and indicates the points where he departs from them in the direction of something new.

There are also books to be written about thinkers of quite a different kind: those who still lived in their inherited world of thought, whose main aim was to preserve the continuity of its tradition, and who did so in accustomed ways, writing and teaching within the framework of the great schools, the Azhar in Cairo or the Zaytuna in Tunis, or of the Sufi brotherhoods. To quote again from Hamid Enayat's book: a special interest attaches to those whose ideas 'are articulated in the recognized terms and categories of Islamic jurisprudence, theology and related disciplines', since their 'credal, epistemological and methodological premises have ensured the continuity of Islamic thought'.[5] In many ways it was such writers and teachers who continued to be dominant throughout the nineteenth century, since most Arabs who acquired literacy and culture still did so within schools of a traditional kind and continued to be affiliated to one or other of the Sufi orders. In the present century they have lost much of their domination, or so it seemed at the point in time when I was writing my book: it is clearer now than it was then, at least to me, that the extension of the area of political consciousness and activity, the coming of 'mass politics', would bring into the political process men and women who were still liable to be swayed by what the Azhar said or wrote, and what the shaykhs of a brotherhood might teach.

3

This book was first published in 1962, reprinted in 1967 with a number of corrections, and reprinted once more in a paperback edition in 1970. For this reissue I have been able to make a limited number of small changes where I have found errors of fact or misprints, but I have not attempted to change the text in any major way. I have however been able to add a supplement to the bibliography, in which I do not try to carry the story beyond 1962, but give references to books and articles which have appeared for the most part since that date, and which throw light on the subjects of the book.

---

[4] C. W. Troll, *Sayyid Ahmad Khan: a reinterpretation of Muslim theology* (New Delhi, 1978).
[5] Enayat, ibid.

As before, I should like to express my deep gratitude to the institutions and persons who helped me. My greatest debt is to the President and Fellows of Magdalen College, Oxford, who elected me to a research fellowship and so made it possible for me to start the process of thought and study which led to this book. Part of the matter of it was given in the form of lectures, at the American University of Beirut in 1956–7, at the College of Arts and Sciences in Baghdad in 1957, at Oxford in 1958–9, at the Institut des Hautes Études of Tunis in 1959; I must thank those who arranged for me to give the lectures and the students who, by questions or silence, helped me to see what was clear in them and what was not. I am grateful for encouragement and kindness to Miss Margaret Cleeve, formerly Research Secretary at the Royal Institute of International Affairs, and her successor, Mr A. S. B. Olver; I much admired the courteous suspension of disbelief with which they greeted every assurance that the book was nearly finished and would soon be in their hands. I am grateful also to those friends who read and criticized it in whole or in part: Richard Walzer, Bernard Lewis, Charles Issawi, Walid Khalidi, Malcolm Kerr, Elie Kedourie and Sylvia Haim. I owe a special debt to Miss Ursula Gibson, who typed the manuscript, and Miss Hermia Oliver of the editorial staff of Chatham House, who brought to my typescript, as to so many others,

the sharp compassion of the healer's art.

January 1983   A.H.

NOTE ON TRANSLITERATION AND REFERENCES

W HEN an Arabic name or word has a form which is generally accepted in English I have normally used it. Other Arabic names and words I have tried to transcribe in a simple yet consistent way; but in the bibliography I have given a full transliteration of the titles of Arabic works and the names of their authors, using the system adopted in the second edition of the *Encyclopaedia of Islam*, with slight variations. I have spelt Turkish words and names, even those of Arabic origin, according to the official Turkish orthography. The names of members of the Egyptian royal house posed a special problem: although Turkish by culture, they ruled an Arabic-speaking country. I have decided to spell their names in the Arabic way. Names of Arab authors who have written in languages other than Arabic are normally spelt as they themselves have spelt them.

With a few exceptions, the footnotes refer to works listed in the bibliography. When only one work by an author is mentioned in the bibliography, footnotes normally give his name only; otherwise, they give a brief title as well. The bibliography includes fuller titles, and the dates and places of publication of the editions I have used. Works by Arab authors will be found in section 2 (p. 374) if published in Arabic; in section 3 (p. 382) if in other languages.

I

THE ISLAMIC STATE[1]

MORE conscious of their language than any people in the world, seeing it not only as the greatest of their arts but also as their common good, most Arabs, if asked to define what they meant by 'the Arab nation', would begin by saying that it included all those who spoke the Arabic language. But this would only be the first step, and it would carry them no more than one step farther to say it included all who claimed a link with the nomadic tribes of Arabia, whether by descent, by affiliation or by appropriation (through the medium of language and literature) of their ideal of human excellence and standards of beauty. A full definition would include also a reference to a historic process: to a certain episode in history in which the Arabs played a leading part, which was important not only for them but for the whole world, and in virtue of which indeed they could claim to have been *something* in human history.

The process opened with the preaching by Muhammad, an Arab of the tribe of Quraysh, of a message which he claimed to have been entrusted to him by God through the medium of the Archangel Gabriel, and which, to the minds of his followers, is so important as to have altered the nature of history. In his preaching Muhammad called on men to repent before it was too late and try to do what was pleasing to God, and defined also those beliefs and acts which God has commanded. Men, he taught, must believe that God is unique, that He has revealed His will through the medium of the prophets, that Muhammad is the last of the line of prophets, that the message revealed through Muhammad, the Quran, is the literal word of God, containing the expression of His will for man; they must act in accordance with the commands it contains, and the world will end with a Judgment at which their acts will be weighed and they will be held responsible for them. To the Prophet's

---

[1] This chapter has drawn largely on the works of L. Gardet, H. A. R. Gibb, M. Mahdi, E. I. J. Rosenthal, and R. Walzer listed in the bibliography.

followers it seemed clear that the revelation of which he was the instrument, since it was the last, must also be the most complete, and that the Quran, together with his own precepts and example, must contain explicitly or by implication all that was necessary to live rightly. In course of time the text of the Quran was fixed and the traditions (*hadith*) of what the Prophet did and said (*sunna*, the Prophet's practices) were collected and examined, and scholars devoted themselves indeed to distinguishing the true among them from the false. In course of time too there evolved from Quran and *hadith* a comprehensive system of ideal morality, a moral classification of human acts which would make clear the way (*shari'a*) by which men could walk pleasingly in the sight of God and hope to reach Paradise. When there was a clear text of the Quran or a *hadith* of which the validity could be accepted this was not difficult; otherwise, those who possessed the necessary intellect and training must deduce the answer from the texts, by using their minds in accordance with the rules of strict analogy or some other process of reasoning (*ijtihad*). Gradually the results of this process became generally accepted by the common opinion of the learned, and when this general acceptance (*ijma'*) existed it came to be regarded as conferring on precepts or laws an authority no less binding than that of Quran or *hadith*. But there still remained differences of opinion about how the *ijma'* could be known, what it validated in fact, and, beyond the bounds of the *ijma'*, about the ways in which human reason could be used and the results its use would lead to; and in course of time these differences were codified into a number of systems (*madhhab*), all of them equally legitimate for a believer to accept.

This system of ideal morality, in its various forms, created a new society as well as a new type of individual. The essential acts of Islamic devotion had each its social aspect. Muslims prayed together in the mosque on Fridays; their annual fast in the month of Ramadan had the aspect not only of an individual act of self-discipline but of a great corporate ceremony; clothed in the white of consecration, they went together on pilgrimage to Mecca at the appointed season; they paid their stipulated alms into the central treasury. The *Shari'a* covered men's relations with each other as well as with God, and these also therefore were acts of religious significance, commanded or forbidden. To refuse to pay the taxes laid down in the *Shari'a*, and deny the obligation to pay them, was no less apostasy than to deny the existence of God or the validity of the prophetic message.[2] The religion of Islam created not only a structure of rights and duties, but also a moral solidarity to support it; Muslims believed themselves obliged to keep their neighbours' consciences as well as their own, not only to do right but to exhort and help others to do so.

'Other prophets before me were sent only to their peoples, I have been sent to all humanity.' It is true, Islam was preached by Arabs first of all, and regarded by some at least of them as being a wholly Arab religion; but this *hadith*, whether authentic or not, expresses what Muslims in course of time came to believe about their religion. Each previous prophet had been sent in the first instance to warn and guide a limited community, an *umma*, and each *umma*, after accepting his message, had ignored or misunderstood it or even tampered with its text. Hence the need for further revelations. The last, that of Muhammad, differed from the earlier in two ways: it was a message for all mankind, and it contained within itself a guarantee of its truth and its correct transmission. 'My community will not agree on an error': so runs the *hadith*, and once more, whether it is valid or not, it expresses what Muslims have accepted. The Islamic revelation claimed to be eternally true, and to supersede all previous revelations; the Islamic *umma* therefore was potentially universal and superseded all others. Since it was universal it was also united, and its members were equal. All Muslims, whatever their culture or racial origin, and whether of ancient or recent conversion, were equally members of the *umma*, possessing the same rights and responsibilities. Moral unity existed even between those who held different beliefs about the truth of Islam. The *umma* soon split on questions of policy and doctrine: one secession was that of the Kharijites, who broke away because they refused to make any compromise with expediency; another was the great schism between Sunnis and Shi'is, in origin a political dispute about the succession to the Prophet, but which gradually acquired undertones of difference in doctrine, law, and custom; and from Shi'ism there sprang a number of sects—Isma'ilis, Nusayris, Druzes—who carried

[2] al-Mawardi, *al-Ahkam al-sultaniyya*, p. 54 (Fr. trs. p. 115).

certain Shi'i doctrines to extremes, and grafted on to them others of alien origin. Strictly orthodox Muslims tended to regard these last as lying beyond the bounds of tolerance, since their teaching was a threat to the essential beliefs of Islam; but between Sunnis and Shi'is—and between various divisions of each—there was a sense of community, based on the profound conviction of Muslims that to live together in unity was more important than to carry doctrinal disputes to their logical conclusion. So too with the Christian and Jewish communities which continued to live under Muslim rule, in Egypt, Syria, Iraq, and elsewhere: they were not of course regarded as part of the Muslim *umma*, but they were recognized as 'People of the Book', who believed in God, the prophets, and judgment, who possessed an authentic revelation and so belonged to the same spiritual family as the Muslims. As such, they were 'protected peoples', allowed life and property, the exercise of their religion and the preservation of their laws and customs, in return for loyalty and the payment of a special tax.

The *Shari'a* told men what right action was, but it also laid down precise worldly penalties for doing wrong. It was a system of laws as well as a system of morality. To uphold the *Shari'a* and impose the penalties, to watch over the performance of all duties commanded by God, to defend the *umma* against its enemies, to spread the bounds of the faith by holy war (*jihad*): all these involved a leader with authority, in other words political power. Thus the Islamic community could not be complete unless it was also a State, and political action was a way of serving God: 'it is a duty to consider the exercise of power as one of the forms of religion, as one of the acts by which man draws near God'.[3]

Thus, according to the belief of most Muslims, to found and lead a community was part of the essential function of the Prophet and of his legitimate successors. They did not all agree, however, about the succession to the Prophet. The Shi'is held that Muhammad's authority had passed first of all to his son-in-law 'Ali, then to a line of his descendants, the last of whom had disappeared; they differed among themselves about whether this was the fifth, seventh, or twelfth of the line. The members of this line, the imams, possessed, in Shi'i belief, not only political

[3] Ibn Taymiyya, *al-Siyasa*, p. 174 (Fr. trs. pp. 173–4).

authority but the power of infallible interpretation of the Quran.

The Sunnis, on the other hand, held that Muhammad's authority had passed to the caliphs, leaders designated and accepted by the community, but that the caliphs inherited a part only of the Prophet's functions and powers. True sovereignty in the *umma* rested with God, not only in the sense that He was the source of all authority but also in the sense that He wielded it. Rulers, like other men, were not independent agents but the channels through which God worked. For a Muslim ruler, as for all Muslims, to be good or bad was to submit to God's purposes or revolt against them. The *Shari'a*, the statement of God's will, was therefore supreme in society, and a whole sphere of political activity—that of legislation—was in principle removed from the competence of the ruler. The caliphs, in theory, possessed neither God's power of making laws nor the Prophet's function of proclaiming them. They inherited only the judicial and executive power. The caliph, it was generally believed, should lead the community in peace and war, collect the canonical taxes and supervise the application of the law. He was also the imam, the leader in prayer, and he should himself be learned in the law and competent to exercise the power of interpretation. It was only in this limited sense that he was successor of the Prophet (*khalifat al-rasul*), but even in this sense he was indispensable to the community, ruler by divine right, and ruler, in principle, over the whole community; for most, although not all, jurists held that the unity of the *umma* implied a unity of political authority. 'He who dies without having known the imam of his time is as one who died in the age of paganism.'

There was a consensus of Sunni opinion that the ruler of the *umma* possessed, under God, the sole responsibility for ruling. In the last resort he was responsible to God and his own conscience alone. It is true, while some caliphs were designated by their predecessors, others in the earliest age were chosen by a group of leaders in the community, and the idea of a choice was always preserved, and symbolized by the ceremony of *bay'a*, the formal acknowledgment of a new caliph and pledge of loyalty to him by the notables of the *umma*. But after the first age this was no more than a formality, and even in theory it was not, in the

full sense, a process of election. It was rather a recognition than a
choice; in the view of most thinkers, in the *bay'a* the community
acquiesced in authority, it did not confer it. By implication, the
first duty of the community towards the ruler was one of obedience. But obedience should be neither passive nor without
conditions. According to the theory generally held, the ruler
should consult the leaders of the community (*shura*) and they
should give him moral advice and exhortation (*nasiha*), although
there was no clear idea *who* exactly should be consulted and
should warn, and how far the ruler should be bound by what
they said. For thinkers of the earlier period, the duty of obedience only held so long as the caliph ordered nothing which was
contrary to the *Shari'a*. In later thought, as we shall see,
obedience tended to become an absolute duty, and even an unjust
ruler was regarded as better than none at all; only a minority
of later thinkers taught that revolt could be legitimate, but even
the majority, while teaching that obedience should be general,
did not assert that it should be given without reserve. Thus
al-Ghazali (1058–1111), after teaching the duty of obedience to
unjust princes, points out that one must not, through obedience,
condone their injustice. The devout Muslim should avoid the
court and company of the unjust ruler, and should rebuke him:
by words if he can safely do so, by silence if words might
encourage rebellion.[4]

In the Islamic view of the true society there was implicit a
series of interrelated contrasts. First and most fundamental,
while the world worshipped idols or joined their worship to that
of God (*shirk*), Muslims proclaimed and worshipped the one
God alone (*tawhid*). Secondly, and connected with this, came a
contrast in the ordering of society. The society which did not
know Islam was ruled by custom, evolved by men for their own
purposes and in ignorance of the commandments of God
(*jahiliyya*—ignorance of the truths of religion); Islamic society,
as well as those founded by earlier prophets to the degree to
which they had not corrupted their scriptures, was ruled by the
Shari'a. Again, the link between human beings in pre-Islamic
society was that of natural relationship, based on blood or
analogous to that which was based on blood. It was the solidarity
of the clan or tribe ('*asabiyya*); but the link between Muslims in

[4] al-Ghazali, *Ihya' 'ulum al-din*, ii/4, chs. 5–6, pp. 124 ff.

the *umma* was a moral link, a common obedience of the law, an acceptance of the reciprocal rights and duties laid down in it, and mutual support and exhortation in carrying it out. Once more, political power in the pre-Islamic community was natural monarchy, created by a human process, controlled by human sentiments or purely human calculations of means and ends, and directed towards worldly goals (*mulk*); but in the Muslim *umma* power was a delegation by God (*wilaya*) controlled by His will and directed to the happiness of Muslims in the next world even more than in this.

For an orthodox Muslim, history was the process by which the society of religious ignorance, directed to worldly ends, held together by natural solidarity and ruled by kings, was replaced by the ideal Muslim society. In a sense the struggle had been going on throughout history, wherever and whenever God had sent prophets to a specific *umma*. In a sense too it was still happening, wherever the *umma* faced the unconverted world. There had however been one period of particular importance, when the final revelation was fully embodied in the institutions of society. To devout Muslims, at the time and later, there lay a special significance in the early history of Islam, when the community was expanding and flourishing, the Quran and the Prophet's words were taken as principles of action, and the *umma* was one in outer manifestation as well as in spirit. For the moral imagination of Sunnis, the early centuries of Islam have always been a compelling drama in three acts: the early days of the Prophet and his immediate successors, the golden age when the *umma* was what it should be; the Umayyad period when the principles of the Islamic polity were overlaid by the natural human tendency towards secular kingship; and the early 'Abbasid age when the principles of the *umma* were reasserted and embodied in the institutions of a universal empire, regulated by law, based on the equality of all believers, and enjoying the power, wealth, and culture which are the reward of obedience. In later ages this period of history served as a norm for rulers and ruled alike, a lesson of what God had done for His people, a lesson too of the evils of division and the rejection of God's will. It provided material for reflection on the moral problems of the corporate life of the *umma*: the struggle for the caliphate between 'Ali and Mu'awiya, then between Umayyads and

'Abbasids, the death of Hasan and Husayn, the massacre of the Umayyads, the withdrawal of the Kharijites from a community which they regarded as being hopelessly involved in sin, the breach between Sunnis and Shi'is—all these are living moments of the Islamic conscience, the points at which it becomes aware of the difficulties of embodying God's will in the life of society. With the full articulation of the message of Muhammad in a universal community obedient to divine command, what was significant in history came to an end. History could have no more lessons to teach, if there was change it could only be for the worse, and the worse could only be cured, not by creating something new but by renewing what had once existed. Inherent in this view of the past was a sense of decline: according to a famous *hadith*, the Prophet had said that his generation was the best of all, that the one which would come after him would be the next best, and after that each succeeding generation would be worse. But the popular mind consoled itself with the belief that in each century there would arise a renovator (*mujaddid*), and with the expectation of a *mahdi*, one sent by God to restore the rule of the saints and prepare the coming of Jesus and the end of the world.

History is what men need to remember of the past, and it is only at rare times and among small groups that the historical sense takes the form of a desire to reconstruct the whole of the past. For Muslims, the great age of early Islam served as an image of what the world should be. We ask different questions of the past, and can see what was to them, in a sense, irrelevant: the fact of historical development. In the light of this fact the contrasts become less sharp. It is still possible for a Muslim to maintain that, during the age of the caliphate, the principles of Islam were embodied in a community, but we can see more closely the process by which this took place. At the heart of the process of development stands the living tradition of *ahl al-sunna wa'l-jama'a*, the self-appointed, self-recognized, unorganized body of 'concerned' Muslims, believing in the revelation of Muhammad, wishing to preserve it unaltered amidst the changes of time, seeking in it guidance in the new problems cast up by those changes, defending it and drawing out its implications not so much by a rejection of what was new as by a discrimination between what could be absorbed into Islam and what could not.

It was through them that the system of orthodox beliefs was built up, by reaction to a succession of challenges: from Greek philosophy, from mystical practice and theology, from Shi'ism and its offshoots. Of Greek philosophy they accepted the technique of logic and certain concepts of natural theology, while rejecting the tendency to turn the living God of Bible and Quran into an abstract principle, a postulate of thought; they took from mysticism its emphasis on inner devotion, on sincerity of intention as well as correctness of act, while looking with suspicion on the monistic theology which blurred the distinction between God and His creatures, and repudiating any suggestion that to know God by direct experience was more important than to obey His laws. They shared the Shi'i reverence for the family of the Prophet, while condemning the gnostic ideas implicit in extreme Shi'ism, in particular the tendency to replace the idea of a human prophet by the idea of an emanation of God.

A similar process of development took place on another level. Gradually, the customs and practices of early Islamic society, many of them inherited from the pre-Islamic worlds—of Byzantium, Persia, and pagan Arabia—were absorbed into the body of Islamic law; it would perhaps be more correct to say, Islamic law was created by the blend of such customs and practices with principles and edicts drawn from the Quran and the authentic *hadith*. No doubt this process involved some 'adulteration' of law and tradition, the creation of new traditions in order to give a cover of Islamic respectability to what was not Islamic by origin; but it also worked in the opposite way, by the selection of customs and practices, the rejection of some and acceptance of others, and the modification even of those which were accepted, in the light of the teaching of Islam. By this slow process, never completed and never indeed capable of completion, the social systems of the many countries converted to Islam were permeated by its moral ideals, and a profoundly unified Islamic society was created.

It is doubtful whether the process could have taken place had the community not possessed, during its first and formative epoch, a unified political and administrative structure. It was under the caliphs, and thanks to their authority, that the distinctive law and society of Islam grew up, and it is not surprising that then and long afterwards the existence of the caliphate was regarded as a necessary condition for the maintenance of law and society. So long as it existed and flourished, its necessity did not have to be defended, but from the ninth century the political unity of Islam began to disintegrate, or at least to change its form. The Turkish mercenary soldiers, on whom the 'Abbasid caliphs had come to rely, began to exercise ever more power in the capital, making and unmaking caliphs and interfering in policy and government; in the provinces, new dynasties began to grow up, still in principle acknowledging the caliph's sovereignty and governing in his name, but in effect ruling independently over limited territorial States; and Shi'ism, revived and developed in the form of Isma'ilism, challenged the right of the caliph to rule and the form of Islam which he defended. In these circumstances, those who believed in the necessity of the caliph's power found themselves obliged for the first time to state explicitly the nature of the caliphate and the reasons for its existence. The most famous of such statements, that of al-Mawardi (991–1031) in *al-Ahkam al-sultaniyya*, defines the caliphate as being a necessity derived from the divine law rather than from reason; the Quran enjoins men to obey those set in command over them,[5] and this implies that there should be a caliph, to replace the Prophet so far as the maintenance of religion and the administration of worldly interests are concerned. His functions are political as well as religious: to maintain orthodoxy, execute legal decisions, protect the frontiers of Islam, fight those who refuse to become Muslims when summoned, raise the canonical taxes, and in general, himself to supervise the administration of affairs without delegating too much authority. He must possess certain qualifications, physical, intellectual, and spiritual, as well as the extraneous qualification of belonging to the same tribe as Muhammad, that of Quraysh; and he must be designated for his office by someone else—either by choice of the leaders of the community, 'those who bind and loose', or by choice of the previous caliph. Once chosen, the people owe him obedience, from which they can only be released if he is immoral, holds unorthodox opinions or has physical infirmities which make it impossible for him to perform his functions.[6]

Even as this doctrine of authority was being stated the movement of history was making it inadequate. The division of

---

[5] Quran, iv.58.   [6] Mawardi, pp. 3 ff (Fr. trs. pp. 5 ff).

authority between 'Abbasid caliph and Turkish dynast was irreversible, just as was the shift of power from Baghdad to other capitals. After the Mongols destroyed Baghdad in the middle of the thirteenth century, the caliph continued to exist only as a shadow, at the court of the Mamluke sultans of Egypt, and few jurists were prepared to recognize his claims in this form. The transfer of power brought with it a change in political institutions. The new States which arose, and of which the Mamluke sultanate of Egypt was the culmination, had a different structure from the caliphate. Power lay in the hands of a military group, central Asian, Turkish, Kurdish, or Caucasian by origin —the sultan, his freedmen, and their dependants. It originated in seizure, its first aim was to maintain itself, and for this purpose it kept in its own hands control of the army and all officials. The link which held the ruling group together was that of common interest and the natural solidarity of language although not of origin. Where the interests of the State were concerned, its laws were the edicts of the sultan, administered directly by him or his governors and derived from considerations of State interest. In essence then it was natural kingship (*mulk*); but it was *mulk* tempered by respect for Islam, for the caliph and the doctors of religion ('*alim*, pl. '*ulama*'), and indeed deriving from this its moral claim. The shadow-caliph was in effect an official of the sultan's court, deprived of power, but serving as a guarantee of orthodoxy, against the insidious threat of Shi'ism in its many forms, and as a moral basis for the sultan's power. Having installed himself by the seizure of power, the sultan was formally invested by the caliph and his authority then acknowledged by the leaders of the people at the ceremony of *bay'a*. The '*ulama*' and what they stood for were also treated with respect. They were the guardians of Islamic morality and law, and of the Arabic language and culture which went with them. The law they studied and interpreted, and the judges who dispensed it, were protected and honoured by the sultan, even if—exercising the right given to the ruler by the law itself—he delimited the cases with which the judges were competent to deal. He maintained also the schools (*madrasa*) where Islamic law and the Arabic language were transmitted, and by drawing the permanent officials of the State from these schools he strengthened the Arabic character of the government. The '*ulama*' were not only

judges, teachers, and officials; they were consulted and used for
foreign negotiations, they took part in the politics and revolutions
of the palace. Although in general docile towards the princes,
and reluctant to participate in revolts against their power,
they served in a sense as leaders of the indigenous opinion of
Egypt and Syria against the Turkish or Caucasian military
class.[7]

These changes raised once more the whole question of
authority. The caliphate had been one, at least in principle; it
had been universal, resting on a formal equality of rights and
functions as between all believers; its head had been, by his own
claim and general recognition, the successor of the Prophet in
his political function, and he had exercised his function in
accordance with the *Shari'a*. None of this was true of the sultans
who had taken over his power. Their rule was territorially
limited. The limits, it is true, were *de facto* only, there was no
idea of a legal frontier separating one Muslim State from
another, and by maintaining the caliph at their court the Mamlukes legitimized in advance any conquests they might make;
nevertheless, neither they nor any other ruler of the time could
claim to be ruling the whole *umma*. Political power moreover was
in the hands of a single ethnic group maintaining itself by co-
optation from the same stock. The sultan might be formally
invested by the caliph, but there was no concealing that his
power rested on seizure or descent, not on what had been regarded by the jurists as the legitimate process of choice—whether
that choice was exercised by the *shura* or by the previous caliph.
Although the *Shari'a* and its judges were respected, side by side
with them there were the edicts and decisions made by the sultan
and administered by him or his officials in his audience-chamber.
Thus the *Shari'a* tended to be no more than a negative principle,
something which the ruler should not transgress, not something
which directed his conduct; his positive aim was to maintain
and strengthen his authority, and to use it, in the light of natural
equity or interest of State, in order to regulate the different
classes of society. This was the view expounded in a new type
of political writing, the books of practical advice for rulers. At
the same time the *Shari'a* was challenged from outside. Since the
tenth century there had been a renewed immigration of Arab

[7] Laoust, *Essai sur Taki-d-Din Ahmad B. Taimiya*, pp. 41 ff.

tribes into the Syrian desert and across Sinai into the Nile valley and the North African littoral, and they brought with them into the heart of the settled world the *'asabiyya* of the tribe and the pagan customs of the age of ignorance.

The reign of secular kingship seemed to have come again; but on the other hand the power of the Turks and Caucasians was necessary for the *umma*. They defended it against dangers from within and without; they had restored the rule of doctrinal orthodoxy as against the challenge of Shi'ism and Isma'ilism. It was difficult to fit the sultanates into the political doctrine of the caliphate, but it was impossible to condemn them out of hand. Once more then the fundamental problem of political thought was posed: in what sense could the new rulers be said to have the right to rule in the Islamic community? If they had no right, did the community founded by the Prophet and entrusted to his successors still exist?

Writing while the transfer of power was still incomplete, al-Mawardi had tried to answer this question. The caliph, he said, could delegate his power to a military commander (*amir*) in an outlying region of the empire, and to a 'minister by delegation' (*wazir*) in its heart. This delegation could be made freely, or else in view of conquest or other circumstances. In this way the legal and moral basis of government could be preserved: 'a defective state of affairs is thus regularized and what was forbidden becomes admissible'.[8] In return, the *amir* should recognize the necessity of the caliphate, show a pious obedience, preserve the *Shari'a* and apply the fiscal principles it contained. Moreover he could only exercise power for the caliph; the caliph kept his political and administrative functions even if he no longer exercised them directly.

To maintain that the sultan derived his power from the caliph was increasingly difficult as it became clear that in fact the caliph was set up and deposed by the sultan. In references scattered throughout the works of al-Ghazali, writing two generations later, we can see a recognition of what this involved. For Ghazali, what is important is that there should be 'an imam who is obeyed'; who he is, and how he is chosen, are important but logically secondary. The imam is necessary because religious order is necessary, and because religious order involves worldly

[8] Mawardi, p. 32 (Fr. trs. p. 67).

order, that is to say, security of life, livelihood, dwelling, and so on.

Both these orders involve law, and the essential function of the imam is to uphold the legal system. For this he needs two qualifications. He must possess certain personal qualities, but he must also have been designated by someone else. In traditional theory, designation could be by the Prophet or the previous imam; to these two ways al-Ghazali now adds a third—delegation (*tafwid*) by the possessor of power. He goes even farther than this: the conditions can be waived if necessary. An imam can appoint himself, if he possesses the necessary qualifications; and even if he does not possess them, but is willing to consult the *ulama* in the exercise of his functions, he should not be deposed, unless it can be done without civil strife. This stipulation shows the root of al-Ghazali's thought, which is that 'necessity makes legal what would otherwise not be legal'. Any imamate is better than none, for any authority is better than 'confusion of opinions'. If there is no imam, marriages and other legal processes are not valid, law ceases to exist, and so the community ceases to exist. The same argument holds good of temporal rule. Any ruler is better than chaos, no matter what the origin of his power. He should try to do natural justice, and do it in a way which is not contrary to the *Shari'a* (and Ghazali himself wrote a book of maxims for rulers); but even an unjust ruler should not be deposed if strife would follow.[9]

Implicit in such a view is the principle that political power is a necessity of human life; all power is therefore in a sense from God, and must be obeyed. But there is still a distinction between good and bad rule, and this distinction is concerned with law. The ruler should act within the bounds of the Islamic law and should uphold it. Law involves an imam, and the imamate is a necessity; but the person of the imam is a secondary consideration, and the qualifications which the jurists regarded as necessary can be waived if otherwise civil strife would result. This view met the needs of the new States well enough to be accepted as the moral basis of their power. Three centuries later a similar view was put forward by an official apologist for the Mamlukes, Badr al-Din ibn Jama'a (1241–1333). The ruler is a necessity,

no dis c

---

[9] Ghazali, *al-Iqtisad*, pp. 105 ff.; cf. A. K. S. Lambton, 'The Theory of Kingship in the *Nasihat ul-Muluk* of Ghazali', *Islamic Q.*, i (1954).

without him there can be no justice; he is 'the shadow of God on earth'.[10] Because he is necessary, the community must accept him whoever he be. This is as true of the imam as of other types of ruler. The imam can either be chosen or can impose himself by his own power, and in either case he must be obeyed, 'in order that the cohesion of the Muslims shall be maintained and their unity assured'. If he is deposed by another, the other must equally be obeyed—'we are with whoever conquers'.[11] If this is true of all Muslims, it is no less true of the imam himself. If a king imposes his rule over a country by force, the imam must delegate matters to him and call on the faithful to obey him, for fear that the *umma* should be divided and weakened. But the link between ruler and ruled remains a moral link. They can demand from him protection of the true religion, the maintenance of its observances, the execution of legal decisions, the collection of the taxes sanctioned by religion, the protection of religious endowments (*waqf*, pl. *awqaf*)—in a word, justice in all its forms. In return, they owe him obedience (except in so far as he infringes the law), advice, respect, and help in carrying 'the burden of the interests of the *umma*'.[12] He must obey God just as his officials obey him, and for this reason he should consult the '*ulama*', the guardians of God's law. But if he does wrong he should not be deposed as an official is dismissed, because of 'the disturbance of conditions'.[13]

The centre of political thought, it is clear, has shifted from the origin of political power to its use, and this shift, although its origin may be found in the changed conditions of the *umma*, was perhaps helped by the development of a different type of thought, and one of which the influence can be seen in the ideas of al-Ghazali. From an early period the doctrines of Islam had been permeated by Greek philosophy; or it might be more accurate to say that as the *umma* expanded, Islam was accepted by men whose minds had been formed by Greek thought and who therefore thought about Islam in terms of Greek philosophy. There grew up a doctrine of the imamate interpreted in the light of Plato's *Republic* and *Laws* and Aristotle's *Ethics* (it is not certain that his *Politics* was translated into Arabic). This doctrine tried to answer the questions, who was the legitimate ruler of the

---

[10] Ibn Jama'a, pt. i, p. 355.
[12] Ibid. pp. 359 ff.
[11] Ibid. p. 357.
[13] Ibid. pp. 363–4.

Islamic community and what should he try to do, in terms of a
general theory of government and society.

The philosophers started from the Greek doctrine that there
is an inherent harmony between human nature and society, such
that man can only attain his natural end in the community. The
virtuous life is that of the individual performing his proper
function in the virtuous State, and the State is therefore a
necessity of human nature. The best State is that which is ruled
by the best man, and the best man is he who possesses not only
the moral virtues required to rule over others but the wisdom
of knowing what goodness is. His aim as a ruler will be to
establish justice, and justice consists in the right relationship of
classes, each performing a necessary function according to its
natural capacities.

Of these propositions, some could easily be reconciled with the
tenets of Islam, others not so easily. For the Greeks, the perfect
man who should rule was the philosopher, the man in whom the
capacity to know was fully actualized; for Muslims, the founder
and first ruler of the community, and its human exemplar, was
the Prophet, the man chosen by God for the communication of
His commands. For Islam, the basis of society was the law, and
the law was the will of God; but for Plato the perfect ruler was
unlimited except by the truth, of which his own reason gave him
knowledge, and law was necessary only for the ruled, and even
then was only the human product of the lawgiver's mind, while
for Aristotle it was a product of human wisdom, freer from
passion than any individual could be and tending to form good
habits in the citizen. Was the prophet or the philosopher the
best of men and the ruler of the best society? Was the Islamic
umma the best society? To put it in even stronger terms: was
prophecy necessary, and was revealed law necessary, if man was
to fulfil his nature? These were urgent questions for the Muslim
philosophers, because they were not only philosophers but
Muslims. While accepting Plato and Aristotle as 'masters of
those who know', they still believed that in some sense Muhammad was a prophet and the *Shari'a* was the will of God. The
dilemma could only be resolved if there could be found an
explanation of prophecy and the law which would satisfy the
philosophic mind. It was this that al-Farabi (870–950) tried to
give in his *Ara' ahl al-madina al-fadila* (Ideas of the Citizens

of the Virtuous City). Prophecy, he declared, was a function of the imagination. The philosopher was a man of powerful and perfect intellect who had reached the highest metaphysical knowledge through contact with the Active Intellect, one of the beings which emanate from God and are intermediary between Him and man. If he also has a powerful and perfect imagination, this too will attain to direct contact with the Active Intellect, and will be able to reproduce the intelligibles which come to it from their invisible forms, in symbols of the utmost beauty and perfection; and it may also receive the knowledge of present and future particulars and of the higher beings. Such a man would be prophet as well as philosopher; as philosopher he would teach the few who can see the truth as it is, but as prophet he would teach the many through persuasion and imagination. He would also have another function, that of giving laws and being the founder and head of the virtuous State. The virtuous State is that in which all co-operate in pursuit of a common good, all have knowledge of the good, directly or by analogy and representation, and all are ordered in a hierarchy according to their nature and their moral habits voluntarily acquired; only he who is both philosopher and prophet can create and rule such a State. But it rarely happens that all the qualities required, of theoretical and practical reason and of imagination, meet in one person; if they are not to be found all together, it will be enough if the ruler possesses those of reason without those of imagination (in other words, is philosopher but not prophet), or if authority lies with a combination of persons, or if the laws given by the founder of the State are maintained by rulers who could not themselves have created them but know what they are and can interpret them (in other words, the caliphs). What is essential is that knowledge of the good should reside somewhere in the city and its ruling element; if it is absent, the city is not virtuous, it is ignorant, immoral, or mistaken in its ideas, its different elements have conflicting interests, and it has no common good but is held together by something else—by force, or contract, or some natural affinity such as common descent, character, or language.

In the theory of al-Farabi, prophecy is no longer a free gift of God, it is a natural human state; and it is a state of the imagination not of reason, giving access to no general knowledge

not attainable by philosophy. The function of the prophet is less
theoretical than practical and even political, to found and rule a
virtuous State, and even this is not a function exclusive to
Muhammad, for just as all true religions are symbolic repre-
sentations of the same truth, so 'there can be virtuous nations
and cities of different religions, for all tend towards one same
happiness and identical objects'.[14] By later philosophers some
of these positions were modified. Ibn Sina (Avicenna, 980–
1037), for example, while maintaining that prophetic illumina-
tion was a natural state, declared that it was a state of the intellect, not the imagination alone, and indeed that it was the
highest state of the human intellect. Its essential function was
to give laws which all men must obey; but the content of the
divine law was attainable in principle by the unaided human
intellect, and failing a prophet a good system of law could grow
up in society in other ways. To the strictly orthodox, however,
this view was no more acceptable than that of al-Farabi; both
alike tended to 'rationalize' the process of revelation, to turn the
relationship of divine and human wills into one of theoretical
intelligences. As the orthodox reaction gathered force, the study
of the philosophers became marginal if not suspect, although
individual scholars carried it on and the tradition of Ibn Sina
remained strong in the Shi'i schools of the east. But no movement of thought vanishes without remainder, and there was a
submerged philosophical element in all later Islamic thought.
The philosophers had taught that rulers were to be judged by
their intentions rather than their title-deeds, and that the unity
of the *umma* was derived from its common good; the jurists of
the later period accepted this even when they rejected the general
ideas of the philosophers. So much is apparent in the political
treatise of Ibn Taymiyya, *al-Siyasa al-shar'iyya*. The author
(1263–1328) was an adherent of the Hanbali school of theology
and jurisprudence, which was strongly opposed to all attempts at
reducing the principles of Islam to a construction of the human
intelligence, but showed great flexibility in applying them to the
problems of social life. The problem which he faced was that of
the two systems of government—the ideal government of the
caliphs, which no longer existed, and the actual government of
the Mamluke sultans of which he was an official—and of two

[14] al-Farabi, *al-Madina*, p. 123 (Fr. trs. p. 96).

systems of law—the *Shari'a*, where the door of *ijtihad* had virtually been closed, and the rules of political expediency and natural equity which the government followed and applied. He resolved it by working out a different conception of the legitimacy of government, the unity of the *umma*, and the methodology of law.

The essence of government, for Ibn Taymiyya, was the power of coercion, which was necessary if men were to live in society and their solidarity was not to be destroyed by natural human egoism. Since it was a natural necessity of society, it arose by a natural process of seizure, legitimized by contract of association. The ruler as such could demand obedience from his subjects, for even an unjust ruler was better than strife and the dissolution of society; 'give what is due *from* you and ask God for what is due *to* you'.[15] But nevertheless there was a difference between just and unjust rule, and its root was to be found in the essential purpose of human life: that is to say, obedience to the will of God. The function of the ruler was to impose on all a just law derived from God's commands and ensuring the spiritual and material welfare of the community. The divinely instituted rule of Muhammad and the early caliphs had been just; but the caliphate had broken up into 'kingdoms', and just as kings like caliphs had a right to obedience, so they must obey God and maintain a just law. By implication, all rulers who did this were legitimate; there could be more than one ruler, even more than one imam, without the *umma* being destroyed thereby. The unity of the *umma* was essentially one of minds and hearts, not of political forms. Muslims shared a doctrine, a language, a law, and a purpose, and all these common elements should be valued and strengthened. Muslims should live together in mutual tolerance of differences of rite, although not of differences on the very bases of the faith—Ibn Taymiyya wrote several legal opinions (*fatwa*) on the legitimacy of war against such sectarians as Druzes and Nusayris, and he had a certain suspicion of Christians and Jews, in whom he saw an intellectual as well as a political danger. Muslims should unify their language as far as possible, using Arabic not only for doctrinal and liturgical purposes but for all the purposes of daily life. They should give their final social loyalty to the *umma* as a whole, above the sect or State. Above all, they should try to rise from external

[15] Ibn Taymiyya, p. 29 (Fr. trs. p. 26).

submission to the law to the love of it and the exclusive service of
God. All this involved activity: mutual exhortation, co-operation
among the faithful, between government and governed and
between the various classes and groups within the *umma*. The
ruler should consult the community—the *'ulama'*, the leaders of
opinion, those qualified to give an opinion of value on the matter
in hand.

The organizing principle of the community was the *Shari'a*.
It followed therefore that the law must be sufficient for all the
purposes of life and government. This meant that two extreme
positions must be avoided. On the one side stood the strict
jurists claiming that the ruler should be guided by the law alone
in a form which by now had grown rigid; on the other the rulers,
claiming the power of deciding freely, in the light of circumstances, and looking on the law as a negative principle only, setting
bounds which should not be infringed. Ibn Taymiyya believed
that there was a middle position. The concept of the *Shari'a*
should be enlarged in such a way as to bring within its scope all
that the ruler by his very function was compelled to do, and that
discretionary power without which he could neither maintain
himself nor provide for the welfare of the community; and if this
were done the *Shari'a* would become once more the guiding
principle of government and community. To this end he gave a
new development to the juridical idea of 'public interest'
(*maslaha*). All Sunni schools of law regarded reasoning by strict
analogy (*qiyas*) as a necessary process of legal interpretation, but
each of them had found it necessary to add some further principle
by which *qiyas* could be directed (for example, when it was
necessary to choose between two analogies) or, within strict
limits, supplemented. One such principle was that of *maslaha*:
since God's purpose in giving laws was human welfare, the
choice between different interpretations of the law should
be directed by concern for welfare. Like other jurists, Ibn
Taymiyya did not apply this principle in the sphere of worship
(*'ibadat*); in these matters there was no way of knowing what
God's purposes were. In the sphere of human relations
(*mu'amalat*), however, the principle should be applied. Everything which conduced to human welfare, and was not specifically forbidden, was not only allowed but even by implication
enjoined. The task of *ijtihad*, of deciding what conduced to

human welfare, could never cease. There could be an infallible *ijma'* of the Companions of the Prophet, who had been faithful to his words and deeds; there could be no infallible *ijma'* of later jurists.

This could easily have been a justification of the *status quo*, but in Ibn Taymiyya's hands it became something else. His doctrine assured the legitimacy of the Mamluke government, but also contained precepts about how it should be carried on. Good government depended on an alliance between *amirs*, political and military leaders, and *'ulama'*, interpreters of the law. In the Mamluke State where the *amirs* were Caucasians or Turks while the *'ulama'* were mainly of Arabic speech and culture, this theory carried with it a plea that government should not be in exclusively foreign hands. But Ibn Taymiyya was not only thinking of the Mamluke State; he was prepared to generalize his idea, and maintain that in a Muslim State power should not be in the hands of *any* limited group. The claims of justice and unity must take precedence over those of any natural ties, whether of friendship, ethnic solidarity, or blood relationship:

> It is a duty for anyone who directs any part of the public affairs of the Muslims ... to employ the most suitable person he can find in each position which is under his control ... If he rejects the worthiest and most proper candidate in favour of another, because that other is his relation, friend or freedman, or because they belong to the same country, legal sect, religious order or ethnic group—Arab, Persian, Turkish, Anatolian—or because he has accepted a bribe or service from this man, or for other reasons, or because of some personal animosity towards the worthier candidate or some enmity between them, he cheats God and His Prophet and the faithful.[16]

To derive glory, outside of Islam and the Quran, from one's birth, country, race, legal school or religious way is to fall into the vanities of paganism.[17]

The vanities of paganism and the dangers of natural *'asabiyya* were more than theoretical ideas to those who wrote at a time when the pressure of the beduin on the settled lands was strong. By implication, the doctrines of Ibn Taymiyya are a protest against the anarchy and pagan customs of the Arabian nomad, who had never really known Islam, as well as of the Turkish soldiers. He drew once more the distinction between *jahiliyya*

[16] Ibn Taymiyya, pp. 6–7 (Fr. trs. pp. 5–6).
[17] Ibid. p. 104 (Fr. trs. p. 99).

and Islam, between ʿasabiyya and religious solidarity. In another
thinker of slightly later date, but similar historical experience, the
contrasts are still there, but are presented with a greater sense of
the complex ways in which the two extremes may be linked. Like
Ibn Taymiyya, Ibn Khaldun (1333–1406) was aware of the challenge thrown down by the beduin to the settled and civilized life.
Places that fall under their control, he says, are quickly ruined,
for their natural disposition is the very opposite of civilization;
they are not concerned with law, each of them wants to be a
leader and (except when held together in the bonds of religion)
they will not subordinate themselves to anyone.[18] But he thought
they had another role to play. They destroyed civilization, but
they founded States. Concerned as he was with the classical
question of political thought, that of the legitimacy of power,
he also had another concern, and one almost unique among the
thinkers of Islam: with the process by which power is seized and
maintained, the changes it undergoes, and the product of
successful power, which is civilization (ʿumran), the life of cities.
He acknowledges as fully as Ibn Taymiyya the essential role
of a common good and a divine law in maintaining the stability
and prosperity of States, but he believes that another element is
necessary if they are to come into existence at all; that element
is natural solidarity based on blood relationship or something
analogous with it, and aiming at the acquisition of power—the
ʿasabiyya which is stronger among the beduin than in any other
human society. ʿAsabiyya, abstractly considered, may be the
opposite of the sense of a common good derived from revealed
law, but unless ʿasabiyya, common good, and law are combined
in some form, stable States cannot come into being. They can
be combined in different ways, and it is possible to construct
therefore a 'scale' of types of authority: from the 'natural' form,
based on ʿasabiyya and tending towards the good of the ruler
through the 'political', governed by natural insight into the
principles of natural justice, whether its object be the good of
the ruler or that of the ruled, up to the State whose principle is a
divinely revealed law and whose aim is the good of the next
world as well as this.[19] This is the highest attainable State, for
the ideal State of the philosophers has never in fact existed.[20]

[18] Ibn Khaldun, i.270 ff. (Eng. trs. i.302 ff).   [19] Ibid. i. 344 (Eng. trs. i. 387).
[20] Ibid. ii. 127 (Eng. trs. ii. 138).

Ibn Khaldun shows that these categories are connected genetically as well as logically: one tends to rise out of the other in a regular sequence. Royal authority arises in the first instance out of necessity: men must co-operate in order to live, and they can only do so if their selfish inclinations are held in check. It is created by a natural process, by means of a group held together by *'asabiyya*, that is to say, 'mutual affection and willingness to fight and die for each other'.[21] Possessing as they do this *'asabiyya* in a special degree, and having more fortitude and courage than city-dwellers usually possess, the beduin are the basis and reservoir of civilization and cities. But once the State has been set up the mass of people lose the *'asabiyya* which made it possible. Its place as basis of the ruler's power is taken by two other things: first, the force of imitation which makes the vanquished want to imitate the victor (for man always sees perfection in the person who dominates him),[22] or else the apathy which comes over a people which has lost control of its own affairs,[23] and secondly the creation of a new group of mercenaries or clients on whom the ruler can rely. They develop an *'asabiyya* of their own which makes it possible for the ruler to dispense with that which gave him power in the first place. Then follows a period of unchallenged power, when the ruler still has complete authority and independence of judgement, and civilization flourishes, for urban life and the prosperity which comes from division of labour need a strong political power. But with contentment decay creeps in: the ruler loses his independence of judgement, the *'asabiyya* of clients and soldiers (never so strong as blood relationship) grows weaker, extravagances lead to heavier taxes, the dynasty may divide into two or the State lose its outer provinces. Urban civilization may for a time survive the weakening of royal authority, through the growth of an urban *'asabiyya* and an oligarchy of city families; but in the end it vanishes, perhaps to be replaced by a new dynasty drawing power from a new group.

Such is the 'natural life span' of dynasties,[24] but it can be checked at any point by the introduction of another factor, a religious law preached by prophets. By itself this cannot create a State, but superimposed on an *'asabiyya* which already exists

---

[21] Ibid. i. 278 (Eng. trs. i. 313).   [22] Ibid. i. 266 (Eng. trs. i. 299).
[23] Ibid. i. 268 (Eng. trs. i. 300).   [24] Ibid. i. 306 (Eng. trs. i. 343).

it can strengthen it. It can provide the strength necessary to found a stable and enduring State; the Arabs, for example, only became a political force when 'religion cemented their leadership with the religious law and its ordinances'.[25] At a later stage of the natural life-span, when the first *'asabiyya* declines and the link between ruler and ruled grows weak, religion can create a new bond of unity and provide a new basis for the virtues by which States are maintained.

Political virtue, stability, civilization: all are bound up with each other, and all rest on a certain relationship not only between different elements in society but between different elements in the human soul. Natural affections and ties are not to be destroyed but to be canalized by rational or religious insight. Such a harmony exists in all types of State which endure, but this is not to say that all have an equal virtue. The moral scale is quite clear in Ibn Khaldun's thought: the State guided by revealed law is unquestionably the highest State. The caliphate is at best a matter of public interest and social organization, not an article of faith;[26] it existed to protect religion and exercise political leadership, and any kingdom which does this possesses the same type of authority. Like kingship, it is based on a natural blood link, that of the family of Quraysh;[27] it is subject to change, and indeed has passed away. The *'asabiyya* of the Arabs, which created first the Umayyad and then the 'Abbasid State, led in time to the establishment of a kingship, first with Islam as its aim and then with self-interest as its aim; and this kingship in its turn led to the decay of the Arab *'asabiyya*.[28] For Ibn Khaldun, the caliphate is essentially a product of the Arab age of Islam; the rise of other types of *'asabiyya* led to other sorts of kingship. It is inevitable that political power should be wielded by those who share in the dominant *'asabiyya*, for only they are capable of performing the functions of government. The new *'asabiyya* is Turkish in the eastern Islamic world, Berber in the western; the *'ulama'*, being mainly of Arab origin, can have no share in the process of government.[29]

[25] Ibn Khaldun, i. 275 (Eng. trs. i. 307).
[26] Ibid. iii. 39 (Eng. trs. iii. 50).
[27] Ibid. i. 352 (Eng. trs. i. 399).
[28] Ibid. i. 364 ff. (Eng. trs. i. 414 ff.)
[29] Ibid. i. 401 ff. (Eng. trs. i. 457 ff.)

II

THE OTTOMAN EMPIRE[1]

FOR Ibn Khaldun, the Islamic State, like all stable and virtuous States, is a blend of kingship (*mulk*) and *Shari'a* State. True as this was of the sultanates of its time, it was true also of the Ottoman Empire, which in a sense was the heir of the whole political development of Islam. First of all it was a dynastic kingdom, with its loyalty focused upon an individual—or rather a group of individuals, a family. It was never thought to be illegitimate to depose a sultan regarded as unfit to rule and declared to be so by the guardians of the law, but with rare exceptions those who rebelled did not question the right of the house of Osman to rule. The right was maintained by a military group held together, and kept fast in its loyalty, by natural 'asabiyya or its equivalent. This group, however, changed its nature (as Ibn Khaldun maintained that all such groups must) once the ruling family had seated itself firmly on the throne. The group which had created the empire was formed of free-born Turks or turkized Muslims of other ethnic origin who were the cavalry and made the conquests of the early sultans. As the Ottoman domains expanded, the group assumed the position of a ruling class: their leaders were given by the sultan the right to collect and keep the land-tax from a certain district in return for military service, and from being warriors they became land-owners. There was at first, and there remained in principle, a sharp distinction between 'askar and ra'aya: between the military group from whom the ruling positions were filled, and the subjects, whether Muslim or Christian, who paid taxes but were excluded from an active share in government. In course of time, however, the distinction became blurred. The 'feudal' cavalry decayed as a military force, and as fiefs fell in their holders were not replaced; the right to collect the land-tax was given instead

---

[1] It will be clear to the reader how much this chapter owes to Bernard Lewis, *The Emergence of Modern Turkey* and H. A. R. Gibb and H. Bowen, *Islamic Society and the West.*

to tax-farmers, who in their turn formed a class of hereditary landowners, but one with less power of its own. To supplement the free Turkish cavalry, a new military caste was built up in the fifteenth and sixteenth centuries, out of the slave-corps which had formed part of the army since early times. Slaves of Balkan Christian or Caucasian origin, acquired by purchase or periodical levy, were trained in the military and palace schools, and according to ability became soldiers in the Janissary or other corps, servants of the palace or high officials of the sultan's government. In its great days this élite of slaves was free of blood ties: by enrolment, conversion, and education it had lost its original ties, and it could acquire no others, for as long as they were soldiers the slaves could not marry, and when they married their children could not enter the corps. In place of natural *'asabiyya* they acquired something else: a professional *esprit de corps*, with its loyalty directed towards the sultan's throne.

From the beginning, however, religious loyalties had reinforced those of blood or professional bonds. The empire had begun as a warrior State, engaged in holy war on the Byzantine frontier, and its first conquests were made at the expense of the Christian empire. Religion indeed did not provide the only motive of its foreign policy, and it allied with Christian States as well as fighting them; but it was the struggle against Christendom which attracted to it the loyalty and aid of the *umma*, and brought to its help volunteers from other Muslim peoples, who in time were absorbed into the Turkish military group. At first the religion of the sultans and their warriors was touched by the heterodox mysticism of Hurufis and Bektaşis; this strain continued in the popular Islam of the Turkish people, but as the empire expanded, and in particular after it occupied the centres of orthodoxy in Egypt and Syria, and found itself faced with the enmity of the revived Shi'ism of the Safavid Empire in Persia, its orthodox Sunni character became more marked. But its Sunni orthodoxy was that of its age, the product of the whole long development of the *umma*, not in any sense an attempt to revert to the pristine simplicity of the early caliphs. It protected the schools where the orthodox doctrines were taught, and founded new ones in Istanbul, and it drew its officials largely from their graduates; but it protected even while it controlled the brotherhoods of mystics (*tariqa*, pl. *turuq*). Their leaders were given financial support, and a special reverence was given to their spiritual fathers: the shrine of Jalal al-Din al-Rumi in Konya was maintained as a place of pilgrimage, and a splendid tomb was built for Ibn al-'Arabi in Damascus. By this time, indeed, the theology of the schools and that of the mystics had made peace with one another, in spite of the differences between them; and many of the *'ulama'* were affiliated to one or other of the brotherhoods.

While the sultan, along with the Moghul emperor in India, was the greatest of Sunni rulers, the defender of Sunnism against the Shah of Persia, no attempt was made (until the end of the eighteenth century) to claim that he was also the caliph, in the sense in which the immediate successors of Muhammad had been caliphs. The great scholar Sayyid Murtada al-Zabidi (1732–91), writing his commentary on al-Ghazali's *Ihya' 'ulum al-din* at the end of the eighteenth century, had no doubt at all, even if he had a note of regret, that the caliphate had passed away. The caliphate, he points out, is acquired by merit, the sultanate by force. If the caliph, besides merit, has also force and *'asabiyya* to rely on he can rule, otherwise sultans and *amirs* must rule, while keeping the name of caliph. After the Mongol conquest of Baghdad, the caliphate continued in name only, and later 'the possessors of power occupied the land, and the name of the caliphate disappeared'. Again, when al-Ghazali says 'authority now only follows power', the commentator adds: 'and *'asabiyya*. This was so even before the time of our author, and indeed has always been so, as Ibn Khaldun suggests in the introduction to his history. . . . Thus Mu'awiya and not 'Ali won the day.'[2]

Although the sultan was not caliph, al-Zabidi would not have suggested that Muslims did not owe him loyalty and religious allegiance. His claim was based not on apostolic succession from the Prophet, but on the divine right of those who had established their effective power and used it in the interests of Islam. The sultan defended the frontiers against Christians and Shi'is; he protected the Holy Places and organized the Pilgrimage with care; he paid respect to the *Shari'a* and its guardians. In principle, all his acts and edicts were subordinate to the *Shari'a*. Of the four main legal systems, that of the Hanafis was the one

[2] Zabidi, iv. 122.

which was officially recognized by the State, although the others were tolerated; the chief Hanafi mufti, the *Shaykh al-Islam*, was head of the religious organization, and as such had a right to disapprove of actions of the government as being contrary to the law. The sultans did in fact enact laws by firman; but in principle their collections of rules (*kanunname*) were regarded as lying within the bounds of the *Shari'a*, or restorations of such sound customs as the *Shari'a* approved, issued by the sultan not by his independent political power but in virtue of the discretionary power left to the secular ruler by the *Shari'a* itself. But of course the control was not all on one side; the greatest of Ottoman jurists formulated the rule that judges of the *Shari'a* must follow the sultan's directions in dispensing justice.[3]

Although the sultan, his grand vezir, and provincial governors had their audience-chambers (*diwan*) where justice was done, the judges (*qadi*) who administered the *Shari'a* were recognized as the only regular judges. In fact, it was the Ottomans who first gave regular form to the *Shari'a* courts and a regular organization to their officials. The judges who dispensed the law, the jurisconsults (*mufti*) who interpreted it, the teachers who taught it in the schools, as well as officials of the mosques, were formed into an official corps, with regular grades and a system of promotion. This corps indeed formed an essential part of the machinery of government, with the military and administrative systems. They played in fact a necessary role as the moral link, and to some extent the administrative link, between the sultan and his subjects, particularly in the Arab Muslim provinces. His acts and decrees were issued to the people through them. Through them alone he could influence Muslim 'public opinion', but in their turn they were spokesmen of opinion, able to bring to the ear of the sultan not only the grievances of various sections of his people, but the voice of the conscience of *ahl al-sunna wa'l-jama'a*. They took part in the political activities of capital and provincial cities, issuing *fatwas* for example to justify the deposition of rulers, but not in popular movements against the sultan, to whom they were loyal, and to whom they brought the loyalty of the people. The brotherhoods of mystics on the other hand, did sometimes serve as channels of popular discontent, at least in the Turkish provinces.

[3] *Encyc. of Islam*, 2nd ed., 'Abu'l-Su'ud' (by J. Schacht).

Whether by choice, or because of the necessary limitations of ruling a vast and varied empire, the sultan's functions were those enjoined on the ruler by the later rather than the earlier political theorists. He did not impose uniformity, but rather ordered and regulated the various classes and elements in the empire, in such a way that they should live at peace with each other and contribute their due share to the stability and prosperity of the whole. The government provided a framework of order, just as the *Shari'a* created a structure of rights and duties; within the framework, each community was free to live in accordance with its own beliefs and customs. To preserve customs, where necessary to restore them, and to keep them within the bounds of the *Shari'a*, was indeed the purpose of the *kanunnames* issued by the sultans of the great period.

The empire then was not so much a single community as a group of communities each of which claimed the immediate loyalty of its members. These communities were regional, religious, or functional; or, to some extent, a mixture of all three. The fundamental divisions—one might say, the constitutive divisions—were two: that of *'askar* and *ra'aya*, rulers and subjects, and that of Muslim and non-Muslim. The State was primarily a Sunni Muslim State. There was a sense in which all Sunni Muslims, irrespective of race or language, were full and equal members of the political community, and no one else was. There existed indeed other Muslim communities. There were Shi'is in what are now Turkey, Iraq, Lebanon, and the Yemen. They were looked at askance, not only because of the long centuries of theological hatred but because of their religious affinities with Shi'i Persia; in times of war between Ottoman sultan and Persian shah, the Shi'is of Iraq, so near to the Persian frontier, were regarded as possible traitors. Their law was not recognized, but their residence in distant places, in mountain valleys or on the edge of the desert, secured them a certain tolerance, and they lived as a closed community grouped around their holy cities and with the great families of scholars as their leaders. In Syria, Lebanon, and northern Iraq there lived also certain sects which were offshoots of Shi'ism, with a mixture of elements from outside Islam—Druzes, Isma'ilis, Nusayris, and others. They too, although not recognized as separate communities, could hope for sufferance as long as they lived far from the centres of government and paid their taxes; but refusal to pay taxes might lay them open to punitive expeditions.

From the time of the capture of Constantinople, the Christian and Jewish communities were given a more formal recognition. At that time the Orthodox and Armenian patriarchs and the Grand Rabbi of the capital were recognized as political no less than religious heads respectively of the whole Orthodox, Armenian, and Jewish population of the empire. (There were other Christian bodies as well—Copts in Egypt, Maronites, Nestorians, and Syrian Orthodox in Lebanon, Syria, and Iraq. Living far from the capital, they had fewer contacts with the government, but their patriarchs also were given such recognition from time to time.) Patriarchs and rabbis received official investiture from the sultan and dealt with his government on all matters affecting their flock; inside their community, their decisions and edicts had the force of law. They were responsible for collecting the poll-tax, and so long as it was paid regularly —so long also as Christians and Jews presented no danger by alliance with foreign Powers—the government scarcely interfered in their internal affairs. Matters of personal status and civil cases they dealt with themselves in accordance with canon law and custom. They were subject to the sumptuary provisions of the *Shariʿa*, but how far these were applied varied from one place or another, according to the will of the local ruler or the state of public feeling; they were more strictly applied, for example, in Damascus than Aleppo. Most of them lived in special quarters of the towns and villages and, although in some places there was a Christian peasantry, most of them were town-dwellers specializing in certain trades, crafts, and professions. Some of them indeed had a position of influence, playing an essential part in the life of the State—the Armenian bankers of Constantinople, the Jewish bankers of Baghdad, the Greek families of the Phanar quarter who served as interpreters in foreign negotiations and as governors of the Rumanian provinces.

Of the functional organizations, the most important were the trade and craft guilds. They went back far beyond Ottoman times; perhaps of Ismaʿili origin, they had a long connexion with Islamic heresy and the mystical brotherhoods, a connexion which might be dangerous to the strictly orthodox State. They were therefore kept under strict control by the government; the local head of the guild received official investiture and was responsible for keeping the members loyal, but within these limits they were tolerated and indeed had a social position of respect. In a similar way, the village was recognized as a social unit, responsible as a whole for taxation and its members' crimes. The headman of the village was officially recognized. So also were the leaders of nomadic tribes, or at least those tribes near enough to the settled lands to be amenable to some control, however flimsy. Shaykhs received official investiture, robes of honour, and subsidies to let the pilgrimage or trading caravans pass without harm. But if need be punitive expeditions were sent, or one faction or tribe was set against another; the empire was primarily an empire of the cities, and inherited from its whole Islamic past the urban hostility towards the beduin, the disturbers of trade and cultivation, the enemies of civilization, and the last repositories of the customs of the age of pagan ignorance.

As the empire expanded, provinces large and small were added to it piecemeal and without consistency, but in the sixteenth century the system of provinces was reorganized and given the form which it retained in essentials until the nineteenth century. The empire was divided into provinces, each ruled by a governor or pasha of varying rank (*basha*, *wazir*) and directly responsible to the central government. With variations from time to time, there were four provinces in what is now Iraq—Basra, Baghdad, Mosul, and Shahrizur—, four in geographical Syria—Aleppo, Damascus, Tripoli, and Sidon—, two in Western Arabia—Hejaz and the Yemen—and four on the North African coast—Egypt, Tripoli, Tunis, and Algiers. The governor, the officials in charge of districts, the tax-collectors, and the *Shari'a* judges were sent from Constantinople, in principle for a year only, to prevent their acquiring local roots or a local following; but the leaders of local opinion too were associated with the government. The provincial council or *diwan* normally included not only the chief officials and military commanders but the leaders of the local *'ulama'*, who usually held most of the positions in the religious hierarchy except that of *qadi*. It might also include representatives of the *a'yan* (the local notables who had acquired power through tax-farming, or in other ways, and gradually obtained official recognition from the government as local representatives),[4] of the merchants, the guilds, and the brotherhoods of mystics.

In the more distant provinces, the balance between central and local elements was soon tilted in favour of the second. In the North African territories the local military corps freed themselves from effective control and ruled their own territories subject to payment of tribute to the sultan: in Egypt, a pasha sent from Constantinople was still ruler in form, but in fact the Mamlukes had regained their power and it was their leaders who ruled; farther west, the power of the militia made possible the rise of local dynasties recognized by the central government. This change led indirectly to greater power for the local '*ulama*', the spokesmen of indigenous opinion, particularly in Cairo and Tunis, where the Azhar and Zaytuna mosque-universities served as rallying points. In the Hejaz and the Yemen the process went farther, and outside the coastal towns which were the centre of Turkish rule power lay in the hands of local families deriving their influence from the respect in which the pious held them: the Sharifs of Mecca, guardians of the holy cities and claiming descent from the Prophet; the imams of the Zaydi Shi'is in the Yemen.

The Syrian and Iraqi provinces were held more closely, at least in the period of Ottoman greatness. They were too important to be allowed to slip away: Damascus because it was the city from which was organized the Pilgrimage, the great manifestation of Ottoman orthodoxy, Aleppo as the centre of international trade, Baghdad because from there the frontiers with Persia must be defended. But only the great cities, the coast, the river valleys, and the plains near the cities were effectively controlled. In the mountains of Lebanon and northern Palestine and Kurdistan in northern Iraq, local dynasties, some of them existing from before the Ottoman conquest and commanding the loyalty of the valleys, were left in control. They were not wholly unrestrained: they must pay taxes and must not encroach on the plains; they were discreetly watched by the governors of surrounding provinces; but within these limits their power was tolerated and indeed recognized. When Kurdistan was conquered in the sixteenth century the Ottoman government made an agreement with the local princes, by which they would help to

---

[4] Cf. *Encyc. of Islam*, 2nd ed., 'A'yan' (by H. Bowen).

guard the Persian frontier in return for acceptance of their hereditary position. They were fitted into the provincial system and the system of 'feudal' landowners, and in the same way the leaders of Lebanon and northern Palestine were fitted into the hierarchy of tax-farmers which grew up later, and treated as chief tax-gatherers of their districts with a virtual right of rule.

Ethnic divisions were not recognized by the Ottoman government, or indeed by any Islamic State after the primitive distinction of Arabs and non-Arab converts was blurred and before the rise of modern nationalism. But there was a certain division of function between languages, and therefore to some extent between linguistic groups. Turkish was the language of government and the army, Arabic of learning and law, Persian a language of polite letters. The special role of the Arabs was indeed recognized to some extent. The descendants of the Prophet (*sharif*, pl. *ashraf*) were recognized as a separate body, with fiscal and legal privileges; in each province they were organized under a head (*naqib*), and the Naqib of Constantinople was one of the great dignitaries of the empire.

Wherever Islam exists, there exists an awareness of the special role of the Arabs in history: the Prophet was an Arab, the Quran is written in Arabic, the Beduin Arabs were 'the matter of Islam' (*maddat al-Islam*), the human means by which it conquered the world. The care given by the Ottoman sultans to the orthodox schools and the law preserved and indeed encouraged the 'national' consciousness of the Arabs. It took the form of pride in language, culture, and ancestry, and a sense of responsibility towards Islam, not that of a desire for a separate political existence; and in this form it had leaders and spokesmen—the local '*ulama*', and more generally the great families of the provincial cities who preserved the tradition of religious learning, of the Arab language and its sciences, and of what the Arabs had done for Islam.

III

FIRST VIEWS OF EUROPE

In so vast and varied an empire, to hold the different communities together required a constant and skilful use of the sultan's regulative power. Even at the height of Ottoman strength, in the reign of Süleyman the Magnificent, there were not wanting voices to remind sultan and ministers how fragile was the structure, and from the beginning of the seventeenth century a decline in strength was clearly noticeable.[1] It was in fact noticed by writers of the time and its causes understood. What was the precise relationship of those causes, and which of them were causes and which symptoms, are of course questions which cannot be answered. We can at least distinguish a number of 'sequences', each closely linked with the others. The machinery of government decayed; the sultan was the centre of the system, and it could only work well if his control was effective, but from the end of the sixteenth century the long line of intelligent and masterful sultans came to an end, and there began a period of rulers weak in character and intellect and ill trained for their work. The result was a struggle for influence between various factions: groups of officials and army leaders, allied with '*ulama*' and with women and slaves of the palace. Towards the end of the seventeenth century the Köprülü family of ministers checked the decay, by shifting the centre of power from the sultan to the grand vezir (*sadr-a'zem*); the vezir's house, the Sublime Porte, replaced as the centre of decision the domed chamber in the palace where the sultan's council had met, and the head of the vezir's chancery, the *reis-ül-küttab*, became virtual Foreign Minister. But the vezir's control was inherently weak: his appointment and dismissal depended on the sultan's will, and besides he no longer had an effective machine through which to work. During the century of confusion the administration had ceased to work properly; the system of tax-collection had lost its efficiency and

[1] For an analysis of the decline of the Ottoman Empire cf. B. Lewis, *Emergence*, ch. 3.

honesty; the old system of 'feudal' landownership had been allowed to decay; the army was losing its discipline. The process might have been reversed, had not the moral basis of the system also disappeared. The professional *'asabiyya* of the slave-élite and the *'ulama'* had grown weaker. The rigid discipline and exclusive loyalties of the Janissaries had broken down: their children were allowed to become Janissaries, free-born Muslims were allowed to enter the corps, and membership of it could be bought, sold, and bequeathed. The highest posts in the sultan's service, as ministers, rulers of provinces or commanders of armies, were held more often by free-born Muslims. The fiction that they were slaves of the sultan was retained, but in fact they tended to be drawn more and more from the Muslim *ra'aya*, and to be Turks; for the common language of the rulers was Turkish, and if not Turk by origin they became so by adoption. In the same way, the upper ranks of the *'ulama'* tended to become an exclusive and privileged clique. Possessing from the start the solidarity of a common education, they sent their sons to the great schools of Constantinople from which almost all the highest posts were filled; they were guardians and beneficiaries of *awqaf*, they had social and political influence, and they had special opportunities for securing grants of tax-farms and becoming landowners; what they gained they could hold, for as a religious group they were comparatively free from the danger of confiscation and could hope to transmit their wealth to their children.

While this political change was taking place, the empire was passing through a long-drawn-out economic crisis. Aggravated no doubt by bad administration, its cause was to be found outside the empire, in the geographical expansion of Europe eastwards and westwards. The establishment of European trading posts in the Indian Ocean dislocated the pattern of trade between the empire and the outer world, both Asia and Europe; and the discovery of America had an even greater effect. It led to a flow of gold and silver into the Mediterranean countries and so to a rise of prices which dislocated the finances of the State and brought hardship to the productive classes. The result was an increase in taxation, the decline of agriculture and crafts, and the depopulation of the countryside.

As both these processes continued, the political and the

economic, the authority of the central government in the provinces weakened, and this gave greater freedom of action to local
forces. In the provincial capitals the Janissary corps had been
the mainstay of order; now they became a threat to order. The
corps became in effect a political party, drawing support from a
populace swollen by the displaced peasantry coming in from the
countryside; it was able to resist authority, and in some places it
split into discordant factions or clashed with other privileged
groups and so maintained a permanent state of tension. In the
countryside, the weakening of the garrisons and drift of peasants
away from the villages made it possible for the nomads to move
into the settled lands and subject the farmers or else drive them
out. The seventeenth century was a time of movement in central
Arabia. New tribes were coming into the Syrian and Iraqi
deserts and challenging the supremacy of older tribes, like the
Mawali, which had established a *modus vivendi* with the sultan's
government; they cut the trade routes, on occasion plundered
the Pilgrimage, and drove the less warlike tribes over the margin
of the settled country. Faced with the challenge of Janissaries
and beduin, the Ottoman provincial government changed its
nature. In the European provinces the central power kept its
control, but in Asia and Africa there grew up semi-autonomous
ruling groups: in Asia Minor the 'Lords of the Valley', local
officials who had been territorial notables and made their power
permanent and hereditary; in Cairo, Baghdad, and Sidon groups
of Mamlukes, Caucasian soldiers of fortune bought, trained, and
freed by those already there; in Damascus and Mosul, local
families accepted by the central government as its governors.
Such groups were able to control the Janissaries and sometimes
hold back the beduin, to give the settled population an effective
administration, to collect taxes and defend the frontiers, and in
varying degrees to keep their provinces ultimately loyal to the
sultan. But they could do so only at a price. To maintain order
they had to raise private armies, and this involved higher taxes.
Moreover their rule gave greater power and scope to those local
forces which, in the great days of the empire, had been held in a
precarious balance by the sultan's regulative power. The notables
and '*ulama*' had greater influence over a local than over the central
government; and in the countryside the great families of the
mountains were able to extend their hold over the surrounding

plains—Ma'n and Shihab, Abi Lam' and Jumblat in Lebanon, Zahir al-'Umar in Galilee, and Baban in Kurdistan.

All these were movements inside the empire, affecting its nature but not, except in the long run, its existence. But from other quarters the empire was faced, in the eighteenth century, with a challenge to its very being. On the desert frontier of the empire, in central Arabia, there arose a movement of reform drawing its inspiration from the Hanbali school of thought. Islam, proclaimed Muhammad ibn 'Abd al-Wahhab (1703–87), is not a mere form of words, an imitation of what others have said: at the Day of Judgment, it will not be enough to plead, 'I heard people saying something, and I said it too'.[2] We must find out what true Islam is: it is above all a rejection of all gods except God, a refusal to allow others to share in that worship which is due to God alone (*shirk*). *Shirk* is evil, no matter what the object, whether it be 'king or prophet, or saint or tree or tomb';[3] to worship pious men is as bad as to worship idols, and it is not simply words and thoughts which constitute *shirk*, but all those acts which imply it—'a man's will to do the acts of this world is a form of *shirk*'.[4] The true Islam, stated Ibn 'Abd al-Wahhab, was that of the first generation, the pious forerunners (*al-salaf al-salih*), and in their name he protested against all those later innovations which had in fact brought other gods into Islam: against the later development of mystical thought, with its monist doctrines, its ascetic renunciation of the goods of the world, its organization into brotherhoods, its rituals other than those prescribed by the Quran; against the excessive cult of Muhammad as perfect man and intercessor with God (although great reverence was paid to him as Prophet); against the worship of saints and reverence for their shrines; and against the return into Islam of the customs and practices of the *jahiliyya*.

Ibn 'Abd al-Wahhab's teaching was not, of course, new: through his own family, who were Hanbali scholars, and through his studies at Medina and elsewhere, he had felt the influence of Ibn Taymiyya,[5] although he interpreted Islam with a firm exclusiveness which was alien to his master. But in the circumstances of his time, his preaching was not only a call to repent, it was a challenge to the dominant social forces: on the one side

---

[2] In *Majmu'at al-rasa'il*, i. 3.
[3] Ibid. iv. 5.
[4] In *Majmu'at al-tawhid*, p. 47.
[5] Cf. *Majmu'at al-rasa'il*, iii. 378 ff.

to the revived strength of the Arab tribes, still living in ignorance
of religion and *Shari'a*, and on the other to the Ottoman Empire,
which stood for Islamic orthodoxy not as the *salaf* were supposed
to have conceived it, but as it had developed over the centuries.
Ibn 'Abd al-Wahhab was really saying that the Islam the sultan
protected was not the true Islam, and he was therefore implying
that the sultan was not the true leader of the *umma*. Like other
such movements in Islam, his embodied itself in a State, and the
challenge of doctrine was also one of power. He joined forces
with a small dynasty in central Arabia, that of Ibn Sa'ud, and
together they founded a State where Muslims could live the
good life in accordance with the *Shari'a* as they interpreted it.
In this State the *Shari'a* was to be fulfilled in every detail, and no
other laws or customs were valid. Authority lay in the hands of
the imam, temporal leader and leader in prayer, but he exercised
it with the advice of *'ulama'* and community. By geographical
accident and by its emphasis on a return to the first days of
Islam, the State was Arab in consciousness; writing of the
imamate, a Wahhabi divine says with pride that, if it is to be
conferred by choice at least 'the Arabs are worthier of it than
the Turks'.[6] Its appeal however was to Islamic not Arabic
solidarity, and in essence it claimed to be *the* Islamic State to
which all could adhere. There was implicit in this a challenge to
the political authority of the Ottomans, and it was a serious
challenge, for its policy in Arabia was to replace the customs of
the *jahiliyya* by the *Shari'a*, and the *'asabiyya* of the tribes by
the sense of Islamic solidarity, and thus to canalize the warlike
energies of the beduin in a perpetual holy war. By the end of the
eighteenth century the Wahhabis were in control of central
Arabia and the Persian Gulf, and a little later they had sacked
Karbala' on the fringes of Iraq, occupied the Hejaz, and were
threatening Damascus.

At the same time, there was taking place beyond the frontiers
of Islam a movement which was destined to be of even greater
consequence for the empire: the scientific revolution in western
Europe, and the growth of military and economic power which
was a result of it. In the sixteenth century the Ottomans had
seemed likely to make themselves masters of Europe; they were
still strong enough, a century later, to capture Crete, threaten

[6] *Majmu'at al-rasa'il*, ii, pt. 3, p. 169.

Vienna, and fight the European Powers on equal terms. But they proved unable to assimilate the new discoveries in the art of warfare as they had accepted those of an earlier age, and by the second half of the eighteenth century they could no longer fight the Powers on equal terms. The result was an increase in the diplomatic influence of the Powers at Constantinople. But since the Powers were at variance with each other and looked on their influence with the sultan as an instrument of rivalry, the growth of influence meant also an increase of conflict, and the Ottoman government was able to snatch from the rivalry a certain precarious independence of action. While the balance was being maintained at the centre, however, it was overturned at the edges. In the war of 1768–74 Russian ships landed troops in Greece and at Beirut, and Russian armies advanced through the Balkans and the Caucasus; at the war's end the sultan had to give up the Crimea, then a mainly Muslim region and the first such to be lost. The British and French navies also sailed freely through what had been once the Ottoman waters of the eastern Mediterranean, and before the end of the century had involved an Ottoman province in their conflict. It was in the course of their struggle with England that the French occupied Egypt in 1798, and it was only with British help that the Turks were able to drive them out.

Even in provinces where there was no military threat, the influence of the Powers was felt. Each European consulate was a centre of influence, around which there grew up a group of protected subjects, Ottoman Christians or Jews who were given some of the privileges of foreign status. European protection extended indeed beyond individuals to whole communities. Since the sixteenth century the Capitulations had given France the right to protect European Catholics, their chapels and chaplains, in Ottoman territory, and she had gradually extended this into a general protection of Ottoman Catholics and European missions working among them. The largest and most important Catholic community was that of the Maronites. Living mainly in Lebanon, they had accepted Papal supremacy during the Crusades and had had direct and continuous relations with the Vatican since the sixteenth century; from 1649 they had direct relations too with the King of France, and French influence was strong among them. As other Catholic communities grew up, they too were under the protection of France, and of Austria to a lesser extent. The sultan had never accepted this formally but he acquiesced in it up to a point, the more so when he needed France's support against Russia. For their part the Orthodox Christians, and particularly the Greeks, had a connexion with Russia. From 1774 Russia claimed a legal basis for it in the Treaty of Kutchuk Kainardji, and the political implications of this were great, for the Orthodox were the largest and most powerful Christian body in the empire.

The Orthodox and other Christian communities indeed were growing in wealth, culture, and influence throughout the eighteenth century. Foreign protection gave them not only political advantages, but commercial and financial also, as middlemen in the trade with Europe. In particular the Greeks, Armenians, and Arabic-speaking Syrian Christians grew rich, and with wealth their standard of culture rose and their communal consciousness was sharpened. This was particularly so of the Greeks, with the still vivid memory of Byzantine greatness. Deprived of political power when Mehmed conquered Constantinople, they had won it back in another way. The Patriarch of Constantinople, always a Greek, was civil head of the whole Orthodox 'nation', and during the eighteenth century he succeeded in bringing it all under his control, either suppressing the other patriarchates or filling them with his nominees. In the same period, the great Greek families of the Phanar filled almost without interruption certain offices of influence in the State: those of Dragoman of the Porte, Dragoman of the Navy, governors of Wallachia and Moldavia. By the end of the century the Greeks had the confident spirit of a people ruling others and conscious of increasing strength, and they were becoming aware of a new world of ideas and riches in Europe and possible friends and allies there. The ideas of the French Enlightenment were brought back by students who had learnt them in the University of Padua, the first national schools were being opened and associations formed, and links with Russia were growing closer.

There had been a time when the Ottomans were quick to learn from Europe if it was in their interest to do so. In the great days of conquest they had made use of the skill and knowledge of renegades from central Europe, and had adopted European improvements in the art of war. Their expansion into Egypt and Syria at the beginning of the sixteenth century had been made easier by their use of gunpowder and firearms, their navy had made full use of the new techniques of navigation and naval strategy, and the geographical discoveries of the Renaissance had soon been known in Constantinople. Sultan Mehmed the Conqueror had some more general interest in European civilization. He invited Italian painters and men of letters to his court and had the works of Ptolemy and Plutarch done into Turkish. Perhaps his interest sprang from military need, for Italian painters were also experts in fortification, and useful information could still be got from Ptolemy, but it seems to have stirred in him a genuine curiosity. Such curiosity, however, was rare in later times. After the first long age of greatness the empire lost its dynamism and much of its political skill, and could no longer adapt itself to change at a time when change was rapid and great. The scientific discoveries aroused no echo—there is no mention of Copernicus in Ottoman literature until the end of the seventeenth century, and then only a fleeting one[7]—and the army and navy did not adopt the new technical improvements. By the middle of the eighteenth century the evidence of decline was too strong to be ignored. The sense of decline indeed seems to have been present since the early seventeenth century. One sign of it was the sequence of works, from Koçu Bey onwards, which set forth with perfect clarity the causes of decline; another perhaps was the interest in Ibn Khaldun, whose *Muqaddima* was translated into Turkish in the eighteenth century and seems to have been widely known. But as the century went on the diagnosis and prescription changed. The earlier writers had exhorted the sultans to restore the institutions of the great past, but now the empire needed something more. To defend itself, it must find European allies against its European enemies, and open itself to the new military techniques of the modern world. It was these needs which were to create the first group of political westernizers in the Near East.

As early as 1720 a special ambassador had returned from France with an admiring report, and from the 1730's the Ottoman government made a number of attempts to create a new

[7] Cf. Adnan, *Science.*

army on European lines. In that decade a French renegade,
De Bonneval, was asked by the sultan to open a school of military
engineering. It did not last long, because of opposition from the
Janissaries, but a generation later, in the 1770's, a school of
mathematics for naval officers was set up. Its first teacher was
an Algerian who knew the languages of Europe and its textbooks
were European works translated into Turkish.[8] In 1789 there
came to the throne a sultan with ideas of reform, Selim III. He
started a far-reaching reform of the army. Training schools were
opened, mainly with French instructors, except in the years after
the invasion of Egypt, when Franco-Turkish friendship was
broken for the moment. Italian and French were studied in these
schools, and some had libraries of French books, mainly but not
wholly technical. By this time, moreover, books on mathematics,
navigation, geography, and history were being translated into
Turkish and printed at the first Turkish press, established in the
1720's under the patronage of the government. There was thus
a certain stirring of thought when the French Revolution came
to strengthen it. It was the first event of European politics which
the Turks observed closely and which had a profound impact on
them, and it led, among other things, to French diplomats mixing
more than before with Ottoman officials and statesmen.[9]

It was these first impulses and ideas which Selim III tried to
canalize. In 1792 he asked the leading persons of the empire to
write reports on what was needed. Most of them agreed that
there must be military reform with the help of European officers
and technicians, but it should be so carried out as to leave the
Shari'a untouched and not arouse the hostility of conservatives.[10]
For the next twenty years Selim tried to carry out these ideas.
But his attempt to create a new model army did in fact arouse
hostility: that of the Janissaries who, seeing their position
threatened, rose in revolt with the support of '*ulama*' and populace and deposed Selim. After a period of confusion there came
to the throne Mahmud II, who had shared Selim III's imprisonment and thought as he did; but, learning the lesson of Selim's
failure, he had to wait twenty years before there came into

[8] Toderini (Fr. trs.), i. 162.
[9] Cf. B. Lewis, 'The Impact of the French Revolution on Turkey', *J. World Hist.*, i (1953), 105–25.
[10] Cf. N. Berkes, 'Historical Background of Turkish Secularism', in R. Frye, ed., *Islam and the West* (1957), p. 56.

existence two factors which enabled him to overcome the opposition of the Janissaries.

The first was the gradual formation of a group of reformers with a certain knowledge of the modern world and a conviction that the empire must belong to it or perish. Some were army officers trained in the new schools, conversant with European languages and acquainted with a modern technique. But there were others, trained in another way, and who in the event were to have greater influence: the young diplomats and diplomatic interpreters. In its early ages the empire had relied for foreign news and diplomatic skill on Jews and European renegades; as the supply of renegades ran out it began to look more to its Greek subjects, and specifically to a few great families of the Phanar, with their inherited political knowledge and skill and their grasp of European politics derived from wide contacts and study in Italy. But their loyalty was not always above suspicion, and relations between the Ottomans and Europe were becoming too close and delicate to be conducted through interested intermediaries. From the end of the eighteenth century the Porte began to open embassies in Europe and send young officials there to study the languages and politics of Europe, and later it opened a translation bureau at the Porte itself.

By the 1820's and 1830's therefore there existed Ottomans who, without being torn from their roots, had become members of the European community and were conversant with its ideas. Such a one was Ahmed Vefik Pasha, whose grandfather had been the first of the new Turkish interpreters, and whose father had worked in the embassy in Paris, where Ahmed Vefik himself was educated. A generation later he was to become grand vezir and as such to have close relations with the British Ambassador, Sir Henry Layard. Layard had known him when he was young, and has left us a portrait of him and of his father. The father was 'a perfect Turkish gentleman, of the most refined manners, and of very dignified appearance, with his snow-white beard and his turban and robes'. What a world of difference seems to separate him from his son:

His acquaintance with English and French authors would even have been remarkable in one who had received the best European education. . . . We read together the best English classics—amongst them the works of Gibbon, Robertson, and Hume—and studied political economy

in those of Adam Smith and Ricardo. . . . We also made him read . . .
the plays of Shakespeare, which he understood and appreciated, and
the novels of Dickens, into the spirit of which he thoroughly entered. . . .
He took so much delight in 'Pickwick' and the other works of Dickens
which had then appeared, and was so well acquainted with them, that
he was constantly in the habit of quoting from them in afterdays . . .[11].

Another such was Mustafa Reşid Pasha, who had his early
training in the 1830's as a diplomat in Paris, and there 'acquired
the French language, and through it had studied much of the
political literature of Europe'.[12] It was from this study that he
derived the convictions which were to direct the policy of the
empire for half a century, through him and others like him. The
empire must become a modern centralized State, and this involved several conditions: first of all, the creation of a modern
army and therefore of an educated corps of officers; then the use
of the army to re-establish the control of the central government
over the semi-autonomous and virtually independent provinces,
and by so doing to lessen the danger of revolt and foreign intervention; and the creation, throughout this reunited empire, of
a new system of law and administration based on the principle
of the equality of all citizens.

In 1821 there came to the surface of Ottoman life another force
which was to play as large a part in the subsequent history of the
empire as the idea of 'westernizing' reform, and which indeed
was an expression of it. There broke out, in Rumania and Greece,
a revolt of the Greeks. In one aspect it was an attempt to overturn
the religious and therefore also the political balance in the eastern
Mediterranean, and replace Turkish Muslim by Greek Orthodox
supremacy; but it was also a national revolt, drawing its inspiration from the memory of ancient Greece rather than
Byzantium, and aiming at the creation of a free State in the
ancient homeland of the Hellenes. The Ottoman army showed
itself unable to master the revolt, which ended—after European
intervention—in the recognition of independent Greece. This
was a decisive event in the history of the empire. From then on,
the other Christian peoples began to think increasingly of national
revolt and rallying the forces of liberal Europe in their favour.
Among those who wished the empire to continue, the idea of
reform gathered strength, for only through reform could the

[11] Layard, *Autobiography* (1903), ii. 47–50.   [12] Ibid. p. 87.

loyalty of the subject peoples be won and the support of western Europe assured. In 1826 Mahmud felt strong enough to take the first, indispensable step towards reform. He disbanded and destroyed the Janissaries, and not a finger was raised in their defence even among the religious conservatives; perhaps their failure to suppress the Greek revolt had broken their hold on the popular imagination. This event opens a half-century of reforms (known collectively as the *Tanzimat*). After that it was possible to create a new army with the help of French and Prussian instructors and use it to end the autonomous rule of 'lords of the valleys' in Anatolia, some of the princes of Kurdistan, and the Mamlukes of Baghdad. Other reforms too were carried out: schools were established to train officers, doctors, and civil servants, educational missions sent to Europe; an official newspaper was created; the last fiefs were abolished and the administration of *awqaf* reformed; the central government was reorganized, and—a symbolic act—modern dress adopted for official purposes.

All these, however, were piecemeal reforms, and did not touch the central problem, which was that of the moral and legal basis of the empire, and the place of the Christian subjects within it. It was not until 1839, shortly after the death of Mahmud, that his successor Abdülmecid, at the instigation of Reşid Pasha, issued the first general statement of the principles of reform, the Gülhane decree:[13]

All the world knows that in the first days of the Ottoman monarchy the glorious precepts of the Koran and the laws of the empire were always honored. The empire in consequence increased in strength and greatness, and all the subjects, without exception, had risen in the highest degree to ease and prosperity. In the last one hundred and fifty years a succession of accidents and divers causes have arisen, which have brought about a disregard for the sacred code of laws and the regulations flowing therefrom, and the former strength and prosperity have changed into weakness and poverty; an empire in fact loses all its stability so soon as it ceases to observe its laws. . . .

Full of confidence, therefore, in the help of the Most High, and certain of the support of our Prophet, we deem it right to seek by new institutions to give to the provinces composing the Ottoman Empire the benefit of a good administration.

[13] Text in *Düstur*, i. 4 (Eng. trs. in Hurewitz, i. 113 ff. and Ubicini, *Letters*, i. 527).

The starting-point of this preamble is the traditional Islamic theory of the State. States are virtuous when they obey the *Shari'a*, and when they are virtuous they are also stable. But what is new is the deduction made from this premiss: when virtue and strength grow weak, there is a need not only for moral reform but for a change in institutions. The decree then goes on to ask what the new institutions should be. They

must be principally carried out under three heads, which are

1. The guarantees insuring to our subjects perfect security for life, honor, and fortune.
2. A regular system of assessing and levying taxes.
3. An equally regular system for the levying of troops and the duration of their service.

And, in fact, are not life and honor the most precious gifts to mankind? What man, however much his character may be against violence, can prevent himself from having recourse to it, and thereby injure the government and the country, if his life and honor are endangered? If, on the contrary, he enjoys in that respect perfect security, he will not depart from the ways of loyalty, and all his actions will contribute to the good of the government and of his brothers.

If there is an absence of security as to one's fortune, everyone remains insensible to the voice of the Prince and the country. . . . If, on the contrary, the citizen keeps possession in all confidence of his goods, then he feels daily growing and doubling in his heart . . . his devotion to his native land. These feelings become in him the source of the most praiseworthy actions.

A number of practical steps were then suggested: the abolition of tax-farming, fixed and limited expenditure on the army and navy, regular conscription, public and regular justice, guarantees for the rights of property and against arbitrary confiscation, regular payment of officials and strict laws against corruption. These measures would apply equally to all the sultan's subjects, of whatever religion or sect they might be. In the presence of the *'ulama'* and the great men of the empire, the sultan would swear to carry them out, and they too would swear to it. The decree would also be communicated to the ambassadors of friendly Powers, so that they might be witnesses of the grant of these institutions.

The general nature of the proclamation is clear from its own words. It was a unilateral declaration of the sultan's intentions as absolute monarch, but given by him something of the nature of a contract with his subjects and with the Powers of Europe. It left the structure of Islamic law formally untouched but in fact aimed at changing the State from an Islamic sultanate to one in which adherents of all religions would equally be members of the political community, and in which all would share in the sentiment of patriotic loyalty. In the next twenty or thirty years its intentions were partly translated into law. Central and local government were reorganized further, conscription introduced, civil, criminal, and commercial courts set up, a new penal code and a new commercial code promulgated. In 1856, during the Crimean War, the sultan issued a further declaration of principles: the *Hatt-i Humayun*, which defined his aim as being the happiness of all his subjects alike, confirmed all the guarantees given in the previous decrees, and all spiritual privileges ever given to non-Muslim communities, and declared that there would henceforward be no inequality on grounds of religion, language, or race, in regard to the holding of government offices, entry into government schools, the payment of taxes or the rendering of military service.[14] In the Treaty of Paris, which ended the war in the same year, the contracting Powers took note of this decree, communicated to them by the sultan and declared to have 'issued spontaneously from his sovereign will'; but they stated that this communication did not give them the right to intervene either collectively or separately in the relations of the sultan with his subjects or the administration of his empire.[15]

The careful phrases of the treaty showed the weakness inherent in the method of reform. All depended on the will of the sultan. In 1845, it is true, an assembly of provincial notables was summoned to discuss the affairs of the empire, but it had no effect; government remained in the hands of the sultan, and in fact his power was tending to increase, as old institutions which had exercised a check on it were replaced by new ones emanating from his will, and the new codes of law grew up alongside the *Shari'a* which had for so long been sovereign. Abdülmecid and his successor Abdülaziz were on the whole willing to work with the reforming statesmen, but they were weak, capricious, and at

[14] Text in *Düstur*, i. 7 (Eng. trs. in Hurewitz, i. 149).
[15] Fr. text in *State Papers*, xl. 8.

the mercy of their advisers. It was only intermittently, and with the aid of the British and French ambassadors, that Resid Pasha and his disciples Fuad and Ali (both of them former diplomats) were able to secure the ear of the sultan and carry out the reforms they believed to be necessary.

Against them they had the religious conservatives, who wished to preserve the traditional basis of the Ottoman State, either because their own interests were bound up with it or because they regarded it as being in conformity with the will of God, and the only guarantee of stability: for example, they successfully delayed the application of the new commercial code, claiming that it dealt with a sphere of life in regard to which the prescriptions of the *Shari'a* were detailed and precise. Opposition came also from those who did not object to the reforms in principle but believed they could not be applied in a State such as the Ottoman Empire. Declarations like those of 1839 and 1856 would in fact give the Powers a new opportunity to intervene, no matter what the treaty of Paris said. Not only that, they would give a new freedom to the subject peoples to strengthen themselves and revolt. The Christian peoples of the Balkans had their own national sentiments and desired independence; the sentiment of Ottoman patriotism existed scarcely at all. Thus the reforms, these critics suggested, rested on an untried principle which nobody really believed in, and would destroy those principles on which the strength and indeed the being of the empire depended: the authority of the Islamic law and the supremacy of the Turkish Muslim element. It would be better therefore to preserve the ancient system but purify it of corruption and inefficiency, while waiting for the slow change of sentiments which would make it possible to introduce new institutions safely. Such was the view of Ahmed Vefik, the lover of *Pickwick*:

An attempt to introduce, wholesale, European institutions into Turkey, and to engraft European civilisation upon the ancient traditionary Turkish political system, before it was prepared for so great an innovation, could not possibly prove successful, and must inevitably so weaken the Ottoman Empire that it would lose the little strength and independence that it still possessed.[16]

(In his old age this same Ahmed Vefik was able to put his principles into practice. After the grant of the Ottoman constitution

[16] Layard, *Autobiography*, ii. 89-90.

in 1876, he became president of the first elected chamber, and his firm control of the debates showed he had lost none of his suspicion of institutions he regarded as out of place and dangerous.)

This indeed was to remain the problem of the empire throughout the last century of its existence: how to introduce into the body politic those changes in institutions and political morality which, in the modern world, were the sources of strength? There were distant provinces of the empire, however, where government was autonomous and the population homogeneous, and where reform therefore posed no such problems and had more success. Such was Egypt, to which the ideas of the French Revolution came embodied in a European army. The last great historian of the ancient tradition, al-Jabarti (1756–1825), was living in Egypt when Bonaparte's army landed, and in his description of the coming of the French we can see implicit the whole ambivalent relationship of modern Egypt and modern Europe. He describes how one day English ships arrived off Alexandria. A small boat was lowered and ten Englishmen came ashore. They met the notables of the city and told them they were searching for the French fleet. 'You will not', they said, 'be able to drive them off. We shall stay here with our fleet to defend your port, and we want nothing of you except water and food.' But the notables replied: 'This is the sultan's country, neither the French nor any other people have any rights in it. Please go away.' Their defiant spirit was echoed by the Mamluke *amirs* when the news came to Cairo: they received it with indifference, saying 'Let all the Franks come, and we shall crush them beneath our horses' hooves.'[17]

On the morrow of his occupation of Alexandria, Bonaparte issued an Arabic proclamation. It began with the traditional Muslim invocation—'In the name of God, the Merciful, the Compassionate; there is no god but God, He has no offspring and no partner.' But the next phrase invoked a new principle: this proclamation, it declared, was issued by the French Government, which was 'built on the basis of freedom and equality'. It then proceeded to apply these principles to Egypt. In the eyes of God all men were equal, except in intelligence and virtue. The Mamlukes had neither intelligence nor virtue, and therefore had

[17] Jabarti, iii. 2 ff.

no right to rule Egypt and control all that is good in it. They had
ruined 'this best of countries', destroyed the great cities and
canals for which it was once famous. Now their rule was over, and
henceforth nobody among the people of Egypt would be excluded
from high position. The men of virtue and learning among them
would direct affairs and the state of the *umma* be improved. The
proclamation ends with a rousing peroration: 'God curse the
Mamlukes and improve the condition of the Egyptian *umma*'.[18]
(The same lesson was repeated in another proclamation, issued a
little later when the great *diwan* was established: the Turks
have ruined Egypt by their greed. Now the French nation
(*ta'ifa*) have come forward to free Egypt from her present state
and give her people rest from the oppression of this government.')[19]

The main appeal is then to national sentiment, but mixed
with it is an appeal to religious sentiment:

It has been said to you that I have only come to this country in order
to destroy your religion. This is a clear lie; do not believe it. Say to the
slanderers that I have come to rescue you from the hands of the
oppressors. I worship God (may He be exalted) far more than the
Mamlukes do, and respect His Prophet and the glorious Quran . . .
O shaykhs, judges and imams, officers and notables of the land, tell
your people that the French also are sincere Muslims; the proof of it is
that they have occupied great Rome and ruined the papal see which was
always urging the Christians to attack Islam, and from there they have
gone to the island of Malta and expelled from it the Knights of Malta
who used to claim that God wanted them to fight the Muslims. At all
times the French have been sincere friends of the Ottoman sultan and
enemies of his enemies.[20]

This was not simply what the modern world would call
'propaganda'. As a child of the French Enlightenment, Bonaparte may well have regarded Islam as being nearer to the
religion of reason than was Christianity, and until the end of his
life he kept his lively interest in it. Moreover in denouncing the
Mamlukes and professing respect for the 'men of virtue and
learning', he was sketching out the policy he proposed to
follow: to transfer local power from the Mamluke *amirs* to the
'ulama', the popular leaders of Egypt and the only alternative
ruling class. Even had his stay in Egypt lasted longer, however, it

[18] Jabarti, iii. 4–5.   [19] Ibid. p. 23.   [20] Ibid. p. 4.

is unlikely that he would have succeeded in ruling in partnership with them, for in the eyes of the '*ulama*' no benefits he could
bring to Egypt would have outweighed his being a non-Muslim
ruling a Muslim land in defiance of the sultan, and it is unlikely
that any Muslim was taken in by his assurances. Jabarti was
himself a shaykh of the Azhar, and he begins his account of the
French occupation by saying that this was the beginning of a
reversal of the natural order and the corruption or destruction of
all things.[21] He does not hesitate, it is true, to give credit to the
French when he sees things of which he can approve—the
Institute with its pictures, maps, and books, its scientific
collections and experiments; the French *savants* with their
enthusiasm for learning, and the warmth of their welcome to
Muslim visitors who shared a genuine interest in science. But
he was always conscious of the danger to religion and morality
inherent in non-Muslim rule: the arming and training of
Christian soldiers, the powers given to Coptic tax-collectors, the
'pernicious innovations' introduced into the legal system, and
the corruption of women—for even the daughter of the greatest
religious notable, the Shaykh al-Bakri, had mixed with the
French and dressed like a French lady, and was executed for it
when the Turks came back.[22]

Possibly some memory of the proclamation and the Institute
lingered on among the shaykhs of the Azhar, and perhaps too
the methodical French administration, which Jabarti admired,
left its mark on the mind of Muhammad 'Ali, who came to power
in the confusion caused by the departure of the French. By
1805 he had established himself as ruler and been recognized
by the people of Cairo and the sultan. He started to modernize
Egypt on lines similar in some ways to those of Selim and
Mahmud. By the massacre of the Mamlukes and the confiscation
of their lands, he destroyed the main obstacle to his own power
and to reform, and on the ruins of their army and government he
built his own. He created a modern army and navy, trained by
French officers, and a relatively efficient, centralized system of
administration and taxation. His reforms were less doctrinaire
than those of Selim and Mahmud, and carried out primarily to
strengthen his own position *vis-à-vis* his sovereign, his subjects,
and the Powers of Europe. Himself a man of no education, who

[21] Ibid. p. 2.   [22] Ibid. pp. 35–36, 171, 142, 20, 170, 202.

only learnt to read in his forties,[23] he was not so responsive to
the political ideas of modern Europe as were the sultans of his
time. He had, it is true, some interest in books, but only for
what they could teach him in the art of government. Books about
Napoleon were translated and read to him, and he had Ibn
Khaldun's *Muqaddima* copied from North African manuscripts
and translated into Turkish.[24] He listened with less admiration
to a translation of Macchiavelli made at his command by his
minister, Artin. Artin relates that he translated it for the pasha
at the rate of ten pages a day:

> But on the fourth [day] he stopped me. 'I have read', he said, 'all that
> you have given me of Macchiavelli. I did not find much that was new
> in your first ten pages, but I hoped that it might improve; but the next
> ten pages were not better, and the last are mere commonplace. I see
> clearly that I have nothing to learn from Macchiavelli. I know many
> more tricks than he knew. You need not translate any more of him.'[25]

Muhammad 'Ali issued no proclamation of rights, and made
no attempt to reform the political institutions of the country.
Apart from one large advisory council called in 1829, he governed
in the traditional way: decisions were made by him personally,
after full and free discussion with his advisers. The *'ulama'* were
not among his closest advisers; as spokesmen and leaders of the
people of Cairo they had helped to put him in power, but that a
ruler should destroy those by whom he has attained power was
one of the lessons he knew without reading Macchiavelli.
Whether he intended it or not, his destruction of the systems of
tax-farms and interference with the *awqaf* struck at the root of
their social position and of the system of Islamic schools. In their
place and that of the Mamlukes he formed a ruling group which
included Turkish, Kurdish, Albanian, and Circassian soldiers,
and also Europeans, Armenians, and others conversant with the
politics and finances of Europe. Popular interest in politics was
discouraged: to a student who told him that he had studied civil
administration in Paris, he replied sternly: 'It is I who govern.
Go to Cairo and translate military works.'[26]

But he had a certain vision of modern Europe, of a dynamic
society rationally exploiting its resources and administering its

---

[23] Senior, *Conversations*, ii. 174.   [24] Rustum, iv, no. 6249.
[25] Senior, ii. 174.   [26] Heyworth-Dunne, p. 168.

affairs, with national strength as the criterion of law and policy. Although he sometimes acted as champion of Ottoman Islam, for example when he destroyed the Wahhabi power in Arabia at the request of the sultan, his policy on the whole was one of religious equality: Christians and Jews of all nations were welcome in Egypt, their rights were guaranteed and their commercial activities encouraged, and among his closest collaborators were Armenians. He was more fully aware than his Turkish contemporaries of the real basis of western strength, the scientific organization of production. He created the basis of Egypt's modern economy, the intensive cultivation of cotton on irrigated land, and he began also to create a modern system of transport and marketing. With less success he tried to create modern industries, for which there existed neither the skilled labour nor the internal market. In all this he may have been influenced by the followers of Saint-Simon who spent some years in Egypt in the 1830's, working as doctors, engineers, and teachers, and helping him to design and execute the first great modern work of irrigation in Egypt, the barrages on the Nile. Saint-Simon's vision of a model society directed by a priesthood of scientists, and with the system of scientific truth taking the place of the religious systems which had broken down, is not likely to have appealed to him, even had it been explained in familiar terms; but the exaltation of industrial development and the planned economy was in line with his own interests.

It was largely in the interest of his military policy that he opened professional schools, sent students to Europe, set them to translate technical works when they returned, established a press to print the translations, and an official newspaper to publish the texts of his decrees and decisions. He needed artillery officers, doctors, and engineers. It was not his intention that they should acquire more than a necessary skill: they were kept under strict control, and when a group of students asked his permission to make a tour of France and acquire a knowledge of French life at first hand he refused it.[27] But with new skills new ideas were bound to enter, and the schools and scholastic missions had an influence greater far than he could have intended. The first teachers in his schools were Italians, and Italian—then the *lingua franca* of the Levant—was the first European language

[27] Heyworth-Dunne, p. 166.

to be taught. But it was soon replaced by French, and with French there came in the ideas of Voltaire, Rousseau, and Montesquieu. As early as 1816 their works were in the library of one of the schools.[28] From 1826 onwards organized missions were sent to France: they read French books and saw French life at one of those moments of revolution when the conflict of general ideas is embodied in the clash of opposing forces. Most of the students of the first schools and missions were Turks or Levantine Christians, but later the Egyptian element grew larger, and it was this element which was to form the first intelligentsia of modern Egypt. Already in the 1830's it was beginning to play a part in affairs: its members were translating and publishing other than purely technical books; it worked closely with the Saint-Simonians to bring about a reorganization of the schools,[29] and from its ranks came the first considerable political thinker of modern Egypt, Rifaʿa al-Tahtawi.

To the Arab Muslims of Syria the new knowledge and ideas came more slowly. The great families of the cities played their part in local politics but took almost no direct share in the government of the empire as a whole. It was not indeed until the end of the nineteenth century that they began to send their sons into the civil administration by way of the professional schools. At the beginning of the century their connexions were rather with the religious order, which was still untouched by ideas of reform when not hostile to them. Nor did they feel, as did the similar class in Egypt, the intellectual and social shock of European occupation. Bonaparte tried but failed to occupy Syria. Had he succeeded, it is not certain that he would have attempted to apply the same policy, of relying on the religious notables as the spokesmen of national opinion. In the proclamation which he addressed to the peoples of the country he made no appeal to 'Arab' or 'Syrian' feeling. Once more he declared it to be his intention to drive out the Mamlukes (by 'Mamlukes' here he meant the military group formed by the ruthless Jazzar, governor of Sidon), and promised to do no harm to the people or their religion. But he addressed himself not to a 'nation' like the 'Egyptian *umma*', but simply to 'the inhabitants of the districts of Gaza, Ramle, and Jaffa'.[30]

[28] Heyworth-Dunne, p. 110.   [29] Ibid. pp. 181–204.   [30] Jabarti, iii. 49.

The Christian population of Syria, on the other hand, had already been touched by some aspects of European thought. It was in the sixteenth century that the Catholic Church began to establish its first regular contacts with the eastern Christian communities. Jesuit and other missionaries were sent to the Near East, not only to bring the dissident Churches into the Roman fold, but to reform the doctrine and discipline of the Maronites and such other elements as already accepted Rome's supremacy. The Maronites made a Concordat with Rome in 1736, and from that time had a regular relationship which guaranteed their hierarchy, liturgy, canon law, and customs, while safeguarding their doctrinal orthodoxy and acceptance of the Pope's supremacy. The work of the missions gradually created similar Uniate groups within the other eastern Churches —Orthodox, Armenian, Coptic, Syrian Orthodox, and Nestorian. After a struggle for power within the patriarchates and bishoprics in the early eighteenth century, these groups emerged as *de facto* separate Churches, each under its own patriarch, although they received no civil recognition from the Ottoman government until the nineteenth century. Thanks to the missions, and under the protection of France, there grew up a network of Catholic schools wherever there were Catholic, or potentially Catholic communities, but particularly in Lebanon and at Aleppo. At the heart of the Catholic Church, in Rome, there were created a number of colleges to form an educated and orthodox Catholic priesthood: the Maronite and Greek Colleges, and the College of the Congregation *De Propaganda Fide*.

From the Christian communities created or strengthened by the missions, there sprang a group of educated men aware of the new world of Europe and indeed in some sense a part of it. By the end of the sixteenth century there was an educated priesthood, in particular among the Maronites and Greek Catholics, of exemplary life and discipline, and with a knowledge of Latin and Italian and the culture to which they were the key, as well as a deeper knowledge than before of their own oriental languages and antiquities and the history and customs of their communities. Some of them, like the famous scholars of the Assemani family in Rome, and the Maronite priests who taught Arabic at the Sorbonne, made great contributions to European knowledge of the Near East, and some of them widened the horizons of their

c

own communities by translating or adapting works of western Catholic theology. The *Summa Theologica* of St Thomas Aquinas was translated in full at the beginning of the eighteenth century.

It was under the impulse of the colleges and missions too that monasteries following the rules of western monasticism began to be created at the end of the seventeenth century, particularly in Lebanon, in the free and secluded mountain valleys and under the protection of the great families, the Jumblats who were Druzes as well as the Khazins who were themselves Maronites. These monasteries too became centres of learning and education, for local seminaries and village schools grew up under their shelter. Such schools taught laymen as well as clergy, and so in course of time there grew up a class of educated laymen, who found scope for their talents as clerks and confidential men of affairs for the local rulers. Already in the seventeenth century the prince of the mountain, Fakhr al-Din, had begun to use Maronite priests in his delicate exchanges with the courts of Europe, and later the Turkish rulers of the Syrian coast, the governors of Tripoli and Sidon, began to employ in their financial administration Christians of supple mind and with a good knowledge of Arabic. Before the end of the eighteenth century Syrian Christians had taken over the administration of the customs in Egypt, and when Muhammad 'Ali succeeded the Mamlukes he too made use of them in his financial control as well as his relations with the local rulers of Syria.

These educated laymen were scholars as well as officials. In the early eighteenth century a number of Christians in Aleppo set themselves to master the sciences of the Arabic language, acquiring them from the only group which possessed them at that time, the shaykhs of the Muslim religious hierarchy. Some of them wrote poetry and prose correctly and with love, and it was from them that the flame of Arabic literature was carried to Lebanon. Those who wished to be officials studied Arabic avidly as part of their professional training, and passed on what they had studied to their children. Whole families of men of letters grew up in this way, and it was from such families—Yaziji, Shidyaq, Bustani—that there came, in the early nineteenth century, the founders of the literary renaissance of the Arabs.

In the eighteenth century trade between the Near East and

Europe was changing its character. The European merchant
colonies in the Ottoman towns were dwindling, partly because
of the difficulties of trade in insecure regions, and partly because
they could find higher rates of profit elsewhere. Trade was
passing therefore into the hands of oriental Christians and Jews,
who had the advantage of consular protection and a knowledge
of European languages and business methods. The Arabic-
speaking Christians and Jews of Damascus, Aleppo, and the
coastal towns, like the Greeks and Armenians, were able to build
a trading network reaching from their own native towns to
Alexandria, Livorno, Trieste, and Marseilles, and in this way
there grew up yet another group with a direct knowledge of
European life, the first Near Eastern group to have mastered the
technique of modern trade and finance.

In so far as these groups, priests, clerks, and merchants,
acquired a European culture, it was mainly a theological culture.
The literature of Catholic theology and devotion they accepted
and read, but neither the polite literature of Europe nor its
political ideas seem to have impinged on them until well on into
the nineteenth century. But the new interest in the Arabic
language had of course a profound influence on their mental life.
It led first of all to a new stirring of historical self-consciousness.
Some of the educated clergy studied with eagerness the antiquities of the Arabs as well as the history of the eastern Churches,
and among clergy and laity alike there grew up also an interest
in secular history. In Lebanon there grew up a school of historians
the centre of whose interest was the peculiar history of the
mountain: the formation of its two religious communities,
Maronites in the north and Druzes in the south, the growth of a
princedom and a hierarchy of noble families which included
them both, the establishment and maintenance of virtual independence as against the Mamluke and then the Turkish rulers
of the surrounding country.

The first important historian was the Maronite Patriarch,
Istifanus al-Duwayhi (1603–1704). Educated in the Maronite
College at Rome, he knew Latin and Italian as well as Arabic
and Syriac, and made use of William of Tyre as well as al-
Mas'udi. In form, his main work—the *Ta'rikh al-azmina*—was
a history of the Maronite Church and people, their patriarchs
and secular chiefs, their struggles against the Jacobite heresy and

the intervention of Muslim rulers; but in its later part it became a history of the emergence of Lebanon as a territorial unit, of the establishment of its autonomy and unity. The writing of local history started by Duwayhi was carried farther by a sequence of historians, both clerical and lay, and culminated in two comprehensive works, summing up the political history of Lebanon and containing by implication a doctrine of what Lebanon was. The Amir Haydar Shihab (1761–1835) wrote a history of the country which was in effect the history of his own family. He had a number of collaborators, and one of them, Tannus al-Shidyaq (1794–1861), wrote a history of the noble families of Lebanon, Maronite, Druze, and Muslim; its concept of Lebanon is of a hierarchy of families, where family alliances and the common interest of preventing the encroachments of the Ottomans outweigh differences of religion.[31]

Haydar Shihab is not unaware of the history of Europe, and indeed he interrupts his local narrative to describe the French Revolution and Bonaparte's occupation of Egypt. For him, as for the Turkish historians of the time, the Revolution is primarily destructive, an upsurge against the established authority of the king. But some consciousness of the positive doctrines lying behind the Revolution seems to have come into Lebanon through Lebanese merchants who had contact with the French army in Egypt and some of whom acted as interpreters. In a writer of the next generation, we have a record of a self-taught mind awakening to the scientific ideas and speculations of the French Enlightenment. Mikha'il Mishaqa (1800–88), although of Greek origin, was born in a village of Lebanon and brought up in the little mountain-town of Dayr al-Qamar. His family was not devoid of culture and his father taught him the rudiments of learning; but he was largely self-educated, under the impulse of a curiosity which awoke at an early age and led his mind far beyond the confines of his village:

Mikha'il's thoughts turned to the knowledge of arithmetic, but at that time there was nobody in Dayr al-Qamar who knew more than addition, and if for example someone wanted to find out how much seven *rutls* would cost, when the price of a *rutl* was $17\frac{1}{4}$, he had to write the price down seven times and then add it up. . . . He used to hear from the Jews about eclipses of the sun and moon before they

[31] Cf. Salibi; Hourani, 'Historians of Lebanon', *in* Lewis and Holt.

happened. They claimed, as they still do, that their rabbis knew how to calculate the times of the eclipses, and did not admit that they received them in the yearly almanac from Europe; and I used to believe their lies. ... I attached myself to one of them ... who told me he was an expert in fixing the times of eclipses, and at the time I did not know what that meant in the way of precise calculations ... so I asked him to teach me and paid him for his teaching. I continued to go to him for some months, and he made me promises but never admitted his ignorance, until I despaired of him and left him. ... Then, in the year of 1814, there came to us from Damietta my maternal uncle Butrus 'Anhuri. ... He got out his books and I looked at what was written on their spines: I found on the spine of one of them *The 'Science of Astronomy* by the Frenchman De Lalande', on a second 'De Lalande—*The Position of the Stars*', on a third 'The commentary of the Archimandrite Anthimus Ghazi on the book of the Englishman Benjamin about natural science' ... with other books on other subjects. ... I opened them and found them all written by hand in Arabic, for those which were originally in a foreign language had been translated by Basili Fakhr, French Consul in Damietta. And when I came upon them ... I was exceedingly joyful, for I believed that once I should know them the secrets of the universe would be spread before me. ... I asked my uncle, 'Do you know astronomy, and if so how did you learn it?' ... and he said to me ... 'When Bonaparte came to Egypt with the French army and occupied it in 1799 the English blockaded him from the sea and trade came to a standstill; I did not waste my time, but I worked hard learning the French language. There were many learned men among them, and from them I became aware of the new discoveries in astronomy and natural science and geography' ... Then in the year 1817 my father sent me to Damietta to my paternal uncle. ... [There and then] my thoughts about matters of religion were troubled ... especially when I saw many of the people of Damietta, Muslims and Christians, more troubled than I was. And my disquiet was increased by reading the book of voyages of the Frenchman Volney, in which he talks about his journey in Lebanon and his visit to the ruins of Palmyra (for at that time M. Basili Fakhr was occupied with translating books into Arabic and translated this book, although there were then no presses to print them in the land of Egypt). ... In this year also I worked hard at mastering the science of music and the art of playing musical instruments both string and wind.[32]

Like all strong rulers of Egypt, Muhammad 'Ali wanted a friendly or subservient régime on his eastern frontier, and by the 1820's he was in a position to secure it: he had created an

[32] Mishaqa, *al-Jawab*, pp. 61–65.

army strong enough to master any opposition from his suzerain the sultan, and established a position of influence with the local rulers of Syria. In 1831 he sent his army into Syria, and conquered the country with small difficulty. For almost a decade his son Ibrahim Pasha ruled it. Here as in Egypt the age of Muhammad 'Ali began a new phase in the knowledge of Europe. The country was opened more widely than before to European travellers and residents, to traders, missionaries, and curious observers. It was placed for ten years under an administration of a new type, and one based on the principles spread by the revolutionary government of France: centralization, a trained and disciplined army, the scientific exploitation of natural resources, equality as between adherents of all religions. The equality of Christians and Muslims seems indeed to have been emphasized by Muhammad 'Ali more in Syria than in Egypt. They sat side by side in the local councils which he established; Christian soldiers from Lebanon were used to put down Druze and Nusayri risings; and Ibrahim's chief advisers were the Christian financier Hanna Bahri and the prince of Lebanon, Bashir Shihab, whose own beliefs were obscure but who relied for support on the Maronites and himself died a Catholic.

By a paradox, however, it was the modern nature of Muhammad 'Ali's government which in the end aroused Syrian opposition, and the new sense of religious equality which he tried to create found expression in an alliance of religious communities against him. In the late 1830's Ibrahim tried to extend to Lebanon and other mountainous districts the modern principles of regular taxation, disarmament of the civil population, and universal conscription. The result was widespread discontent. At the same time, Ibrahim, having defeated the Ottoman army at Nezib, marched into Asia Minor, and this was taken by all the European Powers, except France, as a threat to the existence of the empire and therefore to their interests. A coalition was formed to compel Muhammad 'Ali to withdraw his armies not only from Asia Minor but from Syria, and one of the measures of compulsion was to give arms and other help to the discontented elements in Lebanon. There broke out a revolt against Ibrahim and against Bashir, who remained loyal to him; and in the documents of this revolt we can hear a new note—that of men of different religions co-operating in defence of interests derived

from living in a common home country. In May 1840 leaders of
the different communities met together in the church of St Elias
at Antilyas near Beirut, and swore to work together loyally in
common resistance to the attempt of Bashir and the Egyptians
to impose disarmament and conscription:

We, the undersigned, Druzes, Christians, Shi'is and Sunnis, living
in Mount Lebanon and drawn from all its villages, have met at St Elias
and sworn on the altar of the saint that we shall not betray nor harm
each other. We shall speak with one voice and have one opinion.[33]

Europeans played a large part in preparing and organizing the
revolt. There were British agents in Lebanon, in particular
Richard Wood, a young member of the staff of the British
Embassy in Constantinople, a master of the languages and
politics of the Near East, who had performed already a delicate
function in Kurdistan and was sent to Lebanon to establish
contact with the potential opponents of Egyptian rule. He lived
there for two years under pretext of learning Arabic. There were
also one or two Frenchmen in Lebanon at the time, who in spite
of the general policy of their government, were opposed to
Ibrahim and supported the movement against him. Perhaps one
can see the influence of such men in the proclamation issued by
the insurgents to their fellow countrymen, and which brings us
at a jump into the modern world of mass movements and
national spirit:

Patriots!
You all know of the injustices committed by the Egyptian government, the heavy taxes and extortions under which the whole of Syria is
crushed, so that ruin has fallen on many families. In spite of their well-
known spirit of independence the people of Lebanon have borne with
patience the oppressions of tyrannical authority, out of respect for the
Amir Bashir, and in the hope that at least this patience of theirs would
secure their honour, freedom and existence.

If we have not taken up arms earlier to deliver ourselves from an
oppressive power, it is because we have placed our hopes in the
benevolent and patriotic intervention of our prince, which would have
secured a respite from our sufferings. But alas, this iniquitous government has shown him no gratitude for the services he has given it. . . .
Let us be sure in advance that late regrets will not save us if we are
divided, or if we hesitate an instant to make a common effort for the
recovery of our freedom.

[33] Khazin, i. 2.

So that we should act with dignity and force ... there should be held a meeting of those among us who are best known for their high position and intelligence. This meeting should be composed of five leaders elected by a majority in each district, and all or some of them should form a council to meet in some convenient place in order to establish a perfect organization. ... The members of this council should be constantly in touch with one another, so that we should be able to provide quickly for the defence of our threatened fellow countrymen, to save ourselves from slavery and injustice, and to confound all the tricks of a hated government which will never succeed in dividing us. Already the Greeks have given us an example, and secured their freedom with the help of God.[34]

In spite of the mention of the Greeks, this is not an appeal to independence. The revolt was taking place with the help of the Powers, whose policy was to restore the authority of the sultan in Syria. The insurgents professed willing obedience and submission to the sultan.[35] But the idea of freedom is in the proclamation by implication, and those who issued it were quite clear where it came from; for at the same time they issued an appeal to the French Ambassador to abandon support of Muhammad 'Ali and help them to escape from oppression:

France, that great and magnanimous nation which has spread freedom in every place and has shed so much blood over the centuries to establish liberty in its government ... now refuses us her powerful support so that we may enjoy this same blessing.[36]

Ibrahim Pasha and his army withdrew to Egypt, Ottoman rule was restored, Bashir was deposed in favour of a weak member of his family. A little later the new prince was in his turn deposed by the Turks, and the princedom came to an end. Lebanon was divided into two districts, ruled by a Maronite and a Druze governor respectively. There followed twenty years of crisis, during which the growth of European influence and the spread of western ideas added a new dimension of danger to local conflicts. The removal of the framework of political unity, the intervention of Britain and France, the attempts of the Turkish government to impose direct rule on Lebanon, as well as the measures which Bashir had taken during his reign to weaken

[34] Khazin i. 3; cf. Testa, iii. 74.
[35] Ibid. p. 11; cf. Testa, iii. 81.
[36] Ibid. p. 13; cf. Testa, iii. 82.

the power of the Druze nobles: all these factors led to a tension between religious communities such as had not existed earlier. But the communal tension was something more as well; it contained in itself undertones of social and intellectual unrest. The social balance between Druzes and Maronites was shifting; but so also was the internal balance of the Maronites themselves. The landowning families in the mountain were losing their local authority in the face of two challenges: that of the religious hierarchy, growing in influence and sometimes using it to support the peasants in their conflicts with their lords; and that of the merchants of the ports, both Europeans and Levantines, who imported manufactured goods and exported silk, and were gradually taking over the economic functions of the landowners. The Christian educated class was also increasing rapidly. Under the Egyptians Catholic and Protestant missions were able to work more freely than before. They began to establish schools on a larger scale and a higher level, to write or translate textbooks and print them at their presses, and from the schools there was emerging a new class of educated men with a knowledge not only of Arabic but of one or more European languages, and some knowledge also—whether their teachers intended it or not—of the ideas of the nineteenth century.

The tension and the crisis to which it led, had therefore two aspects: it was a struggle of Druzes to maintain their traditional supremacy, but also a struggle of Maronite nobles against the forces of change. The religious conflict of 1860 was preceded by a social conflict: in 1858 the peasantry in the purely Maronite district of Kisrawan revolted against their lords of the Khazin family. Led by a village hero, Tanyus Shahin, they evicted the Khazins at the beginning of 1859 and set up a 'republican government' with a rough system of popular representation.[37] When war between Maronites and Druzes came in 1860, it led to a Druze victory and a massacre of Christians in Damascus. The Powers intervened, France with an army and the others diplomatically, and after discussion in Beirut and Constantinople an Organic Law was drawn up which settled alike the social and the religious conflict. Lebanon was to be ruled by a Christian governor appointed by the Sublime Porte, but he was to be assisted by central and local councils representing the different

[37] Yazbak, *Thawra*, p. 87 (Eng. trs. p. 53).

communities and chosen after consultation. The communities would be equally represented; all individuals would be equal before the law and all 'feudal' privileges were abolished.[38]

Far to the west, the Regency of Tunis had been a dependency of the Ottoman sultan since the sixteenth century, but had soon become virtually independent, paying tribute but managing its own affairs and to a great extent its foreign relations. From the seventeenth century power had been in the hands of a local military group, and since the early eighteenth a family springing from that group, the Husaynis, had held the office of Bey. In the first half of the nineteenth century the Beys found themselves faced with a decline in internal order and security and the extension of the commercial influence of Europe. To restore their authority they began to build up a modern army and change the methods of administration; and to pay for the army and civil service and restore prosperity they began to encourage foreign merchants to settle. But this created new problems. The growing interests of the foreign merchants and money-lenders gave the Powers a chance to intervene, and the officers of the modern army became the carriers of new political ideas. To remove the legitimate grievances of the foreign communities, to rally the support of the men with new ideas, and to create among all parts of the people firmer roots for their rule, Muhammad Bey issued his own version of the Turkish reforms, the *'ahd al-aman* of 1857.[39] In the preamble, reference is made to the public interest (*maslaha*) as the principle of interpretation of law: 'God ... who has given justice as a guarantee of the preservation of order in this world, and has given the revelation of law in accordance with human interests'. The document then goes on to expound the principles on which public interest depends: first liberty, for man cannot attain prosperity unless his liberty is guaranteed, and he is certain of finding a shelter against oppression only behind the ramparts of justice; secondly, complete security; thirdly,—and this is implied in the second point— complete equality between Muslims and non-Muslims. They should be equal before the law, for this right belongs equally to all men; and foreigners too should have the same rights as

[38] Fr. text in *State Papers*, li. 288.
[39] Text in Bayram, ii. 11 (Fr. trs. in Fitoussi & Benazet, i, app., p. iii).

Tunisians, they should be able to exercise all trades freely and buy property. Three years later, in 1860, a sort of constitution was issued.[40] The first constitution to be issued in any Muslim country in modern times, it is not clear whose ideas were behind it. They may have been those of Richard Wood, the British Consul-General, whom we have already met in his early life in another country; but Tunis is not far from Italy, there were Italian political exiles at the Bey's court, there were Tunisian officials who knew French and had visited France, and it is not difficult to find several sources through which the idea of a constitution may have come. It is in any case a cautious document, admitting the principle of representation only within limits and leaving executive power in the hands of the ruler. The ruler must swear to do nothing contrary to the 'ahd al-aman, and is responsible for his acts before the Supreme Council; but the Supreme Council itself is to include ministers and officials as to one-third of its members, while the other two-thirds are to be nominated by the ruler in the first instance, and then to co-opt new members at regular intervals.

The experiment in constitutional government did not last long, but broke down a few years later because of financial crisis, unrest among the tribes, the pressure and rivalry of England and France, and the desire of the Bey to keep his unrestrained power. But this period left its mark: it helped to form a new political consciousness in Tunis, and to bring to the front a group of reforming statesmen, officials, and writers who were to play a considerable part, in the face of difficulties, until they were scattered by the French occupation in 1881.[41] This group had two origins: one of them was the Zaytuna mosque, the seat of the traditional Islamic learning, where the influence of a reforming teacher, Shaykh Muhammad Qabadu, was felt; the other was the new School of Military Sciences, established by Ahmad Bey, with an Italian administrator, British, French, and Italian teachers, and the same Shaykh Qabadu as teacher of Arabic and the religious sciences.[42] The students of these two schools achieved position and exercised influence in the army, as ministers and as government teachers; their unquestioned

[40] Fr. text in Fitoussi & Benazet, i, app., p. x.
[41] Cf. Ibn 'Ashur, *al-Haraka*, lecture I.
[42] Monchicourt, p. 298.

leader was the first supervisor of the military school, Khayr al-Din, then a young Mamluke in the Bey's service, but later to become Prime Minister at a critical moment and the author of a book we shall consider.

IV

THE FIRST GENERATION:
TAHTAWI, KHAYR AL-DIN,
AND BUSTANI

By 1860 there had come into existence little groups of officials, officers and teachers, alive to the importance of reforming the structure of the empire, and convinced this could not be done unless some at least of the forms of European society were borrowed. The reforming group in Constantinople included few if any Arabs at this time, but the great proclamations of reform and the laws which resulted from them had an influence all over the empire, and Ottoman officials of the new way of thought held positions in the Arab as in other provinces. In Egypt men with some amount of French education were already filling important posts, and in 1863 one of them, Isma'il Pasha, came to the throne; in Tunis too the leader of the young reformers, Khayr al-Din, was beginning to be important in the affairs of the State. The Christian students of the mission schools in Lebanon and Syria were unable to play so direct a part in the government of what after all was still an Islamic State, but they already had some indirect influence as interpreters in the local governments and foreign consulates, and in the 1860's were to acquire a new power as the first journalists of the Arab world. Among all these groups, all involved in some way in the process of change, the *idea* of reform had taken root, and in the 1860's it found expression in a movement of thought, directed in the first instance at the specific problems of the Near East, but raising once more by implication the general questions of political theory: what is the good society, the norm which should direct the work of reform? Can this norm be derived from the principles of Islamic law, or is it necessary to go to the teachings and practice of modern Europe? Is there in fact any contradiction between the two? We can see such questions come to life in the minds of certain writers of the time, committed as they are in some way to the movement of reform, but also in another sense upholders of Islamic tradition and wishing to show that modern reform was not only a legitimate but a necessary implication of the social teaching of Islam.

In Constantinople these themes had already been touched upon by writers of the first half of the nineteenth century, such as Sadık Rifat Pasha, but they were first expounded fully by a younger group who became prominent during the 1860's: Şinasi, Ziya Pasha, Namık Kemal. Acquainted as they were with the literature of Europe, conversant with its ideas and admirers of its strength and progress, they were still not whole-hearted westernizers. They were conscious of belonging to an Ottoman community which included non-Turks and non-Muslims; they wanted the Ottoman Empire to enter the modern world; but they were aware also of an Islamic fatherland in which they were rooted. They set high value on the social morality of Islam, and tried to justify the adoption of western institutions in Islamic terms, as being not the introduction of something new but a return to the true spirit of Islam. In political matters they were democrats, believing that the modern parliamentary system was a restatement of the system of consultation which had existed in early Islam and was the sole guarantee of freedom; and this brought them into conflict with the government, of which they criticized the autocratic nature even when they supported its reforms. They found a channel for their ideas and criticism in the Turkish newspapers which began to spring up from 1860 onwards, both in the empire and in western Europe; and in the mid-1860's they went a stage farther and made the first attempt to organize a political group. Under the patronage of a member of the khedivial family of Egypt, Mustafa Fazil Pasha, a 'Young Ottoman' group, with Ziya Pasha and Namık Kemal as members, was formed in Istanbul and then moved to Paris; the journal they published had a certain influence, but after 1871, when the leaders were allowed to return from exile, the group dissolved.

The Young Ottomans were liberals, but they were also patriotic Turkish Muslims, and there was a hidden tension in their thought which was only to become explicit in a later generation. In Cairo another group was thinking similar thoughts, in which Ottoman Islamic liberalism was intertwined with something else; but there the 'something else' was Egyptian territorial patriotism. The writer who first made articulate the idea of the Egyptian nation, and tried to explain and justify it in terms of Islamic thought, was Rifaʿa Badawi Rafiʿ al-Tahtawi (1801–73).[1] A member of an ancient family with a tradition of religious learning, settled in the town of Tahta in Upper Egypt, he found himself pushed by circumstances from the old world into the new. Muhammad ʿAli's confiscation of the tax-farms (*iltizam*) deprived his family of their wealth although not their learned tastes, and in 1817 the young Tahtawi went like his ancestors to study at the Azhar. There he pursued the normal studies of the ancient curriculum, but perhaps had his first glimpse of a new world. The teacher who had most influence on him was Shaykh Hasan al-ʿAttar, one of the great scholars of the age, and twenty years earlier Shaykh Hasan had been one of the Egyptians who had visited Bonaparte's Institut d'Égypte and seen there something of the new sciences of Europe. Tahtawi may have learned something of them from him, but he owed more than this to his teacher, for it was ʿAttar who secured his appointment as imam of a regiment in the new Egyptian army and then as imam of the first substantial mission sent by Muhammad ʿAli to study in Paris. Both these experiences left their mark on him. The new army was the nucleus of a new Egypt, and all his life Tahtawi remained conscious of the military virtues and the achievements of Muhammad ʿAli's soldiers. But Paris had a deeper effect on him; he remained there five years, from 1826 to 1831, and they were the most important of his life. Although sent there as imam and not as student, he threw himself into study with enthusiasm and success. He acquired a precise knowledge of the French language and the problems of translating from it into Arabic. He read books on ancient history, Greek philosophy and mythology, geography, arithmetic, and logic; a life of Napoleon, some French poetry, including Racine, Lord Chesterfield's letters to his son; and, most important, something of the French thought of the eighteenth century —Voltaire, Condillac, Rousseau's *Social Contract*, and the main works of Montesquieu.

The thought of the French Enlightenment left a permanent mark on him, and through him on the Egyptian mind. Some of its leading ideas would not indeed have been strange to one

---

[1] For lives of Tahtawi cf. works by al-Shayyal, Badawi, & Majdi listed in the bibliography.

brought up in the tradition of Islamic political thought: that man fulfils himself as a member of society, that the good society is directed by a principle of justice, that the purpose of government is the welfare of the ruled. Rousseau's conception of the legislator, the man who has the intellectual ability to conceive good laws and is able to express them in the religious symbols which the generality of people can understand and recognize as valid, has some affinity with the ideas of the Muslim philosophers about the nature and function of the Prophet. But there were new ideas as well, of which the influence can be seen throughout Tahtawi's writings: that the people could and should participate actively in the process of government; that they should be educated for this purpose; that laws must change according to circumstances, and those which are good at one time and place may not be so at others. The idea of the nation too he could have derived from Montesquieu. Montesquieu emphasized the importance of geographical conditions in moulding laws, and this implies the reality of the geographically limited community, the society constituted by living in one place; and he taught too that the rise and fall of States was due to causes, that the causes are to be found in the 'spirit' of the nation, and that the love of country is the basis of the political virtues—'l'amour de la patrie conduit à la bonté des moeurs',[2] and vice versa. These were more than abstract ideas for Tahtawi. At the same time as he was becoming acquainted with them, his experience in Paris was suggesting how they could be relevant to his own society. He met the orientalists of his day, such as Silvestre de Sacy, and no doubt it was through them he became aware of the discoveries of the Egyptologists in the first great age of that science. The idea of ancient Egypt filled his mind and was to contribute an important element to his thought.

It was not Muhammad 'Ali's wish that his students should see too much of French life, but Tahtawi managed to make precise observations of the modern world as well as the ancient, and acquired a wide knowledge of the institutions and customs of the greatest and most flourishing society of his day. Shortly after his return to Egypt he published a description of his stay in Paris, *Takhlis al-ibriz ila talkhis Bariz*. It achieved great fame and was translated into Turkish. It contains many interesting and

---

[2] *L'Esprit des lois*, Book v, ch. 2.

accurate observations of the manners and customs of the modern French. Tahtawi was not an uncritical admirer—the French, he thought, were nearer to avarice than to generosity, and their men were slaves of their women—but he found much to praise: cleanliness, the careful and prolonged education of children, love of work and disapproval of laziness, intellectual curiosity ('they always want to get to the root of the matter'),[3] and above all their social morality. Loving change in outward appearances, unstable in little things, they were steadfast in great: their political convictions were unchanging, and in personal relations they trusted each other and rarely betrayed.

When Tahtawi returned to Egypt, he worked for a time as translator in the new specialist schools, and in 1836 was made head of the new School of Languages, set up to prepare students for the professional schools and to train officials and translators. At the same time he acted as inspector of schools, examiner, member of educational commissions and editor of the official newspaper, *al-Waqa'i' al-misriyya*. But his most important work was done as translator. In 1841 a bureau of translation was attached to the School and placed under his direction; it had a number of translators doing their work subject to his revision. His own work during this period included about twenty translations, most of them books of geography, history, and military science, but those he suggested or supervised were far more numerous. Among them were histories of the ancient world, the Middle Ages, and the kings of France; Voltaire's lives of Peter the Great and Charles XII of Sweden, and Robertson's history of the Emperor Charles V; a book on the Greek philosophers, and Montesquieu's *Considérations sur les causes de la grandeur des Romains et de leur décadence.* This list shows the direction of his own interests as well as those of his master. The ruler took a personal interest in the work of translation, and was fond of having read to him the lives of great rulers and soldiers, whose careers might be compared with his or from whose example he might learn something. But the choice of Montesquieu must have been Tahtawi's own, and shows his life-long preoccupation with the question of the greatness and decline of States, and the answer he would give to it: 'la vertu politique dans la république' was 'l'amour de la patrie';[4] the Romans were distinguished by

---

[3] Tahtawi, *Takhlis*, p. 60.   [4] *L'Esprit des lois*, 'avertissement'.

this, but 'ils mêlaient quelque sentiment religieux à l'amour qu'ils avaient pour leur patrie'.[5]

The favour shown to Tahtawi by his master was withdrawn when Muhammad 'Ali died. His chosen successor Ibrahim had died before him, and he was followed by his grandson 'Abbas. In 1850 Tahtawi was sent to open a school in Khartoum, and the next year his School of Languages was closed. He seems to have incurred the new ruler's displeasure, and he regarded his four years in Khartoum as years of exile. He occupied himself with translating Fénélon's *Télémaque*; but once more a change of rulers brought a change of fortune, and when Sa'id succeeded 'Abbas in 1854 Tahtawi was allowed to return to Cairo. Once more he became head of a school with an office of translation attached to it. When Isma'il succeeded Sa'id he remained in favour and was indeed one of the group which planned the new educational system. He was a member of several commissions, but still found time for his scholarly work. He encouraged the Government Press at Bulaq to publish the Arabic classics; among them was the work of Ibn Khaldun, and this too shows the bent of his mind. He continued also to direct the translation bureau, of which the main work now was to put into Arabic the French legal codes. From 1870 until his death he edited a periodical for the Ministry of Education, and wrote a number of original articles for it. He also wrote several works on a larger scale: the first two volumes of what was intended to be a complete history of Egypt, a book on education (*al-Murshid al-amin li'l-banat wa'l-banin*—which may be loosely rendered Guiding Truths for Girls and Youths) and a general work on Egyptian society, *Manahij al-albab al-misriyya fi mabahij al-adab al-'asriyya* (to translate loosely once more, The Paths of Egyptian Hearts in the Joys of the Contemporary Arts).

It is this last work which will most concern us here, for it contains the most complete statement of Tahtawi's views about the path which Egypt should take. In form it is mainly a treatise on economic activity (*al-manafi' al-'umumiyya*): what it is, how Egypt had it in the past and then lost it, and how she can recover it. But it is far more than that. This book, like all that Tahtawi wrote at this time, was designed to provide edifying reading for the students in the new schools. It is written in an old-fashioned discursive way, with digressions and long stories to prove the points; and from what Tahtawi says can be deduced a theory of politics and of the nature and destiny of Egypt. It is a theory which deserves notice because it makes articulate the ideas current among the new ruling group of Egypt and which under-lay the reforms of the age of Isma'il.

Tahtawi's ideas about society and the State are neither a mere restatement of a traditional view nor a simple reflection of the ideas he had learnt in Paris. The way in which his ideas are formulated is on the whole traditional: at every point he makes appeal to the example of the Prophet and his Companions, and his conceptions of political authority are within the tradition of Islamic thought. But at points he gives them a new and significant development.

In spite of what he has seen in Paris, his view of the State is not that of a liberal of the nineteenth century. It is a conven-tional Islamic view. The ruler possesses absolute executive power, but his use of it should be tempered by respect for the law and those who preserve it. That government should be in the hands of 'the people' was an idea familiar to him from his reading and experience in France: he had witnessed the revolution of 1830, and gives a long description of it in his book on Paris. But it was not, he thought, an idea which was relevant to the problems of Egypt. His country was ruled by a Muslim autocrat, and the only hope of effective reform was that the autocrat should use his powers properly. The ups and downs of his own career showed what a difference the character and intentions of the ruler could make. He felt much gratitude to Muhammad 'Ali, who had sent him to Paris and, after his return, followed his career with un-doubted personal interest; and also great admiration for the man who had freed Egypt from the grip of the Mamlukes and set her on the path of progress.[6] He called him the second Macedonian; Muhammad 'Ali himself indeed was aware of the parallel with Alexander, whose life he used to read with pleasure.[7] Later Tahtawi wrote of Sa'id and Isma'il with discreet and conventional flattery, but his attitude to 'Abbas was naturally unfriendly. It was not only perhaps the beauty of Fénélon's style nor the in-terest of the story which led him to spend his years of exile translating *Télémaque*. Written as moral reading for Fénélon's

[6] Tahtawi, *Manahij*, p. 206.   [7] Ibid. pp. 212 & 214.

pupil the Duc de Bourgogne, it contains an implied criticism of the uncontrolled despotism of Louis XIV, a moral lesson for autocrats which could well be applied to 'Abbas. The evocation of the happiness and beauty of Egypt under Sesotris must have appealed to someone whose love of a country was as warm as Tahtawi's, but it might also serve to remind 'Abbas of the state of Egypt under his predecessor:

cette fertile terre d'Égypte, semblable à un jardin délicieux arrosé d'un nombre infini de canaux . . . des villes opulentes . . . des terres qui se couvraient tous les ans d'une moisson dorée, sans se reposer jamais, des prairies pleins de troupeaux . . . des bergers qui faisaient répéter les doux sons de leur flûtes et de leurs chalumeaux à tous les échos d'alentour. . . .

Heureux . . . le peuple qui est conduit par un sage roi! . . . Aimez vos peuples comme vos enfants. . . . Les rois qui ne songent qu'à se faire craindre, et qu'à abattre leurs sujets pour les rendre plus soûmis, sont les fléaux du genre humain. Ils sont craints . . . mais ils sont haïs, détestés.[8]

In the warning that even good rulers tend to choose bad advisers, flatterers who do not fear to betray, and to withdraw their confidence from 'wise and virtuous men whose virtue one fears',[9] there can perhaps be heard an echo of some personal intrigue which led to Tahtawi's exile. On the other hand, Fénélon's advice about how to rule must have seemed to Tahtawi to be applicable to the Egypt of his time: rulers should have full and direct knowledge of their country, they should encourage trade and agriculture, pay due attention to education, produce the armaments necessary for defence, and above all, respect the principles of moderation and justice.[10]

If Tahtawi accepted the authority of the ruler, he laid emphasis too on the limits imposed on him by the existence of moral norms. To explain the Islamic idea of the *Shari'a* as standing above the ruler he refers to Montesquieu's distinction of the 'three powers',[11] and the idea of restraints on the monarch's absolute power was certainly strengthened by what he saw in France: in writing of the revolution of 1830, he gives a clear definition of limited monarchy and the republic. But in the *Manahij* his argument for limits on the exercise of authority

8 *Télémaque*, Book i i, pp. 26–27. 9 Ibid. Book x, p. 286.
10 Ibid. pp. 298 ff. 11 *Manahij*, p. 349.

starts from a traditional idea, that of the division of society into
'orders' or 'estates' each with a specific function and status.
Following a principle long established, he distinguished four
estates: the ruler, the men of religion and law, soldiers, and those
engaged in economic production.[12] He gives special attention to
the second of these and its role in the State. The ruler should
respect and honour the *'ulama'*; he should treat them as his
helpers in the task of government. This is a theme common to
Islamic jurists, and perhaps for Tahtawi, as for them, it had
'nationalist' undertones, for under Muhammad 'Ali, as under
Mamlukes and Ottomans, power lay in Turkish or Caucasian
hands, and the body of *'ulama'* formed the only institution
through which the indigenous population of Egypt could take
an active part in public affairs. By this time, however, a new
educated group was arising, and it is in reflection of this that
Tahtawi gives a new turn to the idea of the *'ulama'*. In his view,
they are not simply guardians of a fixed and established tradition.
Himself well-versed in the religious law, a Shafi'i by legal rite,
he believed it was necessary to adapt the *Shari'a* to new circumstances and that it was legitimate to do so. The 'door of *ijtihad*'
had been closed, according to the traditional saying, and it was
for a later generation than his to push it open, but he took the
first step in that direction. There was not much difference, he
suggested, between the principles of Islamic law and those
principles of 'natural law' on which the codes of modern Europe
were based.[13] This suggestion implied that Islamic law could be
reinterpreted in the direction of conformity with modern needs,
and he suggested a principle which could be used to justify this:
that it is legitimate for a believer, in certain circumstances, to
accept an interpretation of the law drawn from a legal code other
than his own.[14] Taken up by later writers, this suggestion was
made use of in the creation of a modern and uniform system of
Islamic law in Egypt and elsewhere.

If the *'ulama'* are to interpret the *Shari'a* in the light of
modern needs, they must know what the modern world is. They
must study the sciences created by human reason. Tahtawi
quotes from the intellectual autobiography of a shaykh to show
that the tradition of philosophy and the rational sciences had

---

[12] Ibid. p. 348.   [13] Tahtawi, *al-Murshid*, p. 124.
[14] *Manahij*, pp. 387–91.

been alive in the Muslim world until recently;[15] but it had died, and the Azhar in the present age did not accept the new sciences which were necessary for the welfare of the nation. The *'ulama'* must come to terms with the new learning; and the specialists of that learning should have the same social position as the *'ulama'*. Doctors, engineers, all who had mastered sciences which were useful to the State, should be honoured and consulted by the ruler.[16] In other words, the traditional idea of a partnership between ruler and *'ulama'* has been brought up to date, and the idea of the *'ulama'* reinterpreted in terms of Saint-Simon's 'priesthood' of scientists.

Beyond rulers and *'ulama'* alike lay something else, the community as a whole. For Tahtawi as for other Muslim thinkers there was a sharp distinction between the function of ruling and that of obeying. The ruler was God's representative, answerable to God alone, and under God his own conscience was his only judge; his subjects owed him absolute obedience.[17] But sharply distinguished as they were in function, rulers and ruled were closely linked to each other by rights and duties. The subject should obey, but the ruler should try to please his subjects within the limits imposed by his obedience to God. Fear of God could impel the ruler into good actions, but so too could fear of public opinion,[18] and in the modern world opinion played an active part in the life of the State. In the past, government had been a secret activity of the ruler, but in the modern age it must be based on 'good relations between rulers and ruled'.[19] There must therefore be universal political education. Officials should be properly trained, for even to be the headman of a village needed training,[20] and the ordinary citizen who did not serve the State directly should still understand its laws and know his rights and duties.

When Tahtawi emphasizes that the *'ulama'* should have a modern education and all citizens should have a political education, he is implying that the nature of society and the function of government were different from what they had been in the past. He would no doubt have accepted in principle the Islamic idea of political stability, of the function of the government as being to regulate the different orders of society and keep them within the

---

[15] *Manahij*, p. 372. [16] Ibid. p. 370. [17] Ibid. pp. 354 & 368.
[18] Ibid. p. 354. [19] Ibid. p. 352. [20] Ibid. p. 365.

Shariʿa. But we can see breaking in on him a new idea, of change as a principle of social life, and government as the necessary instrument of change. In his book on Paris he records, as one of the strange aspects of French character, the desire of each man to go further than his ancestors: 'Everyone who is master of a craft wishes to invent something which was not known before, or to complete something which has already been invented.'[21] In the same way the *Manahij* starts from the assumption that society has two purposes: to do the will of God, but also to achieve well-being in this world. So far there is nothing new; but what is new is the meaning given to welfare. It is identified with progress as Europe of the nineteenth century conceived it, and in this sense welfare has two bases: the first is 'the training of character in religious and human virtues', and the second the economic activities which lead to wealth and the improvement of conditions and contentment among the people as a whole.[22]

In the *Manahij* Tahtawi is mainly concerned with the second of these bases, and since he is writing about Egypt, when he talks about economic change he means first of all progress in agriculture. In Egypt, as he well knows, the nature of economic life and therefore the state of public welfare depend on the nature of government; good rulers of Egypt have always been attentive to irrigation, and he gives a detailed description of Muhammad ʿAli's policy, as well as an analysis, drawn from a European writer, of the economic possibilities of the country, which are great and capable of full exploitation in a short time.[23]

But it is characteristic of his thought to insist that national wealth is a product of virtue. When the social virtues have been strong Egypt has been prosperous; and the key to virtue is education. Most of his life was spent as a teacher and organizer of schools, and he had a clear view of what should be done. He put forward his ideas in his book on education. Teaching, he asserts, must be linked with the nature and problems of society; it should aim at 'nourishing in the hearts of the young the feelings and principles which are current in their country'.[24] Primary education should be universal and the same for all, secondary education should be of high quality and the taste for it encouraged. Girls must be educated as much as boys, and on the

[21] *Takhlis*, p. 60.   [22] *Manahij*, p. 7.
[23] *Manahij*, pp. 225 & 285.   [24] *al-Murshid*, p. 6.

same footing: in saying this he was reflecting the new interest
and policy of Isma'il's time, and indeed the cause of his writing
the book was an order from the Ministry of Education to write
something which would be equally suitable for teaching boys and
girls. The teaching of girls was necessary for three reasons: for
harmonious marriages and the good upbringing of children; so
that women could work, as men work, within the limits of their
capacity; and to save them from the emptiness of a life of gossip
in the harem. (He does not seem to suggest that they should
come out of seclusion and take part in public life, although there
is a suggestive chapter on famous women rulers, including
Cleopatra, but he wishes them to be better treated in the family.)
Polygamy is not forbidden, he maintains, but Islam only allows
it if the husband is capable of doing justice between his wives.
By later writers this point was taken up and turned into a virtual
prohibition on having more than one wife.[25]

The aim of education should be to form a personality, not
simply to transmit a body of knowledge; it should inculcate the
importance of bodily health, of the family and its duties, of
friendship and above all of patriotism—*hubb al-watan*, the love
of country, the main motive which leads men to try to build up
a civilized community. In the *Manahij*, as in the book on education, the word *watan* and the phrase *hubb al-watan* occur again
and again. The duties of citizens towards their country are
enumerated: unity, submission to law, sacrifice. So too are their
rights, above all the right to freedom, for freedom alone can
create a real community and a strong patriotism.[26] Sometimes
when Tahtawi uses the term he seems to be doing no more than
teach in general terms the rights and duties of members of any
community; *hubb-al-watan* then has the same meaning as
'asabiyya in the doctrine of Ibn Khaldun—the sense of solidarity which binds together those who live in the same community and is the basis of social strength. But at other times he is
using it in a more restricted and a new sense. The emphasis is
no longer on the passive duty of the subject to accept authority,
it is on the active role of the citizen in building a truly civilized
society; it is no longer exclusively on the mutual duties of members of the Islamic *umma*, but also of those who live in the same
country. *Hubb al-watan* thus acquires the specific meaning of

²⁵ *al-Murshid*, pp. 62, 4, 66, 104, 148, 128.   ²⁶ Ibid. p. 128.

territorial patriotism in the modern sense, and the mother-country—'la Patrie'—becomes the focus of those duties which, for Islamic jurists, bound together members of the *umma* and that natural feeling which, for Ibn Khaldun, existed between men related to each other by blood.

The transition to this new way of thought can be seen in a passage of the *Manahij*. Tahtawi is talking of brotherhood in religion. He quotes the *hadith*, 'the Muslim is brother of the Muslim', and then adds:

and all that is binding on a believer in regard to his fellow believers is binding also on members of the same *watan* in their mutual rights. For there is a national brotherhood between them over and above the brotherhood in religion. There is a moral obligation on those who share the same *watan* to work together to improve it and perfect its organization in all that concerns its honour and greatness and wealth.[27]

What is this natural community, this *watan* to which Tahtawi refers? It is Egyptian and not Arab. In his thought there is indeed some shadowy idea of Arabism, but it belongs to the old rather than the new element in it. He praises and defends the part played by the Arabs in the history of Islam;[28] when he talks of patriotism, however, he does not mean the feeling shared by all who speak Arabic, but that shared by those who live in the land of Egypt. Egypt for him is something distinct, and also something historically continuous. Modern Egypt is the legitimate descendant of the land of the Pharaohs. His imagination indeed was filled with the glories of ancient Egypt, first seen, by a paradox, during his years in France. He wrote poems in praise of the Pharaohs, and it is characteristic of his style of thought that, when writing of the vice of idleness, he should first quote the *hadith* and other Islamic texts, and then go on to talk of the way in which lazy people are depicted in the art of ancient Egypt.[29] But ancient Egypt for him was more than a source of pride; it had both the constituent elements of civilization, social morality and economic prosperity,[30] and what it had possessed modern Egypt could regain, for 'the physical constitution of the people of these times is exactly that of the peoples of times past, and their disposition is one and the same'.[31]

[27] *Manahij*, p. 99.　[28] Ibid. pp. 150 ff.
[29] Ibid. p. 120.　[30] Tahtawi, *Anwar Tawfiq*, pp. 13–14.
[31] *Manahij*, p. 187.

If this is so, however, it is necessary to explain how it was that Egypt lost the virtues and prosperity of ancient times. It was, Tahtawi maintains, because of the historical accident of foreign rule: the rule of the Mamlukes in the later Middle Ages and then, after a brief revival under the early Ottoman sultans, the long misrule of the Circassians. In saying this he echoed the proclamations of Bonaparte, and started a line of thought which was to be generally accepted by later Egyptian writers and finally applied to the ruling family whom Tahtawi served.

Among the works of his later years, his two volumes on the history of Egypt have been mentioned. They were intended to be the first two of a series, which in the event his son finished after his death, and to be a work of national education, a summary of what the modern Egyptian should know about his *watan*. It illustrates the blend of elements in his thought that the first volume is a history of ancient Egypt, based on modern European sources, while the second is a life of the Prophet, drawn from the traditional Muslim sources, used intelligently and not uncritically. In the modern western fashion, he divides history into two main categories, ancient and modern; but as a Muslim, his dividing line is not the fall of the Roman Empire but the rise of Islam. He regards this as the most important event in history, but he still believes pre-Islamic history to be worthy of study. Egypt is part of the Islamic *umma*, but she has also been a separate *umma*, in ancient and modern times alike, and as such is a distinct object of historical thought.[32] Although Muslim, she is not exclusively so, for all who live in Egypt are part of the national community. Once more, while the conclusion is modern, the train of thought is traditional: it begins with the Islamic concept of Christians and Jews as 'protected peoples', *ahl al-dhimma*, and argues for the most liberal attitude towards them. They should be allowed entire religious freedom, and it is legitimate for Muslims to frequent their company.[33]

Tahtawi's patriotism was a warm personal feeling, not just a deduction from the principles of political philosophy. There is no mistaking his pride in the past greatness of Egypt, his concern for her future. He wrote a number of patriotic poems, *wataniyyat*, in which, mixed with praise of the ruling family, there is praise of ancient Egypt and also of the Egyptian army. But he is said

[32] *Anwar*, pp. 8–10.   [33] *Manahij*, p. 405.

also to have translated the *Marseillaise*, and this is significant. When he uses the term *watan*, it is clearly the equivalent of the French *patrie*, and the *patrie* of the French Revolution was not the self-regarding, self-worshipping nation of modern ideologies, it was the servant of the universal. For Tahtawi too the new Egypt could serve something beyond herself: the modern sciences, which were bringing in a new age and changing the lives of the communities of the east.

Tahtawi lived and worked in a happy interlude of history, when the religious tension between Islam and Christendom was being relaxed and had not yet been replaced by the new political tension of east and west. He was in France at the time of the occupation of Algiers, and wrote about it in his book on Paris, but in his thought there is no sense of Europe's being a political danger. France and Europe stood not for political power and expansion but for science and material progress. His was an age of great inventions, and he wrote of them with admiration: the Suez Canal, the plan for a Panama Canal, the trans-continental railways in America. He seems indeed to have been particularly struck by the changes in communications, and wrote a poem in praise of the steam engine.[34] Such novelties, he thought, marked the beginning of a process which would continue, and must in the end lead to the coming together of peoples and their living together in peace. Egypt must adopt the modern sciences and the innovations to which they would lead, and she could do so without danger to her religion. For the sciences now spreading in Europe had once been Islamic sciences: Europe had taken them from the Arabs, and in taking them back Egypt would only be claiming what was her own. The best way to do so was through easy intercourse with foreigners and good treatment of them. They should be encouraged to settle in Egypt and teach whatever they had to teach. Once more, Tahtawi uses an analogy from ancient Egypt: had not Psammtek I encouraged Greeks to settle in Egypt and treated them as if they were Egyptians?[35] Once more, he sees in Muhammad 'Ali and his successors the legitimate heirs of the Pharaohs, trying to revive the glories of Egypt by following the same principles; they too have given equality to all, subjects and foreigners alike.

But civilization, we must remember, has two bases and not

[34] Ibid. p. 126.   [35] Ibid. p. 188.

one only, and moral virtue is more important than material welfare, for the latter is in the long run the product of certain virtues. Europe does not appear to Tahtawi as a political danger, but he is conscious of a certain moral danger. The French, he says, believe in human reason alone. Their constitution does, it is true, embody a certain principle of justice, but it is far from the precepts of the divine law.[36] They are Christians in name only, and their real religion is quite different:

The French are of those who believe that it is human reason which ascribes goodness or badness to things. [Moreover] they deny that miracles can occur and believe it is not possible for the laws of nature to be broken. They believe too that religions have come only to encourage men to do good and avoid what is opposed to it, that national welfare and human progress can take the place of religion, and that . . . the intelligence of their learned men is greater than that of the prophets.[37]

For thinkers of a later generation, this positivism was to be the trend of European thought which interested them most, and they set themselves to show that it was not incompatible with the principles of Islam rightly understood. But Tahtawi is still deeply rooted in his inherited convictions, and to him what is clear is the contradiction between the two, not their possible reconciliation.

In the writings of Tahtawi we come for the first time on many themes later to be familiar in Arabic and Islamic thought: that, within the universal *umma*, there are national communities demanding the loyalty of their subjects; that the object of government is human welfare in this world as well as the next; that human welfare consists in the creation of civilization, which is the final worldly end of government; that modern Europe, and specifically France, provides the norm of civilization; that the secret of European strength and greatness lies in the cultivation of the rational sciences; that the Muslims, who had themselves studied the rational sciences in the past, had neglected them and fallen behind because of the domination of Turks and Mamlukes; and that they could and should enter the main stream of modern civilization, by adopting the European sciences and their fruits. All these ideas were to become the commonplaces of later thinkers, but some thinkers at least were to see that they contained problems, not perhaps insoluble but at least needing to be

[36] *Takhlis*, p. 81.   [37] Ibid. p. 65.

considered. How to reconcile the claims of divine revelation with those of a human reason proclaiming itself the only adequate path to knowledge; or those of the *Shari'a* with those of modern codes of law springing from quite other principles; or the idea that the *Shari'a* was sovereign with the claims of governments to be sovereign, and to decide freely in the light of expediency and human welfare; or loyalty to the religious community with loyalty to the nation?

In another thinker of Tahtawi's age, and one whose book was known to him,[38] one at least of these problems was raised: that of divine and human law. Although not absent from Tahtawi's thought, it was not the centre of his attention. For him, as for the Islamic thinkers of the later Middle Ages, law was a negative restraining factor. It set the limits within which the ruler must act, not the principles in accordance with which he should act. Muhammad 'Ali and Isma'il did not infringe those limits. They were benevolent autocrats of a type familiar to Islamic thought and posing no new problems. They issued no new statement of principles which might be, or seem to be, in contrast with those of the *Shari'a*, and their innovations were mainly in the spheres of economic life and administration, about which the *Shari'a* says little, rather than in the basic institutions of society or the realm of personal status, about which it says much. Moreover, they were ruling a State where effective power had for long been in the hands of a military group, and the *'ulama'* could offer, even if they would, no effective obstacle to its use. The question of how far the changes were compatible with the *Shari'a* scarcely needed to be raised. But in the main body of the empire and certain regions tributary to it this was a real question. The *Tanzimat* aimed not only at changing the military and administrative system of the empire but at giving it a new moral and legal basis. They met with bitter opposition both from those who disapproved in principle and those whose monopoly of the legal system and possession of political and social influence were threatened. For the defenders of the *Tanzimat* therefore the question of law was the centre of attention. They had to show that the reforms were not incompatible with the *Shari'a* and indeed were enjoined by it. In Constantinople this process took place in Turkish, and few echoes of it seem to have crept into

[38] Cf. *al-Murshid*, p. 98.

Arabic in the first half of the nineteenth century. But there was a province of the empire where similar reforms were carried out and raised similar objections: the '*ahd al-aman* in Tunis was also a statement of new legal and political principles and so posed the problem of the law. It is this problem which is the starting-point of the thinker we must now consider, Khayr al-Din Pasha.

Born in the Caucasus, probably between 1820 and 1830, Khayr al-Din was taken to Istanbul in his youth, like so many of his countrymen, to seek a military or political career by way of the household of some leading man.[39] Taken into the service of Ahmad Bey of Tunis, he was given a modern as well as a religious education, and learnt French in addition to Arabic. When his studies were finished he entered the army, where his talents soon won him the favour of the Bey. He was for a time in charge of the Military School, and in 1852 was sent by the Bey to Paris to deal with a difficult problem, that of certain claims made by a former minister against the government. He remained in Paris for four years, and for him as for Tahtawi they were a formative period. He observed the life of a great political community and applied what he learnt to his own world. On his return he became Minister of the Marine, and for six years was at the centre of the movement for constitutional reform. He was a member of the Commission which drafted the constitution of 1860, and was appointed president of the Supreme Council while still keeping his position as minister. This appointment showed the confidence of the Bey, Sadiq, in him. He had already shown it in another way; soon after his accession, in 1859, he sent Khayr al-Din to Constantinople to announce his succession and ask for the customary document of investiture. This was Khayr al-Din's public mission, but he also had a secret one. French ambitions in Tunis were already obvious and menacing, and in order to close the door to them it seemed expedient to reaffirm the position of Tunis as an autonomous part of the Ottoman Empire; in this way the influence of France could be counterbalanced by calling in that of the sultan, and also that of the Powers which wished to preserve the integrity of the empire. Khayr al-Din's secret object was therefore to persuade the Porte to recognize the

[39] For the life of Khayr al-Din cf. Inal, pt. 6; the articles by Demeerseman listed in the bibliography; and his own account, 'A mes enfants', in *R. tunisienne*, xviii–xx (1934).

autonomy of Tunis and the hereditary right of the Husaynid family, in return for the Bey's acknowledgment of Ottoman sovereignty and the payment of tribute.

The sultan was not in a position to offend the French, and the mission failed, just as the constitutional experiment failed. But for the next twenty years the two poles of Khayr al-Din's policy were the attempt to call in Turkey as a counterbalance to European influence, and the attempt to establish some constitutional control over the power of the Bey. It was this second line of policy which led to his losing the Bey's favour. In 1862 he resigned as minister after a disagreement about whether ministers should be responsible to the Bey or the Supreme Council. But the Bey still needed his diplomatic skill, and in 1864 he went once more to Constantinople on the same mission, and once more without success. This failure and that of the constitutional reforms impelled him to withdraw for a time from political life, and in this period of withdrawal he wrote a treatise on government, which was published in 1867.

In 1869 the worsening situation of the Tunisian finances led to the creation of an International Commission to administer the revenues, and Khayr al-Din became president of its executive section. In 1871 he was sent yet again to Constantinople, and this time he was successful; weakened by the war with Germany, France could make no effective opposition to the issue of a firman confirming the position of Tunis as an autonomous part of the Ottoman Empire, although she never recognized it. By this time Khayr al-Din had been made minister in control of the interior, finance, and foreign affairs, and in 1873 he became Prime Minister. He held the position for four years, and used it to carry out many reforms: improvement of administrative procedure, reorganization of the *awqaf* and of procedure in the religious courts, urban improvements, reform of the teaching at the Zaytuna mosque, improvement and enlargement of the Government Press, the creation of a public library and of a modern school, the Sadiqiyya, where Turkish, French, and Italian were taught as well as Arabic, and the modern sciences as well as those of the Islamic religion.[40] But once more he came up against the same obstacles: the ambitions and rivalries of the Powers, the desire of the Bey to preserve his authority. It was

[40] Cf. his own account in 'A mes enfants', pp. 193 ff.

his policy to maintain a balance between the three States which had interests in Tunis, England, France, and Italy, trying neither to make too many concessions to any of them nor to alienate it completely. A policy of balance carried out by a State which has no power of its own is always dangerous and delicate, and in the end Khayr al-Din lost the support of all. He encouraged first British, then French enterprises, and when the Russo-Turkish War broke out in 1876 found himself in an impossible position. The British Consul wanted Tunis to send aid to her suzerain the sultan, the other Powers did not. Khayr al-Din inclined towards the British enough to anger the French, not enough to satisfy Consul Wood. Deprived of foreign support, he could no longer stand against the Bey, whom he had alienated by efforts to curb the royal power, and who in 1877 was strong enough to dismiss him.

His political career in Tunis finished, Khayr al-Din started a new one in Constantinople, invited there by the young sultan, Abdülhamid, who had seen his book.[41] Within a short time of arriving there he had obtained some influence with Abdülhamid. He was able; he was a devout Muslim and convinced that the survival of an independent empire was necessary for the welfare of Islam; as a foreigner, who did not even know Turkish well, he would be quite dependent on the sultan's favour and could scarcely engage in dangerous intrigues. In December 1878 he was made grand vezir. His term of office was marked by one important act, the deposition by the sultan of the Khedive Isma'il of Egypt. It was appropriate that Khayr al-Din should have been the minister formally responsible for this, since Isma'il had gone against one of the basic principles of his policy: by loosening the ties which bound Egypt to the sultan he had opened the door to European intervention.

As grand vezir, however, Khayr al-Din soon ran into difficulties. Some, although not all, were of his own making. His personality was not such as to make relations with his colleagues easy. The British Ambassador, Layard, who worked with him closely and on friendly terms, has thus described him:

He was a stout, burly man, with a somewhat heavy countenance, which was however occasionally lighted up with a very intelligent and

41 *A mes infants'*, p. 213.

not unpleasant expression when he became excited in conversation. His manners were considered haughty and overbearing, and as he was in the habit of treating his colleagues and the Turkish officials and notables in general with something like contempt he soon added to the unpopularity to which his foreign extraction and the mode of his introduction into high offices would under any circumstances have exposed him. The manner in which he thus added to the number of his enemies and the difficulties of his position was not a proof of wisdom. It was difficult to tell his age as he dyed his hair and beard of a hard and deep black colour which did not improve his appearance or soften his features.[42]

Even with his sovereign, so the Master of Ceremonies reported, his relations were not easy: 'His tone and bearing, during his interviews with the Sultan, besides a few other little failings, had rendered him personally . . . disagreeable to His Majesty'.[43]

Apart from his 'little failings', the vezir found himself faced with the same problems as in Tunis: financial chaos, a struggle for influence between the Great Powers, the wish of the sultan to keep his power unchecked. He had the support of Britain and France, but this was not enough. His attempts to carry out internal reforms were spoiled by the hopeless state of the finances, and Salisbury refused to give him the loan he asked for. He had to face the opposition of the army and conservative Muslims, supported by Russia; and although the sultan at first seemed to be with him, this was only in appearance. The history of Tunis repeated itself. Khayr al-Din tried to force on the sultan a programme of reforms; the sultan turned against him and, although Layard and Salisbury used their influence in his favour, got rid of him in 1879. He lived on in Constantinople in virtual retirement,[44] and died in 1889.

Apart from official papers, and a memoir published long after his death, Khayr al-Din's one literary work is a political study, written in Arabic under the title *Aqwam al-masalik fi ma'rifat ahwal al-mamalik* (The Road Most Straight to Know the Conditions of the State). First published in Tunis in 1867, it was later

[42] British Museum, Add. MSS. 38, 938: Layard, 'Memoirs', viii, f. 13.
[43] Public Record Office: F.O. 78/2955, no. 649, 22 July, 1879, Layard to Salisbury, enclosing memo. by Sir A. Sandison.
[44] For his activities in these last years cf. 'À mes enfants', pp. 372 ff.; 'Mon programme', in Mzali & Pignon, 'Documents sur Khéredin', *R. tunisienne*, xxi (1935), 51 ff.

reissued in Constantinople; a French translation of the introduction, made under his own supervision and published in Paris as
Réformes nécessaires aux États musulmans aroused much interest
at the time.

There seems to have been some idea in his mind, when he
wrote the book, that he would do for the modern age what Ibn
Khaldun had done for an earlier one. Both were Tunisians, both
wrote their books in a moment of withdrawal from political life;
both books are concerned in some way with the problem of the
rise and decline of States, and each consists of an introduction,
laying down general principles, and several parts. The comparison goes no farther: the bulk of Ibn Khaldun's book is taken
up with the history of the Muslim dynasties, while most of
Khayr al-Din's is concerned with the history, political structure,
and military strength of the European States. The importance
of the book lies in the introduction. At the beginning Khayr
al-Din explains why he wrote it. He had two purposes:

First, to urge those who are zealous and resolute among statesmen
and men of religion to adopt, as far as they can, whatever is conducive
to the welfare of the Islamic community and the development of its
civilization, such as the expansion of the bounds of science and learning
and the preparation of the paths which lead to wealth . . . and the basis
of all this is good government.

Secondly, to warn those who are heedless among the generality of
Muslims against their persistence in closing their eyes to what is praiseworthy and in conformity with our own religious law in the practice of
adherents of other religions, simply because they have the idea engraved
on their minds that all the acts and institutions of those who are not
Muslims should be avoided.[45]

In other words, he wished to show what were the causes of the
strength and civilization of societies, and more specifically the
role of the State in society, and to do so by an analysis of those
societies which, in the modern world, were strongest and most
civilized; to argue that in the present age the only way of
strengthening the Muslim States was by borrowing ideas and
institutions from Europe, and to convince orthodox Muslims
that to do so was not contrary to the *Shari'a*, but in harmony
with its spirit. His argument indeed is directed primarily towards

[45] Khayr al-Din, *Aqwam*, p. 5 (Fr. trs. pp. 7–8).

orthodox Muslims, and his starting-point is the traditional
theory of the State. The specific object of his thought is not, as
with Tahtawi, the nation, it is the Islamic *umma*. Sometimes, it
is true, he uses the same phrases as Tahtawi, *watan* and *hubb
al-watan*,[46] but he uses them more in a general sense, as equivalent
to 'the political community' and 'public spirit', than in the
specific sense. He is far removed from the spirit of modern
nationalism, for which each nation is unique; what he has to say
applies to all Islamic States because they are Islamic. But the
centre of his interest is the greatest of Muslim States, the
Ottoman Empire, 'the seat of the caliphate'.[47] Similarly, the
question he poses is the traditional one: when power is in the
hands of an autocratic ruler, how to ensure that it is used justly?
Justice is the only sound basis for the State, and in normal
circumstances the only guarantee of it is that the power of the
ruler should be limited. There may, it is true, be a ruler who acts
rightly by innate goodness and the knowledge given him by
reason, but such men are rare, and there is no assurance that they
will continue in the paths they have chosen. In general, the
power of the ruler should be limited in two ways: first by law,
either revealed or natural (*Shari'a* or *qanun 'aqli*) and secondly
by consultation (*mashwara*). There are two classes whom the
ruler should consult, the *'ulama'* and the notables or men of
affairs (*a'yan*). They must be able to speak freely to him, guide
him in the right path and prevent him from doing evil. Apart
from the accident of a ruler with innate rectitude, the best State
is that in which both types of limitations exist, and stable laws
are guarded by those qualified to interpret them. The Islamic
umma in its original form was such a State and so long as it
respected the *Shari'a* it had been prosperous, strong and highly
civilized.[48] (In a manner characteristic of later writers, Khayr
al-Din proved the greatness of Islamic civilization by quotations
from modern European writers, Victor Duruy and Emmanuel
Sedillot.[49]) After this first golden age came a decline, itself
followed by a brief restoration under the early Ottomans. They
had given new energy to the Muslim world, and restored the
bases of its prosperity: they had given due respect to the *Shari'a*
and appointed *'ulama'* and ministers who could keep the sultans
on the right path. It had even been accepted that the guardians

[46] e.g. ibid. p. 43.   [47] Ibid. p. 49.   [48] Ibid. pp. 10–15.   [49] Ibid. p. 22.

of the law had the right to depose the sultan if he should go astray.[50] Later the Ottoman State too had declined because of the bad choice of ministers and decay of the Janissaries: the result was to loosen the ties of loyalty—rulers of distant regions did as they pleased, the Christian subjects looked to foreign protectors, the Great Powers began to interfere, and one by one the provinces to drop away.

So far the analysis is what any Ottoman writer of the age of decline might have given, and it is supported by quotations and references which show the author to have been widely read in the traditional sciences. Besides the Quran and *hadith*, he quotes Ibn Khaldun, al-Ghazali, Ibn al-'Arabi, al-Mawardi; but among them we come across references of another kind—to Thiers, Montesquieu, Polybius, 'the translator of John Stuart Mill', and Tahtawi's Parisian journey—and they are used to point a new moral. The *umma* can only be restored to strength if it learns wherein lies the strength of Europe and adopts it. But what exactly should it learn? As a soldier and statesman, Khayr al-Din was concerned first of all with strength, military and economic alike. But he knew that strength was a product of something else: material power depended on education, and education in its turn depended on political institutions. The basis of Europe's strength and prosperity was 'political institutions based on justice and freedom',[51] in other words, responsible ministries and parliaments. Freedom of person, of the press, of participation in government: without this, material prosperity is not possible. Freedom inspires men to work by giving them the assurance that they will receive the reward of their work; economic prosperity is not possible without the free movement of goods and people, and also that free economic association to which modern Europe owes its material achievements. Khayr al-Din gives an admiring picture of the progress of Europe: as with Tahtawi, what impresses him in particular are the new methods of transport, the Suez Canal and the trans-American railways, but he also mentions great corporate enterprises, like the Banque de France and the East India Company which had conquered an empire, and the great exhibitions with their prizes for inventors. Without freedom

---

[50] Khayr al-Din, pp. 31ff.
[51] Ibid. p. 8. Cf. the ideas of the Turkish writer Sadık Rifat Pasha (1807–56) quoted in B. Lewis, *Emergence*, p. 129.

too there can be no diffusion of knowledge: libraries and academies, for example, had grown in number in France since the Revolution.[52]

Something of modern Europe had already passed to the Ottoman Empire with the *Tanzimat*, of which Khayr al-Din approved in general. He gives a long defence of them against those who oppose them. The opposition, he says, comes largely from vested interests working on public opinion, and certain foreign interests which do not want the empire to reform itself. He is aware of a factor which had not yet impinged on the Egypt of Tahtawi's day: the factor of European pressure and intervention. Reform was impossible so long as certain European governments refused to allow their citizens to be subject to Ottoman law, and they did so because some at least of them did not want the empire to become strong again. But there were also opponents of the *Tanzimat* who were moved by a genuine misunderstanding of their nature and results. Some believed that the reforms would involve extra taxation to pay for more officials; on the contrary, it is despotism which increases taxation, and in a free society people decide themselves what taxes they will pay. Others complained of the waste of time and loss of rights, now that the old summary justice of the pasha had been replaced by the new courts with their elaborate procedure; but this was only temporary, until new officials with a proper public spirit had been trained.[53] Others again protested that the new institutions were contrary to Islam; and here we reach the heart of the problem.

The progress of Europe, Khayr al-Din assures his readers, is not in any sense due to its being Christian. Christianity is a religion which aims at happiness in the next world and not in this. If it were a cause of worldly progress, the Papal State would be the most advanced, not the most backward State in Europe.[54] Thus if the Muslim countries try to adopt the causes of European progress they will not be adopting Christianity. They will simply be adopting the modern equivalent of the ancient institutions of the Islamic *umma*. He is at pains indeed to make the parallel clear. What are the characteristic institutions of modern Europe? They are responsible ministers, parliaments, freedom of the press. But the modern idea of the responsible

[52] Khayr al-Din, pp. 80 & 71. [53] Ibid. pp. 33, 48, & 45 ff. [54] Ibid. pp. 8–10.

minister is not very different from the Islamic idea of the good *wazir* who gives counsel without fear or favour,[55] and parliaments and press are equivalent to 'consultation' in Islam. Members of parliament are what the '*ulama*' and notables were in the Islamic State—'those who bind and loose' (*ahl al-hall wa'l-'aqd*).[56] Thus to adopt European institutions is really to fulfil the spirit and purpose of the *Shari'a*.

To prove this, he puts forward an interpretation of the law which he seems to have derived from the later Hanbali jurists, although the channels by which it came to him are not clear. The *Shari'a* is of divine origin, and the basis of prosperity in this world and the next. But it is not a fixed and detailed code which lays down everything an individual or government should do and prohibits everything it does not enjoin. On the contrary, everything it does not explicitly forbid is allowed, if it is in accordance with social necessity. The principle of *maslaha*—of choosing that interpretation or ruling from which the greatest good will flow—must be the supreme guide of the government Khayr al-Din quotes Ibn Qayyim al-Jawziyya, one of the Hanbali jurists, as saying that the government should avoid putting itself in opposition either to the explicit principles of the law or what can legitimately be deduced from them, but need not confine itself only to doing what the law commands: whatever it does in pursuit of the good is in fact in accordance with the law, even if it has neither been indicated by the Prophet nor revealed by the spirit of God.

But circumstances change, and what is beneficial and necessary for society also changes; therefore laws and policies also must be altered. They should be agreed upon between the '*ulama*' and the men of affairs. It is for the second to propose what is necessary in the interests of the community, and for the first to say whether what is proposed agrees with the principles of the *Shari'a*. Thus the first condition of a healthy reform is that '*ulama*' and statesmen should be in agreement. But this implies that the '*ulama*' should be in touch with the spirit of the times. If they are too remote from political life their advice will have no weight and the men of affairs will have to be left free to follow their passions and inclinations:

That the '*ulama*' should frequent the men of State, and both should

co-operate for the purpose we have specified, is among the most important of their moral obligations in regard to the general welfare; and
the essential pre-condition of this is that the *'ulama'* should be acquainted
with the facts, on knowledge of which depends the application of the
law. . . . The application of the provisions of the law involves a knowledge of texts, but it involves also a knowledge of the circumstances
which must be taken into consideration when the texts are applied.[57]

At one time indeed Khayr al-Din seriously considered
applying this principle so as to create a modern and uniform
system of Islamic law. His friend and collaborator, Muhammad
Bayram, relates that when he was Prime Minister he formed
a project for this purpose. There was, he argued, a large colony of
European merchants in Tunis. They formed an indigestible
element in the community, and a dangerous one because of the
political use made of them by European governments. They
would continue to be dangerous until they were brought within
the law of the land, that is to say, the *Shari'a*. But they could not
be expected to submit to the jurisdiction of Islamic law so long
as there were different interpretations of it, and each judge and
court applied it in a different way. He therefore appointed a
commission, composed of *'ulama'* of the Hanafi and Maliki rites
(the former being the rite of the Ottoman Government and the
Bey, the latter the rite of the people of Tunis) as well as one of
the Muslim merchants, to draw up a single authorized code of
Islamic law. For this purpose it was to draw on the Hanafi and
Maliki codes, the modern laws in force in the Ottoman Empire
and Egypt, and the customs of the country. But nothing came of
the project, for when he ceased to be Prime Minister the commission ceased to exist.[58]

The principle of *maslaha* could be used in two different ways.
It could justify a change of institutions when circumstances were
propitious, but it could also condemn a change when they were
not. Khayr al-Din had helped to create the Tunisian constitution
and had tried to make it work, but he was more doubtful whether
it was possible to introduce real parliamentary institutions into
the empire as a whole. There had been, he pointed out, a recent
demand for an elected Assembly—he was thinking no doubt of
the 'Young Ottomans'. He approved of it in principle but thought
it dangerous in fact. The motives of the Ottoman Muslims

[57] Ibid. p. 41.   [58] Bayram, ii. 65–66.

who asked for it were good, but could they be certain of the intentions of others—by implication, the Ottoman Christians—who were associated with them? The real object of these was to throw off the authority of the Ottoman State, and in this they were being encouraged from outside. Political liberty implied equal rights, but how could there be equal rights for all unless all were loyal to the empire? It was the diversity of the empire which was the main obstacle to the grant of political freedom.[59]

In his later years Khayr al-Din continued to be cautious. When he became Prime Minister of Tunis in the 1870's he was much criticized for doing nothing to restore the constitutional laws. He replied to his critics in a memorandum setting out his motives: if constitutional laws were to have any meaning, two things were necessary—a ruler who was willing to promulgate them, a people who understood them and were willing to accept them. Neither condition existed in Tunis, and the constitution was therefore 'a word without a meaning'.[60] When he became grand vezir of the empire, the Ottoman constitution had already been granted and then suspended by Abdülhamid. But the reforms he advocated were not designed to call back parliament and give it power, they were rather intended to strengthen the position of the ministers as against the sultan. It is true, he demanded the reopening of the Chamber of Deputies, but he suggested that the electoral law and internal regulations should be changed, as they were 'much too liberal even for the most constitutional countries of Europe'. The main emphasis of his demands was on ministerial responsibility. A homogeneous ministry should be formed; it should exercise a proper authority over its officials, who at present often dealt directly with the palace; and when it had reached a decision on matters of importance submitted to it, the sultan should either accept the decision or refer the matter to a new ministry.[61] In short, Khayr al-Din's problem is not that of modern democracy: how should the people govern themselves? It is rather the problem of Islamic thought—how should the governor be restrained?—and it gives the traditional answer in a new guise: a strong, responsible ministry should exercise the functions of the good *wazir*.

[59] Khayr al-Din, pp. 33–36.
[60] Bayram, ii. 82 ff.
[61] Public Record Office: F.O. 78/2955, no. 654, 23 July, 1879, Layard to Salisbury, enclosing Khayr al-Din's memo.

The main problem of Tahtawi and Khayr al-Din, although expressed by each in a different form, was this: how to become part of the modern world while remaining Muslims? Brought up in the traditional way before coming into effective contact with French civilization, and writing as they were for other Muslim Arabs who had not had such contact, they had to defend modern civilization in traditional Islamic terms. The Arabic-speaking Christians, themselves brought in contact with Europe through the mission schools and through trade, had not this problem, but a distinctive one of their own. Europe was not alien to them as it was to Muslims: in accepting its ideas and ways they need have no uneasy feeling of being untrue to themselves, no need to justify themselves to their fellows or their ancestors. But modern European thought was thought about rights and duties, about the nature and virtues of society: it posed questions to which, in their position as members of closed communities shut out of political life, there could be no answer. The questions were posed more insistently still by the great declarations of principles issued by the sultans in 1839 and 1856,[62] and which had different implications for Muslims and Christians: while for Ottoman Muslims what was important was the revival of strength, for Christians what mattered was the statement of rights.

To this factor was added another. The careful study of the Arabic language, undertaken by Christians in the eighteenth century for practical reasons, had led to something else: a passionate love of the language and its literature. In the first half of the nineteenth century Christian Lebanon produced for the first time a great master of Arabic, Shaykh Nasif al-Yaziji (1800–71). After a youth spent in the service of the Prince of Lebanon, the Amir Bashir, he settled in his native village near Beirut as a teacher of Arabic. In his poetry and rhyming prose (*maqamat*) he showed a complete mastery of the language and its traditional styles, and almost all the Arabic writers of the century were directly or indirectly his pupils. But his interest was mainly in the manner of saying things. In other writers the concern with the language was equally great but took a different form. It became above all a concern to make Arabic suitable as a means of expressing the life and ideas of the modern world, and a

[62] See pp. 45 and 47 above.

concern too with those who spoke and read it. Many of the
Christians of Lebanon and Syria were Arab by origin, and of
those who were not most had accepted the Arabic language and
with it a whole culture; in a sense it was theirs but in a sense it
was not, since it was an Islamic as well as an Arabic culture.

These changes posed two questions for Arabic-speaking
Christians: first, how to break out of their closed religious communities, which had been for so many centuries their world?
By education and linguistic pride they were becoming aware of
two worlds beyond the Church. From being a protection, the
religious community came to seem a barrier, and there were
specific reasons for this in each community. Among the Maronites
the clergy had played a large part in the events of the critical
years between 1840 and 1860: both in the struggle of peasants
and lords and in that of Maronites and Druzes. Not everyone
had approved of their part, and there appeared a certain tension
between clergy and laity as well as between higher and lower
clergy. Among Orthodox, there was tension between the hierarchy, who were almost entirely Greek, and the lower clergy
with the laity, who were almost entirely Arab: a tension which
increased when the Greeks broke from the empire and became independent, and also as the Arabic-speaking Christians
became more conscious of their Arabic speech. Among the
Christians of the empire as a whole, there was a growing tension
between hierarchy and community, particularly after the *Hatt-i
Humayun* of 1856, which laid down that each community should
be given a constitution allowing due weight to the voice of the
laity. Such movements prepared the minds of Christian students
for the secularist thought which they imbibed with knowledge of
English and French. It is not an accident that a number of those
who were to become famous as writers broke away from their
communities into the comparative freedom of the new Protestant
community created by American and British missionaries, and
recognized by the sultan in 1850; and that in their writing can
be seen an 'anti-clerical' element absent from that of their
Muslim contemporaries.

The second question was linked with this: having broken
away from the closed world of the minority, what community
could they belong to? In spite of everything, the Ottoman
Empire was still a Muslim empire; the principles proclaimed in

1839 and 1856 would have to be really carried out, and the empire turned into a secular State on the European model, with equal rights for all citizens and a national feeling which embraced them all. Christians could support such ideas without the hesitations of Muslims, whether Arab or Turkish, because they did not possess that deep and final loyalty to the empire, as the shield of Sunni Islam, which almost all Muslims had, and which was indeed the cause of their hesitations. The transformation of the empire, and indeed its disappearance, would cause them no pangs of conscience. On the contrary, the events of 1860, in Lebanon and Damascus, made more urgent the need for change. They may on the one hand have embittered relations between the communities, but to some of the Christians at least they taught another lesson: that religious loyalty was a dangerous basis for political life, and some ground for co-operation between those of different faiths must be found.

These currents of thought were to have their echoes far beyond the Christian communities, because of an important change which took place in the 1860's: the growth of the periodical press. Until then, the only important newspapers had been those published by the government, in Cairo and Constantinople, and containing mainly (although not exclusively) official news. There had also been a few papers published in French, Greek, and Armenian, but virtually nothing in Arabic, until in the 1860's the increase in the number of printing-presses, of Arabic writers and of the reading public, as well as the comparative liberalism of the Turkish and Egyptian régimes, made possible the creation of private newspapers and periodicals. For the next thirty years these were to be mainly in the hands of Lebanese Christians, whether they were published in Beirut, Cairo, or Constantinople; for a whole generation then the reading public of the Arab countries lay open to the ideas of the new writers and thinkers of Lebanon.

The first of them to win fame and influence was Faris al-Shidyaq (1804–87), brother of the historian Tannus. The Shidyaq family was Maronite, of ancient lineage, and had provided leaders in the Maronite districts of the north for 300 years, and officials for the nobility of the centre and south. The father of Faris and Tannus served the Shihab princes, but had already incurred some difficulty with them when a new trouble fell on the family.

Another brother, As'ad, employed by the American missionaries to teach them Arabic, became a Protestant, and was imprisoned and done to death by the Maronite Patriarch. These events started Faris on a life of wandering. He too seems to have become a Protestant and was sent by the American missionaries first to Egypt and then to Malta, where he worked in the mission press as a translator. In 1848 he travelled to England to help in an Arabic version of the New Testament, spent some time at Cambridge and Oxford, and then went to Paris where he stayed for a number of years. He wrote a description of England and France, less perceptive than that of Tahtawi; and while in Paris published a long, strange, original book—*al-Saq 'ala'l-saq fi ma huwa'l-Faryaq*. Written with the purpose of demonstrating the capacity of the Arabic language, and modelled to some extent on Rabelais, it is part autobiography, part social criticism, with a strong implied attack on the Maronite hierarchy who had killed his brother. In Paris too he met Ahmad Bey of Tunis, where he spent some time. It may or may not have been at this time that he became a Muslim and added the name of Ahmad to his own. From Paris he went to Constantinople at the invitation of the sultan, and there he launched, in 1860, an Arabic newspaper, *al-Jawa'ib*, which continued to appear until 1883. He died three years later, and it is a sign of the steadfastness which underlay the changes of his career that he asked that his body should be buried in Lebanon, and is said to have become a Catholic once more before he died.

There is no sign of superior political insight in his writing, nor of a consistent political doctrine. Whatever the nature of the inner struggle whose existence is clear enough from the vicissitudes of his career as well as occasional hints in *al-Saq*, his explicit concern was first of all with language, and it was this indeed which made first the Bey of Tunis and then the sultan eager to have his services. *Al-Jawa'ib* indeed was the first really important Arabic newspaper to be published: the first to circulate wherever Arabic was read, and to explain the issues of world politics. In it, Shidyaq analysed in detail the course of the Franco-Prussian War and the Eastern Crisis of the 1870's, and published translations of important diplomatic documents. He expounded social problems with the authority of one who had spent years in Europe, and compared European life favourably with that of the east. Europeans, he maintained, were orderly, industrious, and productive; they had a social unity which transcended differences of belief; at least in the Protestant countries, religious leaders did not interfere too much in politics; their women shared fully in the life of society; children were well brought up, not in the neglectful and slovenly way common in the east.[63] Politically, he was indeed used by the sultan to defend his policy, and his claim to be caliph, outside the empire as well as inside. His vigorous prose aroused echoes far away: travelling in central Arabia in the 1870's, Doughty found that *al-Jawa'ib* was known there:

I marvelled at the erudition of these Arabian politicians! till I found they had it of a certain Arabic newspaper (which is set forth in face of the 'Porte' at Constantinople).—The aged editor was of Christian parentage in Mount Lebanon. . . . [He] afterward established himself at Stambûl; where he made profession of the Turks' religion: and under favour of some great ones, founded the (excellent) Arabic gazette, in which he continues to labour (in the Mohammedan interest). His news-sheet is current in all countries of the Arabic speech: I have found it in the Nejd merchants' houses at Bombay.[64]

Of no less influence, although in another way, was a man of the next generation, but also of the same Maronite community, Butrus al-Bustani (1819–83). Of a family which produced many scholars, he was educated like Shidyaq at the Maronite seminary of 'Ayn Waraqa, and there laid the foundations of his knowledge of Arabic and many other languages. At that time a young man of education could best find a field for his talents in the service of foreign consulates or missions; he worked for a time at the British and the American consulates in Beirut and formed a more permanent link with the American Protestant missionaries, whose faith he accepted and whose translation of the Bible into Arabic he assisted. He taught in their schools, and in 1863 founded his own National School (*al-madrasa al-wataniyya*) based, as its name implies, on a national not a religious principle, and where the Arabic language and the modern sciences were taught well. To revive the knowledge and love of the Arabic language was indeed half his life's work: his Arabic dictionary, *al-Muhit*, his Arabic encyclopaedia, *Da'irat al-ma'arif*, the

[63] A. F. Shidyaq, *Kanz al-ragha'ib*, i. 87 & 101 ff.
[64] *Arabia Deserta*, ii. 371.

periodicals which he edited, all contributed to the creation of modern Arabic expository prose, of a language true to its past in grammar and idiom, but made capable of expressing simply, precisely, and directly the concepts of modern thought. From the circle which gathered around him—his sons and relations, his friends and pupils—there came the modern novel and drama in Arabic as well as modern Arabic journalism.

The other half of his work was to spread the idea that the Near East could only revive through knowledge of the thought and discoveries of modern Europe. Not that he wished the borrowing to be without discrimination: to accept customs because they were foreign was as absurd as to reject them because they were foreign, and was something to which the Syrians were prone. They should be accepted or rejected on their own merits. Viewed in this light, he found much to criticize in European manners (which he only knew at second-hand): for example, the excessive freedom of European men in their dealing with women.[65] But there was also much which was good, and there should be no hesitation about adopting it. 'The difference of human temperaments, of places and times, makes necessary a difference of customs.'[66] The Arabs had a great civilization in the past; there is no mistaking his pride in it, or his conviction that all who speak Arabic, whether Christians or Muslims, are Arabs. When the Arabs were great, Europe learnt from them. Then the Arabs lost their taste for learning, not by inner deterioration, but because of 'many conditions and varied causes',[67] and learning passed to Europe. Now the Arabs should take it back from them and in so doing they would take back what was their own. There had been much progress in recent times, thanks to Muhammad 'Ali and the missionaries, Catholic and Protestant; but more was needed, and it was false to believe that the Arabs contained in themselves all they needed for their own revival. If they were willing to learn, however, they could learn far more quickly than Europe had done; they could adopt in a short time what it had taken Europe long to develop.[68]

What was it then that the Near East should take from Europe? First of all, it should learn the importance of national unity, the willingness of all who share the same country to co-operate on

---

[65] Bustani, *Khitab*, pp. 17, 23 & 40.   [66] Ibid. pp. 16 ff.
[67] Bustani, *Khutba*, p. 31.   [68] Ibid. pp. 25 ff.

a level of equality. How could this come about? We have to recognize that all religions are in the end the same: we all, eastern and western, have one human nature, are descended from the first parents, worship the same God.[69] Here he was stating a position more easily justifiable in terms of Muslim than of Christian doctrine, but which was to be shared by all the Christian writers of his school. We must also try to encourage the growth of a sentiment of patriotism. 'Love of country is an article of faith' (*hubb al-watan min al-iman*): this phrase, attributed to the Prophet and much used by the Young Ottomans, was the motto of the most famous of his periodicals, and it was a lesson pointed by the events of 1860. In the heat of the crisis, he issued eleven numbers of a broadsheet, *Nafir Suriyya*. Each contains an address to his 'fellow countrymen' (*abna' al-watan*) signed by 'him who loves his country' (*muhibb al-watan*). He writes as an Ottoman subject, and there is no hint that he would wish to break away from loyalty to the sultan, but his appeal is to those who belong to a smaller unit within the empire and, as with Tahtawi, the unit is a territorial one. 'Syria' as a whole is his *watan*. All who live there share a land, customs, and also a language; he is perhaps the first writer to talk with pride of his 'Arab blood'.[70] If Syria is to flourish again, they must love her, and, what is no less urgent, they must be on friendly terms with each other. More than Tahtawi and Khayr al-Din, Bustani lays his emphasis on religious freedom and equality, and mutual respect between those of different faith. This can be explained, not only by the circumstances in which he wrote, but by the direction his own life had taken. He had himself broken out of the closed community of the Maronites to become a Protestant, and self-exile may well have turned his mind to the thought of some wider community to which he could belong. In a sense he is still writing as a Christian to Christians, calling on them to love their enemies and avoid the spirit of revenge.[71] But he draws a sharp contrast between two different types of religion: between the fanaticism (*ta'assub*) which has ruined Syria,[72] and the mutual respect between faiths which should exist and did once exist. The appeal is to the patriotic conscience, but it is

[69] *Khitab*, p. 31.
[70] *Nafir Suriyya*, i (29 Sept. 1860); viii (14 Dec. 1860).
[71] Ibid. iii (15 Oct., 1860).
[72] Ibid. iv (25 Oct., 1860).

also, by implication, to the Ottoman authorities. Making
allowance for local conditions, Bustani shares the outlook of the
Ottoman reformers. If Syria is to be truly civilized, she needs
two things from her rulers: just and equal laws suited to the
times, looking to the matter at issue and not to the person, and
based on a separation between the religious and secular realms;
and education in Arabic. Syria must not become a Babel of
languages as she is a Babel of religions.[73]

The object of this education should be to understand the
modern sciences and what lay behind them, the precise and
reasoned way of thinking and of acting. It is at this point
that the two sides of Bustani's work come together: in adapting the Arabic language to the expression of modern concepts, his aim was to change the minds of those who read and
spoke it, to make them citizens of the new world of science and
invention. In the last analysis, his most important work was the
vast encyclopaedia which he and his family began to issue in
1876, with financial help from the Khedive Isma'il.[74] It occupied
him for the rest of his life, and was carried on by his sons after
his death; although it was never finished, eleven large volumes
were published, full of the sciences and medicine, the engineering works and liberal ideas of Europe and America, and showing
how far the Arab mind had moved since Mishaqa stumbled on
his book of astronomy and Tahtawi landed at Marseilles.

[73] *Nafir Suriyya*, vii (19 Nov. 1860) & x (22 Feb. 1861).
[74] Bustani, *Da'irat al-ma'arif*, i, Introd., p. 3.

V

JAMAL AL-DIN AL-AFGHANI

WHEN Tahtawi and Khayr al-Din looked at Europe, what they saw were its new ideas and inventions rather than the irresistible power it derived from them. Khayr al-Din indeed was aware of the dangers inherent in the growth of European influence over the affairs of the empire, but thought they could be resisted with the help of the liberal Powers themselves; they had not yet become so great as to constitute the central problem of political life, and the main problem was still what it had been for the Ottoman writers of the seventeenth and eighteenth centuries— internal decline, how to explain and how to arrest it. The political ideas and practical skill of Europe were necessary for the one and the other alike, and Europe therefore was first of all a teacher and political ally for those who wished to reform the life of the Ottoman community. Had Tahtawi and Khayr al-Din written their books a few years later they would no doubt have written with a different emphasis, for in the years between 1875 and 1882 there took place events which were to give a new turn to the relationship between Europe and the Near East. The eastern crisis of 1875–8 showed that the armies of a European Power could penetrate to the heart of the empire, and could only be checked there by a threat from another Power; and the Treaty of Berlin which ended it showed that the fate of the empire and each of its provinces was no longer in its own hands. The occupation of Tunis by France in 1881, of Egypt by England in 1882, pointed the moral, and from that time there took place a radical change in the political thought of the Near East. For some of the Near Eastern Christians, indeed, the advantages of the European presence might outweigh its disadvantages; European domination did not challenge their whole view of the universe, and it might hold out hopes of influence and culture for their community, of prosperity for themselves. For a Muslim, however, whether he was Turkish or Arab, the seizure of power by Europe meant that his community was in danger. The *umma* was, among other things, a political community expressing itself in all the forms of political life, and a community which has no power may cease to exist. The problem of inner decay still exercised men's minds, but there was grafted on to it a new problem, that of survival: how could the Muslim countries resist the new danger from outside?

In the first instance the crisis seemed to give added strength to the arguments of the Young Ottomans. If the Bulgarians and Bosnians were rising in revolt, that was because the reforms of the nineteenth century had given the Christian subjects freedom without giving them a principle of loyalty; their freedom had enabled them to liberate themselves from the Empire, and the foreign Powers, particularly Russia, were encouraging and helping them in this. What was necessary was 'grouper tous ces éléments autour d'un principe vivifiant et régénerateur qui eût cimenté leur union; il aurait fallu créer pour ces differentes races une patrie commune qui les rendît insensibles aux suggestions du dehors'. Such a principle could be given them by a constitution, which alone would ensure that rights and duties were equal and that 'les améliorations dont on veut doter une partie de la population ne constituent pas le malheur et l'infortune de l'autre'.[1] But since an Ottoman constitution, being new, could not possess 'la consistance et l'autorité des vieilles constitutions européennes', it was necessary for liberal Europe itself to provide a substitute for what was lacking, by actively supervising the execution of the charter.[2]

The words are those of Midhat Pasha, an intelligent and successful official who had held high office and whose views were in the main those of the Young Ottomans, although he did not always agree with them and they had some suspicion of his autocratic tendencies. In May 1876, after the revolts had started and Russian intervention threatened, he led a coup d'état which deposed Abdülaziz and replaced him by his nephew Murad V and then, when Murad proved insane, by another nephew Abdülhamid II. At the end of the year the Ottoman constitution was promulgated: it provided for a responsible ministry, an appointed Senate, an elected Chamber of Deputies, and a hierarchy of local councils. In 1877 the first Chamber was

---

[1] Midhat, *La Turquie*, pp. 14 & 23 (Eng. trs. p. 986 & 990).
[2] Ibid. p. 28 (Eng. trs. p. 992).

elected. The elections took place under pressure from the local officials; not all the deputies could speak Turkish, or knew how parliamentary debates should be conducted; the Speaker was Ahmed Vefik Pasha, whom we have met in his youth, and who in his old age had not changed his view that nothing should be done which weakened those forces which held the empire together, the authority of the sovereign and the domination of the Muslim element. In spite of all this, however, the debates were real: political ideas were expressed, ministers and court officials were criticized and an opposition group emerged.[3] But the constitution had its enemies: the *'ulama'*, the conservatives, the sultan himself, who, although before his accession he had had some contact with the Young Ottomans, was not willing to give up his personal power. He had only accepted the constitution because of the pressure of the Powers; once the pressure was relaxed he could destroy it at his leisure. The opposition in the Ottoman parliament was becoming increasingly bold, naming ministers in whom it had no confidence and demanding the indictment of the former Prime Minister and the generals who had failed in the recent war against Russia. Abdülhamid prorogued parliament indefinitely and suspended, although he did not abolish, the constitution. Its author, Midhat Pasha, had already been sent into exile; allowed to return, he was arrested, accused of the murder of Abdülaziz (who in fact had killed himself soon after he was deposed), and sentenced to death. The sentence was commuted, he was sent into enforced residence in the Hejaz, and there quietly murdered a few years later. With him the first constitutional movement died. Abdülhamid was supreme and seemed to have taken up again the policy of his predecessors: administrative reform, but reform from above. In his early years at least he carried on the main lines of their policy: modernization of the system of justice and administration; centralization, made possible for the first time by the use of the telegraph and the building of railways; repression of the beduin and support for settled agriculture; the creation of schools, primary and secondary as well as higher. But as the reign went on, a change took place not only in his policy but in the nature of its appeal. The image of the sultan as a benevolent liberal monarch, father of all his peoples alike, Muslim, Christian, and Jewish, and leader of

[3] Fesch, *Constantinople*, pp. 267 ff.

all the forces of westernizing reform—an image which had
gradually been formed since the days of Mahmud II—was not
destroyed, but it was gradually overshadowed by another: that
of the sultan of Sunni Islam, shadow of God on earth, appealing
to all Muslims to rally round the throne in defence of the *umma*.
Emphasis was placed on the role of the sultan as protector of the
Pilgrimage; the railway from Damascus to Mecca, projected in
1903 and completed in 1908, was designed to rally Muslim
enthusiasm and support. What was more important still, the
claim of the sultan to be caliph was taken up and systematically
pushed. First put forward at the end of the eighteenth century,
mainly as a bargaining point in the negotiations with Russia at
the end of the war of 1768–74, it was not taken up seriously
until the reign of Abdülaziz in the 1860's and 1870's. By the time
the Ottoman constitution came to be drafted it had won general
enough acceptance to be included: 'Sa Majesté le Sultan est,
à titre de Kalif Suprême, le protecteur de la religion Musulmane'.[4]

Under Abdülhamid the claim was pushed even farther. It was
a policy aimed partly at the European Powers: they had Muslim
subjects, the Russians in the Caucasus and Turkestan, the French
in North Africa, the British in India, and might fear trouble
among them if their policy pressed too heavily on the sultan. But
it also aimed at reinforcing the loyalty of the Muslim peoples of
the empire, a loyalty which might be shaken by the secularization
of law, the spread of liberal ideas, or the contagion of nationalism.
For the Turks, the sultanate had a national character, and the
intimate link between sultan and people had not yet been broken,
as it was to be in the last days of the empire; the Islamic appeal
did not need to be addressed to them so much as to the other
Muslim subjects, Albanians, Kurds, above all Arabs. The Arabs
were the largest Muslim group in the empire, and the one most
able, by the extension of their language throughout the *umma*, to
win support for the sultan-caliph in Asia and Africa. In particular, they were the key to Africa: through them, the empire might
be able to resist European control of the African territories,
perhaps to win new lands where Islam was spreading. The pan-
Islamic propaganda was thus carried on mainly through the
medium of the Arabic language and with the help of men of

[4] Text in *Düstur*, iv. 2 (Fr. trs. in *State Papers*, lxvii. 683).

Arab origin. Ahmad Faris al-Shidyaq was the first to be used, in the reign of Abdülaziz; but Abdülhamid gathered others around him. At his court there were a number of Arab divines, mostly associated with one or other of the orders of mystics, vying with each other to exalt his claims and so to win his favour. There was Shaykh Muhammad Zafir of Mecca, a member of the Shadhili order; Shaykh Fadl of the ʿAlawi family from the Hadhramaut; and, most influential of all, Shaykh Abu'l-Huda al-Sayyadi of the Rifaʿi order.[5] An Arab from the province of Aleppo, he belonged to a family which for at least two generations had had a local reputation in the mystical orders. Gifted with great force of personality, he acquired a far wider fame; travelling first to Baghdad, then to Constantinople, he established a personal ascendancy over Abdülhamid, partly because of his reputation for supernatural powers, partly through his sagacity and political understanding. He played a large part in the sultan's religious policy, and wrote many works, both in prose and poetry, in which the same themes recur: the glory of the Rifaʿi order and his own ancestors; the exposition and defence of the mystical interpretation of Islam, against the attempts of Wahhabism and similar movements to return up the line of development to some imagined purity of primitive Islam; the defence of the sultan's claim to be caliph, and the call to all Muslims to rally round his throne. The caliphate, he proclaimed, is a necessity of faith, transmitted legitimately from Abu Bakr down to the Ottomans; the caliph is the shadow of God on earth, the executant of his decrees; all Muslims should obey him, being thankful if he does right, patient if he does wrong; even if he commands them to break God's laws, before disobeying they should begin with advice and prayers, confident that God is better able to change him than are they.[6]

There was another movement of thought, however, which also aimed at uniting Islam in face of a common danger, but did not think that the personal rule of a Muslim autocrat could serve as a focus of unity, and which, while it was willing to work with Abdülhamid or any other ruler who seemed to be serving the same purposes, was not prepared to be used for purely dynastic

[5] Cf. Hurgronje, *Verspreide Geschriften*, iii. 191 ff.; Yakan, *al-Maʿlum*, i. 100; Abu'l-Huda al-Sayyadi, *Tanwir al-absar*, introd. pp. 2–8.
[6] Abu'l-Huda al-Sayyadi, *Daʿi al-rashad*, *passim*.

interests. It would be truer perhaps to speak of a person than a movement, for this revolutionary pan-Islamism, this blend of religious feeling, national feeling, and European radicalism was embodied in the strange personality of a man whose life touched and deeply affected the whole Islamic world in the last quarter of the nineteenth century. Much has been written about Jamal al-Din al-Afghani (1839–97), and his life was lived very publicly, but there remains something mysterious about him.[7] Even his origins are obscure. He claimed to be a Sayyid, a descendant of the Prophet, and there seems no reason to doubt it. But was he an Afghan, as he himself said, or a Persian, as his enemies claimed? Shaykh Abu'l-Huda, his enemy at the end of his life, called him *al-Muta'afghin*, 'he who claims to be an Afghan', and asserted that he was really a Persian from Mazandaran.[8] The point is of some importance, since if he was a Persian he would have been a Shi'i, and this indeed is what his enemies meant to imply, and what he himself presumably wished to deny in calling himself an Afghan, for the greater part of his career was spent in Sunni countries. There does indeed exist a book, by a Persian claiming to be his nephew, and giving strong circumstantial evidence in favour of his being Persian by birth and upbringing, Shi'i by inheritance and education.[9] He studied, so the book claims, in the Shi'i holy cities of Najaf and Karbala', and there is some internal evidence that this was so. His writings and lectures show an undoubted knowledge of the tradition of Islamic philosophy, particularly of Ibn Sina, and this was a knowledge more easily come by at that time in the Shi'i schools, where the Avicennian tradition was still alive, than in those of Sunni Islam. However this may be, he first comes clearly into view in his early youth in India: already fully educated in the Islamic tradition, he acquired in India his first knowledge of the sciences and mathematics of modern Europe. With one of those rapid changes which recurred throughout his life, he was next in Afghanistan, where he tried to play a leading part in local politics. But what success he had was brief and limited. Next he went to Istanbul, on his way passing through Egypt where he stopped for a short while and made the acquaintance—

[7] For the life of al-Afghani cf. E. G. Browne; Rida, *Ta'rikh*, i. 27–102; and the works of al-Maghribi, al-Makhzumi, & Lutfallah Khan cited in the bibliography.

[8] Cf. *al-Manar*, xii (1909–10), 4.   [9] Lutfallah Khan, pp. 46 ff.

momentous for both of them—of a young student of the Azhar called Muhammad 'Abduh. In Istanbul he once more found a powerful protector, the reforming statesman Ali Pasha; but a lecture which he gave, and which seemed to place philosophy on the same level as prophecy, in the manner of the Islamic philosophers, aroused the hostility of the orthodox. He left for Egypt once more in 1871. A minister of liberal views, Riaz Pasha, secured him a government pension, and he stayed there for eight years, perhaps the most fruitful period of his life. He became the guide and unofficial teacher of a group of young men, mainly from the Azhar, who were to play an important part in Egyptian life and never to shake off the influence of al-Afghani; besides 'Abduh, the group included Sa'd Zaghlul who, fifty years later, was to become the leader of the Egyptian nation. He taught them, mainly in his own home, what he conceived to be the true Islam: theology, jurisprudence, mysticism, and philosophy.[10] But he taught them much else besides: the danger of European intervention, the need for national unity to resist it, the need for a broader unity of the Islamic peoples, the need for a constitution to limit the ruler's power. He encouraged his disciples to write, to publish newspapers, to form a public opinion, and through them he had a part in bringing about the first stirrings of national consciousness and discontent under Isma'il. For a moment he was on friendly terms with Isma'il's son Tawfiq; but Tawfiq as ruler was less liberal than as heir, and when he became khedive he had al-Afghani deported to India, either (as al-Afghani himself thought) under pressure from the British Consul-General or because of fear of his influence over the educated class.

Al-Afghani spent the next few years in India, and at the time of the British occupation of Egypt was kept under restraint by the authorities. But by 1884 he was in Paris, where he was joined by Muhammad 'Abduh, and together they organized a secret society of Muslims pledged to work for the unity and reform of Islam. The extent of the society is obscure, although it is known to have had a branch in Tunis as well as elsewhere.[11] Under its auspices the two of them published eighteen numbers of an Arabic periodical, *al-'Urwa al-wuthqa*. It was devoted partly to

---

[10] Cf. A. Amin, *Zu'ama' al-islah*, pp. 64–65.
[11] Cf. Rida, *Ta'rikh*, i. 284; Ibn 'Ashur, p. 43.

an analysis of the policy of the Great Powers in the Muslim
world, particularly of England in Egypt and the Sudan, and
partly to an exposition of the inner weaknesses of Islam and an
exhortation to Muslims to take thought and cure them. The
language of the periodical was 'Abduh's while the thought was
al-Afghani's,[12] and both for its thought and its language it
became one of the most influential of Arabic periodicals. Although prevented from entering countries under British control,
it circulated widely, and more than one thinker of a later generation has borne witness to the profound effect on him of a copy of
it found and read by chance years afterwards.

During his stay in Paris his personality and ideas aroused much
interest among Europeans concerned with the Muslim world.
He engaged in controversy with Renan about the attitude of
Islam towards science, and in 1884–5 conducted negotiations
with British statesmen about the future of Egypt and the Sudan.
These negotiations were begun through the good offices of
Wilfrid Blunt. A good minor poet, an aristocrat of wayward and
amorous temperament, an old-fashioned patriot shocked by the
vulgarity of the new imperialism, a romantic who disliked the
mechanical civilization of the nineteenth century, a lover of
strange places and Arab horses, Blunt had travelled with his wife
in the Syrian and Arabian deserts in 1877–9, and in 1879 they
had journeyed as far as Nejd, where the little kingdom of Ibn
Rashid, built on the ruins of the first Wahhabi state, with its
rustic equality and patriarchal justice, seemed to them, in spite
of a primitive brutality which they either did not notice or
condoned, to embody the ideal of human freedom. In 1880 Blunt
had settled for a time in Egypt, to improve his Arabic and study
the modern movements and problems of Islam. There he had
met Muhammad 'Abduh and heard for the first time of al-
Afghani, and had become acquainted with the new spirit of
reform in the world of Islam; he embodied his observations and
thought in a series of articles, published in 1882 as a book with
the title, *The Future of Islam*. He had followed closely the events
which culminated in the British occupation of Egypt, and this
experience helped to throw him into active sympathy with
nationalist movements, in Ireland and India as well as Egypt. He
had played indeed a certain part in the Egyptian crisis of 1881–2:

[12] Rida, *Ta'rikh*, i. 289.

he tried to maintain a link between 'Urabi's government and Gladstone, but while he failed to make any impression on Gladstone he perhaps misled the Egyptians about the extent of his influence and about what England was likely to do. He was now concerned about Britain's policy both in Egypt and in the Sudan, where the Mahdi's movement was spreading but Gordon was still upholding the authority of the Egyptian Government in Khartoum. Al-Afghani had some contact with the Mahdi through former Sudanese students at the Azhar, and may even have been given some authority to act on his behalf. There seems to have been an idea that Blunt should go to the Mahdi, acting on behalf of the British government but with a letter from Afghani, to negotiate the release of Gordon and also a more general agreement by which the Mahdi would halt his advance in return for a British withdrawal from Egypt.[13] The plan came to nothing, and it is difficult to believe that it was ever taken seriously. But Blunt had access to the little circle which ruled England, and had powerful friends among politicians who were anxious to withdraw from Egypt. In 1885 al-Afghani spent some time in London as his guest, to discuss the future of Egypt with Lord Randolph Churchill, then at the height of his brief power. At the time al-Afghani thought of Russia as a greater danger to the Muslim world than Britain. Russia was advancing in Central Asia, and he wanted an Anglo-Islamic rapprochement. The stumbling-block was the problem of Egypt, and once more a plan was produced. Sir Henry Drummond Wolff was being sent by the government to Constantinople to discuss the future of Egypt with the sultan, and it was suggested that al-Afghani should go with him to help in the negotiations. But this plan too came to nothing, and al-Afghani's visit to London ended with one of those melancholy scenes which punctuate the lives of political refugees. Two of his oriental friends quarrelled in Blunt's house and beat each other over the head with umbrellas: 'I had to beg them both to leave the house', records Blunt, 'and the Seyyid followed them. . . . I have now suggested to the Seyyid that he should take up his quarters elsewhere.'[14]

Al-Afghani was now disillusioned about the prospect of an Anglo-Islamic agreement. He went to Persia, then to Russia to

---

[13] Blunt, *Gordon*, pp. 542 ff.
[14] Ibid. p. 500.

explore other possibilities, then back to Persia again as adviser to the Shah Nasir al-Din. But within a year he had quarrelled with the Shah over a tobacco concession which the latter was prepared to give to a foreign company. He started a popular agitation against it, was deported in 1891, and began a press campaign designed to arouse opposition to the shah's policy both in Persia and in Europe. Next year he was invited by the Sultan Abdülhamid to Constantinople. For a time he enjoyed the sultan's favour and had influence at court, but once more the story repeated itself. He incurred the hostility of Shaykh Abu'l-Huda; and was generally held responsible for the murder of Shah Nasir al-Din in 1896. Whether he had arranged it or not, he had certainly helped to create the atmosphere which made it possible; the assassin was acquainted with him, and is said to have cried, at the fatal moment, 'Take this from the hand of Jamal al-Din.'[15] Certainly he rejoiced at the act, and the incident, like his whole career, showed that he could never be the docile servant of an autocrat who identified his own interests with those of Islam. The lesson was not lost on Abdülhamid; al-Afghani ended his life a virtual prisoner of the sultan although treated with honour.

On all who knew him he left a strong although not wholly pleasant impression: of a man devoted to his convictions, obstinate, ascetic, quick to anger when honour or religion was touched, wild and untameable; in Blunt's phrase, a 'wild man of genius'.[16]

He was eloquent, knew many languages, was fond of talking endlessly to his friends, in cafés in Cairo or in his gilded prison in Constantinople, and was a stirring public orator. But he did not like writing, and wrote little. Apart from political articles, a few slight works express his general ideas: a refutation of the materialists, a reply to Renan's lecture on *L'Islamisme et la science*, and the leading articles of *al-'Urwa al-wuthqa*. From these, and the reports of his conversation made by some of his disciples, it is possible however to form a clear idea of his teachings.

The greater part of his life was given up to a defence of the Islamic countries threatened by the danger of European ex-

---

[15] Arslan, *Hadhir al-'alam al-islami*, i. 203.
[16] Blunt, *Secret History*, p. 100.

pansion, but his thought was not exclusively political. The central problem of it, the problem which gave it its form, was not that of how to make the Muslim countries politically strong and successful; it was rather, how to persuade Muslims to understand their religion aright and live in accordance with its teaching. If they did so, he believed, their countries would of necessity be strong. The problem would have been essentially the same had there been no danger from outside, but of course the power and pressure of Europe gave it a new urgency. Al-Afghani lived in the age when European power suddenly became as wide as the world, so that there was no country however seemingly remote or securely independent which was not becoming aware of the pressure and rivalries of the European States, no political problem however apparently limited in scope which could be considered without taking European interests into account. At every point in his own life he was made aware of this: when he engaged in the politics of Afghanistan, lived and travelled in India, or helped to create opposition to the power of bondholders in Egypt or the tobacco company in Persia. His experience being what it was, he was more aware of the danger from England than from other countries. There is little in the '*Urwa al-wuthqa* about French, Dutch, or Russian imperialism, although there is a passing reference to the French occupation of Indo-China,[17] and while for a moment he played with the idea of an Anglo-Islamic entente against Russian expansion, in general it was the British government which was, in his eyes, 'the enemy of the Muslims'.[18] It was not only direct military attack that he feared. The British had other, subtler ways of working; they had conquered India by a 'trick', insinuating themselves into the Moghul Empire under pretext of helping the Moghuls.[19] They sowed division, and weakened the resistance of their victims by weakening their beliefs; it was thus that General Gordon had brought missionaries from Egypt to spread the idea of Protestant Christianity in the Sudan, while in India the false gospel of materialism was encouraged.[20]

The European Powers were not, al-Afghani maintained, innately stronger than the Muslim States. There was a prevalent idea that the English were superior, but this was an illusion

[17] *al-'Urwa*, i. 52.   [18] Ibid. ii. 68.
[19] Ibid. p. 14.   [20] Ibid. i. 13; ii. 138.

(*wahm*) and a dangerous one; such illusions make men cowardly, and so tend to bring about what they fear. The successes won by the Mahdi in the Sudan showed what Muslims could do against the British if only they were awakened; and if Muslim successes were few and defeats the rule, that was because Muslims were disunited, ignorant, and lacking in public virtues. Had India and Egypt been really awake and united, Britain could never have secured a foothold.[21] This view may appear naïve and is certainly expressed in too sweeping a way. The '*Urwa* was not a work of precise thought but a tract for the times, with the aim of arousing men's spirits. If al-Afghani says nothing of the industrial and technical revolution, that does not mean he was not aware of it. He knew that the successes of Europe were due to knowledge and its proper application, and the weakness of the Muslim States to ignorance,[22] and he knew also that the orient must learn the useful arts of Europe. But for him the urgent question was, how could they be learnt? They could not be acquired simply by imitation; behind them lay a whole way of thought and—more important still—a system of social morality. The Muslim countries were weak because Muslim society was in decay.

At this point we become aware of a novelty in al-Afghani's thought, or at least a new emphasis. The centre of attention is no longer Islam as a religion, it is rather Islam as a civilization. The aim of man's acts is not the service of God alone; it is the creation of human civilization flourishing in all its parts. The idea of civilization is indeed one of the seminal ideas of nineteenth-century Europe, and it is through al-Afghani above all that it reaches the Islamic world. It was given its classical expression by Guizot, in his lectures on the history of civilization in Europe, and al-Afghani had read Guizot and been impressed by him. The work was translated into Arabic in 1877, and al-Afghani inspired 'Abduh to write an article welcoming the translation and expounding the doctrine of the book. What was it that seemed to him important in this and similar books? It was first of all the idea of civilization, as the most momentous of all historical facts and that by which other facts should be judged. But it was also a specific meaning given to the word: the meaning of active, willed progress, of 'a people who are pressing forward

---

[21] *al-'Urwa*, ii. 200, 203.   [22] Makhzumi, pp. 224–5.

... to change ... their condition', and specifically of progress in two directions—social development, or the increase in social power and well-being, and individual development, that of man's faculties, sentiments, and ideas.[23] According to Guizot, both types of development were within the power of man. Man himself, with his ideas, sentiments, moral and intellectual dispositions, governs the world, the condition of society depends on man's moral state, and there are two aspects of this moral state which are important: on the one hand reason, and the willingness of men to have their inclinations and actions controlled by it; on the other, unity or solidarity, the common acceptance by members of society of the ideas and moral principles produced by reason.[24]

This was Guizot describing Europe, but it seemed to al-Afghani (with one significant change) to be a description of Islamic civilization as well. In its great days, the *umma* had all the necessary attributes of a flourishing civilization: social development, individual development, belief in reason, unity and solidarity; later it lost them. Being of fiery and political temperament, he tended to see both the greatness and the decline in political and military terms, but in reality the military successes of early Islam were for him only a symbol of the flowering of Islamic civilization. What had once been achieved could be achieved again: on the one hand by accepting those fruits of reason, the sciences of modern Europe, but also, and more fundamentally, by restoring the unity of the *umma*.

The appeal for unity is indeed the theme which runs all through al-Afghani's work. Both the common danger, and the values which all Muslims shared, should outweigh differences of doctrine and traditions of enmity. Differences of sect need not be a political barrier, and the Muslims should profit from the example of Germany, which lost its national unity through giving too much importance to differences of religion.[25] Even the deepest of doctrinal gulfs, that between Sunnis and Shi'is, could be bridged. Thus he called on Persians and Afghans to unite, even though the first were Shi'is and the second not, and during the last period of his life he played with the idea of a general reconciliation of the two sects. It was perhaps the possibility of extending his pan-Islamic propaganda into the Shi'i world

[23] Guizot, lecture I.   [24] Ibid. lecture III.   [25] *al-'Urwa*, ii. 124 ff.

which led Abdülhamid to invite al-Afghani to Constantinople. Al-Afghani seems to have had a plan, as always: Persia would recognize the sultan as caliph, the sultan would recognize the shah as independent and give up to him the Shi'i holy cities in Iraq; a general conference of Islamic leaders would be held in Constantinople, to decide questions of common concern and declare a *jihad* against western aggression. Al-Afghani seems to have had correspondence with Shi'i divines and others, but the plan had no issue, although it may have had something to do with the murder of Nasir al-Din, whose personal power was an obstacle.[26]

Political factions and dynastic interests should not be allowed to stand in the way of unity; the Muslim rulers should co-operate in the service of Islam. This belief explains much in al-Afghani's attitude towards the Muslim rulers and the stormy history of his relations with them. He did not think it possible or necessary to impose the rule of any one monarch upon the rest. There is no sign that he had it in mind to create a single Islamic State or to revive the united caliphate of early times. When he talked of the caliphate he meant by it some sort of spiritual authority or else simply a primacy of honour. If the spirit of co-operation existed, the existence of more than one State was of no importance; if it did not exist, then Muslims had no obligation to obey their ruler. Al-Afghani had a low opinion of the Muslim rulers of his day. They were not worthy of their position; they cared about nothing except their own pleasures and caprices, and so had fallen easy victims to the guiles and craft of the British. They had allowed foreign officials, linked with the nation neither by religion nor by race, to insinuate themselves into their counsels. The despot if he was well-intentioned could do things quickly, but the danger of despotism was that all rested on the ruler's character. If there was a bad ruler, the leaders of national opinion should get rid of him before it was too late.[27]

In this statement we can see the explanation of much in al-Afghani's troubled career and endless wanderings. He was not a constitutionalist on principle; his ideal of government was rather that of the Islamic theorists—the just king recognizing the sovereignty of a fundamental law.[28] By temperament he was

---

[26] Browne, pp. 30, 82–83; Lutfallah Khan, pp. 98 ff.
[27] *al-'Urwa*, ii. 42 & 110.
[28] Makhzumi, p. 90.

autocratic and impatient, and all his life was spent in search of
a Muslim ruler with whom he could work for the regeneration
of Islam, as in that partnership of ruler and philosopher which
al-Farabi had suggested as a substitute for the ideal philosopher-
king, who appeared but rarely. Each time he was disappointed.
The ruler turned out neither to be innately just nor to recognize
the authority of the law standing above him. Al-Afghani did not
belong to the quietist majority of Muslim thinkers who believed
that they should protest against injustice but submit to it; he
accepted rather the view of the minority who believed in the
right of revolt. Each time then that a ruler disappointed him he
turned against him violently, and his opposition served to
strengthen the constitutionalist and nationalist movements which
had begun to appear. For their part, the rulers who had hoped
that he would rally Muslim sentiment behind their thrones found
that his real intention was to use their power in the service of
Islam.

But even the best of rulers, though they could do much, could
not do all that al-Afghani thought necessary. When he talked
of Muslim unity, he did not mean only the co-operation of
religious or political leaders; he meant the solidarity of the
umma, the sense of responsibility which each member of it
should have towards the others and the whole, the desire to live
together in the community and work together for its welfare.
Solidarity (*ta'assub*) was the force which held society together,
and without which it would dissolve. Like all human attributes,
it could be perverted; it was not a law unto itself, it was subject
to the principle of moderation or justice, the organizing principle
of human societies. Solidarity which did not recognize this
principle and was not willing to do justice turned into fanaticism.[29]

Solidarity may have different bases: it may spring from a
common religious belief or else from a natural relationship such
as language. It is here that al-Afghani finds a fundamental
difference between European and Muslim civilization. There is
a belief current in Europe, he says, that national solidarity is good
in itself and conducive to progress, while religious solidarity is
always fanatical and prevents progress. (Was he thinking of
Guizot, who, while recognizing the role of the Church in forming

[29] *al-'Urwa*, i. 138 ff.

European civilization and giving it the idea of a divine law
superior to human laws, and the idea also that material power has
no right over the mind and conscience of man, accused it of
preventing progress by rejecting the right of private judgement
and obstructing the exercise of reason?)[30] This may be true of
Christianity but it is not true of Islam, where religious fanaticism has been rare and religious solidarity is essential for progress.

   This is not to say that he denies the importance of national
or other natural ties. There can be, he admits, a virtuous State
based on human reason as well as divine law; in the lecture
which led to his leaving Constantinople, he had maintained this
in words reminiscent of the philosophers: 'Thus is the body of
human society compounded. But a body cannot live without a
soul, and the soul of this body is either the prophetic or the
philosophic faculty.... [But] the former is a divine gift... while
the latter is attainable by thought and study.'[31] The community
based on human qualities and directed by human reason can be
just as stable as that based on religion; it can even be more stable
and survive two or three changes of religion. (No doubt he was
thinking of Persia.) Indeed, language is an essential element in
creating a stable community; human groups which have no
common language can possess no firm unity, and a group which
has no language of its own in which to express its knowledge and
skill can easily lose them.[32] Even the religious community will
be stronger if it also has a language in common: if only the
Ottomans had adopted the Arabic language as that of the whole
empire, its peoples would have had two links instead of one, and
it would have been united and strong.[33] Moreover a religious
link does not exclude national links with men of different faiths;
in countries such as Egypt and India Muslims should co-operate
with others and there should be 'good relations and harmony in
what pertains to national interests between you and your com-
patriots and neighbours who adhere to diverse religions'.[34] There
is even a natural solidarity beyond the nation: that which binds
together all the peoples of the east threatened by the expansion of
Europe. In its opening number, the *'Urwa* announces that it

[30] Guizot, lectures ii & v.
[31] Browne, p. 7; Rida, *Ta'rikh*, i. 30–31.
[32] al-Afghani, 'Philosophie de l'Union nationale', *Orient*, vi (1958), 123 ff.
[33] Makhzumi, p. 232.   [34] *al-'Urwa*, i. 151 ff.

is addressed to 'Easterners in general, and Muslims in particular'.[35]

When all this has been said, however, it remains true that for Muslims no sort of natural solidarity, not even patriotism, can replace the bond created by Islam. Real unity, in a Muslim nation, rests on common religious conviction. If that goes, society itself dissolves, and this in fact is what al-Afghani believes to be happening. His fear was not only that the *umma* would be weak but that it would cease to exist. In the past it had been held together by the political institution of the caliphate and by the '*ulama*' who preserved correct doctrine. But under the 'Abbasids, caliphate and '*ulama*' had split from each other, and later the caliphate had virtually ceased to exist. Independent kingdoms had arisen, and the '*ulama*' remained as the only organ of unity. They had become 'the spirit of the community and the heart of the Muhammadan people',[36] but they too in time had been split by differences of belief, and all except a few of them had diverged from the truth into false doctrines. As a result, the community had in fact dissolved. Abstract conviction was not enough to hold it together, it must be reinforced by real human needs and impulses; there must be a unity of hearts and deeds, for when this did not exist common convictions expressed themselves only in dreams and images. This in fact was what had happened; when a Muslim in one country heard about the misfortunes of those in others, he felt no urge to help them actively, only the kind of ineffectual regret one has when thinking of the dead.[37]

The salvation of the *umma* could not therefore come from virtuous rulers alone. There was no short cut to the regeneration of Islam. Newspapers by themselves could not do it; schools could not do it, although they could do something to raise the standard of public morality and spread the idea of unity. There could be no real reform of Islam unless the '*ulama*' returned to the truth of Islam, and the community as a whole accepted it and lived in accordance with it. But what is the truth of Islam?

This is the question to which, in the last analysis, all al-Afghani's thought is directed. In his treatment of it we are aware of a new element in Islamic thought. He is addressing himself not only to his fellow Muslims to rescue them from the false

[35] Ibid. p. 11.   [36] Ibid. ii. 167.   [37] Ibid. i. 119.

E

ideas in which they have so long been sunk; he is also talking, beyond the *umma*, to the learned world of Europe. He wishes both to destroy false views of Islam held by Muslims and criticisms of Islam made by Europeans. When he maintains that only by a return to Islam can the strength and civilization of Muslims be restored, he does so the more emphatically because it had become a commonplace of European thought that religion in general, and Islam specifically, sapped the will and restricted reason, and progress was only possible by abandoning it, or at least by making a sharp separation between religion and secular life.

While al-Afghani was in Paris in the 1880's he took part in a controversy with Renan. In his lecture on 'Islam and Science', given at the Sorbonne in 1883, Renan maintained that Islam and science—and therefore, by implication, Islam and modern civilization—were incompatible with one another:

Toute personne un peu instruite des choses de notre temps voit clairement l'infériorité actuelle des pays musulmans, la décadence des États gouvernés par l'islam, la nullité intellectuelle des races qui tiennent uniquement de cette religion leur culture et leur éducation. Tous ceux qui ont été en Orient ou en Afrique sont frappés de ce qu'a de fatalement borné l'esprit d'un vrai croyant, de cette espèce de cercle de fer qui entoure sa tête, la rend absolument fermée à la science, incapable de rien apprendre ni de s'ouvrir à aucune idée nouvelle.[38]

Renan admitted indeed the existence of a so-called Arabic philosophy and science, but they were Arabic in nothing but language, and Greco-Sassanian in content.[39] They were entirely the work of non-Muslims in inner revolt against their own religion; by theologians and rulers alike they had been opposed, and so had been unable to influence the institutions of Islam. This opposition had been held in check so long as the Arabs and Persians had been in control of Islam, but it reigned supreme when the barbarians—Turks in the east, Berbers in the west— took over the direction of the *umma*. The Turks had 'a total lack of the philosophic and scientific spirit',[40] and human reason and progress had been stifled by that enemy of progress, the State based on a revelation. But as European science spread, Islam would perish, and elsewhere Renan prophesied that this would

[38] Renan, *L'Islamisme et la science*, pp. 2–3.
[39] Ibid. p. 11.
[40] Ibid. p. 16; *Averroès et l'Averroïsme*, preface to 3rd ed., p. iii.

happen soon. As an example of the way in which Muslim minds were opened by their contacts with Europe, he gave Tahtawi's description of Paris, which was known to him:

La jeunesse d'Orient, en venant dans les écoles d'Occident puiser la science européenne, emportera avec elle ce qui en est le corollaire inséparable, la méthode rationelle, l'esprit expérimental, le sens du réel, l'impossibilité de croire à des traditions religieuses évidemment conçues en dehors de toute critique.[41]

Renan of course was thinking of Catholicism, and of religion in general, when he wrote of Islam. For him Islam, like Christianity, although in a different way, was an example of the tragic result of confusing two realms. Reason should dominate human action, having as its final cause human perfection and the triumph of civilization, and in the modern world science was the form in which reason expressed itself. Religion was necessary too, but as the expression of a moral ideal—'la beauté dans l'ordre morale',[42] the ideal of unselfishness, of which Jesus was the best exemplar. Properly conceived, there was no opposition between them; both had the same enemy, 'le matérialisme vulgaire, la bassesse de l'homme intéressé'.[43] The contradiction only arose when one trespassed on the field of the other: when, as in the French Revolution, reason claimed to govern the world without regard to the needs of the heart,[44] or when religions laid claim (as both Christianity and Islam had done) to a supernatural revelation of truth, and placed restrictions on the human mind. In a reply by no means lacking in perspicuity, al-Afghani met Renan on his own ground. It was true, he agreed, that while religions were necessary to draw men out of barbarism, they tended to become intolerant. In the childhood of the race, man cannot distinguish good from evil by his own reason, his tormented conscience can find in itself no repose; it is religion which

lui a ouvert les vastes horizons où l'imagination se complaît et où elle a trouvé, sinon la satisfaction complète de ses désirs, du moins un champ illimité pour ses espérances. Et comme l'humanité, à son origine, ignorait les causes des événements qui se passaient sous ses yeux et les secrets des choses, elle a été forcément amenée à suivre les conseils de ses précepteurs et les ordres qu'ils lui donnaient. Cette obéissance lui fut imposée au nom de l'Être suprême auquel ses

[41] *L'Avenir de la science*, p. 50.   [42] Ibid. p. 475.
[43] *Origines du Christianisme*, ii, p. lxiii.   [44] Ibid. p. lxiv.

éducateurs attribuaient tous les événements, sans lui permettre d'en discuter l'utilité ou les inconvénients.[45]

But this was only a phase through which religions passed; in a later phase, men liberated themselves from the chains imposed on their reason, and restored religion to its proper place. They had done so in Christendom at the time of the Reformation; Islam was several centuries younger and its reformation was still to come.[46] Islam needed a Luther: this indeed was a favourite theme of al-Afghani's, and perhaps he saw himself in the role.[47] Once this reformation took place, Islam was as fitted as any other religion to play its essential role of a moral guide. The past of Islam proved this: it could not be summed up, as Renan had suggested, as a blind triumph of orthodoxy over reason. The rational sciences had flourished, and they had been truly Islamic and Arab; it is precisely language which constitutes nations and distinguishes them from one another, and sciences expressed in Arabic must be called Arab. Thus the Arabs can claim Ibn Sina as theirs in exactly the same way as the French claim Mazarin and Napoleon. It is true, the conflict between religion and philosophy will always exist in Islam, but that is because it will always exist in the human mind:

Les religions, de quelque nom qu'on les désigne, se ressemblent toutes. Aucune entente ni aucune réconciliation ne sont possibles entre ces religions et la philosophie. La religion impose à l'homme sa foi et sa croyance, tandis que la philosophie l'en affranchit totalement ou en partie. . . . Toutes les fois que la religion aura le dessus, elle éliminera la philosophie; et le contraire arrive quand c'est la philosophie qui règne en souveraine maîtresse. Tant que l'humanité existera, la lutte ne cessera pas entre le dogme et le libre examen, entre la religion et la philosophie, lutte acharnée et dans laquelle, je crains, le triomphe ne sera pas pour la libre pensée, parce que la raison déplaît à la foule et que ses enseignements ne sont compris que par quelques intelligences d'élite, et parce que, aussi, la science, si belle qu'elle soit, ne satisfait pas complètement l'humanité qui a soif d'idéal et qui aime à planter dans des régions obscures et lointaines que les philosophes et les savants ne peuvent ni apercevoir ni explorer.[48]

In saying this, al-Afghani was understating his case. He not

[45] *J. des Débats*, 18 May, 1883, cited in Afghani, *al-Radd* (Fr. trs. pp. 176–7).
[46] Ibid.
[47] Cf. Maghribi, *Bayyinat*, i. 4.
[48] Afghani, *al-Radd* (Fr. trs. p. 185).

only believed that Islam was as true or false as other religions, but that it was the one true, complete, and perfect religion, which could satisfy all the desires of the human spirit. Like other Muslim thinkers of his day, he was willing to accept the judgement on Christianity given by European free thought: it was unreasonable, it was the enemy of science and progress. But he wished to show that these criticisms did not apply to Islam; on the contrary, Islam was in harmony with the principles discovered by scientific reason, was indeed the religion demanded by reason. Christianity had failed—he took Renan's word for it; but Islam, being neither irrational nor intolerant, could save the secular world from that revolutionary chaos, the memory of which haunted the French thinkers of his time. It was one of the secrets of al-Afghani's attraction for his fellow Muslims, that he offered them an Islam which once more could have a universal mission.

This could only be, however, if he could show that the essence of Islam was the same as that of modern rationalism. This was a dangerous process; some of al-Afghani's contemporaries were aware of the danger, and accused him of being willing to sacrifice the truth of Islam for an illusory welfare of Muslims. Even among his acquaintances there were some who doubted whether he really believed in Islam and fulfilled its legal obligations, just as there were some who later expressed the same doubts about his disciple 'Abduh. To see such accusations in their right perspective, however, it should be remembered that al-Afghani's view of Islam was that of the philosophers rather than that of the orthodox theologians: in other words, he accepted the final identification of philosophy and prophecy, that what the prophet received through inspiration was the same as what the philosopher could attain to by use of reason, but coupled with this the distinction between two ways of communicating the truth—by clear concepts to 'the few', through religious symbols to the 'many'.[49] Between this view of Islam and the ideas of nineteenth-century free thought it was perhaps not impossible to build a bridge.

If we remember that this was al-Afghani's view of Islam, there seems no reason to doubt that he was a convinced Muslim. Muhammad 'Abduh, who perhaps knew him better than anyone,

[49] Cf. *al-Jinan*, x (1879), 306.

said that al-Afghani was personally devout, with a tendency towards mysticism in his thought, and that in matters of practice he was a strict observer of the Hanafi code: 'I have seen none stricter than he in adhering to his code in its root and branches'.[50] Indeed it is impossible to understand either al-Afghani's thought or his political activities unless we realize that he accepted the fundamental teachings of Islam with all his mind: the existence of God, the existence of prophecy, that Muhammad was the last and greatest of the prophets, sent to all mankind, and that the Quran contained the word of God uncorrupted. He might make many concessions to modern thought, but he would not concede anything of that. It was precisely because he believed in the truth of Islam, however, that he was insistent that it should be interpreted aright. What then was the true Islam? First of all it was the belief in a transcendent God, the creator of the universe, and a rejection of all those creeds which maintained that the universe was self-created and that the world or man was a fit object of worship. For al-Afghani, this was the essence of Islam; tolerant as he was of divergences in doctrine or law, he would not tolerate any attack on this. This explains his hostility to certain modern movements in Islam, to Babism and the doctrines of the Indian thinker Sayyid Ahmad Khan (1817–98). He had a considerable knowledge of the doctrines of Babism, and there were Babis among his political acquaintances and followers. But he regarded Babism as a danger to the community, for, like other offshoots of Shi'ism, it substituted a doctrine of emanation for that of prophecy, and so blurred the distinction between Creator and created; while at the same time its belief in a continuing succession of prophets, and that Muhammad was neither last nor greatest of them, struck at the very existence of the *umma*.

The same fact explains too his attack on the 'modernist' movement started by Ahmad Khan. After a visit to England in the 1870's, Sayyid Ahmad began to preach a new Islam to which was applied the term 'Nayshariyya' (derived from the English word 'Nature'). The Quran, he taught, was the only essential element in Islam, the *Shari'a* was not of the essence of religion; the Quran must be interpreted in accordance with reason and nature, and the moral and legal code must be based on nature. Al-Afghani became aware of this doctrine when he was in exile

in India after 1879. In spite of appearances, there was all the
difference in the world between his own belief that there existed
a harmony between the truths revealed by Islam and the conclusions reached by human reason properly applied, and Ahmad
Khan's belief that the laws of nature, as deduced by reason, were
the norm by which Islam should be interpreted and human acts
judged. What Sayyid Ahmad was implying was that there was
nothing which transcended the world of nature, and that man
was the judge of all things. Or so it seemed to al-Afghani;
characteristically he ascribed the spread of the doctrine to a
British plot to weaken the faith and destroy the unity of Muslims,
but he also saw it as a new expression of a way of thought which
had always endangered true religion. To expose it he wrote
his longest work, *al-Radd ala'l-dhahriyyin* (The Refutation of
the Materialists). Those whom he attacked under the name of
'materialists' included all, from Democritus to Darwin with their
equivalents in Islam, who gave an explanation of the world
not involving the existence of a transcendent God. He attacked
them not only as endangering the truth, but because as a consequence they were a danger to social well-being and human
happiness. True religions, he maintained, taught three truths
above all: that man was monarch of the earth and the noblest of
created things, that his religious community was the best of all,
and that he had been sent into the world to perfect himself in
preparation of another life. From acceptance of these truths
sprang the three virtues which were the bases of society; modesty
(*haya'*), trust (*amana*), and truthfulness (*sidq*). The materialists
who denied these truths also destroyed the bases of human
society, and 'cast men down from the throne of human civilization to the base earth of animality'.[51] They dismissed modesty as
a weakness not a virtue, and by denying the Day of Judgment
struck at the root of trust and truthfulness. This subtle poison has
been at work whenever civilizations decay. It appeared in the
classical world in the form of Epicureanism, in ancient Persia in
the person of Mazdak. In Islamic history it found expression in
the esoteric movements which interpreted Islam as something
other than itself. It was this esotericism, claimed al-Afghani,
which weakened the community and made possible the disaster
of the Crusades. Some Muslims had kept their original virtues

[51] al-Afghani, *al-Radd*, pp. 31 & 39.

and were able to drive out the Crusaders in the end, but they could not root out the evil from the *umma*, which therefore remained weak; now it was a prey to the new poison of materialism, brewed in France by the freethinkers of the eighteenth century and brought into Islam by Sayyid Ahmad and his like.

First of all, then, Islam is belief in transcendence. Secondly, it is belief in reason. It encourages men to use their minds freely, in the certainty that what they discover will not contradict the truths revealed by prophecy. Islam alone of the great religions liberates the human mind from illusions and superstitions, and allows it to develop all its capabilities:

> The first pillar on which the religion of Islam is built is that the idea of divine unity should burnish the human mind and cleanse it from the weakness of illusion. Among the most important of its bases is the belief that God is alone in the disposition of beings, single in the creation of things which act and those which are acted upon, and that it is an obligation to cast aside all belief that men or inanimate bodies, whether higher or lower, have any influence for good or evil upon creation. . . . It is necessary to reject any belief that God in the Highest has appeared or appears in the garb of human kind or any other animal, to do good or ill; or that the holy essence has suffered the extremes of pain or the pains of disease in certain phases, for the benefit of any created thing.[52]

No other religion teaches in this way that reason is capable of knowing all and testing all, and that every man's reason is so capable; no other therefore gives men the self-respect and sense of equality which Muslims possess—or should possess, did they but know their religion. Judaism and Hinduism, each in its own way, deny human equality; Christianity denies to all but the priesthood the possibility of direct knowledge of divine truth, and teaches moreover certain doctrines which reason cannot accept.[53] Human reason therefore can fulfil itself in Islam alone; the law which the Prophet received from God is the same as the law of nature, which man's mind can discern from a study of the universe.

There is of course a difficulty about this view. If human reason can attain to all the truths necessary for life, what need is there for prophecy? Al-Afghani's answer appears to be that, while

---

[52] al-Afghani, *al-Radd*, p. 70.   [53] Ibid. p. 71.

reason can attain to truth in principle, human nature by itself cannot observe the rules which reason teaches it. Man is full of self-regarding passions and desires, which can only be controlled by the principle of justice in four ways: if everyone defends his own rights by force—but this leads to chaos or oppression; if everyone obeys his own sense of honour—but the idea of honour changes from one society to another, even from one class to another; if everyone is controlled by the power of the government—but this can only suppress a certain type of injustice, it cannot produce real justice; or if men believe in the existence of God, the eternal life and the Day of Judgment. It is this belief alone which provides a stable basis for obedience to moral principles. Prophecy has therefore a practical function: the prophet is sent to establish and maintain a virtuous society. There are two élites which control human society: the teachers who enlighten the understanding, and the moral preceptors who discipline the passions and point out the path of virtue. The prophets belong to the second class, and without them there can be no persistence in doing right.[54]

This view has far-reaching implications. It means that reason should be used fully in interpreting the Quran. If the Quran seems to be in contradiction with what is now known, we should interpret it symbolically. The Quran hints at things which it could not fully explain because men's minds were not ready for them; now that the mind has reached its full stature it should try to uncover the hints. For example, the Quran contains hidden references to modern science and its discoveries, to railways and electricity, as well as to modern political institutions;[55] for the first time, these can now be understood. Since reason can interpret, all men can interpret, provided they have a sufficient knowledge of Arabic, are of sound mind, and know the traditions of the *salaf*, the first generations of faithful guardians of the Prophet's message.[56] The door of *ijtihad* is not closed, and it is a duty as well as a right for men to apply the principles of the Quran anew to the problems of their time. To refuse to do this is to be guilty of stagnation (*jumud*) or imitation (*taqlid*), and these are enemies of true Islam just as materialism is an enemy. To imitate the words and acts of others corrupts alike religion and reason. If Muslims imitate Europeans they do not become

[54] Ibid. pp. 60–76.   [55] Makhzumi, pp. 161 ff.   [56] Ibid. p. 178.

like them, for the words and acts of Europeans only have meaning because they spring from certain principles understood and
accepted. In the same way, if a Muslim simply repeats the words
of his predecessors he will not acquire the true spirit of Islam.

Thirdly, and perhaps most important in al-Afghani's mind,
Islam means activity. The true attitude of the Muslim, he said
again and again, is not one of passive resignation to whatever
might come, as coming directly from God; it is one of responsible
activity in doing the will of God. That man is responsible before
God for all his acts, that he is responsible for the welfare of
society, that his failures are therefore his own, and avoidable:
all these for al-Afghani are the lessons of the Quran, and again
and again he and his disciples quote a verse which, for them,
sums up the whole: 'God changes not what is in a people, until
they change what is in themselves'.[57] The true Islam did
not teach that all things were commanded directly by God. It
was necessary to distinguish between the belief in compulsion
(*jabr*) and the genuine Muslim doctrine of predestination
(*qada'*). The first had been a popular belief at some times in
Islamic history, but it was not the true view, and was no longer
widespread. The second was the authentic view; it implied that
all things in the universe happened by sequence of cause and
effect, and God was the first cause who initiated the whole chain.
The decisions of the human will were necessary parts of the
sequence; they were free, but God had given, through reason
and the prophets, an indication of how they should be made. To
believe in predestination was to believe that if a man acted rightly
God would be with him; far from causing him to be passive, this
belief would stimulate him to activity. All great deeds had been
done by those who thought that God was with them.[58]

This was not true only of activity directed towards individual
perfection and happiness in the next world. It was true also of
activity directed towards happiness and success in this world.
The laws of Islam are also the laws of human nature: if man
obeys the teaching of Islam, he is also fulfilling the laws of his
own nature, and so attains to happiness and success in this world.
What is true of the individual is true also of society: when
societies obey the laws of Islam they become strong, when they
disobey they grow weak, for Islam commands solidarity and

[57] *Quran*, sura xiii, 10 (Arberry's trs.).   [58] *al-'Urwa*, i. 161 ff.

mutual responsibility, and these are the secrets of the strength of nations.

Virtue, civilization, strength are essentially connected with each other. This much, al-Afghani believes, is proved by the history of Islam. In his writings there is a vivid sense of the greatness and littleness of Islamic history: the *gesta Dei* in the beginning, the long and melancholy decline thereafter. When Muslims followed the teachings of the Prophet, the *umma* was great in the worldly sense; and if later the glories faded it was because they denied that truth. Becoming indifferent to God they also became indifferent to each other; solidarity grew weak and with it strength decayed. But here too there is a problem: if the teaching of Islam is in conformity with the needs of welfare and progress in this world, how is it that the non-Muslim countries today are foremost in strength as well as in enjoyment of worldly goods? Al-Afghani resolves the paradox by saying that neither the achievements of Christian nor the failure of Muslim countries are due to their religions. The Christian peoples grew strong because the Church grew up within the walls of the Roman Empire and incorporated its pagan beliefs and virtues; the Muslim peoples grew weak because the truth of Islam was corrupted by successive waves of falsity. Christians are strong because they are not really Christian; Muslims are *weak* because they are not really Muslim.[59]

[59] Ibid. i. 89.

VI

MUHAMMAD 'ABDUH[1]

FROM time to time in the life of al-Afghani we have come upon the figure of Muhammad 'Abduh, the disciple and collaborator moving closely in his wake. But 'Abduh did not remain all his life a pupil of al-Afghani, nor were the years of their collaboration the most fruitful of his career. He was to become a more systematic thinker than his master and have a more lasting influence on the Muslim mind, not only in Egypt but far beyond. His teaching was in the end to be rejected by many of those to whom he addressed himself, but remained working beneath the surface, the unacknowledged basis of the religious ideas of the ordinary educated Muslim.

His origin was very different from that of al-Afghani. Al-Afghani came from some distant place not to be determined with certainty, and passed like a meteor from one country to another; 'Abduh was firmly rooted in an ordinary family of the country where his main work was to be done. He was born in 1849 in a village of the Egyptian delta, into a family belonging to what has been the creative class of modern Egypt: the village families of some local standing and with a tradition of learning and piety. His father was perhaps of distant Turkish origin, his mother of an Arab family claiming descent from one of the early heroes of Islam. Both families had long been settled in a village near Tanta, but in the later years of Muhammad 'Ali they were forced to leave because of the exactions of his tax-collectors, and lived for some time in difficult straits elsewhere. Muhammad 'Abduh himself was born during this period of involuntary wandering, and although the family later returned to its village and recovered something of its position, he kept all his life the memory of what the victories and worldly glories of Muhammad 'Ali had really meant for the Egyptian people.

---

[1] For the life and thought of 'Abduh cf. works by Adams, Goldziher, Horten, and Jomier cited in the bibliography. For a searching critique of his school of thought, cf. Gibb, *Modern Trends in Islam.*

When he was about thirteen years old he was sent to study at the Ahmadi mosque at Tanta, then the greatest centre of religious culture in Egypt outside the Azhar. He was so bewildered by the method of teaching in use there—the learning by rote of commentaries on ancient texts—that after a time he ran away. He wanted to abandon his studies, but was persuaded to return by a maternal uncle, Shaykh Darwish, whose influence was to be the most decisive in his life before that of al-Afghani. It was his uncle who taught him the reality of belief which lay behind the stiff phrases of the books of grammar and doctrine, and many years later, in a fragment of autobiography, 'Abduh revealed something of what he owed him, and the affection in which he held his memory:

I found no divine to direct my conscience in the path it should take, except that shaykh who, in a few days, let me out from the prison of ignorance into the open air of knowledge, from the bonds of literalism to the freedom of true belief in God. . . . He was the key to my happiness, if I have had any happiness in my life. He gave me back that part of myself which I had lost, and revealed to me what lay concealed in my own nature.[2]

He went back to Tanta, and after finishing his studies there went on to the Azhar in Cairo, where he stayed from 1869 to 1877. He was particularly drawn to a shaykh who lectured on logic and philosophy, but even more to mystical theology. Mysticism remained for some time his favourite study, and was the subject of his first published work. For a while he lived a life of extravagant asceticism, shunning contact with other human beings, but from the danger of this he was rescued first by another intervention of Shaykh Darwish, then by his first meeting with al-Afghani. The Afghan was passing through Cairo for the first time on his way to Constantinople:

One of the students of the Syrian *riwaq* [says 'Abduh's biographer] told him that a great Afghan scholar had come to Cairo and was living in Khan al-Khalili. He rejoiced at that and suggested to Shaykh Hasan al-Tawil that they should visit him together. They found him at supper; he invited them to join him and, when they excused themselves, began to ask them questions about certain verses of the Quran, and what the commentators and mystics said about them. Then he began to give his own explanation, and ['Abduh's] heart was filled with wonder and

[2] Rida, *Ta'rikh*, i. 23.

love, because Quranic interpretation and mysticism were his favourite
studies or, as he used to say, the key of his happiness.[3]

When al-Afghani came back to Egypt in 1871 'Abduh became
the most devoted of the students who gathered around him,
attending the informal classes in his house and helping to spread
his ideas. Under al-Afghani's influence he began to study philosophy at this time: two copies of the *Isharat* of Ibn Sina, made
by his own hand at this time, bear witness to his interest, and one
of them ends with a eulogy of al-Afghani.[4] At this time also he
began to make a name for himself as a writer on social and political subjects, with some articles in a journal newly established
in Cairo by two brothers from Lebanon, *al-Ahram*. In 1877 he
finished his studies with the degree of *'alim*, and started the
career which was always to be the most congenial to him, that
of teacher. He taught at the Azhar, but also held informal classes
in his own house. Soon afterwards he began to teach at Dar
al-'Ulum, a new college established to provide a modern education for students of the Azhar who wished to become judges or
teachers in government schools. Among the books on which he
lectured in his house were a work on ethics by Miskawayh and
the Arabic translation of Guizot's *History of Civilization in
Europe*, and at Dar al-'Ulum his first class was on Ibn Khaldun's
Muqaddima, which had been published in Cairo, thanks to the
interest of Tahtawi, in 1857. The choice of books shows the
way in which his mind was moving: Miskawayh's book was an
Islamic version of Greek ethical philosophy and both Guizot
and Ibn Khaldun dealt in different ways with the problem of the
rise and fall of civilizations.

The 1870's were the period when national consciousness
became articulate in Egypt. It was given expression by the new
periodical press, and a new direction by the growth of foreign
influence. The Khedive Isma'il had fallen hopelessly into debt
to foreign bankers, and the European Powers, to safeguard their
interests, imposed a financial control which seemed likely to
become political as well. European ministers took office in the
government of Nubar Pasha, formed in 1878; and when Isma'il
dismissed them and seemed inclined to break away from control
he was deposed by the sultan acting under pressure from the

[3] Rida, *Ta'rikh*, p. 25.   [4] Osman Amin, *Muh. 'Abduh*, p. 29.

Powers. His autocratic rule, and the very high taxes he had imposed to pay the interest on his debts, had made him unpopular in Egypt, but his son and successor was no more popular. In the first years of his rule three overlapping movements of opposition grew in strength: those who, by religious conviction or national sentiment, saw in his subservience to the influence of Europe a danger to the independence of Egypt; those who, from principle or because of interest, wanted to replace absolute by constitutional rule; and the officers of Egyptian origin, who wanted to break the control of the Turco-Circassian officers over the army. The British and French policy of support for Tawfiq gradually blended these groups into a single movement of national opposition, and—as was perhaps inevitable—leadership fell into the hands of the soldiers. Their leader, 'Urabi Pasha, became Minister of War and virtual head of the government at the beginning of 1882. His government was regarded by Britain and France as a danger to their interests, and a period of tension and suspicion was brought to an end by the British bombardment of Alexandria and occupation of the whole country in September 1882. 'Abduh played an important part in these events. His early articles in the *Ahram* reflected al-Afghani's political views and it was perhaps for this reason that, when the Khedive Tawfiq exiled al-Afghani from Egypt, he ordered 'Abduh to retire to his village. But in 1880 he was back in Cairo, appointed by the Prime Minister, Riaz Pasha, as one of the editors, then as chief editor, of the official gazette, the *Waqa'i' al-misriyya*. During the next two years of crisis he played an important part in forming public opinion, by a series of articles on the social and political order, and in particular on national education. He was one of the leaders of the civilian wing of the national opposition. At Blunt's instigation, he and other civilian leaders drew up a statement of their aspirations which was sent to Gladstone and published in *The Times*. At this time he disapproved of the ideas and methods of the military leaders and had no high opinion of 'Urabi Pasha, but when the British attack began he had no hesitation in drawing closer to them and doing what he could to organize a national resistance. After the British occupation and restoration of the khedive's power he was arrested, kept in prison for a time, and maltreated. This, and the collapse of the nationalist movement, had a profound effect on him. Broadley, the English lawyer who was sent out by Blunt to defend 'Urabi at his trial, says that 'Abduh's 'great intellectual strength [was] overclouded for a time by moral and physical weakness. His mind and body alike seemed crushed out beyond hope of recovery by the cruel reaction born of shipwrecked hopes and the agony of despair.'[5]

Sentenced to exile for three years, he went first to Beirut and then joined al-Afghani in Paris, helping him to organize his secret society and publish *al-'Urwa al-wuthqa*. He was drawn deeply into al-Afghani's political schemes, visited London in 1884 to discuss with Hartington and others the problem of Egypt and the Sudan, and, when *al-'Urwa* expired, travelled to Tunis and then entered Egypt in disguise, hoping to go from there to the Mahdi in the Sudan.[6] Like so many of al-Afghani's plans this came to nothing, and 'Abduh returned to Beirut, where he remained for three years teaching in a school newly established by a Muslim benevolent society. It was here that he delivered the lectures on theology which he was later to expand into his most famous book; and in Beirut as in Cairo his house was a centre for young scholars and writers, Christians, Druzes, and Muslims, who came to talk with him about Islam and the Arabic language.

In 1888 he was allowed to return to Egypt by the khedive, on intercession from various quarters including the British Agency.[7] He had hoped to resume his teaching, but the khedive was unwilling to place him where he could once more have influence over the young. He was made a judge in the 'native tribunals' set up in 1883 to dispense the new codes of positive law, and this was the beginning of a new public career which lasted until his death in 1905. In 1899 he became Mufti of Egypt, head of the whole system of religious law. In this position he could do something to reform the religious courts and the administration of the *awqaf*; and his *fatwas* on questions of public concern helped to reinterpret the religious law in accordance with the needs of the age. In the same year he was appointed a member of the Legislative Council, a small body of thirty members, some nominated and some chosen by a restricted electorate, established in 1883; its functions were to deliberate and advise only, but as a matter of public duty he gave much time to its business. At heart however he remained a scholar, a teacher, and an organizer

[5] Broadley, pp. 227–8.   [6] Rida, *Ta'rikh*, i. 380–1.   [7] Cromer, ii. 179–80.

of schools. He helped to found and direct the Muslim Benevolent Society, the purpose of which was to establish private schools, and in 1895 he persuaded the khedive to set up an administrative council for the Azhar. He remained its most prominent member for ten years, and was able to carry out some reforms in the organization of the ancient university. When he could he still taught there, and when he had time he wrote. His most important book was a systematic treatise on theology based on his lectures in Beirut, *Risalat al-tawhid*; but he wrote a number of commentaries on parts of the Quran, and collaborated with one of his disciples, Rashid Rida, to prepare an elaborate commentary on the whole, based on his lectures but unfinishèd at the time of his death. At some time in the second half of his life he learnt to read French, and read widely in the European thought of his age. His library contained, among much else, Rousseau's *Émile* and Spencer's *Education*; the novels of Tolstoy as well as his didactic writings; Strauss's *Life of Jesus* and the works of Renan.[8] He had some contact with European thinkers, wrote a letter to Tolstoy, and went to Brighton to see Spencer; he went to Europe whenever he could, to renew himself, as he said, and because it revived his hopes that the Muslim world could recover from its present state.[9]

Alike through his writings and public activities, he became in later life one of the best known and best loved men in Egypt. A photograph taken on the terrace of the House of Commons when he visited England in 1884 shows a handsome man, well built, dark of complexion, with a tranquil and almost melancholy charm that does not quite conceal the look of conviction in his eyes. In later years the gentleness increased, and those who knew him well were conscious of his kindness and intelligence and a certain spiritual beauty. He was on good terms both with Cromer and with the most eloquent of his critics, Wilfrid Blunt, and he had around him a group of devoted friends and followers who were to become prominent in the life of Egypt. But the intransigence was still there, and while those who liked him liked him very much, there were others who resented his influence or opposed his religious and political convictions: the conservative school in the Azhar, the nationalists of the party of Mustafa Kamil, and the Khedive 'Abbas Hilmi. The khedive and Mustafa

[8] Osman Amin, p. 33.   [9] Rida, *Ta'rikh*, i. 846.

Kamil opposed him for reasons which were mainly political, but there were aspects of his teaching which might well have aroused the anger of the conservatives.

The starting-point of his thought, as of al-Afghani's, was the problem of inner decay, the need for an inner revival. He was conscious, as al-Afghani had been, of a type of decay peculiar to Islamic societies. According to the orthodox Muslim conception, Muhammad was sent not only to preach a way of individual salvation but to found a virtuous society. It followed that there were certain ways of acting in society which were in conformity with the Prophet's message and the will of God, certain others which were not. But as circumstances changed, society and its rulers inevitably found themselves faced with problems not foreseen in the prophetic message, and acting in ways which might even appear to contradict it. How to bridge the gap between what Islamic society should be and what it had become? In what sense could Muslim society still be said to be truly Muslim? This had been the problem of the Muslim thinkers of the later Middle Ages, but it came up again in a graver form as the movement of westernization advanced. By the time 'Abduh began to form his views and express them, Egypt like the Ottoman Empire was in its second generation of change. Isma'il had imparted to the process a new dynamic force. New codes of law had been adopted, schools on the new model were being created, there was talk of new political institutions, and in every sphere life was throwing up problems undreamed of by those who had made the *Shari'a* into a code. In general, 'Abduh did not deplore the changes. From the 1870's until the end of his life he remained convinced that the general line of development was both inevitable and to the benefit of Egypt. But he was conscious of the danger inherent in it: the danger of a division of society into two spheres without a real link—a sphere, always diminishing, in which the laws and moral principles of Islam ruled, and another, always growing, in which principles derived by human reason from considerations of worldly utility held sway. In other words, the danger came from an increasing secularization of a society which, by its essence, could never be wholly secularized; the result was a chasm which revealed itself in every aspect of life.

In 'Abduh's early articles we find already a clear analysis of the problem and its result. There is, for example, a group of articles concerned with the problem of law. For ʿAbduh, as for his predecessors, society to be moral must conform to a law of some sort. All created things had their natural laws; if a being went beyond its laws, it was in danger of destruction. For men and societies, those laws were 'the moral laws which limit human behaviour . . . they are set down by men of knowledge and wisdom in books of ethics and human education, after they have found expression in the divine commandments'.[10]

Once it crossed the limits laid down by its laws, a society would fall into ruin. But 'laws vary as the conditions of nations vary'; to be effective they must have some relation with the standards and circumstances of the country to which they apply, otherwise they will not fulfil the essential function of law, which is to direct human actions and mould human habits—in fact, they will not be laws at all.[11] This, ʿAbduh pointed out, was the position of law in modern Egyptian society. Muhammad ʿAli and his successors had tried to reform Egypt by planting European institutions and laws in her soil. ʿAbduh had a lively admiration for the achievements of modern Europe, for the serious tone of its society, even at this early age before he knew it directly. But he did not believe it possible to transplant its laws and institutions to Egypt. Laws planted in another soil do not work in the same way, they may even make things worse. The new laws brought from Europe are not really laws at all, because nobody understands them and therefore nobody can respect or obey them; Egypt is becoming that worst of societies, a society without laws.[12]

In the same way, there were two separate types of school in the country. On the one side stood the old religious schools with the Azhar at their apex, on the other the modern schools on the European model, whether established by foreign missions or the government. These two had no relations with each other, and neither was satisfactory in itself. The religious schools suffered from stagnation and slavish imitation, the characteristic ills of traditional Islam. They taught religion in a way, but not the sciences which were necessary for living in the modern world. The mission schools, whether consciously or not, brought their pupils near the religion of the teachers; there were instances known of Muslim children being turned into Christians, and

[10] Ibid. ii. 97.   [11] Rida, *Taʾrikh*, ii. 157 & 163.   [12] Ibid. pp. 103 & 157 ff.

even when this did not happen the student who studied a foreign curriculum in a foreign language might become mentally dependent on a foreign nation and estranged from his own. As for the new State schools, they had the vices of both; they were imitations of the foreign schools with this difference, that while the missionaries taught Christianity, the government schools taught no religion except in a formal way, and therefore no social or political morality.[13]

Behind this division of institutions there lay a division of 'spirits'. By the time of 'Abduh the two systems of education had produced two different educated classes in Egypt, each with a spirit of its own. One was the traditional Islamic spirit, resisting all change; the other, the spirit of the younger generation, accepting all change and all the ideas of modern Europe. The ideas of the French Enlightenment were becoming by this time the commonplaces of thought among the younger generation; the knowledge of French was widespread, Montesquieu and Voltaire had been translated. The ideas of positivism, in their original or a distorted form, were widespread. Some Egyptians indeed had drunk at the fountain-head: there is extant a copy of Comte's *Discours sur l'ensemble du positivisme*, presented by the author himself 'à mon ancien élève', Mustafa Mahramji, an Egyptian engineer sent to Paris by Muhammad 'Ali as a member of an educational mission.[14] This meant not only the absence of a common basis shared by the two groups; it meant also the danger that the moral bases of society would be destroyed by the restless spirit of individual reason, always questioning, always doubting. The thought of nineteenth-century France, by which 'Abduh was deeply influenced from an early age, contained full warnings against the dangers of the 'metaphysical' spirit of the previous century. Comte had emphasized that 'social order must ever be incompatible with a perpetual discussion of the foundations of society',[15] and pointed out that, while the doctrines of the metaphysicians had been necessary in order to break up the theological system, they were essentially negative and destructive, 'a complete doctrine of methodical negation of all regular government'.[16] 'Abduh was aware that the danger would be even greater if these destructive weapons were in hands that did not

[13] Rida, *Ta'rikh*, ii. 505 ff.   [14] Collection of Mr M. Wahba.
[15] Martineau, ii. 13.   [16] Ibid. p. 10.

fully understand them. He knew the fragility of the western culture of the gallicized Egyptian, who imitated the outward show of European life: 'It is the appearance of strength which has led the orientals to imitate Europeans in matters in which there is no profit, without perfecting their knowledge of its sources.'[17]

'Abduh's purpose, in all the acts of his later life as well as his writings, was to bridge the gulf within Islamic society, and in so doing to strengthen its moral roots. He thought this could only be done in one way. It could not be done by a return to the past, by stopping the process of change begun by Muhammad 'Ali. It could only be done by accepting the need for change, and by linking that change to the principles of Islam: by showing that the changes which were taking place were not only permitted by Islam, but were indeed its necessary implications if it was rightly understood, and that Islam could serve both as a principle of change and a salutary control over it. He was not concerned, as Khayr al-Din had been in a previous generation, to ask whether devout Muslims could accept the institutions and ideas of the modern world; they had come to stay, and so much the worse for anyone who did not accept them. He asked the opposite question, whether someone who lived in the modern world could still be a devout Muslim. His writings were directed not so much to convinced Muslims doubtful whether modern civilization was acceptable, as to men of modern culture and experience who doubted whether Islam, or indeed any revealed religion, was valid as a guide to life. It was this class which was the greatest danger to the *umma*, if it was won to metaphysical secularism; but equally it was from this class only that the leadership of a revived *umma* could be drawn.

It may not be fanciful indeed to think of 'Abduh's ideas as being constructed on a framework of Comtean positivism. The starting-point of Comte's thought was the French Revolution, when the rationalist élite, having destroyed the rule of the priesthood, had then almost destroyed the civilized order. Two parties, as Comte saw it, faced each other: those who wanted to return to the world of before the Revolution, and those imbued with the revolutionary spirit. The essence of the revolutionary spirit was the exaltation of private judgement, 'the absolute dogma of

[17] Rida, *Ta'rikh*, i. 868.

individual free inquiry',[18] which led to divergences of ideas and sentiments and so also of interests and actions; the way to 'close the revolutionary period' was to find a system of ideas universally acceptable. Once found, it must be embodied in religious symbols and ritual, and guarded by 'a small number of choice minds which shall have been prepared by a high order of discipline and instruction for the investigation of questions so complex and so mixed up with human passions',[19] a new spiritual authority, governing opinions and morals and supervising the system of education. In Comte's opinion, this new system of common beliefs could be reached by extending the rational methods of mathematics and the natural sciences to society, and developing a rational sociology which should also be a rational system of social morality, a norm of social action and a science of human happiness. It was 'Abduh's purpose to show that Islam contained in itself the potentialities of this rational religion, this social science and moral code which could serve as the basis of modern life; and to create the élite who should guard and interpret it—a new type of *'ulama'* who could articulate and teach the real Islam and so provide the basis for a stable and progressive society, a 'middle group' between the traditional and revolutionary forces to which Comte had pointed, and which could so easily be discerned in modern Islamic society.

In asserting that Islam could be the moral basis of a modern and progressive society, 'Abduh did not of course intend to imply that Islam would approve of everything that was done in the name of progress, and that the purpose of the new *'ulama'* was simply to legitimize a *fait accompli*. On the contrary, Islam as he conceived it was a principle of restraint: it would enable Muslims to distinguish what was good from what was bad among all the suggested directions of change. The task which he set himself therefore involved two things: first a restatement of what Islam really was, secondly a consideration of its implications for modern society. Of these, the former was the more important, indeed 'Abduh himself thought it the most important of his life's purposes. At the beginning of his fragment of autobiography, he defines those purposes:

First, to liberate thought from the shackles of *taqlid*, and understand religion as it was understood by the elders of the community before

---

[18] Martineau, ii. 277. [19] Ibid. p. 24.

dissension appeared; to return, in the acquisition of religious knowledge, to its first sources, and to weigh them in the scales of human reason, which God has created in order to prevent excess or adulteration in religion, so that God's wisdom may be fulfilled and the order of the human world preserved; and to prove that, seen in this light, religion must be accounted a friend to science, pushing man to investigate the secrets of existence, summoning him to respect established truths, and to depend on them in his moral life and conduct. All this I count as one matter, and in my advocacy of it I ran counter to the opinion of the two great groups of which the body of the *umma* is composed—the students of the sciences of religion, and those who think like them, and the students of the arts of this age, with those who are on their side.

My second purpose has been the reform of the way of writing the Arabic language. . . . There is still another matter of which I have been an advocate. People in general are blind to it and far from understanding it, although it is the pillar of their social life, and weakness and humiliation would not have come upon them had they not neglected it. This is, the distinction between the obedience which the people owe the government, and the just dealing which the government owes the people. I was one of those who called the Egyptian nation to know their rights *vis-à-vis* their ruler, although this nation has never had an idea of it for more than twenty centuries. We summoned it to believe that the ruler, even if it owes him obedience, is still human, liable to err and to be overcome by passion, and nothing can divert him from error or resist the domination of his passions except the advice of the people in word and deed.[20]

Nevertheless there were some, even among those who knew him well and liked him, who doubted whether he was himself convinced of the truth of Islam. Cromer thought he was really an agnostic,[21] and Blunt recorded in his diary 'I fear he has as little faith in Islam . . . as I have in the Catholic Church'.[22] In the same way some of his Muslim critics hinted that he was not scrupulous in performing the religious duties of a Muslim, even that of regular prayer.[23] Such statements, taken literally, cannot stand against the evidence of his own writings and of those who knew most intimately the movement of his thought. Rashid Rida, his biographer, has borne witness to 'Abduh's personal faith; in these matters, he says, 'Abduh followed the central tradition of Islamic devotion, that of al-Ghazali and those who believed that

[20] Rida, *Ta'rikh*, i. 11.   [21] Cromer, ii. 179–80.
[22] Blunt, *Diaries*, p. 346.   [23] Rida, *Ta'rikh*, i. 1042.

'submission and the presence of the heart in prayer are an obligation, and are one of the pillars of prayer and a condition of its
being valid and acceptable'.[24] With this tradition he had first
come into contact through his uncle, Shaykh Darwish, who had
rescued him from his early doubts and mystical excesses and
taught him the Islam of *ahl al-sunna wa'l-jama'a*: strictly orthodox in theology, suspicious of too free a rational speculation
about the divine mysteries, a little withdrawn from public life
but keeping the conscience of the community, observing strictly
the requirements of the law but softening legalism with a
personal devotion, a practice of the presence of God, far removed
from the pantheism of the mystical theology and based on meditation on the Quran and devotion to the person of the Prophet.
But in another sense the doubts had a certain validity. They
point to an aspect of his thought which, for his critics, might
very well be a sign of weakness: a sort of eclecticism, a blending
into a system of elements taken from different schools. In his
years of study he acquired a wide and precise knowledge of the
orthodox theology, and in his writings the influence not only of
al-Ghazali but of al-Maturidi can be clearly seen; indeed on the
points at issue between the various orthodox schools of theologians, he seems to accept the position of al-Maturidi rather than
al-Ghazali—for example, on the question of whether good and
evil can be known independently of revelation.[25] But the influence
of other studies also can be seen: his thought always bore the
mark of the study of Ibn Sina in which al-Afghani had initiated
him; and it is possible to see also the influence of Mu'tazilism,
that early Islamic rationalism which had been first sponsored and
then suppressed by the 'Abbasid caliphs, had then become a
dormant element in Islam, but since 'Abduh has been one of the
elements of modern orthodoxy.[26]

This eclecticism seems to imply a tendency to evade difficult
questions: for example, he never squarely faces the problem,
fundamental in Muslim theology, of whether the Quran was
created or not. A statement in the first edition of *Risalat al-
tawhid*, supporting the theory of the created Quran, was quietly
removed in later editions and nothing put in its place. It is

---

[24] Rida, *Ta'rikh*, i. 1036.
[25] Cf. M. Kerr, *Muh. Abduh and Rashid Rida.*
[26] Cf. R. Caspar, 'Le Renouveau mo'tazilite', *MIDEO*, iv (1957), 141–202.

perhaps this equivocation in 'Abduh's thought which gave rise to the doubts of Cromer and Blunt, and the criticisms from the Azhar. He does indeed give the impression of picking and choosing out of the mass of Islamic ideas those which best serve two purposes: first, to preserve the unity and social peace of the *umma*, concern for which led him to blur intellectual distinctions and refuse to reopen old controversies; and secondly, to reply to certain questions posed by the religious debates of the Europe of his time. His intellectual problems were those of Islamic thought, but they were also those of nineteenth-century Europe, in particular of the great debate about science and religion. The European books which he read were mainly those of the English and French thinkers of his day who tried to apply the methods of the natural sciences (as they conceived them) to human nature, society, and the universe as a whole; and his closest European friend, Wilfrid Blunt, was a Catholic who had lost his faith through reading Darwin, but kept all his life a longing for an 'evolutionary Christianity' in which he could believe, and had some contact with Father Tyrrell and the Catholic 'Modernists'. He was also influenced by the distinction drawn by such scholars as Strauss and Renan, as well as by Tolstoy, between 'the real Jesus' and his teachings, and the Christianity evolved by St Paul and the Catholic Church. 'Abduh accepted in general the view of Christianity which he learnt from Renan and Spencer or heard from Blunt: that Christian doctrine as traditionally formulated cannot stand up to the discoveries of modern science and the modern concepts of the laws of nature and of evolution. Such teachings fitted in well with the Muslim view of Christianity: the belief that Jesus was a human prophet, whose teaching and nature had been distorted by his followers. But he did not accept the free thinkers' rejection of theism and their materialism —Renan's view of religion as a necessary creation of the human imagination, and of man as 'the summit of the universe',[27] or Herbert Spencer's view of an unknowable power, manifesting itself in force and its various transformations, as 'the fundamental verity under *all* forms of religion'.[28] Islam seemed to him to be the middle path between the two extremes: a religion fully consistent with the claims of the human intellect and the discoveries of modern science, but safeguarding the divine

---

[27] Renan, *Nouvelles études*, p. xv.   [28] Spencer, p. 90.

transcendence which, for him as for al-Afghani, was the one valid object of human worship and stable basis for human morality. Islam indeed was the religion of human nature, the answer to the problems of the modern world, and some day the Europeans would get tired of the corruptions of their own faith and accept it.[29]

To show that Islam can be reconciled with modern thought, and how it can be, was one of 'Abduh's major purposes. He took part in two famous controversies on the matter, one with the French historian Hanotaux, the other with a Lebanese-Egyptian journalist, Farah Antun, and the polemical element was never absent from his thought. But polemics have their danger: in defending oneself, one may draw closer to one's adversary than one thinks. It is significant that both his controversies were concerned, not with the truth or falsity of Islam, but with its being compatible with the supposed requirements of the modern mind; and in the process, it may be that 'Abduh's view of Islam was itself affected by his view of what the modern mind needs. He carried farther a process we have already seen at work in the thought of Tahtawi, Khayr al-Din, and al-Afghani: that of identifying certain traditional concepts of Islamic thought with the dominant ideas of modern Europe. In this line of thought, *maslaha* gradually turns into utility, *shura* into parliamentary democracy, *ijma'* into public opinion; Islam itself becomes identical with civilization and activity, the norms of nineteenth-century social thought. It was, of course, easy in this way to distort if not destroy the precise meaning of the Islamic concepts, to lose that which distinguished Islam from other religions and even from non-religious humanism. It was perhaps this of which his conservative critics were uneasily aware: there was bound to be something arbitrary in the selection and the approximation. Once the traditional interpretation of Islam was abandoned, and the way open to private judgement, it was difficult if not impossible to say what was in accordance with Islam and what was not. Without intending it, 'Abduh was perhaps opening the door to the flooding of Islamic doctrine and law by all the innovations of the modern world. He had intended to build a wall against secularism, he had in fact provided an easy bridge by which it could capture one position after another. It was not an accident

[29] Rida, *Ta'rikh*, i. 939.

that, as we shall see, one group of his disciples were later to carry his doctrines in the direction of complete secularism.

The key to his defence of Islam, indeed to all his thought about it, was a certain conception of true religion: a distinction between what was essential and unchanging in it and what was inessential and could be changed without damage. The real Islam, he maintained, had a simple doctrinal structure: it consisted of certain beliefs about the greatest questions of human life, and certain general principles of human conduct. To enable us to reach these beliefs and embody them in our lives both reason and revelation are essential. They neither possess separate spheres nor conflict with each other in the same sphere. In the pursuit of religious as of all knowledge we must start with reason and follow its lead as far as it will take us: it teaches us first of all that God exists, and then some of His attributes—necessity, knowledge, will, power, choice, and unity.[30] It can tell us also that there is a life to come, that our fate in it is connected with the good and evil of our acts, and that some things are good and others bad.[31] By reason moreover we can know that there exists something called 'prophecy' and men called 'prophets'. Two lines of thought converge on this point. First, there are certain things which we cannot know by our reason. Some of them we do not need to know, and it is best not to speculate about them; we cannot know anything about the divine essence, for our minds and language are not adequate to grasp the essence of things.[32] Others we need to know in order to live properly, but cannot know by our own efforts: certain attributes of God (His word, sight, hearing); the nature of the life to come, its judgement, its pleasures and pains; certain acts of worship which are pleasing to God, but which man by himself could never have thought of. If to know these is necessary to life, they must be known in some way other than by reason. Secondly, there are things which can in principle be known by reason, but which most men do not in fact know, because their reason is imperfect or because of the power of passion to lead their minds astray. For both these reasons, men need a help if they are to live as

---

[30] 'Abduh, *Risalat al-tawhid*, pp. 42 ff.
[31] Ibid. p. 90.
[32] Ibid. pp. 61–62.

God wishes them to: 'a help to whom they can look in defining the principles of conduct and fixing a right attitude to belief'.[33] But this help must himself be a man, so that other men can understand him, and so that they can deduce his divine inspiration from his being better than others in human matters. Such a help is a prophet: that is to say, a man who transmits to others a message concerning God, judgment, and such other things as they must know.

Just as reason can tell us that prophets exist, so it can tell us who is really a prophet, and specifically that Muhammad is. The proofs that a prophetic mission is genuine are, first, the prophet's own conviction and claims; secondly, the continuity of acceptance and faith in him; thirdly, the evidentiary miracles which he is able to perform and which are vouched for by an unbroken tradition. Judged by these standards, 'Abduh has no doubt that Muhammad was a prophet. Unless God was working in him, how explain his acts and influence in history?[34] How explain the miracle of the Quran, for the splendour of its language and the depth of its thought could not have sprung from a human mind?[35] In the same way, there are rational proofs of Muhammad's claim to be the last of the prophets. The line of prophets must have an end somewhere, for at some point the whole of mankind will have received the guidance to happiness that it needs.[36] This point was reached with the Islamic revelation; Muhammad was sent when mankind was fully grown and capable of understanding all that was necessary; the message he transmitted can be shown to satisfy every need of human nature, and through him it was transmitted to all mankind.

At this point, reason must pause. Having proved that the Quran embodies a divine message, it must accept everything that is in it without hesitation; once it acknowledges that Muhammad was a prophet, it must accept the entire content of his prophetic message. The message is contained in the Quran and in the *hadith* of what he said and did: or rather in such of the *hadith* as are validated by a continuous and sound tradition, for 'Abduh showed much reserve in accepting the greater number of them. Quran and authentic *hadith* between them contain certain truths about the universe (both those which reason unaided

[33] 'Abduh, *Risalat al-tawhid*, p. 92.   [34] Ibid. p. 164.
[35] Ibid. p. 169.   [36] Ibid. p. 192.

can reach and those it cannot); the general principles of individual morality and social organization; and the commandment
to perform or abstain from certain acts (in particular acts of
worship) which we could not otherwise have known to be right
or wrong. These clear precepts must be accepted by all Muslims
without question, although even here at least one rational
science is involved, that of the Arabic language.[37] But there
are matters in regard to which Quran and *hadith* give no clear
guidance: because the text of the Quran is not clear; or because
there are doubts about the authenticity of the *hadith*; or because
Quran or *hadith* state only a general principle, not a particular
ruling; or because both Quran and *hadith* are silent. In these
circumstances reason must act as interpreter. Individual *ijtihad*
is not only permitted, it is essential. It operates within certain
limits, it is true: it cannot 'explain away' what the Quran or
hadith lay down, and if there is anything in them which seems
incompatible with reason, it must either search for the real sense
of the words or else submit itself to God and accept without
understanding.[38] Only those who possess the necessary knowledge and intellectual power must exercise their *ijtihad*; the rest
should follow any doctor in whom they have faith. But within
these limits, reason is free and its task unending; the *ijmaʿ*, the
consensus of the community, is not for ʿAbduh a third source of
doctrine and law on a level with the other two. A sort of *ijmaʿ*
does grow up in time, a collective judgement of the community,
but it is never infallible and cannot close the door to *ijtihad*.

   Such are the true principles of the religion Muhammad came
to preach; but his mission was not only to preach, it was to found
a community as well. Only a prophet could do this, for left to
themselves men will misuse their freedom of will under the
impulse of desire;[39] they will not listen to the voice of the philosopher, only to that of the religious leader, for 'religion is the
most powerful factor in the moral system of the many, and even
of the élite'.[40] Only a prophet can insert into human life a regulative principle which his fellow men will accept. What is this
principle, and what is the ideal society which the Prophet
Muhammad created? For ʿAbduh, as for the main line of Muslim

---

[37] ʿAbduh, *al-Islam waʾl-Nasraniyya*, pp. 72 ff.
[38] Cf. Jomier, pp. 81 ff.
[39] ʿAbduh, *Tafsir al-fatiha*, p. 49.
[40] ʿAbduh, *Risala*, p. 145.

thinkers, society was a system of rights and duties held together
by moral solidarity: by the mutual recognition of rights, and
mutual exhortation and help in the performance of duties. The
system of rights and duties was embodied in a law derived from
revelation: but derived from it in a certain way, for 'Abduh
introduced into the theory of the *Shari'a* a concept not without
its origins in Islamic thought, but which also owed something
to the European theory of natural law as well as to Utilitarianism.
Ibn Taymiyya and other thinkers had made a distinction between
acts directed towards the worship of God (*'ibadat*) and those
directed towards other men and life in the world (*mu'amalat*).
'Abduh adopted this and maintained that there was a systematic
difference between the teaching of revelation in regard to the
one and the other. Quran and *hadith* laid down specific rules
about worship; about relations with other men, they laid down
for the most part only general principles, leaving it to men to
apply them to all the circumstances of life. This was the legitimate sphere of *ijtihad*, of human judgement exercised responsibly
and in accordance with certain principles.

For 'Abduh therefore the mark of the ideal Muslim society
is not law only, it is also reason. The true Muslim is he who uses
his reason in affairs of the world and of religion; the only real
infidel (*kafir*) is he who closes his eyes to the light of truth and
refuses to examine rational proofs.[41] Contrary to what its
enemies say, Islam has never taught that human reason should
be checked, it is the friend of all rational inquiry and all science.[42]
This indeed was the subject of 'Abduh's controversy with Farah
Antun. In an essay on Ibn Rushd (Averroës, 1126–98), Antun
had maintained that Islam had killed the philosophic spirit. A
disciple of Renan, Antun had not necessarily meant to imply that
Christianity was any more favourable to science and philosophy,
but so 'Abduh took him to mean. Christianity, he retorted, was
intolerant by its nature, the enemy of rational explanation and
free inquiry; modern western civilization had nothing to do with
Christianity, it had developed precisely because the thinkers and
scientists of Europe had rejected it, and accepted in its place the
principle of materialism.[43] But since Islam was rational, Muslims

[41] 'Abduh, *Tafsir juz' 'amma*, p. 169; cf. Osman Amin, p. 49.
[42] 'Abduh, *al-Islam wa'l-Nasraniyya*, p. 202.
[43] Rida, *Ta'rikh*, ii. 400 ff.

could have the sciences of the modern world without accepting the religion of matter or rejecting their own.

The ideal society is that which submits to God's commandments, interprets them rationally and in the light of general welfare, obeys them actively, and is united by respect for them. This is the virtuous society, but it is also the happy, prosperous, and powerful society, for the commands of God are also the principles of human society. The behaviour which the Quran teaches to be pleasing to God is also that which modern social thought teaches to be the key to stability and progress. Islam is the true sociology, the science of happiness in this world as well as the next; it does not lead men to an excessive renunciation of the goods of this world, but to a just and moderate use of them. So when the Islamic law is fully understood and obeyed society flourishes; when it is misunderstood or rejected society decays.[44] The individual must often wait until the life to come for his reward, but communities, good and evil, have their rewards and punishments in the here and now.

This is the ideal society, but for 'Abduh it is also a society which once existed. His imagination is fixed on the golden age of Islam, the first generation of obedience and the rewards of obedience—political success and an intellectual development almost without a parallel in the speed and manner of its flowering.[45] The early *umma*, the community of the elders, the *salaf*, was what the *umma* ought to be. It remained so throughout the first centuries, for when 'Abduh talks of the *salaf*, he does not use the term in a technical sense to mean the first generation of friends and disciples of the Prophet; he uses it more generally to refer to the central tradition of Sunni Islam in its period of development: the great theologians of the third and fourth Islamic centuries, Asha'ri, Baqillani, Maturidi, are also *salaf*.[46] If this perfect society in the end decayed, it was for two reasons. First, there came into Islam elements alien to it: the philosophers and extreme Shi'is brought in the spirit of excess,[47] and a certain type of mysticism obscured the essential nature of Islam. For the true mysticism, as he conceived it, 'Abduh had a great respect: it was right that Muslims should interiorize their obedience to the

[44] 'Abduh, *Tafsir al-fatiha*, p. 63.
[45] 'Abduh, *Risala*, pp. 214 ff.
[46] 'Abduh, *al-Islam wa'l-Nasraniyya*, p. 198.
[47] 'Abduh, *Risala*, pp. 7, 19.

law. But another type of mysticism he regarded as dangerous to the mind and morals: that type which gave its devotion to the 'saints' (friends of God, *awliya*') and their miracles, and so tended to divert attention from God and to place intermediaries between God and man; which had invented its own liturgies and by implication disobeyed the clear injunctions of the Quran about how God wanted to be worshipped; which taught the believer to neglect his duties in this world in favour of too much preparation for the next; which subjected the disciple to the will of his spiritual director, and so weakened the activity of the individual will, the necessary basis of a flourishing Muslim society; which used technical metaphors with dangerous moral implications; and whose doctrine of 'the unity of existence' tended to destroy the gap between God and created things. On all these grounds the mystical theology of such thinkers as Ibn al-'Arabi, and the practices of the brotherhoods, seemed to him to attack the bases of the community, and when in his later years he was president of a commission to supervise the publishing of Arabic classics he refused to allow the publication of Ibn al-'Arabi's *al-Futuhat al-makkiya*.[48]

There was another way in which the *umma* had declined. Even those who preserved the essentials of the faith began to lose their sense of proportion and forget the difference between what was essential and what was not. They began to regard the detailed social regulations of early Islamic society as having the same status as the principles of the faith and demanding the same unchanging and unquestioning obedience. This too was a sort of excess—an 'excess of adherence to the outwardness of the law'[49] —and from it sprang a habit of blind imitation (*taqlid*) which was far from the freedom of true Islam. For 'Abduh the spread of *taqlid* was connected with the rise of the Turkish power in the *umma*; perhaps we can see the influence of Renan here. The Turks, newcomers to Islam and devoid of the gift of understanding, failed to grasp the meaning of the Prophet's message. In their own interest, they encouraged a slavish acceptance of authority, and discouraged the free exercise of reason among those they ruled. Knowledge was their enemy, for it would teach their subjects how bad the rulers' conduct was, so they

---

[48] Osman Amin, p. 191; cf. *al-Manar*, vii (1904–5), 439.
[49] 'Abduh, *Risala*, p. 19.

introduced their supporters into the ranks of the '*ulama*', to teach the faithful a dull stagnation in matters of belief and the acceptance of political autocracy. When the '*ulama*' were corrupted everything in Islam began to decay: the Arabic language lost its purity, unity was broken up by the strict division into religious schools, education was perverted, and even doctrine was corrupted when the balance between reason and revelation was overturned and the rational sciences neglected.[50]

So Islam was corrupted by its rulers: 'intellectual anarchy spread among Muslims, under the protection of ignorant rulers'.[51] This ignorance, this corruption had continued until modern times. What 'Abduh wrote of the Turks in the Middle Ages he would equally have applied to the Ottoman sultans. They too, in his eyes, were the pillars of unintelligent conservatism in matters of religion; he disliked Shaykh Abu'l-Huda, the intimate adviser of the sultan and advocate of a mystical view of Islam very different from his own.

While the Islamic nations were losing their virtues and so their strength, the nations of Europe were becoming stronger and more civilized, developing in their own way the essential social virtues of reason and activity, and reaping their reward. 'Abduh was convinced that the Muslim nations could not become strong and prosperous again until they acquired from Europe the sciences which were the product of its activity of mind, and they could do this without abandoning Islam, for Islam taught the acceptance of all the products of reason. This involved a change in the institutions of Islamic society: its legal system, its schools, and its methods of government.

Muslims must do once more what they should always have done: that is to say, reinterpret their law and adapt it to modern problems. Two principles were necessary for this purpose: both already accepted by the jurists but given a new extension by 'Abduh. First was the principle of 'interest', *maslaha*. As we have seen, Maliki jurisprudence had always accepted this principle; and 'Abduh was himself a Maliki by rite, although he studied Hanafi jurisprudence at the Azhar. He used the principle, but he gave it a more general meaning than it had had. Traditionally, it had been no more than a rule for the interpretation of

[50] 'Abduh, *al-Islam wa'l-Nasraniyya*, pp. 134 ff.
[51] 'Abduh, *Risala*, p. 25.

F

texts: in explaining the Quran and *hadith*, the jurist should assume that God's purpose in making His revelation was to promote human welfare, and he should therefore choose that interpretation which, in his opinion, best conduced to this purpose. 'Abduh and his school, however, made it a rule for deducing specific laws from general principles of social morality. Only such general principles, they taught, have been revealed by God. They must be applied to the specific problems of social life by human reason, and since those problems change, the application must also change; the guiding rule at any time is the general welfare of mankind at that time. The second principle was that of *talfiq*, or 'piecing together'. The notion that in any particular case a judge could choose that interpretation of the law, whether it came from his own legal code or not, which best fitted the circumstances had been accepted within limits by some classical authorities, but what 'Abduh suggested was something broader: not simply the 'borrowing' of a specific point from some other code, but a systematic comparison of all four, and even of the doctrines of independent jurists who accepted none of them, with a view to producing a 'synthesis' which would combine the good points of all. As Mufti of Egypt, he was able to put these suggestions into practice. When asked for a ruling by the Egyptian government, he had no choice but to give it in accordance with the official Hanafi code; but when approached by private individuals he had more freedom. For example, an Indian Muslim sent to ask him whether it was lawful for Muslims to co-operate with non-Muslims in framing charitable works, and in his reply he first of all asked the shaykhs of all four codes at the Azhar to state the position of their code, and then gave his own opinion, taking the four statements into account but going behind them to the Quran, the *hadith* of the Prophet, and the practice of the first age.[52]

The logical implication of this method was the creation of a unified and modern system of Islamic law. 'Abduh was well aware of this, and in his writings, as well as his decisions as mufti, he took the first steps towards it. The range of his decisions and opinions was wide and covered almost the whole field of law and social morality: whether Muslims should wear European hats, whether they should eat meat slaughtered by Christians or Jews,

[52] Rida, *Ta'rikh*, i. 648.

whether the painting of the human form was permitted by the law, whether polygamy was morally good or bad. By his decisions he started a tendency which has continued in Egypt since his death until it has achieved part of what he hoped for but by no means all. Since 1920 a succession of official laws and decrees has defined, and in the process has modified, the Islamic law which the religious courts have dispensed. The making of such laws could indeed be justified in orthodox Islamic terms by the right which *Shari'a* gives to the temporal sovereign to define the matters in regard to which the *Shari'a* judges shall have jurisdiction, as well as by the principle of *talfiq*. But *talfiq* has been used in a way more sweeping than the orthodox jurists would have approved, to justify interpretations of the law which seem to meet the needs of the modern age, even if they find no support among the doctors of the Hanafi school, or indeed any of the four great schools of law. In this way what is virtually a modern and unified system of Islamic law has been built up. But this is true only of those matters of personal status—marriage, divorce, and testaments—which the modern codes have left to the jurisdiction of the *Shari'a*. In other matters the process which 'Abduh wanted to reverse has continued. There are still secular courts administering civil and criminal codes derived from European models and enacted by the authority of the State. The civil code of 1948, it is true, mentions the *Shari'a* as a source of inspiration; but it is regarded as one source only, along with natural justice and custom, and in fact the body of the code shows little sign of its influence. Finally, in 1956 the separate religious courts were abolished, although matters of personal status are dealt with by the secular courts in accordance with the *Shari'a* as modified by legislation.[53]

A reform of the law would not be effective unless there were trained lawyers to interpret and apply it, and this involved a reform in the system of religious education. The fullest expression of 'Abduh's views on the matter is contained in a memorandum written during his years of exile in Beirut. There should, he thought, be a different type of religious education for each class in society. The ordinary people should be taught the broad

---

[53] Cf. Schacht, 'Islamic Law in Contemporary States', *Am. J. Comp. Law*, viii (1959), 133–47 and *Esquisse d'une histoire du droit musulman*; Anderson, 'Recent Developments in Shari'a Law', *Muslim Wld*, xl–xlii (1950–2).

principles of doctrine without anything being said about the differences of sects, and something of Islamic history, with an explanation of why Islam spread and conquered so rapidly. Those who were being trained as government officials should be taught logic and philosophy, doctrine with emphasis on the rational proofs of its truth and an exhortation to avoid dissension between the different rites, ethics with the same emphasis on its rational basis and a study of the exemplary lives of the *salaf*, and religious history. Those who were going to be teachers and spiritual directors should be more thoroughly trained in the religious sciences. They should first of all master the sciences of the Arabic language, then study the Quran, with an explanation of it which would take into account the customs, traditions, language, and methods of thought of the Arabs at the time it was revealed and so make it possible to distinguish the essence of the revelation from what was incidental; the *hadith* of the Prophet, but only those which were well authenticated; a complete system of ethics on the model of Ghazali's *Ihya' 'ulum al-din*; theology and jurisprudence, taking into account what could validly be deduced from the texts; the arts of persuasion and argument; and ancient and modern history—not only the period of Islamic glory but that of decline with an explanation of its causes.[54]

When 'Abduh reached a position of authority he was able to do something to carry these ideas into practice. A committee was established at his instigation, and with himself as chairman, to advise on reforms at the Azhar, and later a law was issued embodying its proposals: an administrative council was to be set up, new regulations laid down for the admission of students, for discipline and examinations, the curriculum was to be revised.[55] The council was in fact set up and 'Abduh was its most active member. It carried out some of the measures proposed: an attempt was made to replace the textbooks in use by a direct study of the great masters of Islamic thought, and add to the curriculum neglected sciences like ethics, history, and geography. The attempt however met with opposition: from the conservatives in the Azhar, and from the Khedive 'Abbas, who was on bad terms with 'Abduh at this time, and wished also to preserve the close link between the ruler and the Azhar which had existed in Egypt since Mamluke times. In 1905 'Abduh

[54] Rida, *Ta'rikh*, ii.   [55] 'Abd al-Muta'al al-Sa'idi, pp. 58 ff.

resigned from the council, after an attack on him in a public speech by the khedive.[56] After his death the impulse which he imparted to reform in the Azhar never quite died out. More than one of the Rectors of the University during the last fifty years have been his pupils and followers. In spite of opposition from inside and outside they have been able to carry on his work intermittently, and if the Azhar today is different from what it was in 'Abduh's time, it is largely thanks to him.

When 'Abduh wrote of political institutions there was the same ambivalence in his ideas as in those of his master al-Afghani, between the idea of the political unity of the *umma* and that of the nation in the modern sense. But the ambivalence was more apparent than real, as is clear if we look closer at his view of the *umma*. The earliest exposition of it—if indeed it can be taken as such—is to be found in Wilfrid Blunt's book, *The Future of Islam*. Blunt states that the views he expounds are largely those of 'Abduh, and this might be accepted up to a point. As we shall see later, the book puts forward an argument for the transfer of leadership in the *umma* from the Turks back to the Arabs, and implies that the disappearance of the Ottoman Empire is both inevitable and to be desired. It is unlikely that 'Abduh would have accepted this; but the book also contains an exposition of the nature of the Islamic community and the way to reform it, and it is perhaps possible to accept this as a true report of what was thought at the time in 'Abduh's circle.

The starting-point of the book indeed is exactly that of 'Abduh's own writings: the Islamic community is in decline, it must be reformed from within. The adoption of western institutions will not by itself bring about reform: the *Tanzimat* have been 'instituted not by and through religion, as they should have been, but in defiance of it. . . . All changes so attempted must fail in Islam because they have in them the inevitable vice of illegality'.[57] The Wahhabi movement had been nearer to a true reform, for it had attacked the problem at its root, the need for a reformation of morality and doctrine, a return to the fundamentals of Islam. What was fundamental was a small body of doctrines in conformity with the demands of human reason; Islamic law was the rational application of the principles to the changing circumstances of the world. What was needed now was

---

[56] A. Amin, *Zu'ama' al-islah*, p. 324.　　[57] Blunt, *Future of Islam*, p. 78.

to reinterpret the law so as to assimilate what was good in European morality: to accept, for example, the abolition of slavery, and equality before the law for Christians living in Muslim countries. But how could this process avoid 'the vice of illegality'? The law could not be changed unless there was an authority to change it: it was therefore necessary to restore the true caliphate with a spiritual function and claiming spiritual authority alone. The caliph was to be what 'Abduh's disciple Rashid Rida later called the chief *mujtahid* (practitioner of *ijtihad*). He should have the respect of the *umma* but not rule it; the unity of the *umma* was a moral unity which did not prevent its division into national States. There should, 'Abduh suggested at one point, be 'a chief of our Egyptian nation, acting under the religious sovereignty of the caliphate'.[58]

'Abduh was an Egyptian, deeply rooted in the traditions of his own country, and the nationalist element was important in his thought from the beginning. His very first article, published in *al-Ahram*, talks of the great past of 'the kingdom of Egypt',[59] and he was always conscious that the common history and interests of those who lived in the same country created a deep bond between them in spite of differing faiths. The sense of the importance of unity, which affected his view of Islamic reform, coloured also his view of the nation. Unity, he maintained, was necessary in political life, and the strongest type of unity was that of those who shared the same country—not only the place they lived in, but the locus of their public rights and duties, the object of their affection and pride.[60] Non-Muslims belonged to the nation in exactly the same sense as Muslims, and there should be good relations between those who differed in religion. So when the nationalist press attacked Butrus Ghali, a Copt and then Under-Secretary for Justice, 'Abduh intervened to point out that criticism of one person for one act should not become an attack on a whole community.[61] In the same way, Muslims should accept help from non-Muslims in matters of general welfare: an Indian Muslim asked him whether such help was lawful, and to prove it he quoted the Quran, the *hadith*, and the practice of the *salaf*.[62]

---

[58] Blunt, *Gordon*, p. 626.   [59] Rida, *Ta'rikh*, ii. 15.
[60] Ibid. pp. 194–5.   [61] Ibid. pp. 361 ff.
[62] Ibid. i. 647.

The Egyptian nation then existed as a separate fact, but like the whole of the *umma* it was in a state of inner decay, and could not hope to rule itself until it had reformed its life. 'Abduh's ideal of government was more or less that of the medieval jurists: the just ruler, ruling in accordance with a law and in consultation with the leaders of the people. He went farther than Khayr al-Din in identifying this rule with limited, constitutional monarchy, but he did not believe Egypt was yet ready for it. She needed first of all a gradual training in the arts of rule before she could govern herself. There should be local councils first, then an advisory council, then finally a representative assembly.[63]

These were his settled views, already articulate in his early articles and repeated in his later years. But in between he passed through a period when his national feeling was strong and he was ready to support violent measures. In the later years of Isma'il's reign, the influence of al-Afghani and the worsening situation of Egypt drew him into political life, and as the crisis reached its height his views grew more intransigent. He was no less opposed to the autocracy of the khedive than to foreign intervention. 'Every Egyptian', he wrote to Blunt in April 1882, '. . . hates the Turks and detests their infamous memory',[64] and the same bitterness of feeling lasted all through the period when he was working closely with al-Afghani in Paris. When he came to England in 1884, Blunt found that 'the dominant feeling now is hatred for England; and in this is merged the hatred of the Circassians'.[65] During the visit Blunt interviewed him for the *Pall Mall Gazette*, and he repeated the Egyptian claim for independence: 'Do not attempt to do us any more good. Your good has done us too much harm already.'[66]

When he went back to Egypt after the years of exile he returned to the detached moderation of his early years. Some said this was because of an undertaking he gave to the Khedive Tawfiq, when he was allowed to return, but it is easier to explain it by the waning of al-Afghani's influence and of the memory of 1882, which allowed his fundamental convictions to reassert themselves. What Egypt needed was a period of genuine national education; every political and social problem should be seen in the light of this need. If constitutional government hindered the

[63] Ibid. ii. 129.
[65] Blunt, *Gordon*, p. 270.
[64] Blunt, *Secret History*, p. 191.
[66] Ibid. p. 626.

process it was bad or at least premature; if autocratic rule, or even foreign rule, helped it, it was to be tolerated. There was no purely political road to political maturity and real independence, and in later years he criticized his old master al-Afghani for acting as if there were. 'The Sayyid', he told one of his own disciples, 'never did any real work except in Egypt'.[67] Instead of meddling in the intrigues of the palace at Constantinople, he should have tried to persuade the sultan to reform the system of education. He wrote something of this to al-Afghani himself who was angry, and their relations seem to have ended on this note. When al-Afghani died, he wrote no word of eulogy or affectionate commemoration.

He certainly tried to avoid the same mistake. As we have seen, the greater part of his time was given to national education and reform as he conceived it. When he was appointed a member of the Legislative Council he gave long hours to debates and committees, but did not think of it as political work; it was rather part of the task of political education.[68] He did not want it to have more power; in a famous article he spoke of the benefit which could be derived from 'a just despot', who could 'do for us in fifteen years what we could not do for ourselves in fifteen centuries'.[69] But this of course was not an endorsement of absolute rule as such. The despot must be just, and 'Abduh, like al-Afghani, belonged to the minority of Muslim thinkers who thought the community had a right to depose its ruler if he were not just and the general welfare demanded it.[70]

These principles explain his relations with the political forces of his time. Although the British were foreigners and not Muslims, he was prepared to co-operate with them so far as they were helping in the work of national education and provided their stay was temporary. He was on good terms with Cromer and liked him personally, although he did not like all the other British officials.[71] Cromer wrote of him and his group as 'the natural allies of the European reformer', and supported him when the khedive wanted to dismiss him from his position as mufti.[72] But this did not mean that 'Abduh was wholly satisfied with British policy. Even if Cromer were a just despot, he should

[67] Rida, *Ta'rikh*, i. 79.   [68] Ibid. p. 722.
[69] Ibid. ii. 390-1.   [70] 'Abduh, *al-Islam wa'l-Nasraniyya*, p. 84.
[71] Blunt, *Diaries*, pp. 91 & 350.   [72] Cromer, ii. 179-80.

still rule in consultation with the leaders of the people, and this
he was unwilling to do. 'Abduh wanted him to use his influence
with the khedive so that more Egyptians should be appointed
ministers in place of the old group of Turco-Circassian courtiers,
but although Cromer seemed interested in the idea for a moment
he did nothing, since he did not believe that the ministers
suggested would be better than those now in office.

In the same way, 'Abduh was prepared to work with the
khedive if he should prove to be a just autocrat. When 'Abbas
Hilmi succeeded his father, Tawfiq, in 1892 'Abduh was at first
on good terms with him and could influence him in some
respects. But the khedive turned against him when he tried to
prevent the misuse of *waqf* properties for the royal purposes, and
besides he was distrustful of 'Abduh's influence in the Azhar.
'Abduh for his part soon saw that the khedive would never give
up his privileges or share his power with a responsible ministry.
This brought out in him all the latent hostility to the family of
Muhammad 'Ali which was in the hearts of the Egyptian
peasantry: in an article, written on the hundredth anniversary of
Muhammad 'Ali's becoming ruler of Egypt, he pointed to the
dark side of the achievements of the man who was often called
'maker of modern Egypt'. In reality, 'he was not able to bring
things to life, only to kill them'. For his own power he destroyed
all who were noble or eminent in Egyptian life; he gave office to
those who were prepared to be his docile instruments, and
protection and privilege to foreigners of doubtful character. If
his government was strong, it was not based on respect for law;
he built an army, but by methods which did not instil into the
Egyptian people the military virtues. He encouraged agriculture
only in order to swell his own profits, and from being many
estates Egypt became one great estate. He was Muslim only in
name, did nothing for the faith, and on the contrary despoiled
the mosques and schools of their endowments.[73]

On the other hand, the doctrinaire nationalists seemed to him
mistaken in thinking there could be a short cut to independence.
He always remained critical of 'Urabi and the other military
leaders of 1882. 'Urabi, he said in his autobiographical fragment,
had at first no idea of political reform. He was simply concerned
for his own position in the army and hated the Circassian officers

[73] Rida, *Ta'rikh*, ii. 382.

who blocked the promotion of the Egyptians. Later he developed some idea that the calling of a parliament would curb the absolute power of the ruler and would also cover the mutiny he had led with the cloak of legitimacy. But this was no more than a vague idea gathered from newspapers and translations of European books—it was 'a fantasy which played about in his mind'.[74] 'Abduh goes on to describe how he used to argue with 'Urabi and his friends. The people, he would warn them, were not yet ready for self-government. Even had they been ready, it would still have been wrong to demand self-government by military pressure. Whatever was gained in that way would not be lasting, and besides it might lead to foreign occupation: 'I foresee that a foreign occupation will come and that a malediction will rest for ever on him who provokes it'.[75] Twenty years later, when the nationalist spirit revived under the leadership of Mustafa Kamil, 'Abduh made the same criticisms: Kamil's methods were illegitimate, they would produce either no results at all or results which would not be lasting. The two men did not find each other congenial: 'Abduh could not quite take Kamil seriously, and Kamil criticized the mufti because 'he cared too much for having official influence'.[76]

[74] Rida, *Ta'rikh*, i. 198 & 207.   [75] Blunt, *Secret History*, p. 379.
[76] Blunt, *Diaries*, p. 565.

VII

'ABDUH'S EGYPTIAN DISCIPLES: ISLAM AND MODERN CIVILIZATION

In 'Abduh's thought there was always a tension between two facts, neither of which could be wholly explained in terms of the other, but each of them bringing with it certain inescapable demands. On the one side stood Islam, with its claim to express God's will about how men should live in society; on the other, the irreversible movement of modern civilization, beginning in Europe but now becoming world-wide, and by the very nature of its institutions compelling men to live in a certain way. It was 'Abduh's purpose to prove, by an exposition of the true Islam, that the two demands were not incompatible with each other, and to prove it not only in principle but in detail, by a precise consideration of the teaching of Islam in regard to social morality. He never maintained that there was an unconditional harmony between the two: that Islam permitted all that the modern world approved. When there was a real conflict, he was always clear which of the two claims had precedence. There remained for him something fixed and irreducible in Islam, certain moral and doctrinal imperatives about which there could be no compromise; Islam could never be just a rubber-stamp authorizing whatever the world did, it must always be in some measure a controlling and limiting factor. But the tension was a delicate one, and, as we have seen, it was difficult to say where in fact the limits lay: there was always a temptation to relax it through a half-conscious identification of the commands of Islam with the concepts of modern thought.

'Abduh's influence, although greater than that of any other Muslim thinker of his time, was never universal; and both in his time and later there have been those who maintained that the concessions he made to modern thought were dangerous and unnecessary, and that no such rethinking of doctrine or law was necessary. Even among those who had come under his influence and might claim to be his disciples, there were some whose spirit

was different from his. 'Abduh's own writings were controlled
by a deep knowledge of the traditional sciences of Islam, and
—what was more important—a vivid sense of responsibility to
it. But his methods offered a temptation to thinkers of polemical
tendency, more anxious to defend the reputation of Islam than
to discover and expound its truth: the temptation of claiming
that Islam was everything the modern world approved, and
possessed hidden in it all the modern world thought it had discovered. An example of this type of polemical writing is Muhammad Farid Wajdi's *al-Madaniyya wa'l-Islam* (Islam and Civilization). The title of the book is significant: for Wajdi, as for all the
writers of the school of 'Abduh, there are two important and
independent things: Islam with its truths and laws revealed by
God, and modern civilization with its own laws discovered by
sociology. But what to do when there seems to be a contradiction
between the two? 'Abduh resolved it by saying that *true* civilization is in conformity with Islam; but in Wajdi's book we can see
a subtle change of tone and emphasis, an implication that the
true Islam is in conformity with civilization. He accepts the claim
of modern Europe to have discovered the laws of social progress
and happiness, and goes on to maintain that these laws are also
those of Islam. 'What is Islam?' he asks, and answers that it is
first of all the existence of a direct connexion between man and
his Maker, free from the interposition and tyranny of priests,
but it is much more than that: it is also human equality, the
consultative principle in government, the rights of the intellect
and science, the existence of unchanging natural laws of human
life, intellectual curiosity about the order of nature, freedom of
discussion and opinion, the practical unity of mankind on a basis
of mutual toleration, the rights of man's disposition and feelings,
the acknowledgement of human welfare and interest as the final
purpose of religion, and the principle of progress.

In such works Islam was, so to speak, 'dissolved' into modern
thought. But there were other followers of 'Abduh who preserved
his spirit and applied his method with the same sense of responsibility. 'Abduh's modifications of the Islamic teaching on social
morality had been made by a careful extension of principles
already accepted in Islamic thought. How skilfully the method
could be used by others is shown by a book which appeared, it is
true, forty years after his death, but imbued with his spirit: an

introduction to the history of Islamic philosophy by Mustafa 'Abd al-Raziq. The son of a political associate of 'Abduh, 'Abd al-Raziq studied first at the Azhar and then at the Sorbonne under Durkheim, and after years as a teacher of philosophy in the Egyptian University and a short period as minister became Rector of the Azhar in 1945, and made one more of the thankless attempts to reform it, until death released him in 1947. His book, like those of 'Abduh, is written within the context of nineteenth-century rationalism. It is the ghost of Renan which haunts it. The problem from which 'Abd al-Raziq starts is Renan's assertion that Islamic philosophy is neither Islamic nor Arabic in any essential sense; and he tries to refute it by asserting the place of reason in Islam. But he does so by a scholarly examination of the place of opinion (*ra'y*) in Islamic jurisprudence, a cautious stretching of it as far as it will go without distorting the nature or mis-stating the history of Islam. Appeal is made to Islamic thinkers of the past, to prove that *ra'y* had existed in Islam from the time of the Prophet, who had himself used it and allowed his Companions to do so.[1] The careful treatment of historical sources, and the use of the concept of historical development, show the influence of his European training; but they are controlled by a sense of what Islam really is and has been.

Even among those who tried to preserve the tension created by 'Abduh, there was however a gradual shift in the relationship of its two elements. 'Abduh had put forward not so much a definitive view of Islam—to have done so would have been to create a new kind of *taqlid*—as a method of looking at it and at the world. It was natural that some of his disciples should have been more interested in one aspect and some in another of his method, and that by excess of emphasis they should have tended to overturn the balance he had created, perhaps in ways he would not have approved of. In the years after his death, one group of his followers carried his insistence on the unchanging nature and absolute claims of the essential Islam in the direction of a Hanbali fundamentalism; others developed his emphasis on the legitimacy of social change into a *de facto* division between the two realms, that of religion and that of society, each with its own norms.

[1] M. 'Abd al-Raziq, *Tamhid*, pp. 136 ff.

In 1899 one of his Egyptian disciples, Qasim Amin (1865–1908), published a small book on the emancipation of women. Of Kurdish stock and French education, Qasim Amin had already won some distinction as judge and occasional writer on social problems, but this book gave him greater fame and even notoriety. Its starting-point is a familiar one, the decay of Islam seen in the perspective of Darwinism. The Islamic community is in decline: it is too weak to face the pressures on it from all sides, and if weak it cannot survive in a world ruled by the laws of natural selection.[2] But what are the causes of the decay? Amin does not accept either of the explanations usually given. Decay is not due to the natural environment, for there have been ages of flourishing civilization in these same countries; it is not due to Islam, the decline of which is itself a result and not a cause of the decline of social strength. The real cause of the decay is the disappearance of the social virtues, of 'moral strength', and the cause of *that* is ignorance—ignorance of the true sciences from which alone can be derived the laws of human happiness. This ignorance begins in the family. The relations of man and woman, of mother and child, are the basis of society; the virtues which exist in the family will exist in the nation. 'The work of women in society is to form the morals of the nation.'[3] But in Muslim countries neither men nor women are properly educated to create a real family life,[4] and woman has not the freedom or status necessary if she is to play her role.

Is not this in its turn due to Islam? Amin denies it; on the contrary, he claims, the *Shari'a* was the first law to provide for the equality of women with men (except in regard to polygamy, and there were pressing reasons for inequality in this respect). Corruption came into Islam from outside, with the peoples who were converted and brought in their own 'customs and illusions'. They destroyed the original Islamic system of government, which defined the rights of rulers and ruled, and put in its place the rule of despotic force. All through society the strong learned to despise the weak, and men to despise women.[5]

The heart of the social problem then is the position of women, and this can only be improved by education. Amin did not suggest that women should be as highly educated as men, for

---

[2] Amin, *Tahrir al-mar'a*, p. 116. [3] Amin, *al-Mar'a al-jadida*, p. 124.
[4] *Tahrir*, pp. 116–31. [5] Ibid. pp. 12–14.

in this as in other things his suggestions are so modest as to seem timid. But at least they should have elementary schooling if they were to manage their households properly and play their part in society; this should include reading and writing, some notions of the natural and moral sciences, of history and geography, of hygiene and physiology, as well as religious education, physical training, and the training of artistic taste.[6]

Education should not be directed only to the proper management of the household, it should have another aim and an even more important one, that of fitting women to earn their own living. This was the only sure guarantee of women's rights: unless a woman could support herself she would always be at the mercy of male tyranny, no matter what rights the laws gave her, and would have to secure power for herself by devious means. Education would end the tyranny, and in doing so it would also end the veiling and seclusion of women. Once more Amin approaches his subject with caution. His wish, he says, is not to abolish seclusion as such, for in a certain form it is necessary to safeguard virtue; it is rather to restore it to what the *Shari'a* lays down.[7] First of all then it must be asked what the Quran and *Shari'a* really say on the subject. There is, so Amin maintains, no general and strict prohibition on women's revealing their faces; this is a matter left to convenience and custom, and clearly it is not convenient for women to preserve their rights and play their part in society from behind the veil. How, for example, can they make contracts and conduct legal business? Veiling women does not preserve virtue; on the contrary some types of veil increase sexual desire.[8] Nor is there anything in the Quran about seclusion, except for the wives of Muhammad. There is, in other words, no clear text on the matter, and it is therefore necessary, following 'Abduh's principle, to decide the matter in accordance with social welfare. There is no doubt that seclusion is socially harmful; it prevents women from becoming 'complete beings', for a woman is only complete 'if she disposes of herself and enjoys the freedom granted by the *Shari'a* and by nature alike, and if her potentialities are developed to the highest degree'.[9] Seclusion is thus socially harmful, but it is also bad in itself. It rests on lack of trust. Men do not respect women, they

---

[6] Ibid. p. 20; *al-Mar'a*, pp. 161 ff.   [7] *Tahrir*, pp. 27 ff. & 83.
[8] Ibid. pp. 75–78.   [9] Ibid. p. 85.

shut them up because they do not regard them as entirely human: 'Man has stripped woman of her human attributes and has confined her to one office only, which is that he should enjoy her body'.[10] The same contempt for women underlies the practice of polygamy. No woman would willingly share her husband with another, and if a man marries a second wife it can only be by ignoring the wishes and feelings of the first.[11] In some circumstances it is licit, for example if the first wife goes mad or is childless, but even then it is better for a man not to exercise his right, to be chivalrous and forbearing. It cannot of course be denied that the Quran specifically permits polygamy, but while it does so it also warns against its dangers. The Quranic verse reads, 'Marry such women as seem good to you, two, three, four; but if you fear you will not be equitable, then only one',[12] and Qasim follows Tahtawi and 'Abduh in laying special emphasis on the proviso, and pointing out that men in fact cannot be just to all. Divorce too is permitted in case of necessity, but reprehensible in itself. It is best to refrain from it where possible, and only resort to it where unavoidable; Amin is thinking in particular of the 'fictitious divorces' practised under Muslim law for financial or other reasons. If divorce is to be practised at all, women should have the same right to it as men.[13]

In all the matters he deals with, Amin proceeds like 'Abduh by a cautious definition of an Islamic practice rather than by abandoning it. He is scarcely what a later generation would call a feminist. He does not, for example, suggest that women should have political rights. There is, he admits, no reason of principle why they should not, but the Egyptian woman needs a long period of intellectual training before she will be able to take part in public life.[14] Like 'Abduh again he is appealing to those who still accept Islam; at every point he takes his stand on the Quran and the *Shari'a* interpreted, or so he believes, in the right way. That is to say, where there is a clear text in the Quran or *hadith*, then there is no scope for discussion; men must obey, whatever the consequences. But where there is no text, or a text which can be interpreted in different ways, then one must choose among alternatives in the light of social welfare. In such cases, traditional

---

[10] *al-Mar'a*, p. 47.
[11] *Tahrir*, p. 152.
[12] *Quran*, Sura iv. 2 (Arberry's trs.).
[13] *Tahrir*, pp. 165 & 184.
[14] *al-Mar'a*, pp. 83–84.

rules and interpretations are not sacred; they are purely human customs embedded in religion, and which change from time to time and even from one Muslim people to another.[15] It is legitimate to seek a new interpretation 'which meets the need without departing from the general principle of the *Shari'a*'.[16]

In spite of his caution Amin's book aroused a storm. In the few months after its publication it gave rise to a series of books and pamphlets, some attacking and some supporting his thesis. In reply to his critics Amin published in 1900 a second book on the subject of the new woman. In part it is a new statement of the ideas put forward in the first, but its tone is very different. Naturally it is more polemical; but what is more important, the whole basis of the argument has shifted. It is as if, under the shock of anger, the Islamic scaffolding has collapsed, and what is revealed inside is a completely different structure of thought. The appeal is no longer to Quran and *Shari'a* rightly interpreted, it is to the sciences and social thought of the modern west, and the significant name of Herbert Spencer makes more than one appearance.[17]

The standards of judgement now are the great concepts of the nineteenth century: freedom, progress, civilization. Freedom means 'man's independence in thought, will and deed, so long as he remains within the bounds of the laws and respects morality, and his not being subjected, beyond that point, to a will other than his own'.[18] It is the basis of human progress, but the freedom of women in its turn is the basis and criterion of all other kinds of freedom. When woman is free, the citizen is free; and the arguments used against freedom of women are exactly the same as those used against freedom of any kind—for example, of the press. As human society has progressed, so have the rights of women. There have been four main stages in the process: the state of nature when woman was free; the period of the formation of the family, when she was really subjected; that of the formation of civil society, when some of her rights were acknowledged but she was prevented from exercising them by the tyranny of men; finally the period of real civilization, when woman attains her full rights and has practically the same status as man.[19] The

---

[15] *Tahrir*, pp. 6 ff. & 68.   [16] Ibid. p. 186.
[17] e.g. *al-Mar'a*, p. 199.   [18] Ibid. p. 38.
[19] Ibid. pp. 29 & 152.

eastern countries are in the third of these stages, the European in the fourth:

Look at the eastern countries; you will find woman enslaved to man and man to the ruler. Man is an oppressor in his home, oppressed as soon as he leaves it. Then look at the European countries; the governments are based on freedom and respect for personal rights, and the status of women has been raised to a high degree of respect and freedom of thought and action.[20]

Such passages might be simply an attack on the decay of Islam, in the style made popular by al-Afghani, but it soon becomes clear that they are more than that. They are an attack not on the abuses of Islamic civilization, but on the idea that it is 'the model of human perfection'. Perfect civilization is based on science, and since Islamic civilization reached its full development before the true sciences were established, it cannot be taken as the model. Like all civilizations of the past it had its defects. It lacked moral originality, and there is no sign that Muslims of the great age were either better or worse than other men.[21] It lacked also political maturity: its rulers had unlimited power, so had their officials. There was no constitution to compel the ruler to observe the *Shari'a*; the 'sovereignty of the people' implied by the ceremony of investiture was purely nominal, and in fact the caliph alone was sovereign:

It may be said that the caliph used to rule after the members of the Community had formally invested him, and that this shows that his authority was derived from the sovereign people. I do not deny it; but this authority which the people only enjoyed for a few minutes was a nominal authority, and in reality it was the caliph who was sovereign. It was he who declared war, made peace, imposed taxes, made decisions and looked after the interests of the *umma*, relying on his own judgement and without any obligation to take anyone else into partnership in the matter.[22]

Perfection in short was not to be found in the past, even the Islamic past; it could only be found, if at all, in the distant future. The path to it was science, and in the present age it was Europe which was most advanced in the sciences and therefore also on the path to social perfection. Europe is ahead of us in every way, Amin assures his readers; it is comforting to think

---

[20] *al-Mar'a*, p. 17.   [21] Ibid. p. 179.   [22] Ibid. p. 176.

that while they are materially better than us we are morally better, but it is not true. The Europeans are morally more advanced; their upper and lower classes, it is true, are rather lacking in sexual virtue, but the middle class has high morals in every sense, and all classes alike have the social virtues. They have that willingness to sacrifice oneself which lies at the basis of real solidarity, and which explains

why a German gives up his life and leaves his wife and children to help the Boers; why a scientist turns his back on good living and the pleasures of the world and prefers to work at solving problems and understanding causes; how a statesman of great wealth and high position spends his time devising ways to raise the standing of his nation, and deprives himself of rest for the sake of this; what is the motive of the traveller who spends months and years far from his family and home in order to discover, let us say, the sources of the Nile; what are the feelings which reconcile the priest to living among savages, surrounded by hardships and dangers; and what is the emotion which induces the rich man to give thousands of pounds to a charitable society or a work of which the profit goes to his nation or humanity.[23]

The basis of all this is science, for without knowledge good morals can exist but not be stable. The freedom of women in Europe, for example, is not based on custom and feeling but on rational and scientific principles. It is useless to hope to adopt the sciences of Europe without coming within the radius of its moral principles; the two things are indissolubly connected, and we must therefore be prepared for change in every aspect of our life.[24]

In this second book something is made explicit which was already implied in the first, and it is not difficult to understand why both were received with strong hostility. What Qasim Amin was saying, in effect, was that religion does not by itself create a State, a society, or a civilization. The growth of a civilization must be explained by many factors of which religion is only one; if it is to progress, it must have laws which take all equally into account. In other words, Amin has dissolved the relationship established by 'Abduh between Islam and civilization, and created in its place a *de facto* division of spheres of influence. While treating Islam with all respect, he claims the right for civilization to develop its own norms and act in the light of them.

[23] Ibid. p. 196.   [24] Ibid. pp. 198 ff.

This means also that civilizations can be judged by those norms; and while Islam is the true religion, that does not necessarily mean that Islamic civilization is the highest civilization.

Qasim Amin was not alone in developing 'Abduh's thought in this direction. A number of others, while remaining loyal to their master in thought, began in fact to work out the principles of a secular society in which Islam was honoured but was no longer the guide of law and policy. By the early years of the twentieth century they had come to be known as a party, 'the Imam's party' (*hizb al-Imam*), with political principles drawn from the teachings of 'Abduh. In 1907, for reasons to be discussed later, groups of public men in Egypt began to organize themselves officially into parties, and, although 'Abduh himself was now dead, his followers formed a party based on his principles, with the name of 'People's Party' (*hizb al-umma*). At about the same time they began to issue a periodical, *al-Jarida*, which continued to appear until the outbreak of the First World War made the free expression of opinion difficult. It was written for the educated and never had much influence on the mass, but on those for whom it was intended it made a profound mark.

The problem it faced was still that of the relations between Islam and society, but expressed in a different form. Those who formed the party and wrote the newspaper were Egyptians, conscious of a loyalty to a community which could not simply be conceived as part of the Islamic *umma*. By their time the idea of an Egyptian nation was a commonplace universally accepted, and this was a conception far removed from those of Islamic political thought, not simply because Christians and Jews as well as Muslims lived in Egypt, but because the very basis of the Egyptian community was different. What bound Egyptians together was not the revealed law, but the natural link of living in the same country: they had been Egyptians before Islam and its law existed, the Islamic period was only a moment in a continuous history from the time of the Pharaohs. Thus Egyptian Muslims had two independent loyalties, neither of which could be subsumed under the other: to Egypt and to Islam. What was, what should be the relationship between them? A whole body of ideas on the subject lies implicit in the writings of the editor of *al-Jarida*, Ahmad Lutfi al-Sayyid (1872–1963).[25]

[25] For all this section cf. J. M. Ahmed, *Intellectual Origins*.

Born in a village in Lower Egypt, Lutfi al-Sayyid belonged like 'Abduh to a rural family with a tradition of local leadership. But his family had prospered more: both his father and grandfather were *'umdas*, village headmen, and his father was made a pasha. He too had an early education of the Quranic type, but at the age of thirteen was sent to a modern secondary school in Cairo, and then in 1889 to the School of Law. In the Arab countries schools of law tend to be centres of political thought and action, and among Lutfi al-Sayyid's fellow students were some who were later to be prominent in Egyptian life: the leader of the National Party, Mustafa Kamil, and two future Prime Ministers, Sarwat and Sidqi. It was at this time he met 'Abduh and became his friend and disciple. He also met al-Afghani on a visit to Constantinople and much admired him, although there could have been no deep affinity between his rational and detached spirit and the burning, committed enthusiasm of al-Afghani. His studies completed, he spent a number of years in government service, and, although he did not much like it, he owed to these years his intimate knowledge of every aspect of Egyptian life. In these years also he laid the foundations of his knowledge of European thought. The influence of his wide reading can be seen in what he wrote. Some of it arouses no surprise—like other educated Egyptians of the time he read Rousseau and Comte, Mill, and Spencer—; but he also studied Aristotle's *Ethics*, and was deeply moved by the later didactic writings of Tolstoy.

Free from government service, he entered public life as a founding member of the People's Party and editor of *al-Jarida*. Almost everything he wrote was written in the form of articles for *al-Jarida*, and through it he was able to do something to mould the moral consciousness of the Egyptian nation. But there was that in his temperament which made him dislike public life and unsuited him for success in it: the very coolness and fairness of his mind. In 1915, when *al-Jarida* came to an end, he became director of the national library. When the Wafd was founded he was drawn once more into public life, but soon sickened of politics as he saw the break-up of national unity under pressure of personal ambitions. For the next twenty years he worked mainly in the Egyptian University; he had helped to found it during the early years of the century as the 'Popular University', and when it was reorganized and enlarged in the 1920's he became

Professor of Philosophy and later Rector. He retired at the age of seventy into a life quiet but neither forgotten nor without influence on his friends and pupils.

In his later years he translated Aristotle's *Nicomachean Ethics*, but wrote no connected and systematic works. His periodical articles have been collected into a number of volumes, but it is difficult to judge the ideas of a thinker from short occasional works, where they need not be worked out to their logical conclusion. One strong impression at least can be derived from them however: the surprisingly small part played by Islam in the thought of one whose mind had been formed by Muhammad 'Abduh. He is, of course, aware of himself and most of his fellow countrymen as being Muslim by tradition and forming part of the *umma*, but Islam is not the principle of his thought. He is not concerned, like al-Afghani, to defend it, nor, like 'Abduh, to restore to Islamic law its position as the moral basis of society. Religion—whether it be Islamic or not—is relevant to his thought only as one of the constituent factors of society. In a country with a religious tradition, like Egypt, the individual and social virtues cannot be firmly grounded except in religious belief; since the tradition of Egypt is Islamic, it is Islam which must fulfil this role, but in other countries other religions would do just as well. In other words, Lutfi al-Sayyid holds that a religious society is morally superior to a non-religious (at least at a certain stage of development); he does not assert, as his teachers would have done, that an Islamic society is superior to a non-Islamic:

I am not one of those who insist that a religion or a specific ethical system should be taught for its own sake. But I say that general education must have *some* principle which should guide the student from beginning to end, and this is the principle of good and evil, with all its moral implications.

There is no doubt that theories of good and evil are numerous and disparate, but each nation should teach its sons its own beliefs in the matter. Since for us Egyptians the principle of good and evil is grounded in belief in the essence of religion, it follows that religion, seen from this ethical point of view, must be the basis of general education.[26]

Thus the first principle of 'Abduh's thought has been abandoned, and in its place new principles are established and new questions

[26] Lutfi al-Sayyid, *Safahat matwiyya*, i. 118.

asked. Lutfi al-Sayyid's question is not so much, in what conditions does Islamic society flourish and decay; it is rather, in what conditions does any society flourish or decay? The terms in which it is answered are those not of Islamic but of modern European thought about progress and the ideal society.

Lutfi al-Sayyid and his associates seem to have been influenced by two types of European thought. First, he was conversant with the type of thought expressed, in very different ways, by Comte and Renan, Mill and Spencer, and by Durkheim among his contemporaries. According to such thinkers, human society is tending, by the irreversible and irresistible natural law of progress, towards an ideal state, of which the marks will be the domination of reason, the extension of individual liberty, increasing differentiation and complexity, and the replacement of relations based on custom and status by those based on free contract and individual interest. But he was also influenced by the very different, far less hopeful thought of Gustave Le Bon, who had the incidental attraction for Arab thinkers that he praised the Arabs highly for their contribution to civilization, but from whom they learnt something else as well, the 'idea of national character: that each people possesses a mental constitution no less fixed than the physical, created by slow accumulation throughout its history, and which can only be modified slowly and within limits; that in this constitution there are two basic elements, the first that of reason and the second that of 'character', of all the faculties derived from will, perseverance, energy, the power of domination; that religious belief is the most important factor which acts on national character—'when a new religion is born a new civilization is born'—but even religion, once the first enthusiasm is over, is adapted to national character.[27]

The most important among the ideas which Lutfi al-Sayyid derived from his western masters is that of freedom. It is indeed the centre of all his thought, not only the criterion of political action but a necessity of life, 'the necessary food of our life',[28] the natural condition of man and his inalienable right. His conception of freedom, as he proudly acknowledges, is that of the liberals of the nineteenth century.[29] Freedom means, essentially, absence

---

[27] Cf. Le Bon.   [28] Lutfi al-Sayyid, *Ta'ammulat*, p. 55.
[29] Lutfi at-Sayyid, *al-Muntakhabat*, ii. 58 ff.

of unnecessary control by the State. The functions of the State are limited: it must maintain security and justice and defend the community from attack; for these purposes it can interfere with the rights of the individual, but any other interference is wrong. Some kinds are more dangerous than others: in particular, tampering with the freedom of the law courts, or with freedom to write, talk, publish, and associate with those of like opinions. So far it is the classical doctrine of the nineteenth century; but there is something else as well, derived by Lutfi perhaps from his study of Aristotle. At the heart of his image of society is a vision of what the really free man would be and what the good life is: the free man is he who, spontaneously and without external impediments, fulfils his function in society, and in so doing fulfils his human capabilities. In this sense, all men are potentially good, and some time in the future most men will be so.[30]

That is what men should be, but it is not what Egyptian men are. The general ideas of Lutfi al-Sayyid are not different from those of his generation, but they acquire meaning from his own vivid sense of their relevance to Egypt. When he writes, for example, of freedom of the judiciary, he points out that it does not exist in Egypt, because the government is absolute and controls the law courts as it controls all else, and because Egyptian judges have no sense of vocation, but use the bench as a stepping-stone in an official career of which the logical end is a ministry. Similarly he writes of intellectual freedom with Egypt in mind. In the late nineteenth century Egypt had had great freedom of speech and publication, partly because of the Capitulations, which gave foreign protection and privileges to most journals, and partly because of the influence of Lord Cromer. But after 1907 the situation changed: the successors of Cromer did not share his belief that a free press was a safety-valve of popular feeling; besides, they had a different kind of feeling to deal with, now that national consciousness was awakening again and expressing itself through organized political parties. In 1909 the press law of 1881, which had fallen into disuse, was revived in a modified form: it allowed the government to suppress newspapers, although only on certain conditions. Lutfi fought continuously against it, using with a new sense of urgency the classical arguments of Mill.[31]

[30] *al-Muntakhabat*, i. 106.　　　[31] Ibid. p. 296.

Egyptian society was not what it should be, but—what was more important—neither was Egyptian man. Scattered through these essays is a pointed, detailed, sometimes witty analysis of what Egyptians are like. We Egyptians, he says, are hypocritical in our desire to praise and flatter those who are strong, and that is because we do not believe in ourselves as independent human beings. We are easy-going, we say 'Never mind'—*ma'laysh*—to whatever happens; that is a sort of virtue, but one which is rooted in weakness of soul. We are servile and will accept insults and humiliation rather than lose a post or make a protest.[32] We do not trust each other, we speak evil of others and ascribe base motives to them: 'Everyone belittles the value of the other, without intending anything but simply because he does not trust him'.[33] We worship strength: here Lutfi al-Sayyid quotes the songs of joyous welcome sung by the people in the streets of Cairo to greet Bonaparte on his return from Syria.[34] In a word, we lack independence of spirit, the real freedom, and lacking that we are not in the fullest sense human. But if we examine all these weaknesses and others like them, we see that they all spring from one root: a wrong attitude towards authority. We expect too much from the government: we rely on it to do for us all we should do for ourselves, we have surrendered to it our rights and duties. But we do not trust it or love it; we fear and distrust it, try to avoid its attention, think of it as alien and hostile. Hence our sympathy for those who have fallen foul of the law, no matter what the cause:

It does not surprise any of us that most villagers will do all they can to protect anyone who has been accused of a crime against attempts to prove the accusation. The reason for this attitude is not just family feeling or a preference for wrongdoing over justice; it is rather an expression of the fact that the government and its agents are not working for the welfare of the nation, and so the people tacitly obstruct its decrees, even when it is clear that they are just.[35]

But if we go one step farther, and ask why we have this wrong attitude towards the government, the answer is that we have always had the wrong sort of government. Our government has always been despotic, and despotism has bred in us the vices of

---

[32] Ibid. pp. 37, 49 & 53.   [33] Ibid. p. 122.
[34] Ibid. p. 217.   [35] *Safahat*, p. 176.

servitude. We are easy-going and tolerant because we are impotent; we are slavish and hypocritical because the absolute ruler demands nothing less than complete submission.[36]

Despotism long continued destroys the individual human being as well as the community. It prevents man's moral nature developing in all its fullness, in short it makes man less than human. Thus political freedom is a necessary condition of any kind of freedom. Time and again Lutfi al-Sayyid makes the case against absolute government: it creates a wrong relationship between ruler and ruled, that of command and obedience, of 'lord and slave',[37] it breaks up the solidarity of the nation by destroying trust, it checks the activity of the administrative machine. It is contrary to human nature and contrary to science, for it is based on the illusion that some men—the strong, the rulers—are more than human. The true government is that which springs from free agreement in accordance with the innate sense of justice; it is this agreement which constitutes law, and law once formed is binding on government and individuals alike. Limited government based on law is therefore the 'natural' form of government, and every community has a right to it. Here Lutfi disagrees with 'Abduh, or perhaps he is applying 'Abduh's principle anew in a generation more self-confident than his master's. The right of a community to rule itself, he believes, has nothing to do with its level of civilization. It is only in wholly uncivilized communities that despotism is necessary. It is meaningless to ask whether a nation is ready to govern itself. Only freedom can generate the spirit of freedom; absolute government cannot be an education for self-government.[38]

That government should be based on free agreement was one of Lutfi al-Sayyid's convictions, but he believed no less that there were certain human associations so old and stable that they could be thought of as natural and possessing the same rights as individuals. The nation was such a natural association, subject to natural laws and above all the great law of freedom.[39] Because the individual must be free, the nation must be independent. For Lutfi as for earlier Egyptian thinkers, the nation was defined first of all not in terms of language or religion but of territory. He is thinking not of an Islamic or Arab nation, but of the Egyptian

[36] *al-Muntakhabat*, i. 50.   [37] *Safahat*, p. 25.
[38] Ibid. pp. 30 ff.   [39] Ibid. pp. 43–44.

nation, the dwellers in the land of Egypt. He like Tahtawi is
conscious of the continuity of Egypt's history; Egypt has two
pasts, Pharaonic and Arab, and it is important to study the
Pharaonic, not just to take pride in it but because Egyptians can
learn from it 'the laws of development and progress'.[40] Here we
catch an echo of Tahtawi's idea that ancient Egypt no less than
modern Egypt possessed the 'secret' of worldly progress; but
what is original in Lutfi's writing is his physical consciousness
of Egypt and its countryside. In spite of the poverty and squalor
he knows the beauty of village life: he evokes the sights and
sounds of the cotton fields, paints in bright colours the virtues
and happiness of the good peasant, and exhorts the younger
generation to respond to the beauty of nature—to 'add to the
cultivation of the intellect the training of the sentiments'.[41] In this
we can perhaps see the influence of Tolstoy: Lutfi has himself
recorded that, when he first read Tolstoy, the effect was so
profound that he thought for a time of leaving his career and
going back to his village.

Lutfi al-Sayyid's sense of the existence of something called
Egypt is so strong that there is no need to emphasize the other
bonds of unity which, in other nationalist philosophies, themselves create the nation. Most dwellers in Egypt have a common
ancestry, language, and religion, but Lutfi never tries to assert
that only they are real Egyptians. The bond which unites all
those who live in Egypt and are willing to link their fate with hers
is so strong that it more than counterbalances differences of
religion or language or origin. What makes an Egyptian is the
willingness to take Egypt as his first and only mother country.[42]
What he is criticizing here, by implication, is the double allegiance professed by many of those who live in Egypt. He is
thinking in particular of the Levantine and European middle
class, clinging to their foreign nationality or protection in order
to derive benefit from the Capitulations. Their interests, he
reminds them, are the same as those of other Egyptians. They,
like the Egyptians, want to prevent complete control falling into
British hands; the Egyptians, like them, profit from their
economic activities. Writing specifically for the Syrians, he
reminds them that they share a language with Egyptians, and

---

[40] *Ta'ammulat*, p. 16.   [41] Ibid. p. 39; cf. *al-Muntakhabat*, ii. 163.
[42] *Ta'ammulat*, pp. 63 & 66.

have lived there for many generations; it is natural for them to feel they belong to Egypt, let them therefore become Egyptian in sentiment.[43] But he is thinking even more of Egyptians who define their national allegiance in other than purely Egyptian terms: who think of themselves as being first of all Ottomans, or Arabs, or Turks, or Muslims. Islamic nationalism seems to him not to be true nationalism: 'The idea that the land of Islam is the home-country of every Muslim is an imperialist principle, the adoption of which could be useful to any imperialist nation eager to enlarge its territory and extend its influence'.[44] He does not even believe in the idea of pan-Islam as a political force; it is a bogy created by the British in order to arouse European feeling against the national movement in Egypt, and even did it exist it would be bound to fail, since States are based on common interest and not on common sentiment.[45]

Lutfi al-Sayyid was writing before Egyptian nationalism became Arab in colouring, and he spoke of the Arabs rarely, although with sympathy and respect and something of 'Abduh's belief that Islam and Islamic society were to be found in their pure form in the Arabian Peninsula. He did not think of Egyptians as forming part of the Arab nation; but he did not have to emphasize the point, as few Egyptians at the time thought so. The idea of Ottoman nationalism was more important, particularly after the Young Turk Revolution of 1908, which ended the rule of Abdülhamid and restored the constitution. There were some in Egypt who argued that, now the sultan's autocratic rule was ended and a new age of democratic equality seemed to have begun, there was no need for Egypt to hold herself aloof from the other Ottoman territories; they even suggested she should elect members of the Ottoman parliament. This argument seemed to Lutfi to rest on a false premise: that the autonomy won by Muhammad 'Ali and Isma'il had been won for the ruling family alone, and Egypt was simply a province of the empire assigned to a family for a time as a fief. In fact, he declared, Muhammad 'Ali was working not for himself but for Egypt, and the treaty of London in 1841, which recognized his hereditary rule over Egypt, was also a virtual recognition of Egypt's internal autonomy and sovereignty.[46]

---

[43] *al-Muntakhabat*, i. 170 ff. [44] *Ta'ammulat*, p. 68.
[45] *Safahat*, p. 99. [46] Ibid. p. 37.

It is therefore of the Egyptian nation he is thinking when he maintains the natural right of peoples to rule themselves, and he supports the claim with a theory of Egyptian history. The most important fact about Egyptian history, that which explains the moral condition of her people, is that she has always been ruled by force. She never had 'the government based on the principles of political science' which ancient Greece enjoyed, her government was often foreign in race or religion, always foreign in customs, and directed primarily to the interest of the ruler, only incidentally to that of the ruled. In this way the natural character was formed: Egyptians had to pretend to a loyalty they did not possess, and lost their inner freedom, their courage, their moral link with the government. Hence came all the vices of servitude which Lutfi al-Sayyid has described at length. In the middle of the nineteenth century the situation had at last begun to change: there were the beginnings of a real awakening, but a premature military revolution gave the British the opportunity to occupy the land. The foreign occupation restored the moral situation to what it had been before; the people thought of their British rulers just as they had thought of other foreign rulers, with a cynical distrust that no material benefits could disarm.[47]

Lutfi al-Sayyid criticized British rule not because it was foreign but because it was absolute. The benefits it had brought to Egypt were undoubted; he always acknowledged them fully. But to reform the finances and improve economic conditions was not to solve the *real* political problem, which was the absence of a moral relationship between rulers and ruled.[48] Cromer's rule was autocratic and rested not on free choice but, in the last resort, on British arms. When he was succeeded by Sir Eldon Gorst in 1908 the situation grew worse. Gorst was sent by the Liberal government to introduce a new and more liberal policy; but this turned out to be one of giving more freedom of action to the khedive and so breaking his connexion with the nationalists and winning him to the side of the British. Thus the country was subjected to two autocracies, and the unity between ruler and people, which had existed so long as the ruler was on bad terms with Cromer, disappeared.[49]

Autocracy must be replaced by something else, but it was not possible, so Lutfi al-Sayyid thought, to hope for immediate

[47] *Safahat*, pp. 175 ff.   [48] Ibid. pp. 69 ff.   [49] Ibid. pp. 29 ff.

independence. It was necessary to face facts: Britain was strong, she had essential interests in Egypt, she had declared her intention of staying in Egypt until Egypt herself was strong enough to defend those interests. She could not be turned out by force. The false romantic idea of the 'struggle for independence', if accepted, would only postpone the coming of what it sought. That had been the fatal mistake of 'Urabi Pasha; his intentions were not bad, and he was in no sense a traitor, but he had miscalculated the strength of Egypt and had been deceived by 'English provocateurs' (the reference is clearly to Blunt).[50] The only sane policy was to take England at her word. There was indeed some reason to distrust her intentions, since she had produced one excuse after another for prolonging her stay and so gave the impression she would stay for ever.[51] But it was in Egypt's interest to co-operate in any measures she took to build up the country's strength.[52] This policy of course involved both parties; it would not be possible unless the British too were willing to draw Egyptians into the process of government. What was immediately possible was to limit the absolute power of the khedive and move by stages towards constitutional government. When the People's Party was established, it was Lutfi who expounded its programme, and the reforms he suggested were modest and cautious: to extend the power of existing representative bodies (the Provincial Councils and Legislative Council), to change the method of election to them, to establish a revising body for laws.[53] But this was only a first step: full democratic government must be the aim, it could be achieved while the British were still there, and it was in Britain's real interest to help it on.

As each stage of self-government was reached, it could be used to strengthen the national life of Egypt. It is a sign of the gap which separates his age from ours that economic strength plays a small part in his idea of national strength. In principle he recognizes its importance: Egypt must redeem the foreign debt, which was the reason why she lost her independence, and will be a danger so long as it exists; she must build up her industries, without which she cannot be really free.[54] (When

---

[50] *al-Muntakhabat*, i. 252 & 313 ff.   [51] *Safahat*, pp. 137 ff.
[52] *Ta'ammulat*, pp. 48–49.   [53] *Safahat*, p. 198.
[54] *al-Muntakhabat*, i. 181 & 279.

industry did begin to appear, in the 1920's and 1930's, it was the circle of Lutfi al-Sayyid who were responsible for it. Banque Misr and the companies which it sponsored were founded by a school-fellow and collaborator of his, Tal'at Harb, not for profit alone but as a step in the direction of national independence.) But industry is not, in his opinion, the basis of national strength. All his emphasis is on a strong national consciousness: Egyptians must be more aware of their responsibility to the nation, and every step which makes them more aware is good—the establishment of a Legislative Assembly (by Kitchener in 1913), even if its power is limited, the forming of political parties even if they cannot yet share in the process of government. To this fragile, still immature consciousness he saw two opposing dangers: premature ideals of 'socialism' or 'internationalism' on the one hand, despair and lack of self-respect on the other.[55]

It was a commonplace in the school of 'Abduh that the only effective means to national maturity and real independence was education. Towards the end of the century this idea received powerful support from a book now forgotten but which found great favour in its days: E. Demolins' *A quoi tient la supériorité des Anglo-Saxons?* In this book Demolins explains why the Anglo-Saxon peoples were conquering the world and becoming the strongest and most prosperous of all. The reason he suggested was that they had developed individual initiative to an unheard-of degree. For this in its turn there were two reasons: the main object of their education was to train men to live in the modern world, while French education aimed at fitting them only for life in an unchanging society based on the family and the State; and while the French national spirit was militarist, demanding the sacrifice of the individual to the glory and power of the nation, Anglo-Saxon nationalism was 'personal', based on individual freedom and aiming at individual welfare. Demolins' book had much influence on Turkish and Arabic thought: it moulded the ideas of the Ottoman liberal Prince Sabaheddin, and was translated into Arabic by Ahmad Fathi Zaghlul, brother of Sa'd, with an introduction analysing, in vigorous terms not unlike Lutfi's own, the weakness of Egyptian society—lack of science, of patriotic feeling, of stable friendship, of active benevolence and self-reliance.[56]

[55] Ibid. ii. 103.   [56] A. F. Zaghlul, introd., pp. 23–30.

In much the same vein Lutfi al-Sayyid criticized the system of education now existing. The old Quranic schools had corresponded to a social reality in the eighteenth century, but in the modern world they were ineffective in every way; the mission schools by their nature could not give Muslim children a proper moral education; in the government schools the teachers had nothing of their own to give. Each of the three types was bad, and the coexistence of the three was worse still, because it disunited the nation. A proper system of schools would aim at creating a nation morally and mentally united around the modern sciences and the principles implied in them. But such a system could not be created by the government. Any government would use the schools in pursuit of its own interests; schools must be free to serve science alone, and so must be created either by private persons or by popular bodies.[57]

Even more important than the education given in the schools was that given in the family. 'The welfare of the family is the welfare of the nation', and the problem of the Egyptian family was at the heart of the problem of Egypt. In the upper and middle classes the main problem was that of the seclusion of women—in other words, their inequality to men. Among the peasants, this was not so: women were the equals of men, peasant marriages were based on real affection, but men and women alike were ignorant of many things necessary for the good life. Among the educated young men there was a special problem, that of finding wives of equal education in the circle in which they would normally have to marry. Two things then were necessary: the emancipation of women and their education. For Lutfi al-Sayyid and his generation, feminism was an essential part of true nationalism, and it was no coincidence that when, a decade later, Egyptian women began to throw off the veil and claim the right to take part in the common life of society, it was as a by-product of the struggle for independence in the early days of the Wafd.

The nation is the centre of Lutfi's thought, and that in two different senses: the national unit is the object of which he writes, and the interest of the nation is the touchstone of political morality and the principle of law, albeit a national interest conceived in liberal terms, as the sum of individual interests. The Islamic *umma* is almost beyond the horizon of his thought, the

[57] *al-Muntakhabat*, i. 120 & ii. 75 ff.

theory of the Islamic State he does not condemn but ignores, by implication denying its relevance to the problems of the modern world. It was left to another thinker of the same milieu although a rather younger generation to make explicit what he implies, and to assert not only that Egypt should adopt political principles other than those of Islam, but that there are no such things as Islamic political principles. In 1925 'Ali 'Abd al-Raziq (1888–1966), brother of Mustafa, published a work on Islam and the bases of political authority. Like his brother, he had studied at the Azhar and had then come to Europe, but to Oxford and not Paris. There are occasional references in his book to English political thinkers such as Hobbes and Locke,[58] but the direct influence of English thought is not great, and once more we are in the climate of thought created by 'Abduh. But it is twenty years since 'Abduh died, and new problems have arisen to which his methods must be applied. The immediate problem with which 'Abd al-Raziq is concerned is that of the caliphate. In 1922, after the revolution of Mustafa Kemal, the Turkish National Assembly had abolished the sultanate and set up a shadow-caliphate with spiritual powers only; in 1924 they abolished that as well. There was a lively discussion throughout the Muslim world about whether the Turkish action was legitimate and whether the caliphate could or should be revived. In 1922, when the sultanate was abolished, the Turkish Grand National Assembly issued a semi-official statement justifying their act: drawn up by a group of religious lawyers, it was published in Arabic as well as Turkish, under the title of *al-Khilafa wa sultat al-umma* (The Caliphate and the Sovereignty of the Nation). There is such a thing, the statement declares, as a legitimate caliphate, but it can only exist on certain conditions: the caliph must possess certain qualifications, and he must be chosen and invested by the people, for the Islamic people as a whole possesses sovereignty. These conditions were only fulfilled for the first four caliphs, and all others have therefore been fictitious. That does not mean however that there is no legitimate authority in the Islamic community: when there is no caliph, the community itself can choose some other form of government, and make what arrangements it wishes to ensure that it be ruled justly and legally. The form of government it chooses depends on

[58] A. 'Abd al-Raziq, *al-Islam*, p. 11 (Fr. trs. pt. i, p. 367).

G

the needs of the age, and in the modern age a National Assembly having a sacred duty to ensure the welfare of the country is better than a sultan whose only care is to preserve his throne.[59] The logic of this statement points not to the compromise of 1922 but to the decisive step of 1924; and after the caliphate had been finally abolished, it was Mustafa Kemal who with typical frankness explained why it was done. The caliphate had ruined the Turkish people: they had spent themselves in vain for an ideal which was not in their national interest, and was impossible in itself. For the caliphate was essentially political: the very attempt to make it purely spiritual had proved this, since the caliph had become the rallying point of discontented elements. Either the caliph was a head of State or he was nothing; and he could not be a head of State, for there could not be a united Muslim State today.[60]

Orthodox Muslims received such views with horror; but when they themselves thought the matter out they reached a conclusion not very different. In May 1926 a 'Congress of the Caliphate' was called together at Cairo by a group of Egyptian *'ulama'* presided over by the Rector of the Azhar, 'in view of the privileged position which this country enjoys among the Muslim peoples'.[61] The congress reaffirmed the traditional view of the caliphate: it was legitimate, indeed it was necessary, since many legal obligations depended on it. But to be real it must have both spiritual and temporal power. When such power did not exist the caliphate could not really exist, and this was the situation at the present time. All that could be done was to hold successive meetings to discuss the matter, until the time should become propitious: to this one delegate added the hope that, when this time should come, a caliph might be elected by a 'Muslim representative body'.[62]

'Abd al-Raziq's book was a contribution to this debate. It raised in a vivid way the most fundamental question involved: is the caliphate really necessary? But behind this question there was another, more general and even more fundamental: is there such a thing as an Islamic system of government?

[59] Fr. trs. in *R. des ét. islam.*, vii & viii (1933 & 1934).
[60] Kemal Ataturk, *Nutuk*, ii. 198 ff., 302–3 (Fr. trs. pp. 552 ff., 641–2).
[61] Sékaly, 'Les deux Congrès musulmans de 1926', *R. du monde musulman*, lxiv (1926), 3–219.
[62] Ibid. p. 106.

Two theories, the author claims, have been advanced in regard to the basis of the caliph's authority. The first and more generally accepted is that it is derived from the authority of God, the second that it comes from the choice of the *umma*. Both rest on a common assumption: that to accept the authority of the caliph is an obligation (whether derived from rational principles, or from the statements of the law). In support of this assumption the consensus of the Companions and those who followed them is adduced, and it is also argued that the existence of a caliph is indispensable for the due maintenance of worship and the welfare of the community. But against such arguments, 'Abd al-Raziq points out, even stronger ones can be brought. The Quran is silent on the matter, except for vague general statements enjoining respect for those in authority; the *hadith* also is silent, except for statements equally vague about obedience to the imam, without any clear definition of the imam's function or statement of his necessity. Even if the *hadith* is really referring to the caliph when it talks of 'the imam', this does not imply that there must always be a caliph, any more than the Biblical phrase about 'rendering unto Caesar' implies that there should always be a Caesar. There is no real *ijma'* in the matter. That there was no opposition to the caliph's claim to authority does not create a tacit *ijma'*; for the caliph's power was always based on armed force, even when it was invisible and did not have to be used, and free expression of opinion was not possible. Indeed all free thought about politics was impossible, and it is significant that there has been no real study of politics by Muslim thinkers.[63] There was no more opportunity for a free *ijma'* to come into existence than there was in Iraq when Faysal was elected king by a plebiscite taken under the supervision of the British administration. Nor is the existence of the caliph a necessary condition of worship and public welfare. Some sort of political authority is indeed necessary, but it need not be of a specific kind. When the caliphate virtually ceased to exist in Mamluke Egypt, there is no sign that it made any difference to worship or welfare in the Muslim countries. On the contrary, the authority of the caliphate has been harmful to Islam: 'a plague for Islam and the Muslims, a source of evils and corruption'.[64]

[63] *al-Islam*, pp. 18 & 24 (Fr. trs. pt. i, pp. 374, 379).
[64] *al-Islam*, pp. 18, 24, 32 & 36 (Fr. trs. pt. i, pp. 374, 379, 386, 389).

Thus the caliphate is not a necessary part of the religion of Muslims; how then did it come into existence, and how did Muslims come to regard it as an obligation? The first question 'Abd al-Raziq approaches by an inquiry into the political situation in the time of the Prophet. He can find no clear evidence that there was any kind of organized Islamic government during the Prophet's lifetime. The whole subject is obscure, and we must try to discover what was the attitude of the Prophet towards the establishment of a State. Three answers to this question have been given. It has been said that Muhammad's role as Prophet must be distinguished from his acts as political leader and founder of a temporal kingdom; this is a view which cannot be refuted, and finds indeed some support in law and *hadith*, but it is inherently improbable that the Prophet should also have had quite a different function. Others, like Ibn Khaldun, have maintained that the organization of a State formed an essential part of Muhammad's work as Prophet. This, however, is incompatible with the spirit of the prophetic mission. Others again assert that the Prophet created only a very simple form of government suitable to a simple state of things, not a government such as we know.[65] But to say this is to evade the issue; the Prophet's government, if it existed, does not seem to have had the necessary attributes of even the simplest government—it had no budget and no regular administration.

'Abd al-Raziq then gives his own version, and this forms the core of the book. It is, quite simply, that Muhammad had no function except the essential prophetic function of preaching the truth; he was not sent to exercise political authority, and he did not do so.

The prophetic mission is purely spiritual:

The prophet can have, in the political direction of the nation, a role similar to that of the ruler, but he has a role special to himself and which he shares with no one. It is his function also to touch the souls which inhabit the bodies of men, and to rend the veil in order to perceive the hearts within their breasts. He has the right, or rather the duty, to open the hearts of his followers so as to touch the sources of love and hatred, of good and evil, the course of their inmost thoughts, the hiding places of temptation, the springs of purpose and the foundations of their moral character. . . . Prophecy, which is all this and still

[65] *al-Islam*, pp. 44 & 62 (Fr. trs. pt. ii, pp. 168, 183).

more, implies that the prophet has the right to unite himself with men's souls by a communion of care and protection, and also to dispose of their hearts freely and without obstacle.[66]

As a prophet Muhammad possessed the qualities demanded by his mission, and also the authority. This authority was wider than that of a political leader and different in nature. It was a spiritual authority having its source in the free, sincere, and entire submission of the heart, not based, like political power, on the enforced submission of the body. Its purpose was not to regulate the interests of life in the world, but to lead men towards God. By virtue of his authority Muhammad created a community, but not of the type we normally call a 'State'; it was a community which had no essential relationship with one government rather than another or one nation rather than another. Forms of government indeed are of no concern to the divine will; God has left the field of civil government and worldly interest for the exercise of human reason. It is not even necessary that the *umma* should be politically united; this is virtually impossible, and even if possible would it be good? God has willed that there should be a natural differentiation between tribes and peoples—there should be competition, 'in order that civilization should be perfected'.[67]

The unity of the *umma* then is not that of a State. Islam recognizes no superiority, inside the *umma*, of one nation, language, country or age over another, except for the superiority conferred by virtue.[68] The primitive community was only Arab by accident: it had to start with some specific person and in one place, and God in His wisdom chose an Arab to preach first of all to Arabs. The Muslim community was therefore materially Arab in its early phase, but it was potentially universal from the start. It was not an Arab State; the various tribes and 'nations' of Arabia were a unity around the person of the Prophet, but they retained their own forms of government. The Prophet did not interfere in their political affairs, and his commandments had no relevance to their methods of government. The 'union of hearts' brought about by Islam did not constitute a single State. The proof of it is that the Prophet made no

[66] Ibid. p. 67 (Fr. trs. pt. ii, pp. 187–8).
[67] Ibid. p. 78 (Fr. trs. pt. ii, p. 198).
[68] Ibid. p. 81 (Fr. trs. pt. ii, p. 201).

provision for the permanent government of the community after his death; either therefore he died with an essential part of his mission incomplete, which was impossible if he was really sent by God, or else it was no part of his mission to found a State.

It is the second alternative which 'Abd al-Raziq accepts. The Prophet's mission was only prophetic: when he died it came to an end, and with it there came to an end the specific authority he had been given. If anyone had predominance in the *umma* after his death, it was of quite another kind, civil or political. The preaching of Islam had created an Islamic religious community, but it had also, as a by-product, created an Arab nation and set it on the path of progress; and after the Prophet died the Arabs founded a State within the spiritual community he had created. The first caliph, Abu Bakr, was invested with what was essentially a political and royal power, based on force. His State was 'an Arab State built on the basis of a religious preaching'.[69] No doubt it helped to spread Islam, but essentially it was concerned with Arab interests. This however was not clear to all Muslims at the time; since Abu Bakr had religious virtues and modelled his personal behaviour on that of the Prophet, many Muslims thought he had a religious function. The very title he assumed, 'Successor of the Prophet of God' (*khalifat rasul Allah*), although it really meant he had succeeded as leader of the Arabs, could not fail to have religious undertones and arouse religious loyalty. Those who rejected the political leadership of Abu Bakr were accused of having abandoned Islam itself. From this time a false idea of the caliphate took root, and it was of course encouraged by absolute rulers in their own interests: 'This is the crime of the kings and of their tyranny over the Muslims. . . . In reality, however, Islam is innocent of this institution of the caliphate, as Muslims commonly understand it.'[70] Religion has nothing to do with one form of government rather than another, and there is nothing in Islam which forbids Muslims to destroy their old political system and build a new one on the basis of the newest conceptions of the human spirit and the experience of nations.

'Abd al-Raziq's book aroused a violent storm, and the consequences for him were serious. It was refuted and denounced

[69] *al-Islam*, pp. 90 & 92 (Fr. trs. pt. ii, pp. 209, 211).
[70] Ibid. pp. 102–3 (Fr. trs. pt. ii, p. 221).

by Muslim thinkers of another complexion, and formally condemned by a council of the leading 'ulama' of the Azhar. In their
judgment they refuted, by quotations from the Quran and hadith,
seven propositions contained, or so they claimed, in 'Abd
al-Raziq's work; and they pronounced the author unfit to hold
any public function.[71] He was in fact to live for the rest of his life
privately, author of one or two more writings to which no exception
could be taken, and playing no such role as his brother in public
life.

It is not difficult to understand why his book met with such
opposition. It propounded a new historical theory about matters
of which the accepted historical view had something of the nature
of religious doctrine; and this theory was drawn more from non-
Muslim writers on Islam, who might be accused of trying to
weaken its hold on its adherents, than from the fundamental
Islamic sources, the sciences of Quranic interpretation and
hadith. One critic of the book, Rashid Rida, declared it was the
latest attempt of the enemies of Islam to weaken and divide it
from within, and another, Muhammad Bakhit, maintained that
what non-Muslims said of Islam should never be accepted, and
above all what they said about the caliphate, 'the fearful ghost
which, if the bravest man in Europe saw it even in his sleep,
would cause him to rise in fear and panic'.[72] 'Abd al-Raziq, he
asserted, had accepted the historical thesis of Sir Thomas
Arnold in preference to the whole consensus of Islamic thought;
and he set himself, in great detail and at enormous length, to
refute the author's interpretation of Muslim history and cast
doubt on his knowledge and understanding of the sources. He
produced much evidence to refute the idea that there was no
organized government in the Prophet's time, and that the Prophet
never taught his people about political organization,[73] and to
prove that there was as nearly a complete ijma' on the necessity of some sort of imamate as there was on any question of
doctrine.[74]

There was a still graver charge against the book, made by the
'ulama' in their judgment and elaborated by Shaykh Bakhit. By

[71] Text in Hukm hay'at kibar al-'ulama' (Fr. trs. in R. du monde musulman, ix
(1935), 75–86).
[72] Bakhit, p. 43.
[73] Ibid. pp. 113 ff., 298 ff.
[74] Ibid. p. 33.

implication, 'Abd al-Raziq's thesis attacked the whole system of Islamic doctrine in one of its two bases: the theory of prophecy. Muslim theologians had always taught that, while some prophets were sent into the world to reveal a Book only, that is to say, to reveal a truth about God and the world, others were sent also to reveal a law, a system of morality derived from the Book, and to execute it; and that, while Jesus was a prophet of the first type, Muhammad was one of the second.[75] To execute the law was an essential part of his mission;[76] but this implies that he had political power, and that from the start the Islamic community was a political community. Moreover, since the Book and the law were given not for one generation only but for all time, there must always be someone who exercises political power in the *umma*:

> The Islamic religion is based on the pursuit of domination and power and strength and might, and the refusal of any law which is contrary to its *shari'a* and its divine law, and the rejection of any authority the wielder of which is not charged with the execution of its edicts.[77]

If the Prophet was not a political leader, and if the *umma* was not a political *umma*, then either there was no Prophet and no *umma*, or else the conception of them—that is to say, the very essence of Islam—would have to be changed. Worse still, the instrument by which responsible change and development could take place in Islam had been destroyed. The careful method of reasoning by analogy, with Quran and *hadith* as its premisses, the consensus which was both the product and the guardian of the process: all this had been rejected by 'Abd al-Raziq, and in its place he had put the reason, fantasy and passion of the individual mind:

> He has relied . . . on intellectual sophistry, suppositions and poetical proofs, although these matters which he denies, and of which he denies the proofs, are matters of jurisprudence and law, into which one cannot plunge with the intellect alone, and in regard to which there is no alternative but to rely on the Quran, the Sunna, the *ijma'*, or reasoning by analogy.[78]

This would always be dangerous, but it was the more so in an

---

[75] Bakhit, p. 293.   [76] Ibid. p. 238.
[77] Ibid. p. 294.   [78] Ibid. p. 3.

age like the present, when the natural reason of Muslims drew its light not from Islamic but from European, and therefore ultimately Christian, sources. There was a fundamental difference between the social teaching of Islam and Christianity, and it was a difference on this very point at issue, political authority and the nature of the religious community. By implication, 'Abd al-Raziq was denying the difference, and importing into the *umma* a distinction between prophecy and political rule, between the kingdom of God and the kingdom of the world, which was appropriate to Christianity but not to Islam.[79]

The danger, in Bakhit's view, was not theoretical only. In the last analysis, what 'Abd al-Raziq was saying was that there was no such thing as the *Shari'a*. But if there was no *Shari'a*, no law standing above the government, then there was no political society in the true sense, and the *umma* would dissolve into anarchy. Men need a regulator and governor who will keep them within their due limits, prevent oppression and do justice, and rule in the light of a law which all accept; they cannot be left free to manage their worldly affairs by their own reason and knowledge, their interests and desires, for that would simply mean the domination of the strong over the weak and the end of individual security.[80]

This sounds like a voice from the great tradition of Muslim thought. But if we go on to inquire what is the political law which, in Bakhit's view, can be deduced from the principles of Islam, we hear another note. Taking up 'Abd al-Raziq's statement that orthodox thought has always derived the caliph's authority either directly from God or from the *umma*, Bakhit states categorically that the correct view is the second:

> The source of the caliph's power is the *umma*, and he derives authority from it. . . . The Islamic government headed by the caliph and universal Imam is a democratic, free, consultative government, of which the constitution is God's Book and the Sunna of God's Prophet.[81]

In saying this, Bakhit is not simply maintaining that the political institutions of Islam have all the advantages of modern political institutions; he is implying that essentially they are the same. The identification of Islamic with European concepts, put

[79] Ibid. p. 50.   [80] Ibid. p. 352.   [81] Ibid. p. 30.

forward by the earlier writers, is now accepted without question; and Bakhit seems unaware that he has opened the door to that very invasion of Islam by the ideas of western rationalism for which he reproaches his opponent.

EGYPTIAN NATIONALISM

THE writers of the school of 'Abduh saw themselves as a middle group, steering a careful course between extremes: on one side the traditionalists, on the other the secularists. Their object was to accept and encourage the institutions and ideas of the modern age but link them to the principles of Islam, in which they saw the only valid basis of social thought, the 'political law accepted by all' of which Bakhit spoke. In the process they were led ever nearer to the second of the two extremes, simply because it was this and not the first which presented the real danger. Rigid conservatism would in due course show its incapacity to understand and therefore to control the modern world, and in the end might just wither away. But the ideas of the modern world, precisely because they were irresistible, had the power both to destroy and to remake Islamic society—to destroy it if left unchecked, to remake it if harnessed to the eternal purposes of Islam—; and in the attempt to harness them, more and more concessions were made to them.

This was seen clearly in the attitude of the modernists towards the idea of nationalism, the most potent form in which the modern idea of secular society expressed itself. We shall speak in a later chapter of the way in which the Syrian disciples of 'Abduh were led almost imperceptibly from an Islamic to an Arab political idea: that is a path singularly easy to follow, because of the special position of the Arabs in Islam, the consecration of an Arab nationalist principle in the early history of Islam. But the relationship between Islam and Egyptian nationalism was not so simple: the idea of an Egyptian nation, entitled to a separate political existence, involved not only the denial of a single Islamic political community, but also the assertion that there could be a virtuous community based on something other than a common religion and a revealed law. That the relationship was close and positive was due to the position of Egypt after

1882: it was the British occupation which fused Islamic modernism with Egyptian nationalism and finally produced, as we shall see, a nationalism which was created and led by a close associate of 'Abduh, but which had in the process abandoned his first principle.

In the early phases there was indeed no conflict. The *'ulama'* who led the revolt of Cairo against Bonaparte in 1798, and gave support to Muhammad 'Ali in 1805, were acting as leaders of local opinion; but it was not an explicit concept of the nation which moved them. In the mind of Tahtawi, a generation later, the idea of the Islamic community and that of the Egyptian nation existed side by side without his being aware of a potential contradiction. He asserts without argument the existence of two loyalties, one to those who share the same religion and the other to one's fellow countrymen, and he takes it for granted that, in an Egyptian State as in the ideal Islamic State of the jurists, the law will still be supreme. By the time he died, the concept of 'la Patrie' had conquered without a struggle. *Al-Watan* was the name of one of the first important unofficial newspapers of Egypt, founded in 1877; and when, in 1881, a prominent teacher and grammarian of the Azhar, Husayn al-Marsafi, wrote a short book to explain some of the 'words current on the tongues of men', he included both *watan* and *umma* among them. Called *Risalat al-kalim al-thaman* (Essay on Eight Words), the book is not all it claims to be. It does not in fact give a clear explanation of the terms chosen, but at least it bears witness to the way in which they had spread and changed their meaning. *Umma* for Marsafi has a sense far wider than the religious: it may be used of any group of people bound together by some tie, whether of language, place, or religion; and the *umma* created by language best deserves the name, because unity of language best fulfils the purpose of society. Whatever its basis, everyone has an active role in the community; the government should consult the opinion of all, and rulers should not treat the common folk as if they were beasts.[1]

The development of Egypt in the 1870's, and the events which ended with the British occupation of 1882, gave such ideas a new force over men's minds, and a new importance in political life. Around 1879 a number of officers formed themselves into

[1] Marsafi, pp. 2 & 4.

a semi-secret party, the 'National Party' (*al-hizb al-watani*),[2] which attracted to itself a number of civilians, and it was this group, led by Ahmad 'Urabi Pasha, which became the core of the movement and held power in the months leading up to the occupation. As the threat of occupation came nearer, those who wished to prevent it had no choice but to rally around 'Urabi; but this was only a coalition brought about by pressure from outside, and it concealed a profound difference between those whose purpose was to generate national 'feeling' and those who thought it more important to create a healthy national life based on valid principles. We have seen this difference appearing in 'Abduh's strictures on 'Urabi for his ignorance of what was really meant by the words he used; we can see it too if we compare 'Abduh's early articles with others written at the time. It was in this period that the newspaper of opinion began to play an important part in Egyptian political life, and there appeared one of the key figures of the modern era, the political journalist concerned not so much to communicate ideas as to arouse strong feelings by skilful use of language.

One such was an Egyptian Jew, James Sanu';[3] another, who played an important part for a short time in the years leading up to the occupation of 1882, was a Syrian Christian, one of a line who were, as we shall see, to add an essential ingredient to modern Arabic thought. Adib Ishaq (1856–85), educated by French Lazarists in Damascus and Jesuits in Beirut, went to Egypt in his early youth, and edited the newspaper *Misr*, first in Alexandria and then under a different title in Paris. He played no great part in the events of 1882, and was indeed less important as a direct political influence than as a channel through which certain ideas acquired from his French education passed to the Egyptian reading public. Perhaps because he was Syrian Christian by origin, and also because of his strong anti-clerical feelings, the idea of the political community based on some solidarity other than that of religion was prominent in his thought. He put forward several such ideas in fact: of the 'eastern' community, held together by European contempt and opposition to European power; of the 'Arab' community, based on unity of feeling; the

---

[2] For the early history of political parties in Egypt cf. Landau.
[3] Cf. Gendzier, 'James Sanua and Egyptian Nationalism', *Middle East J.*, xv (1961), 16–28.

'Ottoman' community, unified by a common law and authority, and the will to live together; the *watan*, the territorial unit to which belong all who live within its frontiers and have a loving care for it.

There is a strain of rhetoric in Ishaq's writing, an appeal for unity and strength, but it is balanced by a concern for political virtue. The community is not a law unto itself; echoing La Bruyère, he insists that there is no *watan* without freedom, and no freedom without virtue.[4] The Near East urgently needs a political education, that is to say, an education in political morality, since it is just entering the 'political' phase of social development in which men become responsible for their own affairs. In another journalist of the same era the balance is not so evenly kept. 'Abd Allah al-Nadim (1844–96) became, in the time of crisis, the spokesman of 'Urabi and his group, and a power in his own right through his talent as a mass orator. After the defeat of 'Urabi's movement he went into hiding and did not emerge until 1891, when he was caught and banished. When 'Abbas Hilmi succeeded Tawfiq as khedive, he allowed Nadim to return; but, resuming his career as a popular journalist, Nadim soon incurred the new khedive's hostility and was banished once more, to end his life in Constantinople as a pensioner of the sultan. In his articles can be seen the first full expression of the feelings which had by now gathered around the concept of the nation and formed the state of mind called 'nationalism'. He emphasized above all the importance of national unity: he wrote one of the earliest plays in Arabic, called *al-Watan*, and in it *al-Watan* herself appears as a symbolic character preaching the importance of co-operation.[5] This unity included Copts as well as Muslims, but excluded—as it had not for Tahtawi—some of those who lived in the land of Egypt: the foreigners, in particular the Syrians, whom he attacked with a particular violence as foreigners (*dukhala'*), exorbitant money-lenders, and tools of the foreign conqueror.[6] He laid emphasis also on the importance of national education, teaching men to preserve that national culture which was their common good. The young Egyptians who went to Paris came back too often, he said, as strangers cut off from their own nation.[7] He attacked equally the foreign

[4] Ishaq, p. 460. [5] Nadim, ii. 33.
[6] Ibid. p. 82. [7] Ibid. i. 82, 92.

missionaries whose education was dangerous to the language and culture, no less than the inherited religious beliefs, of their pupils. In his writings indeed there is a streak of that 'xenophobia' which may go with strong national feelings. There is something too of the puritanism which often accompanies them as well; in an article criticizing Isma'il, for example, he reproaches him for having brought in Europeans who opened theatres, dance-halls, and other places of corruption.[8] He can in fact be regarded as the first of the popular Egyptian nationalists; but although the element of defensive pride and suspicion is strong in him, he does not believe the Egyptian nation is sufficient for itself and can generate its revival out of its own resources. Europe is the political enemy, but she is still the teacher. 'Why have they progressed while we have fallen behind?' is the title of one of his long articles.[9] Two false explanations he refutes: Egypt is not backward because of climate or religion. She is backward because she does not possess the sources of European strength yet, although she could possess them all: unity of language and religion, the ultimate unity of all Europe in face of the outside world, the economic enterprise of Europeans, their universal education, constitutional government, and freedom of expression.

Nadim was an orator and writer of the false dawn; his nine years' seclusion and silence were a symbol of what happened to the national consciousness of Egypt after the British occupation. For twenty-three years (1884–1907) Egypt was ruled in effect by the British Agent and Consul-General, Sir Evelyn Baring, later Lord Cromer. Cromer's rule gave Egypt financial stability, a better and more extensive system of canals, a better administration of justice; but it also meant the restoration of the authority of the khedive, only restrained by British control, of the financial power of the foreign bondholders, and of the economic and legal privileges of the foreign communities. As Lutfi al-Sayyid said, the fragile self-confidence of the nation, or at least of its small educated class, was shattered. Those who realized, after Tall al-Kabir, the disunity of the nation, the incompetence of its leader, and the absolute helplessness of Egypt in face of a European Power, either retired into silence or drew, like 'Abduh himself, the moral that since Egypt could not drive out the British she must try to profit from their presence. When the

[8] Hamza, ii. 161.   [9] Nadim, ii. 109.

nationalist sentiment begins to find new expression, a half-generation later, its leaders are younger men and its mood more intransigent. This was not only because of the ten years' occupation and the difference between a struggle to prevent it and one to end it, but also because of a new challenge to the national idea. The men of the 1870's were arguing against Islamic conservatism and popular apathy; those of the 1890's had to pit themselves also against a thesis coming from outside. It was the thesis of the British rulers of Egypt, and the foreign communities which controlled her economic life, that Egypt did not form a nation and could not hope for an independent national existence. Although it may be thought of as an expression of the interests of ruling Powers and foreign merchants, it had a certain influence on the minds of educated Egyptians, stated as it was with force by Cromer in his annual reports and later in his *Modern Egypt*. Cromer was read in Egypt, and the desire to refute such views as his inspired both Lutfi al-Sayyid and the new nationalists:

The only real Egyptian autonomy [he maintained], . . . which I am able to conceive as either practicable or capable of realisation without serious injury to all the various interests involved, is one which will enable all the dwellers in cosmopolitan Egypt, be they Moslem or Christian, European, Asiatic or African, to be fused into one self-governing body. That it may take years—possibly generations—to achieve this object is more than probable, but unless it can be achieved, any idea of autonomy, in the true sense of the term, will, in my opinion, have to be abandoned. . . . The ideal of the Moslem patriot is, in my opinion, incapable of realization. The ideal which I substitute in its place is extremely difficult of attainment, but if the Egyptians of the rising generation will have the wisdom and foresight to work cordially and patiently, in co-operation with European sympathizers, to attain it, it may possibly in time be found capable of realisation.

In the meantime, no effort should be spared to render the native Egyptians capable of eventually taking their share in the government of a really autonomous community.[10]

In other words, what Cromer believed was that there was not and could not be a single political nation in Egypt. There were a number of separate communities each with an equal share in the government; if the government were autonomous, there should be an 'International Legislative Council', in which the

[10] Cromer, ii. 568–9.

foreign communities would have a voice out of proportion to their numbers; and Britain should stay in Egypt for many years if not generations. Such ideas were wholly incompatible with those of 'Abduh and his group, and the desire to give them a reasoned answer underlay the political writing of Lutfi al-Sayyid. From another quarter they aroused a sharper response—a reassertion that there *was* an Egyptian nation and it *should* rule itself. The founder and leader of this new nationalism was Mustafa Kamil, and one can say that, in the years before 1914, his followers and those of 'Abduh divided between them the minds and allegiance of educated Egyptians.

Mustafa Kamil was born in 1874, and the date is significant.[11] His political career began in the 1890's and he was dead by 1908, but he belonged to a generation which on the whole came to political maturity much later. He was only eight years old when the British occupation took place; that is to say, he could not really remember what Egypt had been like before the British came. Men of an older generation might hesitate to oppose the British outright, from a sense of weakness or because they could not deny that in many ways the Egypt of Cromer was better than that of Isma'il; some at least of them, moreover, had been discredited by the fiasco of 'Urabi's movement. As national self-confidence returned with increasing strength and prosperity, no one of them came forward to give a lead to the nationalist opposition, and the vacuum was filled by a young man in his twenties with the crude certainty of youth and for whom England was the only and unquestioned enemy.

He belonged too to a generation which was able to profit from the schools established by Isma'il and developed, although within narrow limits, under British rule. Both his father's and his mother's family belonged to the new educated class created by Muhammad 'Ali, and he himself had not the traditional schooling of the Azhar but a modern education. He went to the School of Law in 1891. The next year a French law school was opened in Cairo; Kamil entered it, and in 1894 obtained the *licence* in law of the University of Toulouse. By this time he had already come forward as a leader, of a group of young men who

---

[11] For the life of Kamil see al-Rafi'i, *Mustafa Kamil* (cited as Rafi'i throughout this chapter); Steppat, 'Nationalismus und Islam bei Mustafa Kamil', *Welt des Islams*, iv (1956).

were coming to be loosely known as the 'National Party'. He had
led an attack on the offices of *al-Muqattam*, the most important
newspaper of the time, founded by two Lebanese Christians,
Nimr and Sarruf, and giving general support to Cromer's policy.
He had made two visits to France, lectured there on the aspirations of his country and given declarations to the press, and begun
to establish close relations with French nationalist politicians
whose nationalism at that time was no less opposed to Britain
than was his own.

His leading ideas too were formed by this time, although there
was to be a change in their emphasis as circumstances changed.
He called for the end of the British occupation and thought it
could be brought about with the help of some third force, the
French, the traditional rivals of England in the Near East, or the
Ottoman sultan, the suzerain of Egypt. He believed that there
was an Egyptian nation, but it was part of a larger whole, or
rather of several: it was Ottoman, Muslim, eastern, and should
strengthen its links with all three worlds. Such ideas he spread
by speech—he is said to have been a good orator—and by writing,
for he was one of the first Egyptians to practise with success the
journalist's art. The newspapers of Cairo were mainly owned
by Lebanese, and the establishment of an indigenous press was
due to two men: 'Ali Yusuf, who founded *al-Mu'ayyad* in 1889,
and Mustafa Kamil, who founded *al-Liwa'* in 1900 (and later
added to it an English and French version). His ideas, his
eloquence, and his newspapers won him an influence over the
educated young, but what direct political influence he had he
owed to another factor, the support of the Khedive 'Abbas Hilmi.
Tawfiq had been restored to his throne by British intervention,
and by necessity as well as weakness remained a pliant tool of
Cromer's policy; but 'Abbas was young and resented the domination of an elderly man, he had spent time at the Habsburg
Court and wished to rule, and he had also been touched, even
if only lightly, by the idea of Egyptian nationalism. He found in
Mustafa Kamil a useful instrument for checking Cromer's
power, and Kamil saw in him a way of securing influence; each
thought he was using the other, and on this unstable basis there
grew up an alliance from which both profited for a time. Their
policy was the same: to use the power of the palace and the mob,
the influence of Constantinople and Paris, to prevent Egypt being

wholly and permanently drawn into the British sphere of influence. But gradually the alliance grew weak as the policy revealed its defects: the humiliation of France at Fashoda in 1898 and the Anglo-French Agreement of 1904 made it difficult to believe that France would come to the support of the nationalists. After 1904 the khedive moved towards a rapprochement with the British, which became possible when Cromer retired and was succeeded by Gorst. Kamil came to realize that 'Abbas Hilmi cared more for his own power than Egypt's independence, and besides he grew to need the khedive's support less, for he now had other means of action: the growth of the student class gave him a larger public for his speeches and articles, and the famous incident of Danishway (Dinshaway) brought to the surface the feeling of national humiliation. In 1906 a fight broke out between villagers of Dinshaway, near Tanta in the delta, and a group of British officers who were shooting pigeons in the neighbourhood. Several officers were injured, and one died of shock and sunstroke; a peasant was beaten to death by the British soldiers who found the dead officer. Cromer was absent on leave, and those who were temporarily in charge lost their heads: a special court was set up, a number of peasants were condemned to be hanged, others to be flogged, and the sentences were carried out with barbarous publicity. This event had a profound effect on public sentiment.[12] Under pressure of this feeling, and with a certain relaxation of control by Cromer in his last years and then by Gorst, political consciousness took a step forward and organized political parties appeared. Three were founded in 1907: the friends of 'Abduh founded the People's Party, 'Ali Yusuf the Party of Constitutional Reform, which in fact was that of the khedive, and Mustafa Kamil and his friends gave a form to what had existed for years in effect, and started the National Party. With a growing political consciousness and public excitement, Kamil, already master of the students and the street, seemed capable of becoming that of the government, but he died the next year.

He left behind him an ambiguous reputation. For some Egyptians of his generation he remained, at least until the last few years, the real leader of Egypt, his glory undimmed by that of Zaghlul or Nahhas; but 'Abduh and his friends thought of

[12] Cf. A. Amin, *Hayati*, p. 79.

him as an empty demagogue, and some of his political adversaries denounced him in violent terms. The leader of a short-lived 'Liberal Party', for example, called him 'a vile impostor . . . a traitor to your country, an enemy to your fellow countrymen, urged on by evil, paid to praise the methods of slavery, despotism, decadence and worse ills, which you cloak beneath the names of freedom and faith'.[13] In France he had staunch supporters, but among the British opinions were divided. The Oriental Secretary of the British Agency, a man by no means devoid of sympathy either for Egyptians or for the more rakish side of human nature, called him 'a charlatan of the first order, discreditable in his private life and *bakshished* up to the eyes by all parties',[14] but Blunt gave another version:

He is enthusiastic and eloquent, and has an extraordinary gift of speech . . . a man with perfectly clear ideas . . . and a knowledge of men and things really astonishing. I take him, too, to be quite sincere in his patriotism, and I could not detect throughout the whole of his talk to-day a single false note. He also has great courage and decision of judgement.[15]

Whatever his personal qualities and defects, he was certainly in the eyes of many Egyptians a powerful symbol of their hopes, and his funeral was the first great popular manifestation of the new national spirit. Twice only, wrote Qasim Amin, had he felt the heart of Egypt beating—at Dinshaway and when Mustafa Kamil was buried.

It was not the content of his teaching which appealed to his fellow countrymen. His speeches and writings have indeed a certain content of ideas about how society should be organized. He quotes the famous phrase of the Khedive Isma'il about Egypt being part of Europe,[16] and emphasizes the importance of adopting what is of value in western civilization; no nation can lead a life of self-respect unless it treads that path.[17] But Egypt must not imitate Europe slavishly, she must remain true to the principles of Islam correctly interpreted: the real Islam is patriotism and justice, activity and union, equality and tolerance,[18] and it can be the basis of 'a new Islamic life which draws its strength from science and a broad and elevated thought'.[19]

[13] Alexander, p. 132.   [14] Storrs, p. 85.   [15] Blunt, *Diaries*, p. 564.
[16] Rafi'i, p. 442.   [17] Ibid. p. 211.   [18] Kamil, *Égyptiens et Anglais*, pp. 292 ff.
Rafi'i, p. 212.

The great names of progress and liberty are invoked, the importance of universal education taught, that of national industry mentioned in passing.[20] All this is the commonplace of Egyptian progressive thought since the time of al-Afghani; but it is significant that Kamil's personal contact with the ideas of al-Afghani came through 'Abd Allah al-Nadim, whom he met in 1892,[21] for he has more affinity with the orator of the 'Urabi movement than the more thoughtful members of al-Afghani's school. His main concern was neither to analyse the nature of Egyptian society, nor to educate it in political virtue, but to generate energy for the struggle against the British.

The British for him were the enemies of the Egyptian people, and the enmity would not end until the occupation ended. Their presence was not necessary for reform; even without them 'all the reforms would have been carried out, and even better carried out'.[22] Immediate evacuation without conditions: that was the motto of his party, and remained so long after his death. A generation later, the remnant of the party was the only recognized political group which refused to take part in the negotiations for the Anglo-Egyptian Treaty of 1936. But the British were also the enemies of the Ottoman Empire; Kamil wrote a long history of the eastern question in which the connexion between the policies of the Powers and the internal movements of the empire was made clear, and the dangers of British exploitation of these movements emphasized. England had shown that she was the enemy of Ottoman Muslims and Christians alike. To retain her position in Egypt, she wanted to weaken the sultan and make it impossible for him to assert his rights as suzerain; that was why she wanted to transfer the caliphate from the sultan to a man under her control. The idea of an Arab caliphate Kamil denounces as a British scheme, and he refers to Blunt's *Future of Islam* as a propaganda tract setting out British policy. But for the same purpose, she had encouraged separatist movements among the Christians, and intervened between them and their sovereign in the name of religion; most Christians remained loyal to the sultan, whose government had always treated them well, but some had given their loyalty to foreign Powers, and suffered for it.[23]

[20] Ibid. p. 149.
[21] Ibid. p. 36.
[22] Kamil, *Égyptiens et Anglais*, p. 314.
[23] Kamil, *al-Mas'ala al-sharqiyya*, pp. 6 & 20–21.

Against the power and plans of England, Kamil appealed to the outside world. He appealed to the 'liberal conscience' everywhere, but he thought of it as dwelling above all in France: not only as the rival of England, but as the home of the European culture he knew, the mother of the French Revolution. His first international act, in 1895, was to present to the French National Assembly a letter asking for French help in securing independence, and with the letter there went a symbolic picture: Mustafa Kamil, followed by the people of Egypt, proffers a petition to the figure of France—France, 'which declared the rights of man', has supported progress and civilization, and liberated so many nations.[24] There were a number of Frenchmen and women who encouraged and helped him. One such was the nationalist writer Juliette Adam; another, the novelist Pierre Loti—'my dream', wrote Kamil in 1895, 'is to become a brother of Pierre Loti who loves the east and the Moslems as never Frenchman has loved and understood them'.[25] But the French withdrawal from Fashoda showed him that France neither could nor would challenge the British position in the Nile valley, and the agreement of 1904 ended any hopes he still had: 'I would be an imbecile to believe an instant that France can be the friend of Egypt or of Islam', he wrote to Mme Adam. 'Farewell to all the dreams of the past, I have in France only you'.[26]

In so far as he looked to any outside force in his later years, it was to the Ottoman sultan. The survival of the empire, he maintained, was necessary to humanity, for its collapse might lead to universal war.[27] Muslims must rally around the sultan's throne. This was particularly important for Egypt, for as long as the sultan was sovereign the Great Powers could not do what they liked with her. Britain had only been able to occupy Egypt because sultan and khedive were on bad terms; she would only be able to absorb Egypt into her empire if she could make an agreement with Turkey similar to that with France. Those who wished to see Egypt independent must help to keep Turkey independent. So Kamil and his group supported Turkey in international affairs—in the Greco-Turkish war of 1897 and the Aqaba incident of 1906—;[28] and in 1904 the sultan gave him

---

[24] Rafi'i, p. 50.
[26] Ibid. p. 238 (Eng. tr. p. 240).
[28] *Égyptiens et Anglais*, p. 180.

[25] *Lettres*, p. 16 (Eng. tr. p. 16).
[27] *al-Mas'ala*, p. 13.

the title of pasha. This did not mean, however, that they wanted Egypt to fall under Ottoman rule again; Kamil exclaimed, in a passage which shows both the rhetorical nature of his mind and the ambivalence of his attitude towards the empire, that it would be absurd if, after a hundred years of civilization, Egyptians should want to become slaves again:

Slanderers have cast it at us that we wish to evict the English from Egypt in order to give her to Turkey as an ordinary province: that is to say, that what we want is not independence and self-government but a change of rulers.

What is this accusation, but a proclamation that the arts and sciences of the west, which have been transplanted into Egypt since more than a century ago, have done nothing except increase our attachment to servitude and humiliation; and that our knowledge of the rights and duties of nations has fitted us only to be slaves?

This accusation is an insult to civilization and civilized men, and a judgement on the Egyptian people, that it can never progress or reach the level of other peoples.[29]

In his eyes, the sultan was caliph as well, and as such the focus of loyalty for all Muslims. Muslim solidarity was a reality, although it meant neither the creation of a single State nor a fanatical hatred of those who were not Muslims. But beyond the Muslim world there was something else: the whole world of the orient, united by common resistance to the expansion of Europe and the need to accept European civilization. The victory of Japan over Russia in 1905 was the first sign that this was possible, and for oriental nationalists everywhere the revival of Japan showed in an exciting way that the east was not dead. Kamil shared the excitement and wrote a book about the new Japan, *al-Shams al-mushriqa* (The Rising Sun).

But he did not believe that Egypt could become independent through foreign help alone. In the end, she could not expect foreign help unless she had some strength of her own. The Anglo-French Agreement of 1904 made this clear; it had taught Egypt, he said, that she could only revive by her own efforts, and by this he meant first of all her efforts towards unity. The British occupation could never have taken place had it not been for splits inside the Egyptian camp, encouraged by the British: in particular, the split between 'Circassians' and 'Egyptians',

[29] Rafi'i, p. 491.

unnecessary because both were really Egyptian. For this split he blamed 'Urabi. A plan had been put forward that 'Urabi should leave Egypt for a time, to make possible a reconciliation between the two groups; this would have prevented foreign intervention, and 'Urabi's patriotic sense should have made him accept it.[30]

How could unity be achieved? Like other nationalists of his age, Kamil believed that unity could be based on 'feeling': the sense of belonging to the nation and responsibility for it. Patriotic spirit—*wataniyya*—there lay the secret of European strength and basis of civilization:

everything that exists in those regions, by way of justice, order, freedom and independence, great prosperity and great possessions, is undoubtedly the product of this noble feeling which spurs the members of the nation in their entirety to strive for a common purpose and a single goal.[31]

Once more, as with earlier writers, the object of this feeling is neither language nor religion, it is the land of Egypt. The beauty and great past of Egypt are invoked; it is not 'the Egyptians', it is 'Egypt', 'my country' (*biladi*) which is the god of Kamil's worship:

Egypt is the world's paradise, and the people which dwells in her and inherits her is the noblest of peoples if it hold her dear, and guilty of the greatest of crimes against her if it hold her rights cheaply and surrender control of her to the foreigner.[32]

(Sometimes, however, he speaks in terms not of Egypt alone but of the 'Nile valley', including the Sudan; the two peoples, Egyptian and Sudanese, 'have, across history, formed but one'.[33] He is deeply suspicious that British policy, once the Sudan has been reconquered, will try to make them two.[34] Attending the opening of the Aswan dam in 1902, he is most conscious of this danger: 'if in the future the English should construct reservoirs in the Soudan, Egypt would be at their mercy and would run the greatest dangers'.)[35]

There was no limitation of language, religion, or status upon those who might be included within the bonds of *wataniyya*. In

[30] Kamil, *al-Mas'ala*, p. 229.   [31] Rafi'i, p. 108.
[32] Ibid. p. 669.   [33] Kamil, *Lettres*, p. 94 (Eng. trs. p. 96).
[34] *Égyptiens et Anglais*, p. 126.   [35] *Lettres*, pp. 94–96 (Eng. trs. p. 98).

principle it could include all who lived in Egypt. First of all it should bind together ruler and people. Kamil, we have said, enjoyed the favour of the khedive during his early years, and naturally laid stress on the close tie between khedive and nation. Gradually however he was disillusioned with 'Abbas Hilmi. He came to see the defects of his character as they unfolded them-selves with the years: the greed for money, the lack of stability and persistence. 'He and the whole of his family', declared Kamil to Blunt in 1906, 'are worthless'.[36] After 1904 the two were estranged; there was later a certain reconciliation and then a final estrangement when Gorst put his new policy into practice. It was no doubt because of this that in later years Kamil de-manded a constitutional and representative government. But whatever doubts he might have about the person of the ruler, he believed the royal family had been the creators of modern Egypt. In a speech to celebrate the hundredth anniversary of the coming of Muhammad 'Ali, he praised him for having secured Egypt's independence, reorganized its government, opened all posts to native Egyptians and avoided debts.[37] But he went on to say that in all this the ruler was only the expression of the nation's will, raised to power by the people's choice. In the tangled events of 1805 there had indeed been close collaboration between Muhammad 'Ali and the leaders of the population of Cairo; they had offered him the rule of Egypt, and it was only later that the Ottoman government ratified the choice.[38] At this moment, said Kamil, there had been created a moral bond between dynasty and nation.[39]

Such a bond existed too between Copts and Muslims who 'have lived together for long centuries in the greatest unity and harmony'. This did not mean that either should cease to hold their religion, or Egypt should cease to be primarily Muslim. There were two spheres, religion and national life, and there should be no conflict between them; on the contrary, true religion teaches true patriotism.[40] The principles are unimpeachable, but Kamil was never really trusted by the minorities of Egypt. They felt a certain lack of strength in his convictions, a willingness to sacrifice them in pursuit of power or national interest as he con-ceived it, and perhaps also a danger that he would raise popular

[36] Blunt, *Diaries*, pp. 564–5. [37] Rafi'i, p. 251. [38] Cf. Jabarti, iii. 350. [39] Rafi'i, p. 459; cf. *Égyptiens et Anglais*, p. 272. [40] Rafi'i, pp. 147 & 492.

forces he could not control. The same could be said of his relations with the foreign communities in Egypt. He tried to win them over: foreigners and Egyptians, he repeated, have the same interest, that of preventing Britain taking everything into her own hands. Moreover, the foreigners are of positive benefit to Egypt: they are 'the vanguard of western civilization', 'the guarantee of progress and welfare'.[41] But another note came into his voice when talking of the Lebanese 'intruders' who were helping the occupying Powers: 'L'intrus, l'intrus! voilà le véritable ennemi ... [ils] ont renié leur patrie et n'ont payé la générosité et l'hospitalité de l'Égypte que par l'ingratitude et la haine.'[42]

The ambivalence of Kamil's attitude, and the doubts of foreigners and minorities, can be explained by the methods through which he hoped to achieve unity. He could be a courtier, but he was also the first popular politician of modern Egypt. He believed that Britain could never be persuaded to establish constitutional government by secret diplomacy or rational argument; she would yield only to pressure, and he tried to generate national energy by arousing public interest in politics and directing it in ways which would lead to his goal: through the nation-wide party, the popular manifestation, the student strike. In 1906 he organized a strike at the School of Law which began a long period of student agitation that only came to an end when political activity itself came to an end under the military government of 1952. There were others who thought like him, but there was no one in his time who had the same influence over the public, and in a sense the National Party never recovered from his death. It is true, it played an important part in the troubled years before 1914 and was a force to be reckoned with by British and khedive alike, but it never again found an adequate leader. Its nominal head, Muhammad Farid, was dignified but ineffective; he went into voluntary exile in 1911 and died in 1919. Real power fell into the hands of 'Abd al-'Aziz Shawish, a former lecturer in Arabic in Oxford, a violent orator who developed the ideas of Mustafa Kamil in the direction of pan-Islamism and pan-Ottomanism. (He was himself not an Egyptian by origin but a Tunisian.) His one achievement was to bring the latent suspicion of Muslims and Copts to the surface, for almost the only time in the modern history of Egypt. He too left Egypt,

---

[41] Rafi'i, p. 442. [42] *Égyptiens et Anglais*, pp. 93, 163.

for Turkey during the First World War, and when the war
ended he, like Farid, had lost his influence.

The war indeed changed the nature of Egyptian nationalism.
From a movement of the educated élite it became a movement
which, at the moment of crisis, could command the active or
passive support of almost the entire people. The change was
due to the new ideas and spirit generated by the war, to wartime
promises and declarations which, although not intended for the
Egyptians, still had an effect on them, but also to certain specific
grievances. The Khedive 'Abbas Hilmi was deposed at the
beginning of the war and replaced by a more malleable uncle,
Ottoman suzerainty was abolished and Egypt declared a protectorate: these acts offended those who supported the khedive
and valued the Ottoman connexion, and strengthened the fears
of those who believed that Britain's policy was to make Egypt
permanently a part of the British Empire. Under pressure of the
war, Egypt was in fact treated like a colony: the number of
British officials increased while their quality did not improve,
numerous peasants and their livestock were virtually conscripted
for service with the Allied force in Palestine. The presence of a
large foreign army brought profit to some but also led to incon-
venience and friction, major and minor; the world demand for
cotton made some fortunes, but also caused too much land to be
given to the production of cotton, too little to the growing of
food, and in the later years of the war, when imports became
difficult, food grew dear and scarce. With the change of spirit
came a change of leaders. It was not the National Party founded
by Kamil which gave expression to this new feeling; the lead was
taken by a man who had never been of the school of Kamil, and
a party whose principles were not the same.

The new leader was Sa'd Zaghlul,[43] but he was new only in
his capacity as popular politician. He belonged indeed to a
slightly older generation than that of Kamil and was already well
known as one of the most prominent members of 'Abduh's
group of friends. His origins indeed were much the same as those
of 'Abduh, and once more with him we come upon the class
which created modern Egyptian thought, until the military
revolution of 1952 brought a different class to the centre of the

[43] For the life of Zaghlul cf. al-'Aqqad; E. Kedourie, 'Sa'ad Zaghlul and the
British' (cited in the bibliography).

stage. He was born probably in 1857, in a village of the Gharbiyya
province in the delta. His father was an *'umda*, a large farmer, a
man of some wealth and local standing, and his mother came of a
similar family which had held official positions since the time of
Muhammad 'Ali. There were no modern schools in the province
when he was a boy, and he went first to an old religious school
and then in 1871 to the Azhar. The date is important: this was the
year when al-Afghani came to live in Cairo, and throughout the
1870's Sa'd was one of his inner group of disciples, as well as the
pupil of Muhammad 'Abduh. In 1880 he joined 'Abduh on the
staff of the official gazette and later received other official posts;
but his career was interrupted by the British occupation. What
part he played in the national movement of that time is not clear,
but he certainly sympathized with it, and was in prison for a time
on suspicion of forming a 'Society of Revenge'. He then worked
for almost ten years as a lawyer, and in 1892 was taken back into
favour and made a judge in the court of appeal. For the next fourteen years he worked as a judge, and was associated with 'Abduh,
Lutfi al-Sayyid, and Qasim Amin in what they all regarded
as the most important task of their time: to remould the laws
and institutions of Egypt in response to the needs of the modern
age. But he also took the first steps towards a political career. He
frequented the first political *salon* of the modern Middle East,
that of Princess Nazli; he learnt French and studied at the
French School of Law in Cairo; and he married the daughter of
the Prime Minister, Mustafa Fahmi Pasha, in 1896. Although
belonging to the old Turkish aristocracy, she was to identify
herself wholly with his role as leader of the Egyptian nation, and
to live on for years after his death, much respected as 'Mother of
the Egyptians'.

Through his father-in-law, Zaghlul was drawn into the ruling
element. In 1906, when Cromer was at last convinced of the
need to bring representative Egyptians into the government, his
choice fell on Zaghlul. He forced the khedive to appoint him
Minister of Education, although 'Abbas never liked Zaghlul and
regarded him, with reason, as an opponent of absolute rule.
Sa'd remained in charge of education for four years, and proved
a competent although exacting minister. He increased the number of schools and carried out certain changes—for example,
the partial replacement of English by Arabic as language of

instruction. What was more important, he was the first Egyptian minister to establish his authority over his British advisers and officials, although not always without a struggle. The best of the British officials liked him, and one of them has recorded that, although 'his manner was stiff and uncordial', he was a careful administrator and showed an unusual interest in the details of the ministry's work.[44] In 1910 he was promoted to a more important ministry, that of Justice. But he found it increasingly difficult to take part in the government. He had been on good terms with Cromer, whose photograph he kept in his study along with those of Bismarck, al-Afghani, and 'Abduh,[45] and he had indeed dreamed, like 'Abduh, of a partnership of British and Egyptian reformers to curb the autocracy of the khedive and carry out the necessary reforms. But he was less in sympathy with Gorst's policy of giving greater power to the khedive, and he did not get on well with Kitchener. In 1913 he resigned from his ministry, and shortly afterwards presented himself as a candidate in the elections for the new Legislative Assembly which Kitchener had established. He was elected a member, and then chosen as vice-president. The Assembly met in 1914 for a few months, until the outbreak of war suspended its life. These few months were enough for Zaghlul to establish himself as the leader of opposition to the government, and to the British power which stood behind it. He had been closer to the Umma group than to Mustafa Kamil's National Party, and had indeed been violently attacked by Kamil's followers when he was Minister of Education; but now he began to be the voice of national opinion. Political life came to a standstill during the war, but when, towards the end of the war, Egyptians began to discuss the possibility of forming some sort of representative delegation to present Egypt's case for independence to the Peace Conference, it was natural that he should take the lead. The first discussions appear to have taken place in his house in the country, between himself, Lutfi al-Sayyid, and a few others. After making contact with others who had the same idea, including a number of ministers, he and his associates decided to form a delegation (*wafd*). It seems very probable that the ruler, Fu'ad (who had succeeded 'Abbas Hilmi at one remove, with the title of sultan) knew what they proposed to do and acquiesced in it. On

[44] Bowman, p. 75.   [45] 'Aqqad, p. 588.

13 November, 1918, two days after the armistice, Zaghlul and
two other members of the delegation called on the British High
Commissioner, and asked for facilities to go to London and
present Egypt's case to the British government. From then until
his death his history was that of Egypt. The British government
refused the request. There was some ground for this, since it
would have been difficult to accept Zaghlul rather than the
Egyptian government as spokesman of the national interest; but
the Foreign Office then refused a similar request from the Prime
Minister, Rushdi Pasha. Rushdi resigned, tension grew, Zaghlul
and some of his supporters were arrested in March 1919 and
deported to Malta, and widespread disorders broke out. Rather
unfairly making a scapegoat of the High Commissioner, the
British government replaced him by Allenby, the victor of the
Palestine war, and then replaced repression by conciliation.
Zaghlul was released and allowed to go to Paris to put his case
before the Peace Conference, and it was announced that a special
mission under Lord Milner would study the problem. The
Milner mission arrived in Egypt in December 1919, and was
boycotted by almost the whole country. This boycott, organized
by Zaghlul's followers, not only demonstrated his influence but
increased it; it was indeed the means by which he imposed his
authority over the country. Much impressed by it, the mission,
on its return to England in March 1920, began to negotiate
privately with Zaghlul, who was still in Europe. It offered to
recognize Egypt as an independent State and a constitutional
monarchy, linked with Britain by an alliance which would
grant Britain the right to maintain a force for the sole purpose of
guarding imperial communications. The negotiations broke
down, and the British government then tried to make an agreement without Zaghlul. The Prime Minister, 'Adli Yakan Pasha,
was willing to try; this was a challenge to Zaghlul's position, and,
after an unsuccessful attempt by 'Adli to draw him into the discussions, he set himself to thwart 'Adli's mission. He succeeded
in this: once negotiations began, 'Adli found he could not in fact
make an agreement, for agreement implied compromise, and if
'Adli made concessions Zaghlul could always outbid him and
make his position impossible. He resigned in November 1921,
and shortly afterwards Zaghlul was arrested again and deported
to the Seychelles: but too late, for he had already done what he

intended to, and shown that an Anglo-Egyptian treaty could only be made, if at all, with him and his supporters. There was now only one way to break the deadlock, and that was for Britain to concede unilaterally what she would have been prepared to concede in a treaty. In February 1922 the High Commissioner issued a declaration of Egyptian independence. The protectorate was ended, Egypt was henceforth independent, but Britain reserved to herself four points until agreement should be reached on them: imperial communications, defence, foreign interests and minorities, the Sudan.

Zaghlul had succeeded in securing at least a limited independence for Egypt, without binding himself to anything in return. In September 1923 he was allowed to return to Egypt. By this time a constitution had been drawn up, and elections were now held which resulted in a victory for Zaghlul's supporters, who organized themselves into a regular parliamentary party, the Wafd Party. Zaghlul became Prime Minister and opened negotiations with the British government on the four reserved points. The British Prime Minister of the time was Ramsay MacDonald, who had shown some sympathy for Egypt's claims; but the negotiations broke down, tension grew in Egypt, the publicists of the Wafd denounced British policy with force, and the British Commander-in-Chief of the Egyptian army was assassinated. The High Commissioner held Zaghlul and his followers responsible, and presented the Egyptian government with a stiff ultimatum, in the face of which Zaghlul resigned. There followed a period when the Wafd seemed to have lost its initiative. Power was held by a coalition of palace nominees and independent 'liberals'. But it was an unstable coalition, and soon the palace became all-powerful and the independents made their peace with the Wafd, which pressed for elections. These were held in 1926; the Wafd obtained a majority, but owing to British objections Zaghlul did not take office. He became President of the Chamber, and a coalition of Wafdists and 'liberals' took office. This too was unstable, but was held together through the influence Zaghlul exercised over his followers, until his death in 1927.

The public career of Zaghlul falls clearly into two parts, divided by the war of 1914–18. Close study may indeed show that this like most divisions in history or the life of man is less sharp than it seems, but there remains a difference between the reforming judge and the popular leader. Reflecting this difference there is a change if not in the content at least in the emphasis of his thought about politics and society. Until his full entry into political life his ideas were roughly those of the school of 'Abduh. The unit of his thought was Egypt, conceived as something separate in space and continuous in time, Pharaonic and Arab alike. Egypt should be independent, but true independence could come only by way of reform, and two types of reform were particularly important, that of education and that of law. There should be a legal system rooted in the principles of Islamic jurisprudence, but responsive to modern needs; such a law must rule society if it was not to become anarchy, and government if it was not to be despotism.

This system of beliefs explains his activities before 1914. As a judge, he was distinguished by his care that justice should be done. In case of doubt he inclined to leniency, for it is 'better for a guilty man to go free than an innocent man to be found guilty';[46] on occasion he would break the laws of procedure in order to correct an error in judgement; he condemned the use of threats and pressure by the police, because it was 'more dangerous to the public than that a criminal should be hidden or should evade his penalty . . . it harms the judiciary and renders it an aid to tyranny instead of a help to justice'.[47] Justice then should be done: but what justice consisted of should be decided in the light of *maslaha*, public interest, and public interest should be defined in terms of the sum of private interests. Passing judgment against the irrigation authorities of Alexandria for damage it had done to private property, he proclaimed: 'It is not possible that the purpose of this law should be to permit despotic measures contrary to justice and law, harmful to the rights of individuals, and devoid of public utility'.[48] His work therefore may be seen as an attempt to apply in the secular courts those principles which, in the view of 'Abduh, should underlie a reform of the religious law. When he became Minister of Justice he came into direct contact with the religious law, and founded a school for *Shari'a* judges, in order to give them a modern training.

When he entered political life, as a candidate in the elections of 1913, his election address shows the same concern for reform

[46] Zayyat, p. 272.   [47] Ibid. pp. 389 ff.   [48] Ibid. p. 5.

in the fabric of society. If he were elected, he would press for reforms in the legal system, the extension of education to the children of the poor, greater freedom for the press within the limits of public order, municipal improvements in Cairo, a bettering of the condition of the farmers.[49] When, after the election, he was drawn into the opposition against the government, and so took the first step towards his later fame, this also was a continuation of the same line: the main enemy he was attacking was still lawlessness—the absolute rule of the khedive. To this end he was prepared to make use of the British in so far as he could, although he was not an uncritical supporter of the British presence and did not want too much control and interference.

When Zaghlul became popular leader of Egypt, he did not of course change his personality completely. The same ideas lay at the back of his mind until his life ended, and he remained, at least in a cool hour, the disciple of al-Afghani and 'Abduh. His considered idea of government was still that of democracy: the government should be the servant of social and individual welfare, and for this purpose it could demand positive help from the people: 'The people have looked at the government as a bird at the hunter not an army at its leader. [We must replace this by] trust in the government, and persuade the people that the government is a part of the nation.'[50] In his earlier speeches as political leader, he tried to appease fears by recognizing the interests of all sections: the financial interest of foreigners, the interest of the world in the Suez Canal, the interests of Copts inside the Egyptian national community. The spirit of the early Wafd was that of the 'sacred union', of a national bond compared with which differences of religion counted little: it was perhaps too simple to last, and religious differences cannot be conjured away easily, but there is no reason to doubt that Zaghlul was sincere, and he never lost the support of prominent Copts. In the same way, the nationalism of the Wafd appealed to another suppressed element, the educated women of Egypt. Since Qasim Amin feminism had formed part of the content of nationalist thought, and it was no accident that the heroic days of nationalism were also those when educated Muslim women, led by Huda Sha'rawi, threw off the veil and first took part in public life.

[49] 'Aqqad, p. 154.   [50] Ibid. p. 433; cf. Sa'd Zaghlul, *Athar al-za'im*, p. 54.

H

But hours of reflection came more rarely as the political struggle continued, and it was noticed by all, Egyptians and foreigners alike, that the leader began to speak in a different tone and with another emphasis. He became more imperious, even vindictive, in his dealings with other leaders, and very early the Wafd began to split at the top: not only ambitious politicians like Muhammad Mahmud and Isma'il Sidqi parted company with him, but also the thoughtful, unambitious Lutfi al-Sayyid, his companion in the school of 'Abduh. He became more exacting in his dealings and more exclusive in his conception of the Egyptian nation. 'The most important results of the revolution', he said in one of his speeches,

have been the egyptianization of the Egyptian economy, the abandonment of the veil by women, their participation in the national movement, the destruction of the class of pashas, the seizure of power by the
fellahin, the disappearance of the Turkish element from Egyptian
politics—and independence comes after all this, because external independence has no value unless there is also an internal liberation.[51]

In this list, the first three items would have met with the approval of 'Abduh, but it is doubtful whether the last three
would, for his appeal had always been to social unity (national
as well as religious), to the harmony of all interests, to an idea of
the Egyptian nation which took no account of racial origin.

Why did this change take place? There were those who
believed that power had unbalanced his character. There is
undoubtedly some truth in this. He always had perhaps a
tendency to violence and vindictiveness, and political life by its
very nature encouraged it. This was shown clearly when 'Ali
'Abd al-Raziq was in trouble over his book on Islam and the
foundations of government. Zaghlul might have been expected
to show some sympathy to one who had belonged to the followers
of 'Abduh, whose book was an extension—even if it might be
considered an illegitimate one—of 'Abduh's principles of interpretation, and who had become a martyr of intellectual freedom.
In fact he showed no sympathy, and if anything was rather
pleased that 'Abd al-Raziq was in trouble, because he was connected with the Liberal Constitutional Party, formed by the first
seceders from the Wafd, and the scandal might therefore weaken
a rival party.[52]

[51] Qal'aji, p. 96.   [52] 'Aqqad, p. 518.

Zaghlul was not in the true sense an intellectual. The bent of his mind was practical. His culture was that of a man of action: he read only the books which were relevant to his work; he learnt French not because it was the key to unlock the treasures of modern civilization but because it was essential for the career of an ambitious public man, and later he learnt English because he had to deal with Englishmen, and some German, in the First World War, as an insurance; he was interested in the Quran mainly as a source of useful quotations.[53] If then his point of view seems to have changed in later life, it may well have been not because of a change in his character but in response to certain practical problems with which he was faced. That he should have been less willing than before to co-operate with England is easily explained by the shift in the British position in Egypt and the world: by 1918 English administrative control had increased but it was being used to safeguard British interests rather than carry out an essential work of reform; besides, Wilson's Fourteen Points and other Allied promises had created a new spirit in the world. That Zaghlul was less interested in internal reform than in independence, in spite of speeches like that already quoted, is also easily explained: before 1914 even limited independence had been impossible, and for a practical Egyptian reformer there had been no alternative to accepting the British presence and trying to draw profit for his country from it. Much of what appeared violent and unreasonable may have been due to the nature of the political problem with which he was faced. He was trying to lead a movement of a type new to Egypt, in conditions in which some kinds of action were impossible and others were inevitable. The nature of the acts he had to perform affected the concepts in terms of which he explained and justified himself.

The delegation which visited Sir Reginald Wingate in November 1918 was self-constituted, and its claim to speak in the name of the Egyptian people had no basis except its own assertion that it did so. Since there was no parliament and no other organized and recognized expression of public opinion, it could only establish its claim *vis-à-vis* the British and its rivals by imposing its will on them; and it could only do this by generating some kind of strength to replace that which a parliamentary majority would have given it in a constitutional country,

[53] Ibid. p. 573.

or an army and a network of foreign relations in an independent country. It had thus two essential aims, each connected with the other: to secure for itself some substitute for parliamentary and national strength, and to find a moral basis for its actions—some moral justification for its claim to negotiate on behalf of the Egyptian people, and when necessary to defy constituted authority, whether that of the protecting Power or that of the legal government.

In this process there were two critical moments. The first was the moment of Zaghlul's first encounter with the British in 1918–19. When the Foreign Office rejected his request to proceed to London and Paris and discuss the future of Egypt, it was in fact questioning his claim to speak in the name of the Egyptian people. He was, it is true, a man of some distinction and experience, but there were others such, and some of them were members of the government while he was not. At first, some attempt was made to give the Wafd a legal basis by linking it with the only representative body which could be said to exist, the Legislative Assembly which had been elected in 1913 and had ceased to meet at the outbreak of war, and some members of which (including Zaghlul himself) were members of the Wafd. But gradually another doctrine was put forward: that Zaghlul was not just one political leader among several, and the Wafd was not a political party. In some special way they were representatives of the Egyptian people, were indeed their embodiment, and this imposed on them certain obligations and freed them from contrary obligations; in the end, they alone were the sole judges of what they must do.

The first constitution of the Wafd, drawn up in 1918, declared that 'the Wafd draws its power from the will of the Egyptian people expressed either directly or through their representatives in the representative bodies'.[54] At an early stage, an attempt was made to secure 'powers of attorney' (*tawkil*) signed by Egyptians all over the country, authorizing the Wafd to work for Egypt's independence by all possible means. Documents to this effect were signed not only by the educated classes, but by members of local councils, headmen of villages, and rural notables, with some encouragement from the Egyptian government of the time.[55] It was on this basis that Zaghlul claimed to speak for

---

[54] 'Aqqad, p. 195.   [55] Haykal, *Mudhakkirat*, i. 86.

Egypt in face of Britain. Already in 1918, in answer to Wingate, he had claimed that he and his associates were 'natural representatives empowered by the Egyptian nation itself';[56] and three years later he went farther and drew the logical implication of this claim. In December 1921, in the period of disturbance after the breakdown of the 'Adli–Curzon negotiations, Zaghlul was warned by the then Adviser to the Ministry of the Interior, Sir Gilbert Clayton, to abstain from political activity. He replied that he could not, because the only moral law he could recognize was that of national duty: 'Since I have been delegated by the nation to work for its independence, nothing except the nation has the authority to prevent me carrying out this sacred duty'.[57] This was not only a moral claim; it contained by implication a programme of action. The only way in which Zaghlul could accomplish his ends was by generating popular support: in other words, by making the nation act as if his claim were true. There was, it is true, another instrument he could use: like Kamil, and indeed like all nationalist leaders in the empires of democratic States, he trusted to some extent in the European liberals: 'If no foreign government will help us, among their peoples are many liberals who sympathize with us and help our cause by speech and writing'.[58] But this was a secondary instrument only: his first was popular support, and to use this he had to impose his authority on the Egyptian people, and in this way to place the British in a position where they had to accept him as sole spokesman of Egypt.

By the end of 1919 this process was more or less finished. The boycott of the Milner mission by the whole of unofficial Egypt, the difficulty there was in finding a government which would hold office during the mission's stay in Egypt, impressed Milner and his colleagues so much that they were prepared to negotiate with Zaghlul personally: if he made an agreement the Egyptian people would accept it, if he did not, no one else would. From that moment there was no danger that Zaghlul's credentials as a popular leader would be called in question. But he was still not the Egyptian government. He might defy the British government, whose moral claim to be in Egypt was not of the best; but could he defy the legal government of his own country, and claim that he and not they could speak for Egypt? This was the issue at

[56] 'Aqqad, p. 202.   [57] Ibid. p. 382.   [58] Ibid. p. 295.

stake in the second crisis, that of 1921, when 'Adli was preparing
to negotiate a treaty with Britain. The danger for Zaghlul was
not only that 'Adli had all the authority of the government behind
him, but that he was a possible focus of political feeling. It is
true, he had one great disadvantage. He was a Turk, belonging
to one of the old families who had grown rich and powerful in
the service of Muhammad 'Ali and his successors; he was
perhaps too much of a *grand seigneur* to have the same appeal as
Zaghlul, of whom an English diplomat could write:

> Zaghlul is very human. For example, he likes gambling, bad jokes
> and good food. . . . He is in some ways the first really representative
> Egyptian and one racy of the soil. Whether he thunders like a minor
> prophet or chaffs in dialect like a man of the people, he speaks a
> language that every Egyptian can understand.[59]

But on the other hand 'Adli was a man of some political gifts, of
an honest and pleasing character, a liberal and in his own way a
nationalist. He had encouraged the Wafd in its early stages, and
had gone to Paris at Zaghlul's request in 1920 to help in the discussions with the Milner mission. There, although the two men
had friendly relations, a certain rivalry had begun to appear
between them. The members of the Wafd disagreed about
whether they should accept Milner's proposals, and those who
were willing to do so—including Lutfi al-Sayyid—gravitated towards 'Adli. After the publication of the Milner plan, the British
government declared its willingness to negotiate, and this
widened the breach: 'Adli, now Prime Minister, insisted that
the government should negotiate, although with the approval of
the Wafd; Zaghlul, that the Wafd itself should do so. It seemed
to some Egyptian leaders that Zaghlul was claiming 'that one
man should be able, without any right laid down in the existing
laws, to impose his will on the possessor of the throne and on the
whole land, and to go beyond the bounds of law and order in
order to do so'.[60] Men more cautious and experienced than
Zaghlul, or not prepared to accept his claims, might well find
'Adli a leader easier to work with.

It was essential therefore for Zaghlul to prevent 'Adli negotiating in the name of Egypt; or, if that were impossible, to prevent
the negotiations succeeding. This struggle for power went on

[59] Young, *Egypt*, p. 271.   [60] Haykal, *Mudhakkirat*, i. 123.

throughout the year and although it ended in Zaghlul's second period of imprisonment and exile, it led also to the failure of the conversations between 'Adli and Curzon. In the course of it, Zaghlul developed a new theory of what the Wafd was and what he himself was. The Wafd, he declared, was not a political party:

They ask us, 'Where is your programme?' And we answer, we are not a party, we are a delegation empowered by the nation and expressing its will about a matter which it has assigned to us: this matter is complete independence, and we strive to this end alone. . . . As for internal questions—should education be compulsory, should it be free, should interest be paid on the Debt, should cotton be sown on a third or half of the registered area—these are matters which I leave to men who know more of them than I do. But so far as independence is concerned, we are a nation and not a party. Anyone who says we are a party demanding independence is a criminal, for this implies that there are other parties which do not want independence. The whole nation wants independence, we are the spokesmen of the nation in demanding it, we are the trustees of the nation.[61]

It was a permanent part of the political structure of Egypt, it was the Egyptian nation organized for political purposes. The function of the government was to rule, that of the Wafd and of its leader was to represent public opinion. The government should accept this: it should not try to control public opinion or influence it against the Wafd, and if it negotiated it should submit the result to the Wafd.[62] In other words, to govern is of secondary importance; whether in or out of office, the Wafd is the unchanging guardian of the public interest. Such claims, forged in the heat of conflict, were henceforth to be part of the doctrine of the Wafd, and to have a profound influence on its ideas and its policy.

[61] Sa'd Zaghlul, *Majmu'at khutab*, p. 27.   [62] 'Aqqad, p. 300.

IX

RASHID RIDA

IDEAS such as those of 'Abduh were 'in the air' in the last quarter
of the nineteenth century. We find similar groups of reformers
in all the more advanced of the Muslim countries, and perhaps
it is too simple to explain them in terms of the influence of
al-Afghani and 'Abduh. It could be said, as an alternative, that
al-'Urwa al-wuthqa could only have had its influence because
there were already little groups of Muslims thinking on the lines
which it made popular. In Tunis such a group existed among the
associates and followers of Khayr al-Din: in particular, there
was Muhammad Bayram, one of a line of religious scholars,
who wrote a number of works on reform of the law, as well as
an important history of his age. In Baghdad there were the
scholars of the Alusi family, one of whom wrote a vast commentary on the Quran, a judicious summary of the traditional
learning, while another, a generation younger, wrote a defence
of Ibn Taymiyya against charges of unorthodoxy—a sign of the
influence which such ideas were now beginning to exercise over
educated Muslims of a different tradition.[1] In Syria similar men
can be found in all the great centres of Muslim learning, Aleppo,
Damascus, Tripoli, and Jerusalem. Among those who were
roughly contemporary with 'Abduh, and had some contact with
him, was Tahir al-Jaza'iri (1851–1920). A scholar of Algerian
origin from the entourage of the famous Amir 'Abd al-Qadir, a
writer on literary and linguistic subjects, he had a wider importance through his work for the establishment of modern
schools and the preservation of ancient books; it was he who
founded the Zahiriyya library in Damascus as a home for the
manuscripts scattered throughout the mosques and old schools
of the city. The same concern for a blend of ancient and modern
learning, for an acceptance of the modern world which would not
destroy the convictions and values of Islam, can be seen in the
life and writings of Shaykh Husayn al-Jisr of Tripoli (1845–1909).

[1] Cf. N. Alusi, *Jala' al-'aynayn.*

A student of the Azhar, where he was influenced by the teaching of Marsafi, he later edited one of the early newspapers and founded a 'National Islamic School' in his native town; the curriculum included the Arabic, French, and Turkish languages, the religious sciences, logic, mathematics, and the natural sciences of modern Europe, all studied in Arabic through such works as those of Dr Van Dyke, an American missionary who provided the Syrian Protestant College with many textbooks explaining the modern sciences in a clear and correct Arabic.[2] He also wrote an exposition of Muslim doctrine, *al-Risala al-hamidiyya*, of which the purpose was to present Islam in a new way and one easily understood, and respond to the new interest in Islam which, or so he believed, was being shown by non-Muslims. On many matters his attitude was that of a traditionalist, not that which 'Abduh was making into the new orthodoxy. He maintained for example that the *jihad* was legitimate, not only to defend Islam but to bring into the faith those who obstinately refused it; he defended the Islamic conception of slavery; and he accepted the traditional view that the door of *ijtihad* had been closed after the first three centuries— the scholars of the first ages spoke with more authority than those who came later because they were nearer in time to the Prophet and those who had known him, and after a time all the important questions had been settled.[3] But there is perhaps a new note to be seen in the way he begins, with the personality and preaching of Muhammad, and still more in his insistence on the rights of reason in interpreting Quran and *hadith*.[4] They must, he claims, be interpreted literally unless the literal interpretation clearly contradicts some rational principle; if so, they must be explained figuratively. What cannot be accepted is that there should be a contradiction between all possible interpretations and a conclusive intellectual proof (*dalil 'aqli qati*').

Among Syrians of the next generation there were a group who had been prepared by the teaching of such men to appreciate and accept fully the ideas of al-Afghani and 'Abduh. They included 'Abd al-Qadir al-Maghribi, who spent some years of his youth in close contact with al-Afghani in Constantinople; Muhammad Kurd 'Ali, a Kurd from Damascus; Amir Shakib

[2] Cf. Rida, *al-Manar wa'l-Azhar*, p. 142.   [3] Jisr, pp. 301, 310, 320.
[4] Ibid. pp. 4 & 328 ff.

Arslan, a member of one of the noble Druze families of Lebanon who, while still a schoolboy, fell under the influence of 'Abduh during his years of exile in Beirut; and Muhammad Rashid Rida (1865–1935). Life led them in different paths. Kurd 'Ali and Maghribi, after a youth spent in journalism in Cairo and Damascus, gave their riper age to scholarship: they founded the Arab Academy of Damascus, and Kurd 'Ali became the historian of the city. Shakib Arslan, although he never lost his concern for Islamic reform, was drawn into Arab nationalist politics, and we shall come upon his traces again later. It was Rashid Rida who, more than the rest, preserved the impulse imparted to them by 'Abduh.[5]

Born in a village near Tripoli, of a family not unlike 'Abduh's own, a village family of some standing and with a tradition of learning and piety, Rashid Rida started his education in the ancient way at a local Quranic school; but coming a generation later than his master, he was able to profit from the new education, and at a Turkish government school in Tripoli and then at Husayn al-Jisr's school he imbibed something of the new sciences as well as a certain knowledge of French. But he also mastered the sciences of the Islamic religion and the Arabic language, and his writings bear witness to a solid scholarship of the old-fashioned type.

He has left us something which is not so rare in Arabic as was once thought, a fragment of autobiography describing his mental and spiritual formation during the first thirty years or so of his life.[6] The great intellectual influences stand out clearly. In Husayn al-Jisr's school and through the writings of the Lebanese journalists of Cairo he caught his first glimpse of modern science and the new world of Europe and America. Among the Islamic classics he fell under the spell of Ghazali's *Ihya' 'ulum al-din*, and in a sense this was to remain the deepest influence of his life. Ghazali had struck a balance between external obedience to the law and personal inner devotion; Rashid Rida, like 'Abduh, always laid stress on the importance of such devotion and on good intentions as necessary if ritual prayer and works were to be

---

[5] For the life and thought of Rida cf. Arslan, *Rashid Rida*; Jomier; Kerr, *Muh. Abduh and Rashid Rida* and 'Rashid Rida and Islamic Legal Reform', *Muslim Wld*, 1 (1960); Laoust, 'Le Réformisme musulman dans la littérature arabe contemporaine', *Orient*, x (1959).

[6] Rida, *al-Manar wa'l-Azhar*, pp. 129 ff.

valid. But in later generations the balance had been tilted: inner
devotion within the bounds of the law had become mystical
practices free from the law's restraints and evolving a ritual and
theology of its own. Rashid Rida realized this when, under the
influence of Ghazali, he decided to join one of the orders of
mystics and practise the spiritual life under the direction of a
shaykh. He chose the Naqshabandi order and for a time followed
its teachings, adopting ascetic practices of an extreme severity.
But he gradually became aware of the spiritual dangers of the
mystical systems, and his doubts came to the surface in a dramatic
way when he attended a session of the Mawlawis, the 'dancing
dervishes':

They said to me, 'Won't you come and attend the meeting of the
Mawlawis in their monastery—it is like the heavenly paradise, lying
on the bank of the river Abu 'Ali.' I agreed, and went with those who
were going after the Friday prayers. It was the opening of the season for
these meetings in the spring. I sat in the spectators' space . . . until the
time of the session came, when Mawlawi dervishes appeared in their
meeting-place in front of us, with their shaykh in the seat of honour.
There were handsome beardless youths among them, dressed in snow-
white gowns like brides' dresses, dancing to the moving sound of the
reed-pipe, turning swiftly and skilfully so that their robes flew out and
formed circles, at harmonious distances and not encroaching on one
another. They stretched out their arms and inclined their necks, and
passed in turn before their shaykh and bowed to him. I asked, 'What's
this?' and they told me, 'This is the ritual prayer of the order founded
by our Lord Jalal al-Din al-Rumi, author of the *Mathnawi*.'
I could not control myself, and stood up in the centre of the hall and
shouted something like this: 'O people, or can I call you Muslims!
These are forbidden acts, which one has no right either to look at or to
pass over in silence, for to do so is to accept them. To those who commit them God's word applies, "They have made their religion a joke and
a plaything." I have done what I was obliged to do; now take your
leave, and may God pardon you.' Then I left the place and retraced my
footsteps quickly to the city; as I was going I looked back, and found
behind me a small number who had returned, while the greater number
stayed on. . . .[7]

The suspicion of Sufism thus generated was one of the factors
which in later years was to draw him nearer to the teachings of
Ibn Taymiyya and the practices of Wahhabism, but at the time

[7] Ibid. pp. 171–2.

of which he was writing he knew Ibn Taymiyya only through the works of his opponents, and nothing about the Wahhabis except for the orthodox condemnation of them and such tales as that they stabled their horses in the Prophet's mosque.[8]

No less powerful than this revulsion from the mysticism of his time was the attraction exercised on him by al-Afghani and 'Abduh as soon as he came to know their ideas. He has recorded that his first acquaintance with the *'Urwa al-wuthqa* was in 1884–5, the time of its first appearance. He heard some articles from it read aloud by Egyptian political exiles who were then staying with his family, and at about the same time he met 'Abduh when the latter visited Tripoli.[9] But it was not until almost ten years later, in 1892–3, that he discovered a complete set of the *'Urwa*, and the effect was profound:

I found several copies of the journal among my father's papers, and every number was like an electric current striking me, giving my soul a shock, or setting it in a blaze, and carrying me from one state to another. . . . My own experience and that of others, and history, have taught me that no other Arabic discourse in this age or the centuries which preceded it has done what it did in the way of touching the seat of emotion in the heart and persuasion in the mind.[10]

He thought for a time of going to join al-Afghani in Constantinople, but this plan came to nothing, and the influence of al-Afghani upon him was soon overshadowed by that of 'Abduh. In 1894 'Abduh visited Tripoli again; Rashid Rida met him once more and talked at length to him. From that moment until his death he was 'Abduh's liege man: the mouthpiece of his ideas, the guardian of his good name, and his biographer. There were, it is true, others of 'Abduh's disciples who cast doubt on Rashid Rida's claim to be his spiritual heir, and, as we shall see, the doctrines of 'Abduh suffered a certain change at the hands of his follower, but the reality of his devotion cannot be doubted. In 1897 he left Syria for Cairo, and the next year he published the first number of a periodical, *al-Manar*, which was to be the organ of reform according to the ideas of 'Abduh. He continued to publish it more or less regularly until he died in 1935, and indeed there is a sense in which, from the time of its foundation, the *Manar* was his life. Into it he poured his reflections on the

[8] *al-Manar wa'l-Azhar*, p. 179. [9] Rida, *Ta'rikh*, i. 390. [10] Ibid. p. 303.

spiritual life, his explanations of doctrine, his endless polemics, violent alike in attack and defence, all the news that came to him from the corners of the Muslim world, his thoughts on world politics, and the great commentary on the Quran (*Tafsir al-Manar*), based on 'Abduh's lectures and writings, carried farther by 'Abduh's disciple but never finished. His other activities were numerous, it is true. He wrote a number of books: some were collections of articles first published in *al-Manar*, but others were new and important—above all his life of 'Abduh, the most important source for the history of the Muslim Arab mind in the late nineteenth century. He put into practice an idea which was dear to 'Abduh and created a seminary for Muslim missionaries and spiritual directors (*dar al-da'wa wa'l-irshad*): after he had failed to set it up in Constantinople under the auspices of the Young Turks he finally started it in Cairo in 1912, but it was only active until the beginning of the war of 1914. He took an important part in Islamic politics, and attended the Islamic conferences of Mecca in 1926 and Jerusalem in 1931. As a Syrian, he remained on the margin of Egyptian politics, but as the mouthpiece of 'Abduh was not uninvolved in them. His relations with the Khedive 'Abbas Hilmi were bad while the khedive was on bad terms with 'Abduh, but grew better later. Like 'Abduh, he wrote a severe criticism of Muhammad 'Ali, and by implication of the whole line of policy followed by his family, during the centenary celebrations,[11] but later the khedive gave financial support to the seminary. This change, and also his good relations with 'Ali Yusuf, were connected with his opposition to Mustafa Kamil and the nationalists of his party; 'Ali Yusuf, he thought, was a man of integrity and independent judgement, Mustafa Kamil was not.[12] He played a larger part in the political struggles of Syria, from the Young Turk Revolution until his death: in the Party of Decentralization before 1914, the wartime negotiations with the British, as president of the Syrian Congress of 1920, as member of the Syro-Palestinian delegation in Geneva in 1921, and of the political committee in Cairo during the Syrian revolt of 1925-6. But all such activities were no more than by-products of his essential work as guardian of the ideas of Muhammad 'Abduh.

In general, the view of Islam held by Rashid Rida and his

[11] *al-Manar*, v (1902-3), 157 ff., 175 ff.   [12] Ibid. xvii (1913-14), 68 ff.

friends was that expounded by al-Afghani and 'Abduh. It starts from the question, 'Why are the Muslim countries backward in every aspect of civilization?' and answers it in terms of the essential connexion, in Islam although not necessarily in other religions, between religious truth and worldly prosperity. The teachings and moral precepts of Islam are such that, if they are properly understood and fully obeyed, they will lead to success in this world as well as the next—and to success in all the forms in which the world understands it, strength, respect, civilization, happiness. If they are not understood and obeyed, weakness, decay, barbarism are the results. This is true not only of individuals but of communities: the Islamic *umma* was the heart of the world's civilization so long as it was truly Islamic. Now, in science and civilization, Muslims are more backward than non-Muslims: it is not necessary to compare the Muslims of the Near East with the Christians of Europe, it is enough to compare them with the eastern Christians who live among them. After a century of modern education, how many men of independent judgement are there in Egypt, and how many are there among the Indian Muslims compared with the Hindus and Parsees? The reason for this backwardness is that the Muslims have lost the truth of their religion, and this has been encouraged by bad political rulers, for the true Islam involves two things, acceptance of the unity of God and consultation in matters of State, and despotic rulers have tried to make Muslims forget the second by encouraging them to abandon the first.[13] But what happened in the past can happen again: Islamic civilization was created out of nothing by the Quran and the moral precepts enshrined in it, and can be re-created if Muslims return to the Quran. It is irrelevant to say that modern civilization rests on technical advance, and that Islamic civilization cannot be revived so long as the Muslims are technically backward; technical skill is potentially universal, and its acquisition depends on certain moral habits and intellectual principles. If Muslims had these, they would easily obtain technical skill; and such habits and principles are in fact contained in Islam.[14]

What are the principles which are contained alike in Islam and in modern civilization? First of all comes activity: positive effort is the essence of Islam, and this is the meaning of the

[13] *al-Manar*, ix (1906–7), 357 ff.　　　[14] Arslan, *Limadha*, pp. 82 ff.

term *jihad* in its most general sense.[15] The Europeans have this dynamism more than anyone else in the modern world, and that is why they have conquered the world: they are willing to sacrifice their lives and money for their nation, they have a loyalty which none of them will betray, they have in brief that fanatical devotion which is the basis of the strength of nations.[16] All this the Muslims once had and can have again, but in a different way. The Europeans are active and successful because they have abandoned their other-worldly religion and replaced it by the principle of nationality, but Muslims can find such a principle of unity and loyalty in their religion itself. For the second distinguishing sign of Islam is that it has created a single community: not simply a Church, a body of men linked by faith and worship yet separated by their natural characteristics, but a community in every sense. The long history of the caliphate, the spread of a common culture, and many centuries of mingling and intermarriage, have created an *umma* which is both a Church and a kind of 'nation': it is held together by unity of religion, of law, by equality and mutual rights and duties, but also by natural links, and in particular that of language, since Arabic is the universal language of devotion, doctrine, and law wherever Islam exists.[17]

It is impossible indeed to exaggerate the importance of unity for these writers, and the scandal of disunity. But when they talked of unity, they did not mean a unity based on feeling or tradition alone. They were aware, as al-Afghani had been, how transient and unstable such a merely affective unity could be, and how dangerous when not transient. Nor did they mean that unity should express itself necessarily in the form of a single Muslim State; we shall see later what type and degree of political union Rashid Rida thought to be possible. Islamic unity meant for them, in essence, the agreement of hearts of those who accepted each other as believers and dwelt together in mutual tolerance, and the active co-operation of all in carrying out the commandments of religion. The community which was so constituted held authority from God: this was witnessed by the *hadith*, 'My community will not agree upon an error'. In so far

---

[15] Ibid. p. 19.
[16] Ibid. p. 87.
[17] Rida, *al-Wahy al-muhammadi*, pp. 225 ff.

as any human being exercised authority in it, it was 'those who have the power to bind and loose', a vague phrase which may mean, in general, those who have responsibility for the unity and continuity of the *umma*, or more precisely the doctors of the law and the holders of political power.

But unity is necessarily connected with truth: there can be no real agreement between Muslims unless they are all agreed on the truth, and conversely agreement is a sign of truth. Possession of the truth is the third and most fundamental sign of Islam, and the true Islam is that which was taught by the Prophet and the 'Elders' (*salaf*): a comparatively simple, easily intelligible system of doctrines and practices of which the knowledge is contained in the Quran and the tradition of what the Prophet and his companions said and how they lived. It was fully revealed in the lifetime of the Prophet, who himself proclaimed, in the 'Pilgrimage of Farewell': 'Today I have perfected your religion for you, and I have completed My blessing upon you, and approved Islam for your religion'. Thus the Islam of the 'Elders' is that of the first generation who had known Muhammad, and the only *ijma* which is valid is that of this generation.[18]

Here there is a difference from the teaching of 'Abduh, and it is one which is significant of Rida's mind and method. When 'Abduh talked of the *salaf*, he meant in a general way the creators of the central tradition of Muslim thought and devotion, from the Prophet to al-Ghazali. Either because of a certain vagueness in his concepts, or from a sense of the overriding importance of unity, he had been content to construct a synthesis of elements which might prove incompatible with one another if any of them were carried to its logical conclusion. But Rashid Rida had the spirit of a disciple as well as a certain intellectual force and clarity which made him more rigid in his formulations than 'Abduh had been, and so, in spite of his emphasis on unity, more exclusive. Because of this, the Sunni element in his thought is more prominent than in that of 'Abduh, still more than in that of al-Afghani (who, as we have seen, was probably himself a Shi'i). He believed that unity between Sunnis and Shi'is was essential, and that it rested on two conditions: the first, that the two sects should co-operate in those matters on which they agreed and pardon each other for those about which

[18] Quran, v. 5 (Arberry's trs.); Rida, *Muhawarat*, p. 58.

they differed, and the second, that when an adherent of one sect
maligned the other he should be answered by a member of his
own group.[19] These are fine sentiments, but when disagreement
broke out or unity could not be achieved, he was quick to lay
the blame on the Shi'is and ascribe base motives to those of their
leaders who had incurred his anger: Shi'ism was full of 'fairy
tales and illegitimate innovations';[20] its leaders were preventing
unity from selfish love of money and glory; it sprang from a
doctrinal difference which did not exist in the time of the *salaf*,
and was largely owing to the machinations of the first Jewish
converts to Islam. (The accusation that early Jewish converts
introduced legends and false ideas into the body of the faith is
common in polemical writings of the classical age.) It is not
surprising that his relations with Shi'i writers were not devoid of
tension.

He interpreted Sunnism in the direction of strict Hanbalism,
of which the tradition was more alive in Syria, particularly in
Damascus, than in Egypt. Although he differed from Ibn
Taymiyya in some ways, he derived perhaps as much from his
teachings as from those of al-Ghazali, and through the *Manar*
published a number of his works. Sympathy with Hanbalism
led him, in later life, to give enthusiastic support to the revival
of Wahhabism in central Arabia, and to the policy of its leader,
'Abd al-Aziz ibn Sa'ud. He welcomed the Wahhabi conquest of
the Hejaz and the holy cities, and defended them against charges
of heresy. Their doctrines, he declared, were wholly orthodox.
Their religion was that of the original Muslims; although they
rejected all idea of a superhuman status for Muhammad they
thought of him as having the highest rank among human beings,
and in regard to the saints they objected not to the idea that they
performed exceptional works but to the tendency of the ignorant
to give them the worship they owed to God alone.[21] Ibn Sa'ud
indeed was maintaining and defending the essential principles
of Sunnism better than almost anyone since the first four
caliphs.[22] (It was natural that his enemies should hint that he
had been bought by Ibn Sa'ud: defending himself against this
charge, he said that it was not personal contact but reading and
thought which had caused him to give up his early view that

[19] Rida, *al-Sunna wa'l-Shi'a*, ii. 208 ff.   [20] Ibid. i. 23.
[21] Cf. Rida, *al-Wahhabiyyun*.   [22] Rida, *al-Sunna wa'l-Shi'a*, p. 79.

Wahhabis were an innovating sect; it was only later that he
established contact with Ibn Sa'ud, and even then it was only
on the political level, as part of a plan he had to bring about a
union of Arab rulers against foreign interference.)[23]

Like 'Abduh, Rashid Rida disliked the later development of
mystical thought and practice in Sunni Islam. Like him, he
drew a distinction between the true mysticism and the false. It
was legitimate and indeed necessary that the Muslim should add
to sound doctrine and good acts according to the *Shari'a* something else: 'Truthfulness and sincerity and the making of resolutions and the examination of conscience'.[24] But it was bad when
this led to the development of a false theology and of practices
not sanctioned by the *Shari'a*. There were spiritual dangers in
this kind of mysticism: an excessive submission towards a
shaykh might come between the soul and God; the spiritual
liturgies invented by the orders could lead to neglect of the forms
of worship directly commanded by God in the Quran; the
practice of calling up spirits had dangerous doctrinal implications.
'Abduh would have agreed with this, but it is perhaps typical of
Rida that he casts doubt on the motives of the mystics. This sort
of mysticism, he says, (echoing once more a theme of earlier
polemics), was introduced into Islam by secret Zoroastrians who
wished

to corrupt the religion of the Arabs and pull down the pillars of their
kingdom by internal dissension, so that by this means they could
restore the rule of the Zoroastrians and the domination of their religion
to which the Arabs had put an end in Islam.[25]

There is also a practical criticism of the mystics common to
Rida and his friends. The Sufis are a weakness to society as
well as a danger to religion. They neglect their duties in the
world, studying things which are of no value,[26] and they corrupt
the *umma* by teaching that Islam is a religion of passive submission not strength and activity; their festivals can be an
occasion for drunkenness, drug-taking, and other kinds of
immorality.[27]

Rashid Rida's emphasis on the unchanging nature of Islam
does not, however, mean that his thought is rigid, for, like the

---

[23] *al-Manar*, xxviii (1927–8), 1 ff.   [24] Ibid. xxii (1920–1), 177.
[25] Ibid. p. 177.   [26] Maghribi, *al-Bayyinat*, i. 55.
[27] Kurd 'Ali, *Mudhakkirat*, iv. 1014.

Hanbalis, he distinguishes between what belongs to the essence of Islam and what does not: what is laid down in the Quran and the authentic *hadith* is one thing, the accumulation of practices and traditions which has grown up around them is another. This distinction is connected with another: between acts of worship and those of morality, acts oriented towards God and those oriented towards other men. The first have been laid down for ever and completely in Quran and *hadith*; they can never be changed, and no addition can be made to them; so far as they are concerned, the *ijma'* of the first generation, of those who knew the Prophet and heard his words, is binding. Likewise in matters of personal religious habits, not covered by any strict religious obligation and not involving relations with others, it is usually best for Muslims to follow the example of the early Muslims as laid down in the *hadith*, for to do so will strengthen the bonds of the community; but they should do so freely, as a spontaneous act of conscience, and no one should put pressure on them.[28] But the whole complex structure of human relations has not and cannot be regulated in the same way by explicit texts. When there does exist such a text, precise, explicit, admitting of no ambiguity, well authenticated, then there is no argument, and men must obey it. But to this, two qualifications must be added. First, when a specific command is contradicted by a general one, laying down some such general moral principle as that no injury should be done (*la darar wa la dirar*), or that necessity permits what would otherwise be forbidden (*al-dururat tubih al-mahzurat*), then the principle should be preferred to the specific injunction.[29] Secondly, there are many problems in regard to which there is either no text at all, or else one of which the meaning is not clear or the authenticity doubtful. In such matters, it is for human reason to decide what act best accords with the spirit of Islam. In so deciding, human reason must be guided by the principle of interest, interpreted in the light of the general principles laid down in the Quran and *hadith*.

As we have seen, the principle of interest was not new to the Islamic jurists, and Rashid Rida is able to quote Ibn Qayyim al-Jawziyya, Ibn Taymiyya, and others to support him. In some ways, however, he goes beyond his masters, at least by making explicit what was half-hidden in their writings. For the traditional

[28] Rida, *Yusr al-Islam*, p. 79.   [29] Rida, *Muhawarat*, p. 126.

thought, *maslaha* had been a subordinate principle, a guide in the process of reasoning by analogy rather than a substitute for it. For Rashid Rida, it tends to become itself the positive principle of decision, replacing analogy; and other commands or prohibitions, whether specific or general, have rather a negative function, of laying down the limits within which reason shall work. Since interests vary according to circumstances, the implications of this are far-reaching: what Rashid Rida is saying in fact is that there is and can be no *ijma'*, even that of the first generation, in matters of social morality; or, in other words, that the Muslim community has legislative power. The rulers of the community have not only the executive and judicial powers, they can legislate in the public interest. Thus there can be a body of 'positive law' (*qanun*) subordinate to the *Shari'a* in the sense that if there is conflict it is the latter which is valid, but otherwise independent and with a binding force which derives ultimately from the general principles of Islam; for it is not only the right but the duty of a Muslim nation to give itself 'a system of just laws appropriate to the situation in which its past history has placed it'.[30]

This does not mean, of course, that every Muslim is free to exercise his own judgement and create his own system of rules. The creation and change of social morality and law is the function of 'those who have power to bind and loose': those who have authority in the *umma* or its political divisions, or, to put it in another way, those who have responsibility towards Islam. When he uses this phrase, Rashid Rida is thinking, like the jurists of later Islam after the caliphate broke up, of a partnership between the two types of authority: the just and devout Muslim ruler and the real '*ulama*', those who have the personal qualifications to exercise *ijtihad*. The making of laws, like all the functions of government, should be exercised by consultation (*shura*) between them. But here again the modern note is present. He thinks of the '*ulama*' as an organized body, of the *shura* as a deliberate process, and of the law which it produces as springing from some sort of formal procedure. In other words, having rejected the old conception of *ijma'*, he is introducing a new one: the *ijma'* of the '*ulama*' of each age, a legislative rather than a judicial principle, working by some sort of parliamentary process.

[30] Rida, *al-Khilafa*, p. 90 (Fr. trs. p. 151).

It is Rashid Rida's contention that this is the original conception of legislation in Islam. In course of time it was obscured:
in every age some of the doctors of the law still remembered it,
but except for the greatest they were silenced by fear of the
government, while others lost sight of the distinction between
what was essential and what was not. Thus there crept into
Islam that disease to which he refers sometimes as congealment
(*jumud*) and sometimes as blind imitation (*taqlid*). In the sphere
of law this takes the form of slavish obedience to one or other of
the four recognized legal schools, and as an example of this he
mentions that the *Shaykh al-Islam*, the highest judicial authority
of the Ottoman Empire, refused to give judicial opinions or
allow his muftis to do so in regard to the new code of civil
law, the *Mecelle* (ar. *Majalla*), promulgated by the government
and which, although based on the Hanafi system, incorporated
in it certain changes which did not have the authority of its
founder.

Stagnation and imitation are always bad, but they are more
dangerous than before, now that the Muslim countries are faced
with a new civilization and therefore the need for new laws.
Among Rashid Rida's friends were some who welcomed the
modern civilization of Europe as valuable in itself. Kurd 'Ali,
for example, was full of admiration for what he saw on his
journeys to the west and generous to acknowledge what the
Arabs had learnt, what they could still learn, from it: social
reform, equality before the law, freedom of thought, the importance of national solidarity, above all the virtue of activity.[31]
Rashid Rida, however, was less moved by admiration than by
the thought of necessity. He belonged to the last generation of
those who could be fully educated and yet alive in a self-
sufficient Islamic world of thought. His master 'Abduh had had
close and easy personal relations with a number of Europeans
and had travelled more than once in Europe. Rida went once
only, and then for a specific political purpose; he seems to have
read little or nothing in European languages; he had close contact with one European only, the Under-Secretary of State for
Finance, Alfred Mitchell-Innes, and it is difficult to imagine
what they could have talked about.[32] He disliked the social life

[31] Kurd 'Ali, *Masadir*, pp. 83–84, 111.
[32] Cf. Rida, *al-Manar wa'l-Azhar*, p. 195.

of Europeans, and his references to Christianity were usually hostile; if it were not for the Church, for the politicians, and for the inner decay of Islam itself, Europe, he thought, might well become Muslim.[33] But with his robust sense he recognized the challenge of the modern world, and wanted Islam to accept the new civilization so far, and only so far, as it was essential for a recovery of strength. Always coherent and logical in his thought, he justified this by reference to a principle of Islam. The *jihad* is a binding duty for Muslims, but it is a duty which cannot be performed unless they are strong, and in the modern world they cannot be strong unless they acquire the sciences and techniques of the west. What is an indispensable condition for performing a duty is itself a duty; it is therefore a duty for Muslims to study the sciences and ways of the modern world.[34] He echoes here a thought which had first been expressed by Tahtawi and Khayr al-Din: in accepting European civilization, the Muslims are only accepting what had once been theirs, for Europe had only progressed because of what they had learnt from the Muslims in Spain and the Holy Land.[35]

Because of this new need, the change in law must be greater than ever before. It involves more than a modification of the four existing systems: in fact, the development of a new and unified system. Again and again Rashid Rida urges the *'ulama'* of his time to come together in order to produce a book of laws based on the Quran and *hadith* but in accordance with the needs of the age: it should be free from ambiguity, easy for all believers to understand. At the beginning of each chapter dealing with social morality, it should show clearly what is an article of faith, based on texts, and what is a deduction of human reason. In this way, it would be 'a living refutation of all those who advocate slothfulness in law and religion'.[36] He is not, however, suggesting a complete abandonment of the four traditional schools, but rather a gradual approximation and amalgamation of them. Like 'Abduh he appeals to the principle of *talfiq*, but he wants it to be applied more systematically than before. The use of it, he argues, is not condemned by a consensus of jurists, and it is not in itself contrary to reason or the principles of Islam. *Talfiq* is

[33] Rida, *al-Wahy*, pp. 19 ff.
[34] Rida, *al-Khilafa*, pp. 29–30.
[35] Cf. Jomier, pp. 120–1.
[36] *al-Manar*, x (1907–8), 234; Rida, *Muhawarat*, p. 131.

only wrong when it is used in an uncritical way: to accept blindly
a decision of another legal school is as bad as to accept blindly a
decision of one's own school. But when *talfiq* is used in a rational
way, it is a kind of *ijtihad*, and as such is legitimate in itself.[37]

Much of his thought was given to sketching the outlines of the
new system of law: in separate treatises on specific points, in
his commentary on the Quran, above all in his *fatwas* in the
Manar. A special section of each issue was given to answers to
questions of morality and practice sent in by the readers of the
periodical—and perhaps sometimes contributed by the editor
himself. There is scarcely any problem in the moral life of the
community which is not touched on somewhere in the *Manar*,
and here it will only be possible to take a few examples which
show to what extent, but also within what limits, Rashid Rida
rejected the traditional position in favour of one more in accord
with 'the spirit of the age'. In regard to apostasy, for example,
he gave up the traditional view that the Muslim who abandoned
Islam should necessarily be put to death. Instead, he made a
distinction between the apostate who revolts against Islam and is
therefore a danger to the *umma*, and him who abandons it quietly
and as an individual: the first should be put to death if captured,
the second not. His reasoning in favour of this conclusion shows
the principles of his thought. The condemnation of the apostate
to death is supported, it is true, by the unanimous *ijma'* of the
jurists; but one must go beyond this, and ask if the *ijma'* is based
on a clear text of the Quran or not. In this case, there is no text of
the Quran stating that all apostates should be killed; on the
contrary, there is a text condemning all compulsion in religion
(*la ikrah fi'l-din*). The *ijma'* is therefore in contradiction with
the principles of Islam, and must be rejected.[38]

Similarly in regard to the *jihad*, the duty to wage war against
non-Muslims: Rashid Rida admits its necessity but defines the
limits within which it is legitimate. Once more, one must
distinguish: between a war to spread Islam and a war to defend
it. The second is always lawful, the first only when the peaceful
preaching of Islam is forbidden, or Muslims are not allowed to
live in accordance with their law. To use force to compel the
'people of the Book' to become Muslims would infringe this
same principle of freedom in the faith.[39]

[37] *Muhawarat*, p. 84.   [38] Jomier, p. 290.   [39] Ibid. pp. 272 ff.

In both these matters, Rashid Rida was drawing out the clear
implications of the principles of his two masters, but when he
talked of economic life he made perhaps a more startling break
with tradition. Islamic law prohibits the taking of interest: Rida
was convinced that this was the best system, but he pointed out
that Islam was faced with a danger such as it had not known in
the days when the structure of law grew up—the danger of
economic penetration and domination by the western capitalism.
The principle of necessity can therefore be invoked: necessity
makes legal what would otherwise be forbidden, and in this
case it may compel Muslims to depart from their traditional
interpretation of the law and build their economic life on the
same basis as the western nations:

At all times, wealth has been a mainstay of the life of peoples and
States. In our days, it has taken on an importance such as it never had
before, in particular in the time of the Prophet, when nations, having
no more than limited needs, did not depend for their livelihood upon
traffic with other nations. But God, to whom nothing is secret, in
His wisdom and power revealed this truth in the time of the Prophet:
'Do not give to fools your property that God has assigned to you to
manage' [Quran, iv. 4].[40] In this way God has made us understand how
important is wealth in the life and organization of peoples and how
necessary it is for them. . . . Can one maintain that the law of this
religion demands that its adherents should be poor, and that what is
essential for their livelihood and for the power of their community and
State should be in the hands of covetous men belonging to other
peoples?[41]

The limits of his sympathy with the modern world, and the
strength of his roots in tradition, were shown most clearly
perhaps in his discussion of the rights of women, a contribution
to the discussion started by Qasim Amin. Muslim women
ought to take part in the communal life of Islam, as they had
done in the great days. Their faith is just the same as that of men
and so also are their religious duties, and their social duties in
so far as they are derived from the principles of religion. There
is thus an equality of rights, but there is an inequality of fact, for
men are stronger, more intelligent, more apt for learning and
most types of action. So they have a predominance over women;
but, like that of the ruler over the State, it should be exercised

---

[40] Arberry's trs.   [41] Rida, *al-Khilafa*, p. 98 (Fr. trs. p. 164).

not despotically but by consultation. In this, they should learn from the example of the Prophet, who in his treatment of his wives was the perfect man. His polygamy was just because it was in the interest of the community; indeed, polygamy is always justified if it does not contradict the principle of justice and if there are advantages derived from it. Slavery also is not necessarily in conflict with justice: it protects women from harm and gives all of them a chance to bear children. The principle of Islamic law, so far as women are concerned, is

that every woman should have a legal guardian, to give her all she needs to be an honourable virgin, a virtuous wife, a careful mother, and a respected grandmother. She who is prevented from being wife or mother is not thereby prevented from enjoying protection and honour.[42]

The need to create a system of law which people could really obey in the modern world—which should therefore be law in the real sense, just as it should be Islamic in the real sense—was at the centre of all Rida's thought. It was one of the factors which led him in the direction of Hanbalism, which combines great rigidity of principle with great flexibility of application. (In Saudi Arabia, Hanbali law is still the basis of the legal system, and there alone there has not grown up 'the same distinction between religious Islamic and modern statutory law as in other Islamic countries in the Near East'.)[43] But law, he believed, implies an authority to maintain and enforce it; by its nature Islam is a religion of 'sovereignty and politics and government',[44] and Islamic law cannot be reformed unless the Islamic polity is remade. There is such a thing as a truly Islamic political system: it is based, in Rida's view, on consultation between the ruler and the guardians and interpreters of the law. If it is to be restored, two things are necessary: real '*ulama*', and a real Islamic ruler— in other words, a true caliph.

There are some obscure points in Rida's doctrine of the caliphate. He certainly did not want the caliph to be an absolute ruler; it is not clear how far he wished him to be a temporal ruler at all, and if so what would be his relations with other Muslim rulers, for he certainly did not think it possible to reunite all parts

---

[42] Rida, *Nida' ila'l-jins al-latif*, p. 121.
[43] Schacht, 'Islamic Law in Contemporary States', *Am. J. Comp. Law*, VIII (1959), 138.
[44] Rida, *al-Wahy*, p. 239.

of the *umma* into a single State. His view of the essential function
of the caliph however is clear: it is not to rule, it is to make laws
and watch over their application. The caliph should be the
supreme practitioner of *ijtihad*, the great *mujtahid*: a man
capable by intelligence and special training and with the aid of
the *'ulama'*, of applying the principles of Islam to the changing
needs of the world, and capable. by the respect in which he is
held, of imposing the results of this process on the Muslim
governments: for while, in matters of private morality, a man
should follow his own conscience, in matters of public interest
the *ijtihad* of the caliph should prevail over all others.[45] Only if
such a caliph existed could a real Islamic society exist. He alone
could re-establish the authentic Muslim consultative government, taking counsel with those who bind and loose in questions
which are not the subject of a text in the Quran, an authentic
hadith or *ijma'*, or a previous formal act of *ijtihad*. He alone could
restore Islamic civilization, and graft on to it the sciences and
techniques necessary for national power and prosperity; could
restore the purity of religion and drive out superstition and innovation; and could create an Islamic unity which would include
Shi'is, Zaydis, Ibadis, as well as Sunnis of all four legal schools.[46]

During the first half of Rida's career the Ottoman Empire still
existed and the sultan claimed to be caliph. He and his friends
were not then opposed to the existence of the empire, and indeed
thought it necessary for the Arab and Muslim peoples, since it
alone could provide the strength which they needed to protect
them against foreign pressure. For this reason he was opposed
to the idea, which was already in the air, of founding a new
caliphate to replace that of the Ottomans; this idea, he thought,
was of foreign inspiration and would serve only foreign interests.[47] The Ottoman caliphate could be accepted then as a
'caliphate of necessity', but it was not a real caliphate. The
Ottoman sultans did not possess one of the essential conditions
of *ijtihad*, which was knowledge of the Arabic language, the only
language in which the doctrines and laws of Islam could be
thought about, and in other ways too they were incapable of
ijtihad.[48]

[45] Rida, *al-Khilafa*, p. 79 (Fr. trs. pp. 132–3).
[46] Ibid. p. 105 (Fr. trs. p. 178).
[47] Cf. Maghribi, *al-Bayyinat*, i. 87.
[48] Rida, *Muhawarat*, pp. 94–95.

After the war of 1914–18 the situation changed: the sultan fell under the control of England and France, who had occupied Constantinople, and then was deposed by Mustafa Kemal. For the next few years the problem of the caliphate occupied thinkers all over the Muslim world, and neither Rida's concern for Islam nor his polemical tendencies would have allowed him to stand aside. He took part in the great controversy aroused by 'Abd al-Raziq's book, which he denounced vigorously in the pages of *al-Manar*. The danger of views such as 'Abd al-Raziq's, he said, was that they could be made use of by the enemies of Islam. These enemies fought with ideas as well as the sword; in particular, they were trying to cut the links which bound Muslim peoples to one another so that they would become 'a prey to the wild beasts of imperialism'; they were fighting a 'moral war' which would weaken Islam from within, and in such a war a book like this was a blow struck at Islam.[49] To the discussion he also contributed a long and comprehensive treatise on the caliphate. This was published at the time when the new Turkish government set up a figurehead of a caliph, without power and with purely 'spiritual' functions. Rida, like most other Muslims, did not approve of this act: it took no account of the purpose of the caliphate, which was to ensure the application of the *Shari'a*; it was no more than a political gesture, springing from national feeling and general Islamic feeling, and comparable to the political demonstrations organized in Egypt in favour of Zaghlul.[50] No real caliphate now existed, and it was necessary to restore one. But this could only be done in two stages: first, the establishment of a 'caliphate of necessity', to co-ordinate the efforts of Muslim countries against the foreign danger, and then, when the time was ripe, the restoration of a genuine caliphate of *ijtihad*. For both these tasks, however, certain conditions must be fulfilled. One was the restoration of good relations between Arabs and Turks, who together formed the central bloc of the Islamic world. For all the bitterness generated by the policy of the Young Turks and then the Arab revolt, Rida was convinced that Arabs and Turks needed each other and the *umma* needed both. The Arabs had preserved the true spirit of Islam, and the knowledge of Arabic; the Turks alone had the political cohesion

---

[49] *al-Manar*, xxvi (1925–6), 100.
[50] Rida, *al-Khilafa*, p. 67 (Fr. trs. p. 114).

and power of leadership which the *umma* needed.[51] Rida had at that time a great admiration for Mustafa Kemal: a great man, he remarked, who unfortunately knew nothing about Islam. If he had known what Islam really was, he would have been just the man who was needed.[52]

The other condition was more important still: it was, that 'those who bind and loose' should work together actively for the restoration of the caliphate:

The *umma* as a whole is responsible for [restoring the imamate], for it is sovereign in this matter, as we have shown above. The representatives of the *umma*, 'those who bind and loose', must work actively to this end, as it is they who are responsible for all the interests of the *umma*, and for the question of the supreme authority in particular. They are the guides and leaders of the *umma*: it trusts them in matters of knowledge and action and essential interest, and follows them in what they decide in respect of things religious and worldly.[53]

But where were such people to be found? They could scarcely be found among the Muslim nations which were subject to the European Powers, since among them leaders usually represented only the foreign authority which had appointed them (although of course there were exceptions like 'Abduh and his 'spiritual son' Zaghlul in Egypt, Gandhi and Maulana Abul Kalam Azad in India). Nothing much could be hoped for from the recognized religious institutions, the great homes of learning like the Azhar in Cairo, the Zaytuna mosque in Tunis, or the Deoband seminary in India. Their social and political standing had been destroyed by despotic governments, and their shaykhs were in no sense leaders of their people as were the great scholars of the Shi'i cities. At the other extreme, nothing could be expected of the 'westernizers' who had dominated public life for the last few generations; their principle was that religion was incompatible with modern society, and so they were creating institutions and laws which had no roots in Islam. In their view, national or racial sentiment should be the basis of law, not Islamic conviction; but in fact they were destroying the moral foundation of society.[54] Somewhere between the two extremes however stood

---

[51] *al-Khilafa*, pp. 70 ff. (Fr. trs. pp. 117 ff).
[52] Arslan, *Rashid Rida*, p. 315.
[53] Rida, *al-Khilafa*, pp. 57–58 (Fr. trs. p. 98).
[54] Ibid. pp. 62 ff. (Fr. trs. pp. 105 ff).

a middle group, the 'Islamic progressive party': they had the independence of mind necessary to understand at the same time the laws of Islam and the essence of modern civilization,[55] they would accept the changes which were necessary but relate them to valid principles, in other words they would reconcile change with the preservation of the moral basis of the community. They could only do this however if they were strong, that is to say, if they were united; and positive unity was more easily to be attained in the modern world than ever before. For the improvement of communications made it possible for men of like mind to meet each other: even a real *ijma'* was possible nowadays, since for the first time all the *'ulama'* of the age could be brought together in one place.[56]

Supposing these two conditions were fulfilled, what could be done? There were several ways, thought Rida, of setting up a temporary 'caliphate of necessity'. The rulers of the Arabian Peninsula might proclaim one of their number as caliph—for preference, the Imam of the Yemen, who possessed most of the qualifications required—; or Egypt could take the lead in nominating a caliph, since the other Arab countries liked to take their lead from Cairo; or the Turks might be persuaded to set up something more substantial than their puppet caliphate. However it was established, the question where its seat should be was important. It could not be in the Hejaz, because its ruler was dependent on a non-Muslim Power and also because of the character of the king and his family (we shall return to this later); it could scarcely be in Turkey because of the attitude of the government towards putting power in the hands of a caliph, and towards the Arabic language, and in spite of the arguments on the other side, the quality of leadership shown by the new Turkish government and the aptitude of the Turks for the arts of warfare; it might be in some intermediate place like Mosul, on the borderline between Turks, Arabs, and Kurds.[57] (At that time the fate of Mosul had not been settled: although it was administered as part of Iraq, the Turks were still putting forward a claim to it.)

This could only be the first step, however. At the same time, the 'Islamic progressive party' should set up a seminary to train

[55] Ibid. p. 62 (Fr. trs. p. 104).   [56] Ibid. p. 102 (Fr. trs. p. 172).
[57] Ibid. p. 78 (Fr. trs. p. 131).

real masters of *ijtihad*. The students should study the principles
of international law, universal history, sociology, the organization of religious institutions like the papacy, in a word, all the
subjects which were necessary for a valid application of Islam in
the modern world. So they would form a new body of *'ulama'*
who could preserve the fabric of the *Shari'a* and the unity of the
umma; but they would do more than that, for among them would
be Arabs of Qurayshi stock, and in the fullness of time one such
might be chosen by electors of all Muslim countries, and be
formally invested by 'those who bind and loose' as a genuine
caliph and restorer of that true Islamic government which was
the best of all.

It was the best for Muslims, Rida had no doubt; but was it
also the best for Christians and Jews living in Muslim countries?
He argued that it would be so. The position of minorities in an
Islamic State would be better than in a secular State, for an
Islamic State would be based on justice, on a law which gave
rights and freedom to Christians and Jews, while the secular
State was based on a purely natural solidarity which was not the
ground of a moral system. Justice created a link, while solidarity
divided: the hatred between those who worshipped their own
communities and had nothing else to worship was far worse than
between those who had different religions. If there had been
persecution in the Near East, it was because of the decline of
Islam; a proof of this was the outburst of hatred which followed
the revolution of the secularist Young Turks in 1908.[58]

[58] *al-Khilafa*, p. 108 (Fr. trs. p. 183).

X

CHRISTIAN SECULARISTS: SHUMAYYIL AND ANTUN

MUHAMMAD 'ABDUH and his followers had taken the common-places of European thought and applied them to their own society. The effect had been more drastic than 'Abduh himself perhaps had expected: an attempt to restate the principles of Islamic society had led to the idea of a secular national society where Islam was tolerated, was honoured, even helped to strengthen the affective links between fellow citizens, but no longer provided the norms of law and policy. A similar idea was being taught at the same time by another group of writers from among the Syrian Christians, although, being Christians and a minority, they gave it a rather different twist.

Shidyaq and Bustani had been the forerunners of a school of writers who found new scope for their talents through the growth of the Arabic periodical press. In the 1870's two new types of publication began to appear in Arabic: the independent political newspaper, giving news of world politics and expressing political opinions, and—what most concerns us here—the literary and scientific periodical, with the double purpose of revealing to the Arab mind the ideas and inventions of Europe and America, and showing how they could be written about in Arabic. The greater number of these, whether they were published in Cairo or Beirut, were written by Lebanese Christians educated in the French or American schools; and since for a whole generation they provided almost the only popular reading-matter in Arabic, they gave the Lebanese an influence over the Arabic-reading public great although short-lived.

The first important periodical of this type was *al-Jinan*, appearing under the name of Butrus al-Bustani but written largely by his son Salim. It was published for sixteen years, from 1870 to 1886, and finally ceased to appear because of the growing difficulties of writing freely under the rule of Abdülhamid. It was the same reason which led many of the disciples of Bustani to move from Beirut to Cairo, where the growth of a reading public, the comparative freedom of expression, and the patronage of such men as Riaz Pasha exercised a power of attraction. Of these Lebanese-Egyptian periodicals, the most famous were *al-Muqtataf*, founded in 1876, and *al-Hilal* which first appeared in 1892. The former was started in Beirut by two young teachers of the Syrian Protestant College, Ya'qub Sarruf and Faris Nimr. In 1885 they moved to Cairo, where *al-Muqtataf* continued to be published for half a century with a formula which in essence remained unchanged. To take an example at random: the issue of January 1896 contained articles on infectious diseases, microbes in the air, and the differences between men and women; a philosophical analysis of man's position among the animals; an article on the administration of Lebanon under Rustum Pasha (one of the governors appointed under the arrangement of 1861); a summary of a report by an American commission on the bases of education; a collection of sayings about the dove drawn from Arabic literature; shorter notes about new industrial and agricultural methods and scientific discoveries, and extracts from articles in the foreign press.

The founder of *al-Hilal*, Jurji Zaydan (1861–1914), had also studied for a time at the Syrian Protestant College, but was less deeply marked by it and had a different cast of mind. He paid less attention to the natural sciences, more to ethics and sociology, world politics, geography and history, and the language, literature, and antiquities of the Arabs. To take an example once more: the issue for February 1913 published articles on the history of Lebanon, the siege of Damietta by the Crusaders, Macchiavelli and Ibn Khaldun; on education and the social order, age and ageing, and fatness and how to cure it; a description of the editor's visit to France, England, and Switzerland, and an instalment of his new historical novel on Saladin and the Assassins.

All this may seem without significance, and both periodicals tended to avoid anything bearing directly on local politics or religion, and which might stir up hostility. But behind them both, and others of the kind, there lay certain positive ideas about what truth was, how it should be sought, and what the Arabic reading public ought to know. That civilization was a good in itself, and to create and maintain it should be the criterion of

action and the norm of morality; that science was the basis of
civilization, and the European sciences were of universal value;
that they could and must be accepted by the Arab mind through
the medium of the Arabic language; that from the discoveries
of science there could be inferred a system of social morality
which was the secret of social strength; and that the basis of this
moral system was public spirit or patriotism, the love of country
and fellow countrymen which should transcend all other social
ties, even those of religion: it was largely through the work of
these periodicals that such ideas later became commonplace. In
the end *al-Muqtataf* died because its work was done, while
al-Hilal survived only by appealing to a different public. When
these ideas were first expounded it was with a missionary zeal,
and they were not received everywhere with approval. It is
recorded, for example, that when the first numbers of *al-Muqtataf*
arrived in Baghdad in 1876 the conservatives were opposed to it
in all communities, Sunni and Shi'i, Christian and Jewish,
because it preached new and dangerous doctrines, and only some
of the younger generation welcomed it. Even Nu'man al-Alusi,
leader of an Islamic reformism not dissimilar to that of Muhammad 'Abduh, opposed it, and it took some time for its doctrines
to spread.[1]

Such ideas were for the most part preached by implication,
but there were some among the Lebanese and Syrian writers
who tried to formulate in a connected way their view of society.
Perhaps the first was Fransis Marrash (1836–73), a member of
an Aleppine family who studied medicine in Paris. He died young
and left only a handful of writings, among them *Ghabat al-haqq*
(The Forest of Truth), an allegory mainly in the form of
dialogue, which raised the question of how to establish 'the
kingdom of civilization and freedom'.[2] The ideas of the book
are those of the advanced European thought of the time: the
benefits of peace, the importance of freedom and equality (there
is a denunciation of slavery, perhaps a reflection of the controversies of the American Civil War), and the need of the Arabs
for two things above all—modern schools and 'a love of country
free from religious considerations'.[3] There is also a discussion of
the meaning of civilization which shows how important the

---

[1] *al-Kitab al-dhahabi*, pp. 129 ff.   [2] Marrash, p. 15.
[3] Ibid. pp. 11 & 73.

I

concept was for him. Civilization is 'a law which guides man towards the perfection of his natural and moral conditions'.[4] It can exist only if certain conditions are fulfilled: the first of them is political education, and this means that the ruler must be properly trained for his position and possess the necessary qualities of mind and character, that all should be equal before the law without exception, that laws should be well suited to society, and that the general welfare should be the aim of government. But there are other conditions as well: the proper cultivation of the intellect, the improvement of social customs and morals, the cleanliness and good construction of cities.

The emphasis on hygiene is perhaps a reflection of Marrash's study of medicine in Paris; but he was there before the great revolution in biological thought effected by the theories of Darwin, and it was a writer of the next generation, also a Syrian Christian and also a doctor, who first introduced those theories to the Arab world. Shibli Shumayyil (1850–1917) was an early graduate of the medical school of the Syrian Protestant College, and then studied medicine in Paris before settling in Egypt, where he practised his craft and became a frequent contributor to the *Muqtataf* and other periodicals of the type. He also took an interest in public affairs, and in a small book addressed to Abdülhamid in 1896 (*Shakwa wa amal*) summed up his view of what was wrong with the Ottoman Empire: 'Three fundamental things are lacking: science, justice, and liberty'.[5]

For him, the greatest of the three, and indeed the basis of the others, was science. He belonged indeed to that great movement of the late nineteenth century for which science was more than a method of discovering regularities in the behaviour of objects: it was the key to the secret of the universe, even a mode of worship. For Shumayyil, science meant the metaphysical system constructed by Huxley and Spencer in England, Haeckel and Büchner in Germany, out of the cautious hypotheses of Darwin, and his main work was a translation of Büchner's commentary on Darwin, with notes and additions. The basis of this system was the idea of the unity of all being. All things are formed by spontaneous process from matter, which has existed from eternity and will exist for ever; at each stage the forms—

    [4] Marrash, p. 37.
    [5] Lecerf, 'Sibli Sumayyil', *Bull. d'ét. orientales*, i (1931), 153 ff.

mineral, plant, animal, human—are more differentiated and complex than at the last; each stage arises from the last without a break by the operation of forces inherent in matter itself and which themselves take different forms at different levels, so that what begins as light becomes movement, attraction, desire and love; man is the summit of the process, the first being who is able to control it and consciously to take part in it, by changing his outer circumstances and by replacing the struggle for existence with co-operation and the division of labour; and man is still in process of reaching his own perfection, the development of his intellectual powers, the replacement of conflict by co-operation, of coercion by voluntary organization, of selfish desire for one's own happiness by a striving for the happiness of the whole. This vision of the great chain of being, of the common ground and origin of all things and man as its final aim, stirred Shumayyil's sense of beauty and reverence as it did that of his generation in Europe and America. What, he asks, is more pleasant and useful than the knowledge of the transformation of matter with its forces, and to know that in the end all things are one? It cannot be an accident that he applies to the unity of nature the term used in Muslim theology to refer to the unity of God: *tawhid*.[6]

He proclaims his doctrine with all the fervour of a convert and a revolutionary, and indeed when he first made his translation of Büchner in the 1880's the theory still had the power to shock. There had been an incident only a few years earlier at the Syrian Protestant College, only a few years after Shumayyil had been a student there. The instructor in natural sciences, giving the 'commencement address' for 1882, appeared, in the words of a contemporary report, 'so distinctly to favor the theories of Darwin, that several of his associates and of the managers of the College were constrained to express alarm at the utterance of such views by a Professor of the Institution'. The matter was submitted to the Trustees, whose president expressed the opinion 'that neither the Board of Management, the Faculty nor the Board of Trustees would be willing to have anything that favors what is called "Darwinism" talked of or taught in the College'. The culprit offered his resignation, which was accepted. A number of other teachers resigned in protest; some of the medical students too showed their sympathy and were suspended, but

[6] Shumayyil, *Falsafat al-nushu'*, p. 30.

to return after making an apology.[7] Thus the historian of the College, but an oral tradition which still survives hints at the incident having been more violent and having left profound marks on those who witnessed it. Shumayyil himself refers to it,[8] and does not find it strange that such a statement should have met with such a response, for the religion of science was a declaration of war on older religions. Christianity, in his view, sprang from egoism: from the love of domination on the part of religious leaders, and the ordinary man's desire for individual survival. To grasp and acknowledge the vision of the unity of all matter would free men from the grip of egoism.[9]

The new religion also had vast social and political implications. For the natural sciences were the basis of the human sciences and sound laws could only be derived from valid human sciences. False sciences led to false laws and systems of government. Theocracy and despotism were not only wicked, they were unnatural and false: theocracy because it raised some men above others and used spiritual authority to prevent the true development of the human mind, autocracy because it denied the rights of the individual.[10] Both sprang from the false principle that individual advantage should be preferred to that of society as a whole, and both encouraged the mind to remain stagnant and so obstruct that gradual progress which is a law of the universe. It was possible, however, to conceive of a system of laws and government which was based on the laws of the universe, and which therefore enabled the universal process of development to continue and man to 'live in accordance with himself'. Such a system would spring from the same principles as the laws of nature: that all things were in process of differentiation and change, that the process took place by means of the struggle for existence, that those who survived in the struggle were those who were fittest to survive. But what constituted fitness to survive? Just as a body was best fitted to survive when all its parts functioned in perfect interdependence, so a society functioned best when all its parts worked together for the good of the whole. Co-operation was the supreme law of society; it followed that laws and institutions could not be regarded as infallible or unchanging, only as arrangements for social life, to be

[7] Penrose, pp. 43–44. [8] *Falsafat al-nushu'*, p. 25.
[9] Ibid. p. 43. [10] Ibid. p. 10.

judged according to how they contributed to social welfare, and
to be changed when the conditions of welfare changed.[11] Such
change should however be gradual: in some circumstances indeed
violent revolution was necessary, because in no other way could
poison be expelled from the system, but on the whole the only
reforms which could succeed were those which sprang from a
change in the general will and aimed at the general good.[12] But
there could be no agreement on the general good unless there
was liberty, in particular liberty of thought: in a despotism, one
member and his interests dominated the rest by force. Nor
could there be a general will unless there was an underlying
social unity, and this in its turn involved the separation of
religion from political life. Religion was a factor of division: not
religion itself, but the religious leaders, sowed discord between
men, and this kept societies weak. Nations grew stronger as
religion grew weaker.[13] This was true of Europe, which only
became strong and really civilized when the Reformation and the
French Revolution broke the hold of religious leaders on
society. It was true also of Muslim societies: for it was not
Islam or the Quran but the power of the shaykhs which kept the
umma weak. Shumayyil developed this idea in reply to criticisms
of Islam made by Lord Cromer in his *Modern Egypt*. 'Islam as
a social system has been a complete failure', was Cromer's judgement, and he blamed the failure on the inferior status of women,
the toleration of slavery and rigidity of the law, the exclusiveness
of the faith.[14] He did not believe that any remedy was possible.
Writing of a would-be reformer, the Tunisian Muhammad
Bayram,

> We may sympathize [he declared] with the Mohammed Beyrams of
> Islam, but let no practical politician think that they have a plan capable
> of resuscitating a body which is not, indeed, dead, and which may yet
> linger on for centuries, but which is nevertheless politically and socially
> moribund, and whose gradual decay cannot be arrested by any modern
> palliatives however skilfully they may be applied.[15]

This criticism aroused great interest and a number of replies,
and it may seem strange that the Christian Shumayyil should
have rushed to the defence of Islam; but he wrote about Islam

[11] Ibid. p. 57.
[13] *Falsafat al-nushu'*, p. 81.
[15] Ibid. p. 184.

[12] Shumayyil, *Majmu'a*, ii. 40.
[14] Cromer, ii. 134 ff.

with greater freedom than an Arab Christian of an earlier generation would have done.

The provenance of these ideas is not difficult to find: it must be sought in the pages of Spencer and Büchner. But they clearly had special implications for a society which was still based on the religious community. Many Christian Arab writers of the time of Shumayyil were putting them forward, and drawing the conclusion that there must be a national unity to transcend religious differences. But Shumayyil himself drew a further conclusion. He was not simply trying to replace religious by national solidarity. All types of exclusive solidarity, he argued, had the same danger as religious, because they divided human society. National fanaticism was as bad as religious, and sooner or later loyalty to the limited *watan* must give way to the *wataniyya* of the world. When, in 1909, the question of the prolongation of the Suez Canal concession was being discussed, and the Legislative Council was opposing it, Shumayyil wrote an article suggesting that it would be to Egypt's advantage to prolong the concession and accept the compensation the company was offering. Scientific progress, he asserted, was faster than ever before, and so too, therefore, was social progress: the conception of the *watan* was changing and soon it would embrace the whole world. By the time the present concession came to an end in 1968 the canal would no more belong to Egypt than it did to China and America; let Egypt take the compensation offered while she was still thought to have a right to the canal, and use it for the general welfare.[16]

This opposition to nationalism aroused much criticism at the time, and so too did Shumayyil's professed socialism. Although he did not invent the word, he was perhaps the first to spread the concept of socialism (*ishtirakiyya*) in Arabic. It is clear, however, that his problem was not that of European socialism, the problem of private or public ownership of the means of production. In an Egypt where modern industry did not yet exist this was not a real problem. He was concerned much more with the liberal problem of the limits of State action, and when he called himself a socialist what he really meant was that the government should interfere positively in the social process in order to bring about co-operation in pursuit of the general

[16] Shumayyil, *Majmu'a*, ii. 293.

welfare. It should for example find work for those who could work, ensure that wages were equal, improve public health.[17] In a more ambitious programme for a socialist party in Egypt, written in 1908,[18] he suggested that the party should have both a negative and a positive policy. It should aim at destroying all useless books, the School of Law, the new university which was in process of being established, the Mixed Courts, indeed all courts as now established, companies which monopolized the water supply, and newspapers which spread dissension by talking about 'Muslim and Copt and immigrant' (*dakhil*—this was a reference to Egyptian attacks on the Lebanese immigrants in Egypt). Having thus destroyed almost all existing institutions, it should then establish a real university where the sciences were studied, a technical college in place of the School of Law, very simple local law courts, public institutions for the distribution of water, elementary schools in every village and quarter, and proper newspapers.

Such ideas might be impossible to carry out, but even to spread them was to help in the ferment of thought and action which led to the constitutional movement in Egypt and the Ottoman Empire. In general Shumayyil was a supporter of the Young Turk opposition to the tyranny of Abdülhamid. Not all the Young Turks, he wrote in 1898, were sincere liberals, but they were on the side of cosmic and national progress. They stood for liberty, for a social unity which transcended religious differences, and for the spread of education: with all their faults, they were the forward movement of mankind and the universe.[19] Abdülhamid was not, and it is significant of the harmony which Shumayyil found between the laws of the universe and those of each human society that he ends the introduction of his book on Darwinism with a warning to tyrants: your day is ending, even in the east, as knowledge spreads.[20]

The thought of Shumayyil must be understood within the context of the great debate on science and religion, and the same is true of another Lebanese journalist of a slightly later generation, Farah Antun (1874–1922). He came from Tripoli to Cairo in 1897 and spent the rest of his life there and in New York editing Arabic periodicals, in particular one which was famous

---

[17] Ibid. pp. 152 ff., 179 ff., 185–6.   [18] Ibid. p. 187.
[19] Ibid. p. 90.   [20] *Falsafat al-nushu'*, p. 61.

in its time, *al-Jami'a*. In these and his novels he gave expression
to the 'advanced' European thought of his time, and it was this
which brought him into conflict with Muhammad 'Abduh in a
famous controversy which produced 'Abduh's essay on Islam
and Christianity and a statement by Antun of his views on
society and government. The controversy generated heat and
broke the friendly relations which had existed between the two
men, and between Antun and Rashid Rida. Antun and Rida had
indeed travelled together from Lebanon to Egypt, but whatever
friendship they possessed changed in the stress of conflict into
violent and contemptuous hostility.[21] It is not difficult to see
why if one reads the exchanges, for Antun's views struck at the
root of 'Abduh's convictions.

The origin of the dispute was a long study of the life and
philosophy of Ibn Rushd, published by Antun in *al-Jami'a*. The
choice of subject shows the influence on Antun of Ernest Renan.
He had translated Renan's *Vie de Jésus*, and now, in writing of
Ibn Rushd, he was following a path marked out by his master.
The general views which he expounds are roughly those of
Renan, although without the seduction of his master's voice, of
that extraordinary style, limpid, moving, and not quite serious.
The 'conflict' between science and religion can be solved, but
only by assigning to each its proper sphere. There are two
independent human faculties, the intellect and the heart, each
with its rule of procedure, field of activity, and methods of proof.
The intellect proceeds by observation and experiment, and its
field is the created world; the heart moves by 'acceptance of
what is contained in the [sacred] books without an examination
of their bases', and its proper objects are the virtues and vices
and the after-life. Neither can refute the findings of the other;
let them then respect each other and not invade each other's
territory.[22]

All this sounds innocent enough, but such ideas, injected into
a society organized on the basis of adherence to revealed religions,
could have revolutionary implications. Antun was quite aware
of this. In his dedication, he declares that the book is meant for
'the new shoots of the east':

those men of sense in every community and every religion of the east

---

[21] Antun, *Ibn Rushd*, pp. 173 ff.; Rida, *Tar'ikh*, i. 805 ff.   [22] Antun, p. 122.

who have seen the danger of mingling the world with religion in an age like ours, and have come to demand that their religion should be placed on one side in a sacred and honoured place, so that they will be able really to unite, and to flow with the tide of the new European civilization, in order to be able to compete with those who belong to it, for otherwise it will sweep them all away and make them the subjects of others.[23]

A little farther on he explains why he is writing about Ibn Rushd: it is to bridge the gap between the various elements in the east, to purify their hearts and unite their voices, by showing there is no point in proclaiming the superiority of one religion over another. This way of thought is out of date; the modern age is one of science and philosophy, and modern society rests on mutual respect between religions.[24]

What attracts Antun in Ibn Rushd is what attracted Renan: the assertion of the Islamic philosophers that prophecy is a kind of understanding, that prophets are philosophers, that there is one truth which is dressed by the prophets in religious symbols for the masses but which the *élite* can contemplate in itself. But he has another aim as well. His work, like that of Shumayyil, has something of the political tract even when it seems most theoretical, and his political aim is like that of Shumayyil and the other Lebanese writers of the time. He wishes to lay down the presuppositions of a secular State in which Muslims and Christians can participate on a footing of complete equality. There are two such presuppositions. The first is that what is essential in all religions should be separated from what is accidental. What is essential is a body of principles, what is inessential is a body of laws, both general and particular. If the first are examined, it will be found that they are the same in all religions. (The Trinity is only 'a poetic and figurative matter',[25] Christ is the Son of God not because of any difference of nature but because he possessed in a special degree the 'spirit of God' which we all have, and which makes all of us in some sense 'sons of God'.)[26] If, on the other hand, we examine the body of laws, we shall find that their only purpose is to exhort men to virtue: all that is fixed in them is the moral principle lying behind them, and they must be interpreted so as to fulfil their proper function, even if this

[23] Ibid. Dedication.   [24] Ibid. p. 6.
[25] Ibid. p. 190.   [26] Ibid.

involves interpreting them allegorically (*ta'wil*).[27] In a word, all religions reduce themselves to a single religion teaching certain broad principles; religious laws have no validity in themselves, they are only a means to an end; human nature is fundamentally the same in all religions, and human rights and duties are the same; even those who have no religion are no different from others in their nature or rights.

For Antun, this is the basis of true toleration.[28] But there is a second condition of secularism, and one which is no less important: it is the separation of temporal and spiritual authorities. There are five reasons why this is necessary. First of all, the aims of the two are different and even contradictory. Religion aims at worship and virtue in accordance with the revealed books; each religion believes it alone has the truth, and men must tread its path to salvation, and therefore the religious authorities, if they have political power, will use it to persecute those who disagree with them and in particular the thinkers. But the aim of government is to preserve human freedom within the limits of the constitution; left to themselves, governments would not persecute men because of what they think. Secondly, the good society is based on absolute equality between 'sons of the same nation' (*abna' al-umma*)—an equality which cuts across religious differences. Thirdly, the religious authorities legislate with a view to the next world, and therefore their control would interfere with the purpose of government, which is to legislate for this world. Fourthly, States controlled by religion are weak: religious authorities are weak by their nature, since they are at the mercy of the feelings of the mass, and they are a cause of weakness in society since they emphasize what divides men; to mix religion with politics even weakens religion itself because it is brought down into the arena and exposed to all the dangers of political life. Finally, religious government leads to war: although true religion is one, the different religious 'interests' will always be hostile to each other, and since religious loyalties are strong among the masses it is always possible to stir up their feelings.[29]

Implicit in this lies a theory of what the State should be. It should be based on freedom and equality, its laws and policy should aim at happiness in this world, at national strength and peace between nations; and it cannot be this unless the secular

---

[27] Antun, p. 120.   [28] Ibid. p. 147.   [29] Ibid. pp. 151 ff.

power is autonomous of control. With something of this 'Abduh
certainly agreed, but not with all. He too made a distinction
between what was essential in religion and what was not, but it
was not quite the same distinction: behind all religions there
might lie the same truth, but there was some precise sense in
which Islam, and Islam only, expressed the whole of it. He too
was prepared to allow the government great latitude in its
legislation, but he thought of modern laws as developing out of
the *Shari'a* and not in independence; and he wanted an equal
partnership, not a separation, between those who governed and
the guardians of the law. He was prepared to allow non-Muslims
a position of complete legal and social equality, but the State
should still be an Islamic State. His violent reaction against
Antun's views is not then difficult to explain. It is true, he fastened
specifically on a secondary question raised in passing by Antun:
the question whether Islam had persecuted science more than
Christianity. It was in reply to what he understood Antun to be
maintaining that he wrote his book on Islam and Christianity.
But in fact Antun was not saying exactly this, but something
else which was the real object of 'Abduh's anger. He did in fact
suggest that the separation of the two powers in Christianity
made it easier for Christians to be tolerant than for Muslims,
but he also made clear that the record of the two religions was
much the same, and if European countries were now more
tolerant, that was not because they were Christians but because
science and philosophy had driven out religious fanaticism, and
the separation of powers had taken place.[30] This was in direct
opposition to 'Abduh's belief that religion, if purified, could
still serve as the basis of political life, and was in fact the only
solid basis; and in his replies Antun made the opposition quite
clear. The world has changed, he reminds 'Abduh: modern
States are no longer based on religion, but on two things—
national unity and the techniques of modern science. As an
example of this change he gives the defeat of the Wahhabis by
the armies of Muhammad 'Ali: had 'Abduh's theory been correct, and did religious reform lead to strength, the Wahhabis
would have won, but in fact they lost because Muhammad 'Ali
was the first man in the east who understood how the world had
changed. 'Abduh's hope of an Islamic union was vain: it could

[30] Ibid. p. 124.

not come into existence, and if it did it would make no difference, for it would not generate the strength needed to hold back the danger from Europe.[31] Examples could be brought from Christian and Muslim history alike to prove that religious unity was impossible, and States must find some other kind of unity were they to survive. In the modern world, the way to unity was by the creation of national loyalty and the separation of national from religious authority: without this there can be 'no true civilization, no toleration, no justice and equality, no security or friendship or freedom, no science or philosophy and no progress'.[32] He would not accept 'Abduh's view that the unity and strength of Islam had been destroyed by the Turks, and could be restored if only the centre of gravity moved back to the Arabs. On the contrary, it was the patriotic spirit of the Turks and Persians, and the strength they derived from it, which had enabled the *umma* to survive. The culture of the Persians, the military virtues of the Turks had infused a new strength into Islam: 'The Ottomans took over the Arab heritage by natural selection, and preserved it by their strength from the evils and dangers which beset it'.[33]

'Abduh made a further point. The separation of religion and State was not only undesirable, it was impossible. A ruler must belong to a specific religion, and how could he free himself from its influence in his acts? Man is a unity, not simply two things connected with each other, body and soul: the functions of the two cannot be separated, how then is it possible to separate the authorities which control them? In answer, Antun states the full democratic theory of government. The ruler should not rule according to his own will or personal convictions. He should act in the light of the laws laid down by the Assembly of representatives of the people. The people must possess sovereignty, otherwise there will be despotism or anarchy; and their representatives have greater wisdom than any ruler can have—their corporate intelligence is higher than that of each individual among them.[34]

The Assembly should be superior to religious authorities as well as to the ruler: this is what Antun really means by the separation of spiritual and temporal powers. The danger he knows is that of interference by religious chiefs in the affairs of

[31] Antun, pp. 176–7.   [32] Ibid. p. 160.
[33] Ibid. p. 174.   [34] Ibid. p. 161.

the world; when the government is not only secular but supreme and assigns to the religious power its limits, no confusion will exist, and neither it nor the Church will transgress its bounds. He shows no signs of being aware that there is an opposite danger. What reason, he asks, is there to think that the government will interfere in religious matters? If the Church has no political power it will not attract interference. Its cause is a dying cause: the élite can dispense with its help even in religious matters, while the masses are more interested in the affairs of this world. Socialism, or 'the religion of humanity', is taking the place of the revealed faiths.[35]

From time to time, in Antun's pages, we catch a note which is more than an echo of his European masters: the expression of an active political consciousness among the Arab Christians. For so long they had been content not to be interfered with, and devoted their political talents to the tortuous affairs of their patriarchates. But when Antun calls for a secular State, he is not only demanding that Christians should not be persecuted or that they should be given equal rights. He is calling for a community in which they can take an active part, for a sphere of political responsibility. He is at pains to dissociate the eastern Christians from the western missionaries, and still more from the European Powers who use religion for political purposes. We should not forget the benefits we have received from the missionaries, he admits; but let us not forget the political harm they have done. His is an eastern Christian consciousness: we are the real Christians, he asserts with pride, but perhaps also in a spirit of defence; our religion has not been mixed with politics. We are not responsible for what western Christendom had done; our loyalty is to the east—we have always been faithful to the sultan.[36]

[35] Ibid. pp. 165 ff.   [36] Ibid. pp. 169, 179 & 205.

XI

ARAB NATIONALISM

THAT those who speak Arabic form a 'nation', and that this nation should be independent and united, are beliefs which only became articulate and acquired political strength during the present century. But as far back in history as we can see them, the Arabs have always been exceptionally conscious of their language and proud of it, and in pre-Islamic Arabia they possessed a kind of 'racial' feeling, a sense that, beyond the conflicts of tribes and families, there was a unity which joined together all who spoke Arabic and could claim descent from the tribes of Arabia. All tribes had a common family tree, universally known and accepted, and whether it was genuine or fictitious is not to the point. After the rise of Islam, and when Islam and the Arabic language spread far beyond the peninsula, this 'family' came to include many who were of different origin, while not excluding those, like the tribe of Banu Ghassan, who were Arab by origin but did not accept the new religion.

In the history of Islam, and indeed in its essential structure, the Arabs had a special part. The Quran is in Arabic, the Prophet was an Arab, he preached first to Arabs, who formed the 'matter of Islam', the human instrument through which the religion and its authority spread; Arabic became and has remained the language of devotion, theology, and law. The sharp distinction which at first existed between the Arab ruling class and the new converts was later blurred, and in the eyes of the law all believers were alike except in virtue; but in fact the sense of ethnic difference persisted, and expressed itself not only in the literary controversies of the *Shuʻubiyya*, but also in the struggle for power which lay behind them. Power finally passed to the Turks and kindred groups, and Turkish became the language of government; but even then Arabic kept its privileged position, as the language of religious culture and law, in short of the State in its religious aspect as upholder of the *Shariʻa*. As such, it was the means by which the Arabs could still play a part in the public life of the community.

The empire disintegrated in the eighteenth and nineteenth centuries, and what was a natural process, often repeated in history, had 'national' undertones. Local feeling and opposition in the provinces of the empire found its leaders in the religious families of the great cities, who had managed to preserve their wealth and social position under the protection of the religious system, held local religious offices and so were linked with the religious hierarchy throughout the empire, and often had the privileged position accorded to *ashraf*, descendants of the Prophet. In such families the sciences of the Arabic language were treasured and handed down, as a necessary introduction to the sciences of religion; pride in Arab origin—very often, descent from the Prophet or one of the early heroes of Islam—was blended with a sense of what the Arabs had done for Islam, and both reinforced that sense of responsibility to the community and the past which had always marked *ahl al-sunna wa'l-jama'a*. In a sense, therefore, they could be regarded as spokesmen of 'Arab' consciousness. In another way the Wahhabi kingdom in Arabia was Arab: not only by the accident that it arose in a region where Arabic was spoken, but also because by calling Muslims to return to the primitive purity of Islam it revived the memory of the Arab period in the history of the *umma*. The short-lived empire of Muhammad 'Ali too was Arab by geographical accident: expansion from Egypt was bound, in the first instance, to be expansion in Arab countries. But was it Arab in some other sense than this? Did Muhammad 'Ali aim at creating an Arab kingdom? Nothing in his words or policy seems to show it, although there are signs of it in the words of his son and chief helper, Ibrahim Pasha: 'I am not a Turk. I came to Egypt when I was a child, and since that time, the sun of Egypt has changed my blood and made it all Arab'. This statement to a French visitor has often been quoted, as has the visitor's comment that Ibrahim's aim was to found an entirely Arab State, and 'give back to the Arab race its nationality and political existence'.[1] At the same time he was writing to his father in terms which might bear a similar meaning: the war with the Turks was a national and racial war, and a man should be willing

[1] Douin, *Mission Boislecomte*, pp. 249–50.

to sacrifice his life for the sake of his nation.[2] But there is no clear evidence what he meant by this, or whether it reflected more than a passing mood of his thought.

There are some signs that, under the impact of such movements, and also perhaps of the spread of nationalism among the Balkan subjects of the empire, the consciousness of a difference between Turks and Arabs was growing throughout the first half of the nineteenth century. It is true, nevertheless, that explicit Arab nationalism, as a movement with political aims and importance, did not emerge until towards the end of the nineteenth century. Until then, the political interest and activities of Ottoman Arabs were channelled in the general movements of the empire: in the struggle, at first open and then hidden, which ran all through the reign of Abdülhamid. On the one side stood the sultan and his supporters: not only those who had an interest in preserving the existing system but those who believed that only the strength of the monarchy and the domination of the Muslim element preserved the unity of the empire, and only the empire could preserve what was left of the unity and independence of Islam. Among the closest advisers and supporters of the sultan were Arabs like Abu'l-Huda, the agent of his religious policy, and 'Izzat Pasha, his secretary and political man of affairs, and it is probable that a majority of Arabs, particularly in the Syrian provinces, were not dissatisfied with his rule, alike for religious reasons and because the Arab provinces derived material benefit from the extension of schools and railways. On the other hand stood those who believed that the empire could only be preserved by being turned into a constitutional monarchy, with equal rights for Muslims and non-Muslims, Turks and non-Turks. This idea has found its first expression in the 1860's and 1870's, among the 'Young Ottomans' in Paris and London, and the reforming officials, led by Midhat Pasha, who made the coup d'état of 1875 and thus set on foot the first constitutional experiment.[3] After its failure, and the reimposition of personal rule by the sultan, the organized opposition was broken and discontent went underground. Apart from the short-lived 'Progress and Union' group, founded in 1889 by students in the military schools and virtually dissolved in 1896, opposition

---

[2] Rustum, ii. 52.
[3] For the Young Ottomans, cf. Ramsaur; Lewis, *Emergence*.

was kept alive and expressed only by a small group of exiles in
Paris and elsewhere in Europe; led by Ahmed Rıza, reinforced
in 1899 by a brother-in-law of the sultan, Damad Mahmud
Pasha, and his two sons Sabaheddin and Lûtfullah, they published periodicals in Turkish and French, and organized two
'congresses of Ottoman liberals', in 1902 and 1907, to co-
ordinate action against the autocracy of the sultan.

In this movement too Arabs played a part, but Syrian
Christians more than Muslims. Between the journalists of
Beirut and the reforming officials of Constantinople there seems
to have been some contact since the beginning of the 1860's:
owing perhaps to the presence of Ahmad Faris al-Shidyaq in the
capital, perhaps to the sojourn in Syria of the reformer Fuad
Pasha as Ottoman Special Commissioner to inquire into the
events of 1860. The 1860's and 1870's were years when expression was comparatively free, and we find Arabic periodicals in
Beirut expressing ideas roughly equivalent to those of the Young
Ottomans and Midhat Pasha, although giving to them that
secularist twist which was characteristic of the Christian writers.
Such a one was *al-Jinan*, founded by Butrus al-Bustani in 1870
and directed by him and his family for sixteen years. The east, it
proclaimed, was once prosperous and civilized, then it lost what
it had. The cause of the loss was bad government, the remedy is
good government: good government can only be based on participation, the separation of religion from politics, the separation
of the judiciary from the executive, regular tax assessment, useful
public works, compulsory education—above all, on justice,
unity between those of different religions, and 'love of country'
that is to say, a patriotic feeling which should unite all Ottoman
citizens.[4]

When the first Ottoman parliament met in 1877 *al-Jinan*
reported its early debates, and reported also, in a dispatch
reproduced from *The Times*, the appearance of an opposition
party.[5] But after a time the reports disappeared from the paper,
and this is perhaps not an accident, but an early sign of that
reassertion of the sultan's control and stifling of opposition
which was to end *al-Jinan* itself in 1886, and to shift the centre
of Lebanese journalism from Beirut to Cairo. But the ideas of
the 1870's were not forgotten. Midhat Pasha spent several

---

[4] *al-Jinan*, i (1870), 15, 38, 160; x (1879), 481.   [5] Ibid. ix (1878), 118.

months as governor of Damascus in 1879, after the constitutionalists had failed but before Abdülhamid was certain enough of his strength to imprison and then destroy him. He established contact with the journalists of Beirut and left a permanent mark on them: one of them, Khalil al-Khuri, translated his article on the past, present, and future of the Ottoman Empire into Arabic, and another, Sulayman al-Bustani, a cousin of Butrus, was later to play a part in Ottoman politics after the constitution was restored in 1908. He gained an independent fame as translator of the *Iliad* into Arabic, learning Greek for the purpose and being perhaps the first of all Arabic writers to make a serious study of Greek poetry and poetic theory. Another of his writings is more to our purpose: '*Ibra wa dhikra* (A Lesson and a Memory, or the Ottoman State before and after the Constitution) came out just after the revolution of 1908 and is, as its name implies, a survey of what the empire had been like under Abdülhamid, as well as a programme of action. Its standpoint is that of Ottoman nationalism, its hero is still Midhat Pasha, to whose memory it is dedicated. There *is* an Ottoman nation, the author asserts: it incorporates all national and religious communities within the empire, but with a certain primacy for Turks and Muslims. Until Abdülhamid came it was moving forward on the path of civilization and religious harmony, now it can progress once again; but the first condition of progress is the absence of religious and racial fanaticism and the cultivation of a national spirit.

Even before the revolution of 1908, Lebanese and Syrian writers who were beyond the range of Abdülhamid's police had continued to promulgate constitutional ideas openly. The Lebanese newspapers of Cairo, *al-Muqattam* and *al-Ahram*, attacked the sultan without wearying; and in Paris a Lebanese, Halil Ganem (Khalil Ghanim), was among the leaders of the small group of 'Young Turks' who kept liberal ideas alive throughout the years of disorganization. Ganem was a Maronite, who had been deputy for Beirut in the parliament of 1878, and had made his mark there as an outspoken opponent of the government; after the dissolution he went to Paris and stayed there for the rest of his life as journalist and writer. A book he wrote about the Ottoman sultans throws light on his way of thought. The 'Ottoman nation' has been ruined by two things. The first is despotism, which oblitère les sentiments au fond de l'âme, fausse l'esprit, supprime chez l'homme le sens de l'équité ainsi que la notion exacte de la justice, bouleverse le jugement et rend malfaisants et stupides des êtres qui pourraient briller soit par leur intelligence, soit par leur bonté.[6]

The second is Islam, which, liberal at first, soon became tyrannical, and was equally so under the Arabs—for the caliphs, 'sous leur apparente bonhomie . . . n'en furent pas moins des êtres de basse tyrannie'—and under the Turks, who contracted habits of intolerance during the long struggle with Christendom. The only remedies were a return to the constitution of 1876 and a more careful watch over the education and moral environment of the princes.[7]

If anything, Halil Ganem was anti-Arab: the spirit of persecution, in his opinion, characterized all the Muslim peoples, but the Arabs in particular.[8] This may be a relic of his Maronite origin, or the product of a whole-hearted immersion in the movement of Ottoman reform. Such a complete identification however was rare, and for the most part national preferences and feelings were scarcely concealed beneath the surface of Ottoman unity. Within the Young Turk movement in exile there was a significant difference of approach. Ahmed Rıza and his group were first of all Turkish nationalists, arguing for the continued domination of the Turkish element in the State even when the constitution should have been restored; on the other hand, Prince Sabaheddin and his 'League of Administrative Decentralization' wanted strict equality between races and religions, and considerable autonomy for the provinces. The split was significant, for behind it lay a difference of opinion about the relations between the Ottoman State and its subject peoples. Sabaheddin believed that, if the peoples were free to choose, they would choose to be loyal; Ahmed Rıza, that they would use freedom to secure independence. It is difficult to doubt that Ahmed Rıza was right, and what happened at the 'Congresses of Ottoman Liberals' seemed to prove it. All present were agreed on the need to get rid of the despotism of Abdülhamid, but on nothing else. The Turks wanted a unified constitutional State, the Armenians did not because they did not want to give the empire a new lease of life: in the final pronouncement of the Congress of 1902, they dissociated themselves from

[6] Ganem, ii. 295. [7] Ibid. p. 296. [8] Ibid.

the desire of the other participants for the transformation of the present régime into a constitutional régime, on the grounds that it was 'inopportune and even contrary to their interests'.[9] The Turks were doubtful whether it was wise to call in the European Powers to help in overthrowing the régime, because it might lead to a foreign protectorate; the Christians did not object so much to foreign protection, veiled or not, because it might lead to reform.

The Armenians who supported the Young Turks were, in the last analysis, Armenian nationalists; and the Arabs were taking the steps which would lead them towards Arab nationalism. Among Arab Muslims, perhaps the main force which pushed them in that direction was the Turkish claim to the caliphate, first put forward systematically around the middle of the century. There is evidence that this claim, whenever put forward, met—as it was bound to—with a negative response from Arabs who had inherited the tradition of Islamic learning: they had learned from their ancestors what the true doctrine of the caliphate was, and it was indeed essentially connected with their pride in what the Arabs had done for Islam. They might accept the sultan as sultan, a necessary protector of Islam, but they could not believe in his claim to be more than this. Their equivocal attitude is well described by an observer who lived in Jerusalem in the 1850's and 1860's and had much intercourse with Arabs of this type:

The . . . dwellers in towns are a mixed race of various origins, but there are among them families entitled to the name Arab, their ancestors having been immigrants from Arabia at the time of the Mohammedan conquest. This class forms but a small proportion of the population; but these people are proud of their descent: they know, even the ignorant among them, something of their system of religion, and look back to its Arabian source.

They are on this very account unable to comprehend how a Sultan of Turks, an alien race coming from Tartary, can rightly be regarded as Caliph (successor) of Mohammed the Koreish Arab, or exercise the power of appointing or displacing the Shereef of Mecca.

Among other modes of expressing their dislike of Ottoman pretensions to the Caliphate was the bitter way of their pronouncing the Sultan's title of 'Khân', as though it were an epithet derived from the Arabic 'Khana' (to betray or cheat). I have heard them, with strange

⁹ Ramsaur, p. 71.

amount of emphasis, speak of 'Abdu'l Mejeed el Khaïn' (the betrayer of trust).[10]

These Arabs, as they consider themselves, detest and hate the Turks with an ancient hatred which goes back to the period of the Ottoman conquest of 'Arabistân'. The enmity and jealousy are due to difference of race and traditional remembrance of conquest.

But loyalty to Islâm is a powerful and pervading principle which keeps in check every other feeling. The Sultan is *de facto* Caliph to the learned Arabs; he is also Caliph *de jure*. As a matter of religious obedience they acknowledge and obey him.[11]

The writer of these words wrote his book in 1870–2, but he was describing Jerusalem as he had known it ten or twenty years earlier. At that time the caliphal propaganda had scarcely begun; as it became more insistent Arab doubts seem to have grown stronger, and even those Arabs who worked for Abdül-hamid were not sure whether the sultans were really caliphs, or whether Abdülhamid was the man to save Islam. Abu'l-Huda used to advocate the idea of an Arab caliphate at times, if only to frighten his master;[12] and the son of Ahmad Faris al-Shidyaq (presumably reflecting his father's views) told an English visitor in 1884 that Abdülhamid, although a man of good intentions, and kind to him personally, was ignorant of the world, and 'to tell the whole truth, he is crazy[13]. . . The whole Turkish State was dying. The Caliphate would some day return to Arabia.'[14] If such ideas were entertained in the sultan's camp, they were more prevalent still among the Islamic modernists, whose general view of Islam would tend to encourage them. Between them and Muslims like Abu'l-Huda there was indeed more than a difference of personalities or even of political views. There was a difference in their whole conception of Islam. Abu'l-Huda stood for Islam as it had in fact developed with its traditions, its mystical theology, its Turkish leadership: the *umma* 'cannot agree on an error', and if it has finally taken this shape then it must be accepted as it is. The modernists wished to proceed up the stream of development to the point at which it had gone wrong, and beyond it to the primitive Islam as they

[10] 'In the opinion of this class of the people the modern reforms and liberal measures were a flagrant departure from the pure Moslem laws of the Korân.'
[11] Finn, i. 215.
[12] Yakan, i. 99 ff.
[13] Blunt, *Gordon*, p. 317.
[14] Ibid. p. 305.

conceived it. That the Turkish sultan was now supreme was not important, compared with the fact that, in its great days, the Arabs had been the head and heart of the community. To return to the original purity of Islam meant in fact to move the centre of gravity back from Turks to Arabs; if there was to be a caliph at all, he could only be an Arab caliph.

Blunt's book, *The Future of Islam*, is a sign that such ideas were current in the early 1880's. As we have seen,[15] the book is an argument for the reopening of the door of *ijtihad*, and the restoration of a true caliphate, as the supreme authority which would legalize doctrinal reform. But the book makes clear that the Ottoman sultan could not be a caliph of this kind: he had no legal claim to the caliphate, and the whole tradition of the Ottomans was against the reopening of the door of *ijtihad*. In any event, the future of the empire was obscure. It seemed likely to be absorbed by Russia and Austria, and if that happened the Turks might cease to be Muslims. The reform of Islam depended on the Arabs, in particular on the Arab '*ulama*', who stood at the heart of the Islamic world and were the most capable of exercising *ijtihad*. But they could not do so freely unless the caliphate was restored to the Arabs. When the empire finally collapsed a council of '*ulama*' might be held at Mecca to choose an Arab caliph: a member of the family of the Sharif of Mecca seemed the most likely candidate, with Mecca or Medina as his 'Papal State', although it was also possible that Cairo would become the seat of the caliphate. All elements in the Muslim world except the Turks would accept an Arab caliph, who would reconcile the sects and liberate Islam from the weight of Turkish stagnation.

Blunt implies that 'Abduh himself held such views, but we may doubt that this was so, or at least, even if he held them for the moment, whether they expressed his mature conviction. It is true, he rejected the Turkish sultan's claim to be caliph: it had been put forward, he said on a later occasion, in the interests of the Ottomans themselves and not of Islam, and those who directed the propaganda for it had no idea what the caliphate really was. But as time went on and the pressure of the European Powers became greater he grew more aware of the value of the empire to Islam, and the danger of its disappearance. If the Arabs tried to break away, he told Rashid Rida in 1897, Europe might

intervene and subjugate them and the Turks alike. With all its
faults, the Ottoman Empire was what was left of the political
independence of the *umma*, and if it vanished Muslims would lose
everything and become powerless as Jews.[16]

This same caution, which we have already seen in the attitude
of the notables of Jerusalem as Finn describes it, appears later in
that of 'Abduh's disciple Rida. But we need not conclude from
this that Blunt was ascribing to others what were simply his own
views. There may well have been *'ulama'* in Syria and the Hejaz
who held them at the time he wrote, and in the next quarter of
a century they spread more widely for a number of reasons. On
the one hand, there was the obvious failure of the sultan to
defend Islam against its enemies; on the other, various groups
which had an interest in preparing opinion for a transfer of the
caliphate to the Arabs, and indeed to a specific Arab, the Sharif of
Mecca, immediate ruler of the Holy Places and member of a
family whose claim to descent from the Prophet was at least as
good as any other. This period is still obscure and it is necessary
to speak with caution, but it does not seem unlikely, *prima facie*,
that some British officials in the Near East were already playing
with the idea that, if the Ottoman sultanate should fall under
unfriendly influences in its weakness, the Sharif of Mecca
might be useful as a focus of loyalty and an ally of some local
importance. It appears too that, from some uncertain date,
members of the Egyptian ruling house were playing with the
idea of the sharif as caliph under the temporal protection of an
Egyptian sultan. Blunt, for example, tells us that the ideas of the
caliphate which he expounded in *The Future of Islam* he first
heard from two men, one the Persian Ambassador, Malkom
Khan (himself of Christian origin), and the other a Christian
journalist, Louis Sabunji, who founded an Arabic periodical,
al-Nahla (The Bee), in London in 1877, and carried it on for a
few years. Although a Catholic priest, Sabunji appears by this
time to have had greater sympathy with Islam than with his own
faith, and in his newspaper he preached religious reform, with
an Arab nationalist colouring,[17] and denounced Abdülhamid as
'an usurper of the title of . . . Caliph'.[18] There was, says Blunt,
'a mystery about the financing of this little journal . . . and I have

---

[16] Rida, *Ta'rikh*, i. 912.   [17] Cf. *al-Nahla*, 1 Nov. 1879.
[18] Blunt, *Secret History*, p. 66.

since had reason to believe that the funds to support it . . . came, in part at least, from the ex-Khedive Ismaïl'.[19] What makes this more probable is that Isma'il had his own grievance against Abdülhamid, who had deposed him under pressure from the Powers, and that in 1879 there appeared another Arabic periodical with a similar message, in Naples and under the title of *al-Khilafa* (The Caliphate). Its editor was an Egyptian man of letters in Isma'il's service, and its purpose was to denounce the claims of the Ottoman sultan to the caliphate and support those of the khedive. Then in the 1890's another queer Englishman, Marmaduke Pickthall, wandered up and down Palestine and found that the doctrine of the Arab caliphate was still being preached in secret by missionaries sent from 'Abbas Hilmi, Khedive of Egypt; the idea of an Arab empire, with the khedive as its temporal and the sharif as its spiritual head, appealed to older men who still remembered the rule of Muhammad 'Ali and Ibrahim's 'gospel of an Arab Empire'.[20]

It was perhaps therefore not without encouragement that in the second half of the nineteenth century the Sharifs of Mecca began to put forward a claim to be *par excellence* the descendants of the Prophet, guardians of his faith, and in some sense the spiritual leaders of the Muslim world. They had no firm basis for their claims. Although enjoying a certain respect as rulers of the Holy Places, they had not possessed in any sense a religious position; according to a knowledgeable Dutch scholar who lived for some time in Mecca, they were more to be compared with 'les chevaliers pillards du moyen age qu'avec des ecclesiastiques'.[21] Ruling precariously over the Holy Cities, and not always far beyond them, snatching a fragile autonomy by maintaining a balance between Constantinople and Cairo, their position had taken a turn for the worse after the Wahhabi conquest and then the Egyptian occupation of the Hejaz. When the Turks returned in 1847, they took over from Muhammad 'Ali the control he had imposed over the sharifs and made it stricter. By the 1880's the sharifs could no longer resist the sultan's officials by force; they were indeed themselves chosen by the sultan. It was in order to check this process that they began to look around for possible support; from the khedive, from the religious leaders in Constantinople, from the general sentiment of the Islamic world.

---

[19] Ibid.   [20] Fremantle, p. 47.   [21] Hurgronje, iii. 189 ff., 311 ff.

Such currents of thought as we have expounded were first given full expression in two books written by a member of one of those learned families of the Arab provinces among whom they were widespread. 'Abd al-Rahman al-Kawakibi (1849–1903) belonged to a family of Aleppo, of Kurdish origin. He had an old-fashioned Arabic and Turkish education in his native city, and then worked there as official and journalist until he fell foul of the Turkish authorities and found it best to move to Cairo in 1898. Cairo was his centre for his remaining few years: he wrote for *al-Manar* and other periodicals, frequented the circle of 'Abduh, and travelled in Arabia and East Africa. He produced two books, *Taba'i' al-istibdad* (The Characteristics of Tyranny) and *Umm al-qura* (Mother of the Cities), one of the traditional names of Mecca. In a sense they are not original. His general ideas about Islam were those of the circle of 'Abduh and Rida, he may have been influenced by Blunt's *Future of Islam*,[22] and the framework and some of the ideas of his book on tyranny were probably taken from Alfieri's work on the same subject. In his preface, he himself states that he borrowed a certain amount; this seems to have been widely believed at the time, for Rashid Rida, in an obituary notice, repeats the story, while giving it no credit, for, said he, Kawakibi's picture of eastern society is too exact to have been taken from a western author.[23] Recent research has shown more or less conclusively that he did borrow something from Alfieri's book, and has suggested how he could have learned of it: there was a Turkish translation, made in 1897 by a Young Turk and published in Geneva, and this may well have been known in Aleppo or in Cairo.[24] Nevertheless, there is something original about his writing, owing no doubt to his strong political interests and convictions. He was a strong opponent of the despotism of Abdülhamid, and of his adviser Abu'l-Huda, of whose religious ideas he disapproved and with whom he also had a family quarrel: the religious families of the Aleppo district were always doubtful of the claim of Abu'l-Huda, himself from the same district, to be descended from the Prophet, and resented his using his influence in the palace to secure for his family the post of *naqib* or doyen of the *ashraf* in Aleppo. On

[22] Cf. S. G. Haim, 'Blunt and al-Kawakibi', *Oriente moderno*, xxv (1955), 132 ff.
[23] *al-Manar*, v (1902–3), 279.
[24] Haim, 'Alfieri and al-Kawakibi', *Oriente moderno*, xxiv (1954), 321 ff.; E. Rossi, 'Una Traduzione turca dell'opera "Della Tirannide" ', ibid. pp. 335 ff.

the other hand he was on good terms with the khedive, praised the policy of the royal family of Egypt,[25] and may have undertaken his journeys on his behalf and in furtherance of his ideas about an Arab caliphate. It was no doubt this strong interest which led him to draw out with great clarity certain implications of the teachings of the reformers, and develop them in the direction of Arab nationalism. His starting-point is the one we have already met so often, the decay of Islam, and he gives the same explanation of it. Islam has decayed because of illegal innovation (*bid'a*), in particular the coming in of mystical excesses alien to its spirit; and because of imitation (*taqlid*), the denial of the rights of reason and the failure to distinguish what is essential from what is not. But another cause exists as well. Al-Afghani and 'Abduh had already suggested that the later Islamic rulers had encouraged the false spirit of passive imitation and other-worldly resignation, in order to strengthen their own absolute power; Kawakibi lays greater emphasis on this, and regards it as a separate cause of corruption and decay. Despotic rulers have supported false religion, but their evil doing is not confined to that; despotism as such corrupts the whole of society. The just State, in which men fulfil themselves, is that in which the individual is free and freely serves the community, and in which the government watches over this freedom but is itself controlled by the people; this is what the true Islamic State was.[26] The despotic State is just the opposite: it encroaches on the rights of its citizens, keeps them ignorant to keep them passive, denies their right to take an active part in human life. In the end it destroys the moral relationship of rulers with ruled and citizens with each other; it distorts the moral structure of the individual, destroying courage, integrity, the sense of belonging, both religious and national.[27]

To free Islam from these evils there must be a reform of the law, the creation of a modern and unified system of law by the use of *ijtihad*; there must be proper religious education; but something else is necessary as well—a shift in the balance of power inside the *umma*, from the Turks back to the Arabs. Only the Arabs can save Islam from decay: because of the central position of the Arabian Peninsula in the *umma* and the Arabic

[25] *Umm al-qura*, pp. 188–9.   [26] *Istibdad*, p. 27.
[27] Ibid. pp. 34, 60 ff., 87, 91–92.

language in Islamic thought, but also for other reasons—Arabian Islam is comparatively free from modern corruptions, and the beduin are free from the moral decay and passivity of despotism.[28] The centre of gravity must move back to Arabia: there should be an Arabian caliph of the line of Quraysh, elected by representatives of the *umma*; he should have religious authority throughout the Muslim world, and be assisted in the exercise of it by a consultative council nominated by the Muslim rulers; he should have temporal authority in the Hejaz, assisted by a local council.

Among the Arab Christians too there were undertones of 'nationalism'. Inside their own communities, most of them were engaged in a struggle which had 'nationalist' implications. The Uniate communities, while accepting the Catholic doctrine in its entirety, were jealous of their customs and the privileges granted them by Rome: the jurisdiction of their own patriarchs, the use of Arabic or Syriac in their liturgies. They always reacted strongly against any attempts by western Catholic missionaries to latinize their rites or laws, or by the Vatican to impose too heavy and direct a control. In the Orthodox community the 'national' question was even more acute. The Greek Patriarch of Constantinople had been civil head of the whole Orthodox community of the empire since 1453; and from the seventeenth century the great Greek families of the Phanar quarter in Constantinople had, as we have seen, exercised a great influence in the Ottoman government. Gradually the Greeks had extended their ecclesiastical control over the whole Church: the Balkan patriarchates had been extinguished; the Patriarch of Antioch was normally a Greek; those of Jerusalem and Alexandria were also Greeks, and normally resident in Constantinople, while the revenues and government of the Church in the Holy Land were in the hands of a tight, powerful monastic brotherhood, the Brotherhood of the Holy Sepulchre, with a membership almost entirely Greek. Since most Orthodox in the patriarchate of Alexandria were Greeks, the situation there was relatively stable; but in Syria the great majority of the laity and lower clergy were Arabic-speaking. Even in the eighteenth century there were signs of discontent among them; this increased in the nineteenth, as the sense of ethnic and linguistic difference came to the surface of men's consciousness in the Near East, and still more because

[28] Ibid. p. 14.

of the close connexion of Russia with the Orthodox inside the empire, and her unwillingness to accept Greek control of the Church. Matters came to a head at the end of the nineteenth century, with a disputed election to the patriarchate of Antioch; the Russian government supported an Arab against the Greek candidate, and the Ottoman government, under pressure from Russia, secured the election of the Arab.

In the last quarter of the century this 'national' feeling began to take also a secular form. Bustani's periodical *al-Jinan*, while appealing for unity within the Ottoman *watan*, made also a special appeal to local feeling. The empire is our *watan*, but our country (*bilad*) is 'Syria'.[29] There is here a certain change of phrasing from *Nafir Suriyya*, which does not however signify a change of fundamental position. In the atmosphere of the 1870's, hopes for Ottoman unity were high; but the warmth of Bustani's feeling is still concentrated on the smaller territorial unit. The Ottoman government is praised for giving local positions to local men—for example, in Beirut in 1870 almost all posts were held by local Arabs.[30]

In 1875 a few young Christians of the circle of Bustani created a little secret society, and in 1879–80 they plastered Beirut with placards calling on the people of Syria to unite, and asking for the autonomy of Syria in union with Lebanon, the recognition of Arabic as an official language, and the removal of restrictions on expression and knowledge.[31] The group may have had a connexion with Midhat Pasha when he was governor of Damascus; certainly his enemies accused him of planning to make Syria autonomous like Egypt, and this would not have been inconsistent either with his ambition or his desire to reform the empire with the help of Europe.

The secret society had little importance,[32] but it is significant of the awakening of the Syrian Christians to political conscious-ness. Their culture and general ideas they had derived from the mission schools, but this made them more and not less anxious to emphasize their attachment to their own people, and to find a community of which they could be fully a part. Such a com-munity, however, did not yet exist. With all the reforms of the

[29] *al-Jinan*, i (1870), 15.
[30] Ibid. p. 38.
[31] Antonius, pp. 79 ff.
[32] Cf. Zeine, *Arab-Turkish Relations*, pp. 56–57 & 68.

period of the *Tanzimat*, the empire remained primarily a Muslim
State. There were some like Halil Ganem who were willing to
accept this and hope to make it a liberal Muslim State; but others
gave their loyalty, once they emerged from their closed sectarian
worlds, to an idea, even a dream, of a nation which might be
brought into existence.

The dream took several different forms. There were some
who found the solution of their problem in the idea of an independent Lebanon, the centre of a free Christian life, and placed
under the protection of a European Power of Catholic faith. This
indeed had been rather more than a dream since 1861: the
privileged sanjaq set up by international agreement possessed
internal autonomy; it had a Christian majority; it was under the
protection of the Concert of Europe. But it was regarded by
those whose national feelings were focused on the idea of
Lebanon as being no more than a stepping-stone towards real
independence, which would some day be achieved with the help
of Europe. This was the point of view, for example, of the
Maronite Bulus Nujaym, who wrote a work on the Lebanese
question under the pen-name of M. Jouplain. Syria, he proclaimed, formed a distinct historical entity; it had been and
would always be the link between different civilizations, Mediterranean and Semitic. But inside it, Lebanon had a special place:
there had been a Lebanese nation since the beginning of history,
it had been able to preserve its special character under all the
rulers of Syria, and even when engulfed in the Ottoman Empire
had still enjoyed a wide autonomy. The whole of Syria should
some day be autonomous and free, and Lebanon would be the
vanguard. It had been formally privileged since 1861, but its
constitution should be more democratic and its frontiers extended
to include Beirut and certain country districts; and for this it
looked to the help of France.[33]

There were others who were moved by the same vision but
expressed it in different words. The 'material' was the same:
the mountains and villages of Lebanon, the church bells ringing
freely, European ships protecting them and European hands
helping them to reform, a new reign of peace and progress with
their Muslim neighbours. But the political form which they
wished to impose on this matter was that of an autonomous

[33] Jouplain, pp. 587 ff.

Syria rather than Lebanon: that is to say, a State embracing the whole of 'geographical' Syria, from the Taurus mountains to the desert of Sinai, and a community which included Christians and Muslims, Druzes and Jews, co-operating so fully that it no longer mattered which was majority and which minority. We have seen this idea emerging in the mind of Butrus Bustani in 1860–1. In 1861 one of the earliest Arabic journalists, Khalil al-Khuri, wrote a little book on *Kharabat Suriyya* (The Ruins of Syria), of which the subject is the country's ancient monuments; and from about that time the name 'Syria' begins to be widely used, and with undertones of pride and self-identification, under the stimulus of factors similar to that which gave rise to the idea of Egypt. The idea was particularly widespread among the graduates of the American mission schools, and it is easy to see why. They were mainly Orthodox and Protestant Christians, and later Muslims and Druzes; for them, the independence of Lebanon meant the domination of the Maronites and of French culture, the pervading influence of the French government. The idea of 'Syria' seemed to offer them a chance of escaping from their position as a minority, without falling under a new domination. But there were also Catholics of French education and inclinations who accepted the Syrian idea. This may have been owing in part to the influence of the Belgian Jesuit Henri Lammens, a great historian of Islam who taught at the Jesuit University in Beirut throughout his career, and who was a staunch believer in the entity called 'Syria'; his dislike of Islam and Arab nationalism is obvious in all his writings, and he drew the sharpest possible distinction between Syrians and Arabs. A Maronite Archbishop of Beirut, Yusuf Dibs, wrote a vast history of Syria in eight volumes, which shows clearly the almost unconscious equivocation between the idea of Syria and that of Lebanon. The early volumes are a history of Syria in its most general sense, dealing with the continuous record of the country in ancient and classical as well as Islamic times, and relying on the work of European scholars. But when it comes to modern times it changes in content and method: drawing largely on local sources, it confines itself mainly to the history of Lebanon and of the Maronite community in particular.

In most of these writers there is an Arab element. They are conscious of a tie of language which should bind together those who differ in inherited religious belief; they are proud of the culture expressed through the language, and their writings communicate this pride to those who read them. In a lecture of 1859 Bustani is already aware of an entity called 'the Arabs', of something called 'Arab culture' in which he claims to participate. Twenty years later Ibrahim al-Yaziji, son of Nasif, called on the Arabs to remember their past greatness and awake, in a famous ode; and the secret society of 1875, of which he was himself a member, spoke in its proclamations of the 'Arab pride' of the people of Syria and rejected the sultan's claim to be caliph as a usurpation of Arab rights. But perhaps it was Jurji Zaydan who did more than any other to create a consciousness of the Arab past, by his histories and still more by his series of historical novels, modelled on those of Scott and creating a romantic image of the past as Scott's had done. Nevertheless, most of the Christian writers felt some doubt about drawing the political conclusions from this, and talking in terms of an 'Arab nation'; for they could not be certain that Arab nationalism would not turn out to be a new form of Islamic self-assertion. This doubt they could only banish in one of two ways. They could identify themselves with the majority in a way which, although equivocal, is not unusual for a minority; for example, Sulayman al-Bustani, arguing for the Ottoman constitution, refutes the suggestion that it is a religious innovation (*bid'a*) by maintaining, exactly as a Muslim would have done, that something like it had existed under the first caliphs.[34] Or else they could fill the concept of 'Arabism' with the same content as that of 'Lebanon' or 'Syria', and dream of an Arab nation divorced from its religious basis, and incorporating Christians and Muslims in exactly the same way, and under the benevolent protection of liberal Europe.

Such was the line taken by Négib Azoury, a Syrian Christian belonging to one of the Uniate communities, and like most of his fellows, of French education. He was for a time an Ottoman official in Jerusalem, but left his post in 1904 for obscure reasons, and went to Paris and later to Cairo, where he lived until his death in 1916. In 1904 he founded a *Ligue de la Patrie arabe*, of which the name clearly echoes that of the anti-Dreyfusard *Ligue de la Patrie française*. The activities of the League, if indeed it ever really existed, were limited to issuing manifestos.

[34] S. Bustani, '*Ibra wa dhikra*, p. 16.

Later he published in Paris a short-lived monthly periodical, *L'Indépendance arabe* (1907–8).

The full exposition of his views is to be found in a book published in French in 1905, *Le Réveil de la nation arabe*. There is, he asserts, an Arab nation—a single nation, which includes Christians and Muslims equally. The religious problems which arise between adherents of different faiths are really political, and aroused artificially by external forces in their own interests;[35] Christians are Arabs no less than Muslims, and indeed there should be a specifically Arab Christianity, an Arab Catholic Church instead of the present multiplicity of rites, worshipping and thinking in Arabic;[36] he defends the Arabic-speaking Orthodox Christians against the Greek hierarchy of their Church.[37] The frontiers of this Arab nation include all the Arabic-speaking countries of Asia, but not Egypt or North Africa. These lay beyond the limits of his interest as an Arab nationalist. Egypt, he maintained, was not Arab in the full sense,[38] and he had a strong dislike for the 'false Egyptian nationalism' of Mustafa Kamil, pro-Islamic and pro-Ottoman.[39] The Egyptians, he asserts, are not fit to rule themselves yet, they should be grateful for good British administration.[40] He did indeed dabble in Egyptian politics in his later years, but scarcely as an Egyptian nationalist. For a time he was 'foreign secretary' of a 'Young Egyptian Party', of which the programme was the gradual creation of representative government in collaboration with the occupying Power.[41]

This Arab nation must be independent of the Turks. The anti-Turkish note is clearer in Azoury's than in previous writings. The Turks, he says, have ruined the Arabs. Without them, the Arabs would have been among the most civilized nations in the world; they are better than Turks in every way —even as soldiers, for the Turkish victories have been due to Arab fighters.[42] It was not, he believed, possible to hope that the empire would reform itself and grant the Arabs a better position. If reform were possible, the Arabs would be loyal subjects; but Abdülhamid would never change his policy, and the Young Turks would never come to power.[43] Independence, then, was

---

[35] Azoury, p. 179.   [36] Ibid. pp. 168–9, 178.   [37] *Indép. arabe*, iv/5–6.
[38] Azoury, p. 246.   [39] *Indép. arabe*, i.   [40] Azoury, p. 89.
[41] Alexander, pp. 277 ff.   [42] Azoury, pp. 25, 210, 232.   [43] *Indép. arabe*, no. i.

the only way out. Arabs, Kurds, and Armenians must break away from the empire, which would then collapse. But how could this happen? Mainly from within and because of the weakness of the structure, but also with help from outside, from the Powers of Europe. Much of Azoury's book is taken up by a long analysis of the Near Eastern interests and policies of the Powers, and the conclusion he draws is that Russia is the greatest danger, from whom everything is to be feared,[44] German expansion in Asia Minor is also dangerous,[45] while everything is to be hoped from England and France with their liberal traditions, but more from France than from England.[46] (Azoury's culture was French, he had French collaborators, he may possibly have been subsidized by the French government.) But there is another danger from outside besides that of Russia: for almost the first time we hear a new note of warning, against the ambitions of Jewish nationalists to return to Palestine.

Deux phénomènes importants, de même nature et pourtant opposés, ... se manifestent en ce moment dans la Turquie d'Asie: ce sont, le réveil de la nation arabe et l'effort latent des Juifs pour reconstituer sur une très large échelle l'ancienne monarchie d'Israël. Ces deux mouvements sont destinés à se combattre continuellement, jusqu'à ce que l'un d'eux l'emporte sur l'autre. Du résultat final de cette lutte ... dépendra le sort du monde entier.[47]

(But he was not entirely consistent: at a later stage he hinted that the installation of Jewish settlements and banks in Palestine might mean that Arab nationalism would be strengthened by the interest of high finance.)[48]

It is only in broad outline that Azoury sketches the structure of an independent Arab State. It should be a constitutional liberal sultanate with an Arab Muslim sultan; but in the Hejaz there should be a temporal kingdom for an Arab caliph, and the autonomy of Lebanon, Nejd, and Yemen should be respected.[49] Who should be sultan, who caliph? He does not make it plain, but it is difficult to resist the impression that a member of the Egyptian ruling family is to be sultan, and the Sharif of Mecca to have the caliphate; once more we come across traces of that 'gospel' which Pickthall had found being preached in Palestine by emissaries of the khedive.

[44] Azoury, p. 91.   [45] *Indép. arabe*, no. iii.   [46] Azoury, pp. 104, 110.
[47] Ibid. p. v.   [48] *Indép. arabe*, no. i.   [49] Azoury, p. 245.

So long as Abdülhamid was supreme, the difference between various tendencies of opposition was held in check, both because it was impossible to write, organize, and act freely, and because of the common interest in changing the régime. From 1906 onwards however things began to change: there was a revival of Young Turk activities inside the empire: a group of army officers founded a secret revolutionary society, which eventually made contact with the exiles in Paris and took the name of their organization, the 'Committee of Union and Progress'. The society was strongest in the army of Macedonia, based on Salonika, and it was there, in 1908, that there suddenly broke out a revolt which spread rapidly and compelled the sultan to restore the constitution he had suspended thirty years earlier. A new government took office, and elections were held for a parliament. From that time the problems of politics changed and the possibility of political action was extended. Newspapers could be published freely: in the years from 1908 to 1914 about sixty new ones (mostly short-lived) appeared in Beirut, and about forty in Baghdad. In parliament matters could be discussed freely, political groups formed, and—what was perhaps most important—men from different provinces could meet each other and work together. From the very first session most of the deputies from the Arab provinces—second only to the Turks in number—began working together.

As was to be expected, the union of interests brought about by the need to end Abdülhamid's despotism began to break up as soon as the common aim had been achieved. The danger from the sultan's supporters was easily dealt with, and when they attempted a counter-revolution in 1909 the sultan was deposed. The real danger, however, came from inside, from the contradiction inherent in the Young Turk movement, and which now came to the surface. The Young Turks wanted constitutional government, which implied freedom and equality for all elements in the empire; but they also wanted to preserve the empire as a unit, and strengthen it against pressure from outside, and this implied centralized government and the predominance of the Turkish Muslim element over others.[50] Connected with this was another contradiction. The Young Turks stood for equality among Ottoman citizens, based on an Ottoman patriotism which

[50] Cf. B. Lewis, *Emergence*, pp. 214 ff.

all should share, and for the unity and strength of the empire; this, in their view, implied that all citizens of the empire should have the same relationship with the government, and all should have a direct relationship with it; this in its turn meant that all should be thought of and dealt with primarily as individual citizens, not as members of racial or religious communities inside the empire. But most non-Muslims, and many non-Turkish Muslims, meant by liberty and equality liberty for the community and equality between communities, and saw their own interest not in strengthening the power and increasing the intervention of the central government, but in maintaining the rights of the communities and strengthening the administrative autonomy of the provinces. The constitutional movement gradually split up: those who were first of all Ottoman nationalists and stood for central control split from those who were first of all Ottoman liberals and decentralizers; the gaps between the Turks and non-Turks grew wider, and Arabs, Albanians, Armenians tended to support the liberals. After a number of troubled years power was seized, in 1913 in the middle of the Balkan War, by a group of Turkish officers, whose ideas were nationalist rather than liberal; they ruled the empire until it collapsed, and in the process the ideas of the Ottoman nationalists changed. There took place a gradual and painful disentanglement of the three ideas of State, religious community, and linguistic nation—a process which can be traced in the thought of the theorist of the Young Turks, Ziya Gökalp.[51] The starting-point of the process was the idea that the only way to resolve the inherent dilemma of the empire was to impose a single national sentiment on it; but it gradually grew clearer that Ottoman national sentiment could not play this role, for it was too fragile and artificial, and rested ultimately on nothing except loyalty to the ruling family. The only effective nationalism was that which was rooted in some objective unity such as language or race, and thus Ottoman nationalism gradually turned into Turkish nationalism. The basis of the empire should be the national unity shared by all who spoke Turkish and were of Turkish origin, its policy should be directed to furthering the interests of Turks outside the empire as well as inside, for the empire was or should be the homeland of all Turks. This idea implied that an attempt should be made

[51] Cf. Gökalp, pp. 76 ff.

to strengthen the hold of the Turkish element in government and
administration and even to turn other ethnic groups into Turks
by insisting on the use of Turkish in schools and government;
and in the last few years of the empire's life there were some signs
that the Young Turk government was moving in this direction.

There was, it is true, another side to the rule of the Young
Turks. They improved local government and public security,
built public works, expanded education, and encouraged the
emancipation of women. But in the eyes of their subject peoples,
this was more than outweighed by the threat to their languages
and political rights implicit in the tightening of central control,
the policy of 'Ottomanization', and the idea of Turkish nationalism. By reaction against the new Turkish nationalism, that of the
Armenians was strengthened, that of Arabs, Albanians, and
Kurds came to political life. Among the Arabs, there were some
who continued to support the Young Turks, from the belief that
at all costs the empire must be preserved; one of the leaders in
fact was an army officer from Baghdad, Mahmud Shawkat Pasha,
although it is true he was of Georgian and not Arab origin, and
was in any case assassinated in 1913, when the policy of turkization was still new. On the whole, however, the effect of the new
policy was to drive the political leaders into opposition: they
tended to gravitate to the main opposition group, the *Entente
libérale*, but what was to be more important, their opposition
became more consciously Arab. Thus there grew up the first
effective and organized Arab groups, both open and secret:
numerous, some important, and some almost unreal, merging,
splitting off, ceasing to exist in a way difficult to follow. No
attempt will be made here to trace their history in detail; it is
enough to distinguish two types, whose history and programmes
illustrate the development of the national idea.

The politicians, the Islamic reformers, the local notables and
deputies, the men of standing, tended to express their opposition
within the constitutional system, and in agreement with the
Ottoman liberal decentralizers whose most prominent leader was
Prince Sabaheddin. In 1912 a number of Arabs living in Cairo,
mainly Syrians, founded a party designed to give expression to
their ideas: the 'Ottoman Party of Administrative Decentralization'. It had connexions with the Turkish liberals, and even with
'Izzat Pasha, the former secretary of Abdülhamid and an exile

since 1908;[52] it also had a network of 'committees of reform' in the Ottoman Arab towns, notably in Beirut. Its explicit aims, as its name implied, were administrative rather than political. It wanted Arabic to be recognized as an official language in provincial business; most local officials to be Arabs; the local authorities to be consulted about the appointment of officials; military service to be performed locally in time of peace; some local revenues to be applied to local needs; provincial councils to have wider powers; and foreign advisers to be appointed to reorganize the police and gendarmeries, justice and finance.[53] These aims it proposed to pursue by open and legitimate means; whether, as the Turks later claimed, it had other, secret aims going as far as autonomy on the Egyptian model, under a local ruler and with foreign protection, is uncertain, but it does not seem inherently improbable that its thoughts turned in this direction.[54]

In 1913 a group of individuals, mostly affiliated to this party, organized an 'Arab Congress' in Paris. It was attended by some twenty-five persons, all Syrians in the broader sense except for two Iraqis: some were students or residents in Paris, some men of distinction from Cairo and Beirut; roughly half were Muslims and half Christians; and it had the support of some of the prominent political leaders in Constantinople. The reports of its discussions give a vivid picture of the 'atmosphere' of moderate Arab nationalism at that time. It was an atmosphere of 'westernization': we Arabs, the speakers declared, want to reform the empire because we want to participate in modern civilization, and we look to Europe for help. There are complimentary references to France, appeals to the European conscience, hopes expressed of European pressure on the Ottoman government, refutations of the idea that Europe is a danger—the real danger lies within, in our own decay.[55] No less fervently, loyalty is pledged to the empire, and the desire expressed that the empire should be strong; although there is an occasional mild threat— the degree of our loyalty depends on how we are treated. The strength of States, it is declared, rests in their systems of government: Ottoman government must be really democratic, and in a

---

[52] *La Vérité sur la question syrienne*, p. 122.
[53] Jung, i. 61 ff.; Rossi, *Documenti*, p. 10.
[54] *La Vérité sur la question syrienne*, pp. 73, 103, 114, 117.
[55] *al-Mu'tamar al-'arabi al-awwal*, p. 38.

multi-national empire this implies provincial liberty. There should be effective participation by Arabs in the central government, and administrative autonomy in each Arab province; Arabic should be an official language, in parliament as well as local government; within the national community, Christians and Muslims are as one.

At first the Young Turk government seemed to take these suggestions seriously. They sent a delegate to confer with the leaders; but it soon became clear that the concessions they intended to make were limited and illusory, and this confirmed the view at which some Arabs had already arrived, that the methods of the decentralizers were useless and their demands did not go far enough. The Arabs must have independence, and could only gain it if willing to use force. This had long been Azoury's view, as we have seen, and he had from the beginning been sceptical about the Congress.[56] But he was not a power to be reckoned with; more important were such leaders as the group of thirty-five Arab deputies who already in 1911 had sent a letter to the Sharif of Mecca, Husayn, through the political boss of Basra, Sayyid Talib. The Arabs, they told him, 'are ready to rise with you, if you wish to break the yoke which weighs on them'; they 'recognize you as caliph of the prophet, the one man responsible for the interests of all the Arab countries'.[57] There may have been a touch of parliamentary rhetoric in this; but in the wake of the notables and deputies was rising a new generation who took such thoughts perhaps more seriously. Under Abdülhamid the system of public schools had been extended: secondary schools had been set up in the provincial capitals, the professional schools for training officers and officials expanded. Muslim Arabs of the great towns of Syria and Iraq began to go to these schools, learn foreign languages, become acquainted with new ideas; and from the schools they began to enter the public service. In the years immediately before 1914 there entered public life and came to political consciousness a group of such young men; pride in the Arab past was reinforced perhaps by the experience of living among those of different origin, and perhaps the unity which a common language confers became clearer in a place where not all shared it; their minds had been formed by the political ideas current in Constantinople as well as those which came to them from Cairo and Beirut; and they had acquired something of the discipline and sense of responsibility inherent in the officer corps of an imperial army, even if of an empire in decline. After the revolution of 1908 they began forming secret societies with far-reaching aims: the *Qahtaniyya*, founded in 1909 by army officers, including one of Egyptian birth, 'Aziz 'Ali al-Misri; the *Fatat*, started in Paris in 1911 by a number of Syrian students; the *'Ahd*, started in 1914 by al-Misri, and consisting almost entirely of army officers, with a strong Iraqi element among them.[58] The real aim of all of them was virtual or complete independence, and their spirit was for the first time anti-Turkish, something which was natural in officers entering a military group with a national tradition other than their own. The Turks are our misfortune, proclaimed an appeal issued by one such society in 1911. They have suppressed our culture and prevented economic progress. All the nations which have broken with them have started a vigorous national life, while those who have remained are condemned to poverty and stagnation. The present government are sacrificing the country to foreigners, and are not even believers in Islam. The Arabs must break away, by violence if necessary, and all Arabs must help in this: 'Muslim Arabs, this despotic State is not a Muslim State. Arab Christians and Jews, unite with your Muslim brothers'.[59]

But such appeals for Arab political unity did not strike a response among all who spoke Arabic. The greater freedom to speak and act after 1908, and the policy of the Young Turks, encouraged the growth of Arab nationalism, but also that of other nationalisms; and those Christians who believed in a Lebanese or Syrian nation also began to organize and express themselves. In Lebanon, two members of the ancient family of Khazin published, in 1910, a defence of the *Perpetuelle indépendance, législative et judiciaire du Liban*, and both there and in other places where Lebanese lived—in Cairo, New York, and Paris—committees sprang up to watch over the interests of the privileged sanjaq. They differed from each other in emphasis, and still more in personalities, but in general their aims were the same: to maintain the privileges they already had, to increase it

---

[58] For the early history of Arab nationalist parties cf. Antonius; Zeine, *Arab-Turkish Relations*.
[59] Rossi, *Documenti*, p. 7.

if possible, to enlarge the frontiers of Lebanon in order to make it economically viable, and in all this to seek the support of the western nations, but above all that of France. The idea of 'Syria' also had powerful champions, particularly in Paris, where two Lebanese Christian men of letters, Chekri Ganem (Shukri Ghanim) and Georges Samné, expounded it with encouragement and support from the Quai d'Orsay. The Syrian nation, they taught, possessing a unity given by nature and strengthened by history, had never yet possessed a social and political unity, and that for two reasons: first because of differences of origin, customs, and above all beliefs, and secondly because it had never had a national government, 'an authority accepted by the people and working in its interest'.[60] It should have such a government, based on the principles of democracy, laicism, and decentralization; its constitution should be a loose federation of largely self-governing districts, each with a stable ethnic or religious basis, and so delimited that each important community had a region in which it was in the majority; its moral basis should be a national sentiment making possible a complete and equal co-operation between those of different faith or race. Such a unity is gradually coming into existence, under the influence of modern education and civilization; there is being created a common Syrian nationality, based on culture, on 'la langue arabe et le trésor commun des traditions antiques, l'héritage des glorieux souvenirs de l'Orient'.[61] But it takes a long time for such a spirit to grow and free itself from the religious loyalties which divide men, and in the meantime Lebanon, with enlarged frontiers, must maintain its existence as the prototype of what all the regions will be in the future. When the time comes to create the secular national Syrian State, Lebanon will take its place as one of the provinces.[62]

Between these different tendencies the lines were not yet drawn clearly. The supporters of Syrian nationalism were proud of their Arab culture, had connexions with the 'Party of Decentralization', and took part in the Arab Congress of 1913;[63] at the same time, they argued for the *de facto* independence of Lebanon. Similarly, those who spoke in terms of Arab nationalism often

[60] Khairallah, 'La Syrie', *R. du monde musulman*, xix (1912), 16.
[61] Ibid. p. 106.
[62] Cf. Samné, *passim*.
[63] Jung, i. 67.

had a special feeling for the human community of Syria, and
when asking for Arab autonomy thought primarily of Syria, with
Damascus as its centre. The advocates of independent Lebanon,
it is true, tended to think in terms of Muslims and Christians
rather than Arabs and Turks, and wished to be independent of
Damascus no less than Constantinople; they saw Lebanon as a
Mediterranean country linked with western Christendom. But
at the same time they were jealous of the autonomy of the eastern
Catholic Churches, proud of the Arabic language and its
literature, aware that they could not turn their backs on their
Syrian and Arab hinterland of economic and cultural influence.
There was no need, before 1914, for lines to be sharply drawn:
all groups had a common interest in changing the policy of the
government, and none of them seemed near to securing independence in any form. The situation changed however when
war broke out in August 1914, and Turkey was drawn in before
the end of the year.[64] The war, it was clear, offered opportunities
and made necessary decisions. It might lead to the collapse of the
empire, the grant of independence or the imposition of a new
control. There was already a group of nationalists who looked to
one or other of the Powers of Europe to help them improve their
position, and some were already in touch with representatives
of England and France. What attitude should they take up towards the war, what action take, what foreign alliances seek? On
all these matters there took place a lively debate, which continued long after the war ended. There were some who were
more or less enthusiastic supporters of the Committee of Union
and Progress: among many of the educated, and perhaps most of
the Muslim masses, national had not yet superseded religious
loyalties, and the strength of Islam, the authority of the caliph,
and the independence of the empire were the main considerations. Others again, while opposed to the policy of the Young
Turks, thought the survival of the empire essential both for the
Arabs and the *umma* as a whole, since if it collapsed it would be
replaced by the rule of a European Power; they therefore
supported the State but hoped for a reform of the system of
government in the direction of provincial autonomy, or the

---

[64] For the history of Arab nationalism during and immediately after the war
cf. Antonius; Kedourie, *England and the Middle East*; Zeine, *Struggle for Arab
Independence*; Longrigg, *Syria and Lebanon*, chs. 2 & 3.

transformation of the empire into a dual monarchy. Others still wanted to take advantage of the war to obtain independence for Lebanon, or Syria, or the Arabs, with the help of the enemies of the empire. This group was however divided in several ways: some relied more on England, some on France; most of the Muslims who supported this policy did so with hesitation, for they knew that England and France had interests of their own which were not the same as those of the Arabs; nevertheless they thought the risk worth taking, for they had much to gain and little to lose. This was the advice given to them by Sa'd Zaghlul, not yet the popular leader of Egypt but already one of its most distinguished politicians:

> Zaghlul's argument . . . was to the effect that the Arab lands in those days had no political or sovereign entity which might perish. There was then no Arab independent State in existence, the very life of which was in jeopardy, as was the case with Turkey. Thus, no gamble was involved.[65]

But some at least of them did not pose the question only in terms of interest, but in those of conscience. The sultan claimed to be caliph; even if they did not accept this, at least he was sultan, legitimized by four centuries of temporal rule, the last great independent ruler of Sunni Islam, the political symbol of the unity of the *umma*. If they revolted against him, not only would they be fighting their legitimate ruler; they would be breaking the *umma* at a time when it needed to be united, and perhaps doing so in the interests of its enemies. There were others, however—although more Christians than Muslims—who had no such doubts, either because they believed implicitly in the good faith of the liberal States of Europe, or because they wanted the protection of England or France, for religious reasons or as a necessary help in building a modern State.

The most important division was about frontiers and systems of government when independence from the Turks should be won. The greater number of Muslim supporters of revolt wanted an Arab State under an Arab king, and many of them looked to the family of the Sharif of Mecca to provide the king; but while some dreamed of a single Arab State with an Arab caliph—a revival of the Ottoman Empire with its centre of gravity moved

[65] Zeine, *Struggle for Arab Independence*, p. 214.

from Turks to Arabs—others still kept the ideas of the Party of Decentralization, and wanted an independent Syria, itself a federation of provinces, and in some sort of loose relationship with an independent Iraq and Hejaz. The link with the Hejaz and the Sharif of Mecca sharpened the opposition of the Lebanese nationalists, either because they feared a revival of Muslim domination or because behind the sharif they saw the policy and ambitions of Great Britain: they came out in favour of a wholly independent Lebanon with enlarged frontiers and Beirut as its capital, under the protection of France, although they did not all agree on the nature and extent of French control. In the same way, the group of 'Syrian nationalists', mainly Christians, small but important because they had the support of the Quai d'Orsay,[66] became more sharply opposed to the Arab idea than before: Syrians are not Arabs, they declared, indeed there is no Arab nation, only 'une prétendue nationalité arabe, création de l'emir Fayçal et des agents anglo-indiens'.[67] In a book full of knowledge and thought, the spokesman of the group, Georges Samné, put forward their plan of a Syrian republic, secular, democratic, and federal, under the protection of France.

So long as the war lasted, these divisions were not urgent. Many Lebanese Christians took service in the French forces. The Sharif of Mecca, in association with the Arab nationalist secret societies, revolted against the Ottoman government on receipt of rather ambiguous assurances from the British, declared the independence of the Hejaz, and formed an 'Arab army' which took part in the Allied campaign which ended in the conquest of Syria. When the war ended, it seemed for a moment that both Arab and Lebanese nationalists would secure the substance of what they wanted. There was a British military administration in Palestine, a French in Lebanon and along the coast to the north; and the French government was clearly committed, by its whole tradition, to support the idea of an independent Christian Lebanon. In the interior however there was an Arab administration, recognized and subsidized by Britain, with a son of the sharif, Faysal, as head, and the leading posts in the hands of members of the secret societies and officers of the Arab army. But neither the administration nor the nationalist movement as a whole had any strength of its own: militarily and diplomatically

[66] Jung, ii. 55.   [67] Samné, p. 574.

it relied on the strength of Britain. It was caught in the inescapable dilemma of a weak group who look to a Great Power to
achieve their ends: they need the strength of the Power, but have
no way of forcing it to prefer their interests to its own. Great
Britain had made other commitments which, in the end, were
irreconcilable with those she had made to the Arab nationalists.
Her own strategic need for southern Iraq and the Palestinian
coast they were ready, if necessary, to accept. But beyond that,
she had committed herself to support for the creation of a Jewish
National Home in Palestine, and this, however she might deny
it, might lead in the end—as certain British statesmen knew—to
the creation of a Jewish State in which the Arab inhabitants of
Palestine would have the choice between becoming a minority
and leaving their homes. To the north, she had committed herself to supporting a virtual French control of whatever Arab
State was set up in Syria, and it seemed unlikely that France
would accept either a wholly independent State or one which
was linked to the Hejaz, both from solicitude for her Lebanese
clients and because she, like them, saw behind the sharif the
shadow of Britain, her traditional rival in the Levant. If it came
to the point, Britain would always prefer her need for good
relations with France to her desire to establish an Arab State in
Syria; and the Zionists could bring greater pressure to bear in
London than could the Arabs. For two years Faysal tried, not
without skill, to retain British support by reaching an accom-
modation with the French and the Jews. But he was caught
between forces stronger than himself: any agreement he would
himself have been willing to make with France would scarcely
have had the approval of his followers in Syria; and he may have
overestimated the support he could expect from Britain. In 1920
a congress of Syrian and Palestinian leaders, meeting in Damascus, declared him king of Syria and drew up a statement of principles which, in one way, was the last expression of the ideas of
the Ottoman Decentralizers and, in another, served as a programme for Arab nationalists for the next twenty-five years.
Declaring that it represented Muslims, Christians, and Jews
alike, the congress called for the complete independence of Syria
within its natural frontiers, from the Taurus to Sinai, from the
sea to the Euphrates. Its form of government was to be democratic, civil, monarchical, constitutional, and decentralized, with

safeguards for the rights of minorities. The congress rejected the idea of a foreign mandate, which had already been adopted in principle by the Peace Conference in Paris; if forced to accept a mandate, it would regard it as equivalent to the rendering of economic and technical assistance without prejudice to complete independence; it refused to accept the Balfour Declaration, Jewish immigration or the creation of a Jewish commonwealth, or the separation of Lebanon or Palestine from Syria. Iraq should be independent, and between her and Syria there should be no economic barriers.[68] Britain and France refused to accept these decisions. A few weeks later, after a period of mounting tension, the French occupied Syria and ended the reign of Faysal, and in the next two years the fate of the Arab countries was settled on very different lines. The Hejaz was left its independence, but the more advanced Arab countries of Syria and Iraq were placed under British and French mandates, which gave the mandataries administrative control, although with the obligation of preparing the way for eventual independence. Iraq, under British mandate, was separated from geographical Syria, which was itself subdivided into four regions—Syria and Lebanon under French mandate, Palestine and Transjordan under British; while Syria itself was subdivided into a number of separate regions. The mandate for Palestine placed on the mandatary the obligation of facilitating the Jewish immigration and the creation of a Jewish National Home.

It has been necessary to go into the events of these years in some detail, because they determined the spirit and aims of the nationalists for the next twenty years, until a new war once more changed the premises of politics. Arab nationalist thought and action, in the countries where it was strong, that is to say, Iraq and the four countries of geographical Syria, were concentrated on three main aims: first of all, the securing of a greater measure of self-government from the mandatory Powers, by demonstrations, by occasional revolts, by refusal to co-operate, by appeals to the liberal sentiments of England and France or to enlightened self-interest. Although Syria was the more advanced of the two regions, it was Iraq which achieved this first, thanks to a British

[68] Zeine, *Struggle for Arab Independence*, p. 265; *Dasatir al-bilad al-'arabiyya*, p. 3.

policy of maintaining control through an indigenous government under Faysal; the Anglo-Iraqi Treaty of 1930 gave her independence and membership of the League of Nations in return for political alliance with England and the maintenance of British air bases. The French were more reluctant to make such agreements, and when they finally made treaties with Syria and Lebanon in 1936 they never ratified them, and it was not until the end of the war that foreign troops left their soil. Second was the attempt to keep alive the idea of Arab unity, of that unity which had existed in a sense in Ottoman days, and was now threatened by the new political divisions, which not only tended to create different systems of administration, law, and education, but also split the Arab movement by giving it, in each region, the different immediate task. This idea found expression in writing, in ephemeral groups, in help and sympathy given from one country to another in its struggle, above all in periodical conferences bringing together men from different Arab countries and ending in the passing of general resolutions: after the Syrian Congress of 1920 there was the Caliphate Conference of Mecca in 1926, Islamic but with a certain Arab colouring, then the Jerusalem Congress of 1931, both Islamic and Arab; then, and perhaps the most important of the series, that held at Bludan in Syria in 1937, with an Iraqi president and with an Egyptian senator and the Orthodox Bishop of Hama among its vice-presidents: it affirmed Arab unity and laid emphasis on the inter-religious character of Arab nationalism.[69]

The third object of activity, and one closely interwoven with the second, was the rallying of support for the Arabs of Palestine in their opposition to Jewish immigration and land purchase and their demand for a unitary government with an Arab majority. This theme was already important at the Jerusalem Congress, and became more so when Jewish immigration increased after 1933. Before that, the Arabs had complained that the policy of establishing a Jewish National Home would prevent Palestine becoming part of an independent Syrian or Arab State, but now there was added to this the fear that the growth of the Jewish community would lead in the end to the subjection or expulsion of the Arabs of Palestine; there were serious disorders in 1929,

---

[69] *Oriente moderno*, xvii (1937), 497–9; R. Montagne, 'Le Congrès de Bloudane', in *Entretiens sur l'évolution des pays de civilisation arabe*, iii. 43.

and in 1936 the methods of protest and demonstration gave way to that of armed revolt. The main object indeed of the Bludan Conference was to affirm the general Arab interest in what was happening in Palestine; for the same purpose, an Arab and Muslim Inter-Parliamentary Conference was held at Cairo in 1938,[70] and in the same year the British government formally recognized the interest of other Arab countries in the problem of Palestine, and the existence of something called an Arab world, by inviting several Arab governments to send delegates to the Round Table Conference to be held in London.

In the attempts to secure self-government and keep alive the idea of an Arab nation, leadership remained in the hands of a small group, mainly former Ottoman officers and officials, whose political outlook had been moulded by the rule of the Young Turks, the secret societies, and the Arab revolt. They had, whether they were Syrians or Iraqis, a common mind, a system of ideas which formed the political orthodoxy of the years between the wars. First of all, they believed implicitly in the existence of an Arab nation: in schools, in barracks, in the Ottoman parliament, in exile in Cairo, and in the Sharifian forces they had come to know each other and acquired the ease of discourse which possession of a common language and a common education gives. But while on the one hand the idea of an Arab nation was spreading as a result of the war and the spread of education, and this gave them a more solid backing than before, on the other, the new political divisions were obscuring the reality of that nation, and this gave to their advocacy an insistence it had not previously possessed. The existence of the Arabs had not been questioned in the later Ottoman Empire, and the various Arab provinces had been thought of as a whole. The division of the post-war settlement called it in question, and threatened to set up the idea of a Syrian, a Lebanese and an Iraqi nation as its rival, sometimes with the encouragement of the mandatory Power.

Laying all their emphasis on the existence of the Arab nation, they also emphasized its unity, and justified the struggle for self-government in each State as only the first step towards a reunification. Each Arab State, it was implied, once independent would use its freedom of action to help those still struggling, and

[70] *Oriente moderno*, xviii (1938), 587–601.

to draw closer to those already free: this was the theory underlying the intervention of the Arab governments in the Saudi-
Yemeni war of 1934, thought of as a fratricidal struggle, and
then in the Palestine revolt, as well as the Treaty of Arab Brotherhood concluded by Iraq and Saudi Arabia in 1936, in consideration of 'the Islamic links and the national unity which unite
them'. Their conception of unity was still that of the years from
1908 to 1922: they thought of the Arab nation as excluding
Egypt and North Africa, with which its links seemed more
religious than national. They meant by 'Arabs' the Arabic-
speaking inhabitants of Asia, of Syria, Iraq, and the peninsula,
and specifically those of Syria and Iraq, more advanced in culture
than those of the peninsula and so more ready for political
existence and national independence. The problem of unity,
therefore, posed itself at three levels: first of all a reunion of the
States of geographical Syria; then a federation of Syria and
Iraq; then a looser link with other Arab States. This had been
the programme of the Syrian Congress of 1920; and a generation
later it was restated by one of Faysal's closest associates, who by
that time had reached a position of authority. In his 'Blue Book'
of 1943, Nuri Pasha al-Sa'id suggested that Syria, Lebanon,
Palestine, and Transjordan should be reunited into one State,
with a measure of autonomy for the Jews in Palestine and (if they
demanded it) a privileged régime for the Maronites in Lebanon;
and there should be created an Arab League to which Iraq and
reunited Syria would adhere immediately, and which could be
joined by the Arab States at will. The League would be presided
over by one of the Arab rulers to be chosen in a manner acceptable to the member-States.[71]

Although Syria was still the centre of Arab nationalist feeling,
and the idea of the Arab nation had first become explicit there,
there was a tendency throughout the 1920's and 1930's to look
to Baghdad as the leader in the movement for independence and
unity; partly because the alliance between the aspirations of the
national groups and the ambitions of the Hashimite family,
created in the days of the Young Turks and cemented by the
Arab revolt, was still unbroken, and a large part of the nationalists
still looked to Faysal as the leader of their movement, and partly
because Iraq, although more backward politically and socially,

[71] Nuri as-Sa'id, p. 11.

obtained relative independence earlier than the States of Syria. This was a role which was, on the whole, accepted by the monarchy and government of Iraq, although political conscious- ness was less widespread than it was becoming in Syria. Their interventions on behalf of Syria and Palestine were tireless and they took the initiative in Arab politics whenever it could be taken. But they had opponents and competitors. Opposition to the Hashimites, in Syria and Iraq alike, was stronger than it appeared on the surface; their administration of the Holy Places was widely criticized, and in general Arab affairs they were accused of having been too ready to identify their interests with those of Great Britain. In 1926 they were replaced, as rulers of the Hejaz, by 'Abd al-'Aziz ibn Sa'ud, creator of the new Wahhabi State in central Arabia, and his influence was growing. His was the only considerable Arab State which was inde- pendent, in the sense that it was not occupied by foreign troops; the Wahhabi ideal of Islam, still uncorroded by wealth, aroused much sympathy among reformers of the school of Rida; and the king himself embodied those archetypal virtues which Arabs liked to believe that they possessed. On the other side stood Egypt, not yet considered as wholly Arab in spite of language and scarcely yet thinking of herself as Arab. This was the period when 'Pharaonic' nationalism was at its height, and Egyptians were concerned primarily with their own problem of independ- ence, child of their own history; the influence of the monarchy had declined, and it no longer followed the Arab-Islamic policy of Muhammad 'Ali and 'Abbas Hilmi. But the beginnings of a change were there. Egypt was already the centre of Arab culture, thanks to her newspapers, publishing houses, films, and broad- casting station; in 1936 the signature of the Anglo-Egyptian Treaty gave her comparative freedom in foreign policy, and as always her natural hinterland of influence was the Arab region to the east of her; already some Arab leaders were looking to her as a possible source of help in the complicated problem of Palestine. At the Bludan Conference, the Egyptian vice-president stated that a Jewish State in Palestine would be a danger to Egypt as much as to its neighbours, and Egyptian delegates took a large part in the Round Table Conference of London.

Explicitly, Arab nationalism was a secular movement. The leaders wished to deprive the French of their most powerful weapon, the existence of Christian and dissident Muslim minorities who looked to them for protection; they wished to state their opposition to Zionism in national terms, in terms of the threat to the interests of Christian and Muslim Palestinians alike, rather than of religious hostility; and they needed the help of what was still by and large the best educated part of the population and the one with most experience of Europe. Moreover, the intellectual atmosphere in which they had grown up, in schools of a western type or under the Young Turks in Constantinople, was one of secularism—of the separation, for the good of each, of the realm of government from that of religion. This implied not only that the national ties which united men were more important politically than the religious beliefs which divided them, but also that in its own sphere the national government should be autonomous and be bound by no norm except its own interest. The teaching was reinforced by the success of Kemal Atatürk and his supporters. Until the crisis of Alexandretta in 1937–9 this exercised a great influence over the political minds of the Arabs, not only because of the success of the Turks in beating back the encroachments of Europe, but because there still remained profound ties, of religion, a shared history and often a blood relationship between Arabs and Turks, and still more because of their uncompromising statement of the rights of the nation. Few Arabs of the older generation approved of the strong anti-clerical element in Atatürk's policy, but they responded to a theory of government which echoed not only the teachings of their European masters but also the later political doctrine of Islam:

Sovereignty and the right to rule cannot be conferred on no matter whom, by the first comer, as a result of an academic discussion. Sovereignty is acquired by force and power and by violence. It was by violence that the sons of Osman seized power, reigned over the Turkish nation and maintained their domination for six centuries. Now it is the nation which, revolting against these usurpers and putting them in their place, itself takes back effectively the exercise of sovereignty.[72]

Nevertheless, it was impossible for Arabs to separate nationalism from Islam to such an extent as the Turks had done.[73]

---

[72] Atatürk, *Nutuk*, ii. 186 (Fr. trs. p. 540).
[73] For the relations between Islam and Arab nationalism cf. the works by Haim cited in the bibliography.

Islam was what the Arabs had done in history, and in a sense it had created them, given them unity, law, a culture. For both Muslim and Christian Arabs, in different ways, there lay a dilemma at the bottom of Arab nationalism: secularism was necessary as a system of government, but how was complete secularism compatible with the existence of an Arab sentiment? In real life dilemmas need not be resolved, they can be lived, and most Arabs who thought about the subject were content to affirm both terms of it; non-Muslim Arabs are fully a part of the Arab nation, but Islam is the basis of the corporate sense of the Arabs. Thus Nuri al-Sa'id, in his 'Blue Book', derives Arab nationalism from the Muslim feeling of brotherhood enjoined on them by Muhammad in his last public speech; it is 'an aspiration to restore the great tolerant civilization of the early Caliphate'.[74] Some of them posed the problem at a more profound level: Islam for them was important not simply as a source of pride and inspiration, but as providing a moral law which should guide the life of nations; the community should not be its own law, it must have a regulative principle standing above it. Thus Faysal's brother 'Abd Allah, Amir of Transjordan and later King of Jordan, in an essay on Arab nationalism added to his memoirs, states as the first principle of Arab political life that the Quran and Sunna must be obeyed. So long as the Ottoman sultans accepted this the Arabs were content to be ruled by them even though they were not themselves Arab. But in the nineteenth century they abandoned the principles of Islam and adopted a western form of government which they themselves did not understand; from that moment the bond of Arab loyalty was loosened and Arabs began to think of an Arab government which would once more be faithful to Islam.[75]

In the same way there was something equivocal in the attitude of the nationalists towards Europe, and specifically towards England and France which were the Europe that they knew. Most of those who had supported the agreement with England and the revolt against the Ottoman government during the war believed that the peace settlement was not in accordance with the undertakings they had been given: few of them would have accepted T. E. Lawrence's verdict that Britain came out of her

[74] Nuri as-Sa'id, p. 8.
[75] King 'Abd Allah, *Mudhakkirat*, p. 318 (Eng. trs. p. 243).

Arabian adventure 'with clean hands'. Among Iraqis, the sense of betrayal was softened by the rapidity with which they were given independence and the mandate was ended; a framework was established within which Iraqi nationalists could co-operate with Great Britain. In Syria, however, it was strengthened by the reluctance of France to relinquish control, and by the growth of the Jewish National Home in Palestine. Thus there came into being a bitterness and distrust similar to those which had existed in Egypt since 1882. The shock of subjugation was all the greater because the Muslim Arabs of Syria and Iraq had been part of the dominant element of the Ottoman Empire, and had played a larger part in its government in the half-century before it ended. On the other hand, they were still under the spell of European civilization. The Powers of Europe were actually (although no longer potentially) the strongest in the world; they had created modern civilization, in a sense they still had 'the secret' of it; the political ideas and institutions of western Europe still seemed to most men not only the necessary basis of national strength but the best in themselves. So, while the nationalists condemned British or French policy, the conclusion they drew was not that England or France was intrinsically bad but that they were being untrue to themselves. The appeal was to the 'true' England and France, and the expectation was that sooner or later they would reassert themselves and understand that their interests were in harmony with those of the Arabs. If this should happen, the Arabs would obtain their independence—at least a relative independence in treaty relations with a Great Power, for in the world of the 1920's and 1930's this seemed the only way in which a small Asian State could hope to enter the community of nations. For the most part, too, it was taken for granted that once independent the Arab States should adopt the characteristic institutions of European liberal society.

In the course of the half generation from 1908 to 1922 Arab nationalism became a conscious political idea, then an organized movement, acquired a programme, was forced—too early for its own good—to make a choice, saw its hopes destroyed, and acquired from the experience a new frame of mind. Nowhere can this process be studied better than in the full, frank and self-revealing pages of *al-Manar*. From the beginning of his life until

the end, the final object of Rashid Rida's political thought was
the re-establishment of a truly Islamic State. He disapproved
of all attempts to create in the Muslim world States based on a
solidarity other than that of religion: among others, national
States in which the nation was the final object of loyalty, national
sentiment the binding force, and national interest the highest
criterion of policy and legislation. This sort of nationalism
seemed to him nothing but a new form of the purely natural
tribal solidarity which had existed in the days before Islam; its
principles were those of the days of religious ignorance—loyalty
and honour—not those of the *Shari'a*.[76] He was therefore in
disagreement with Ibn Khaldun's belief that natural *'asabiyya*
is the foundation of every state and is present as a motive in all
social action, that religious loyalty and law can only be effective
once *'asabiyya* has done its work. This, he maintained, was
untrue in fact, and the history of Islam showed it; the actions of
Muhammad were not directed by the desire for social prestige
or to increase the authority of his clan, and his success was not
due to the strength of the *'asabiyya* at his disposal. On the
contrary, *'asabiyya* was subordinated to the imperatives of
Islam;[77] and when it revived it destroyed the Islamic State. It
was the blind will for domination which led rulers to impose their
personal power on the *umma*, and they had perverted its political
structure by making obedience to themselves an absolute
religious duty.[78]

It may seem self-contradictory that, in spite of this, the element
of Arab national feeling is strong in Rashid Rida's writings, and
stronger still in those of his friend Shakib Arslan. When they
talk of the problems of Islam they are thinking first of all about
Arab Islam, and regard other Muslims, in Arslan's own phrase,
as 'the pupils of the Arabs'.[79] But the contradiction is apparent
only: they believed that, because of the special place of the
Arabs in the *umma*, Arab nationalism could be reconciled with
Islamic unity in a way impossible for any other—even more,
that a revival of the *umma* needed a revival of the Arabs. Islamic
thought could not flourish unless the Arabic tongue flourished:
it was the only language in which Islam could be properly studied

[76] Cf. *al-Manar*, x (1907–8), 459.
[77] Rida, *al-Khilafa*, p. 135 (Fr. trs. p. 227).
[78] Ibid. p. 43 (Fr. trs. p. 75).
[79] Arslan, *Limadha*, pp. 10 ff.

and expounded, and therefore it was the duty of any Muslim who could do so to learn Arabic.[80] Moreover there could be no deep unity in an *umma* unless it was a unity of language, and in the Muslim *umma* this could be none other than Arabic. No non-Arab had ever been able to serve Islam unless he knew Arabic. The Arabic language was a common good of all Muslims:

One of the religious and social reforms of Islam was to bring about linguistic unity, by making its common language that of all the peoples who adhered to it. The religion preserved the language and the language preserved the religion. But for Islam the Arabic language would have changed like others, and as it had itself changed previously. But for Arabic, the different interpretations of Islam would have grown apart from each other, and it would have split into a number of faiths, with the adherents of each accusing the others of infidelity; when they wished to give up following their passions and return to the truth, they would have found no general principle to invoke. Thus the Arabic language is not the private property of the descendants of Qahtan, it is the language of all Muslims.[81]

The Arabs were the guardians not only of the language of Islam, but also of its Holy Places. They had done much for Islam, and were capable of doing more, for in the peninsula at least they were still devoted to their religion and untouched by the corruptions of the west. Those Muslims who belittled the Arabs were in reality weakening Islam. Here we catch an echo of the controversies of the *Shu'ubiyya*. Indeed it was a conscious echo, for Kurd 'Ali throws the name at those who attack the Arabs: his work on Islam and Arab civilization is a defence of the Arab contribution to civilization, both Islamic and European, against those who attacked it, whether Muslim nationalists (like the Pharaonic nationalists of Egypt) or orientalists such as Renan.[82] At times indeed members of this group moved from defence to counter-attack. Rida argued that it was the non-Arabs who had altered the true nature of the caliphate and the *umma*: they had brought into Islam alien theories of a hidden truth and an infallible imam; they had exalted the person of the caliph and effaced the true idea of government by *shura*; and while the

[80] *al-Manar*, xii (1909–10), 904.
[81] Rida, *al-Khilafa*, p. 88 (Fr. trs. p. 148).
[82] Kurd 'Ali, *al-Islam*, pp. 34 ff.

coming of Islam had canalized the *'asabiyya* of the Arabs, that of Turks and Persians had continued to exist uncontrolled and had finally ruined Islam.[83]

In other words, while the *'asabiyya* of other Muslim peoples was in conflict with the interests of the *umma*, that of the Arabs was in harmony with them. Rashid Rida explains this further when he deals with the traditional belief that the caliph should be of the family of Quraysh. This condition might seem to run counter to the universalism of Islam, and for this reason has not been accepted by all jurists. In fact, argues Rida, the contrary is true. Any ruler or ruling family is bound to possess a corporate pride and interest, but only that of Quraysh must always and necessarily be in harmony with the pride and interest of Islam. The Quraysh are the family of Muhammad, and therefore their glory is linked with that of Islam; in them, as in no other family, religious zeal and the pride of race reinforce each other.[84] Himself claiming to belong to this stock, Rida proudly affirms the eternal identity of Islam and Arabism:

I am an Arab Muslim and a Muslim Arab, of the family of Quraysh and the lineage of 'Ali, of the seed of Muhammad the Arab Prophet, whose line goes back to Isma'il the son of Abraham, and whose community of true belief is that of his ancestor Abraham: its base is the sincere affirmation of the unity of God and the turning of the face in surrender (*islam al-wajh*) to God alone. . . . My Islam is the same in date as my being Arab. . . . I say, I am an Arab Muslim, and I am brother in religion to thousands upon thousands of Muslims, Arabs and non-Arabs, and brother in race to thousands upon thousands of Arabs, Muslims and non-Muslims.[85]

Arab feeling was implicit in Rashid Rida's doctrine from the beginning, but it was only gradually, and under the pressure of political circumstances, that it led him to become an advocate of Arab national independence. Before 1908, although a loyal supporter of the empire for the same reasons as 'Abduh, he was openly critical of Abdülhamid on two grounds: his personal despotism, and his encouragement of what in Rida's view was a false kind of Islam. (For this he incurred the hostility of Abu'l-Huda, who objected to his criticism of the *turuq* and praise of

[83] Rida, *al-Khilafa*, p. 123 (Fr. trs. p. 209).
[84] Ibid. p. 20 (Fr. trs. p. 34).
[85] *al-Manar*, xx (1917–18), 33.

al-Afghani, and who—at least according to Rida himself—tried to have him expelled from Egypt, prevented *al-Manar* from entering Syria, and offered him titles and positions if he would give it up.)[86] He founded a political society, the 'Ottoman Society of Consultation', dedicated to the union of all Ottomans and the replacement of despotic by consultative government; and criticized the Committee of Union and Progress because in fact although not in name it was entirely Muslim.[87] At first he had great hopes of the revolution of 1908; but his disapproval of the policy followed by the new government towards the Arabs was strengthened perhaps by personal disappointment when he failed to obtain from them support for his plan of a seminary for Muslim missionaries. In 1909, while in Constantinople, he published an important series of articles on 'Turks and Arabs',[88] in which he was at pains to stress the loyalty of the Arabs to the Ottoman State. European imperialists were trying to encourage Arab separatism, in order to divert Turkish forces from Macedonia and Anatolia and so weaken their hold there, but they had met with no success, and even in the worst days of Abdülhamid no Arab had called for independence except a few Christians.[89] Until recently there had been no Arab hatred of their Turkish rulers: they had not indeed thought of them as foreign, in the sense in which British rule was foreign, for Islam had abolished the racial *'asabiyya* of the Arabs. After the revolution, most Arabs were in favour of the new régime, and if their ideas were now changing it was because of the Turkish attitude towards them. The Turks had always had a kind of hatred or contempt for the Arabs, and to this they had now added a policy of turning the empire into a Turkish State: for example, by dismissing Arab officials and neglecting the teaching of Arabic in official schools. Such a policy could not succeed: one racial element could not be changed into another by force, and Turkish *'asabiyya* would simply arouse that of the Arabs. This in turn would bring disaster on the empire, for the Arab provinces formed its largest and richest part, the Arab peoples had intelligence and a potential military strength, and their language was that of the legal system as well as the official religion. It was still possible to restore good relations, by a change in the

---

[86] *al-Manar*, xii (1909–10), 1 ff. [87] Ibid. p. 13.
[88] Ibid. pp. 813–32, 913–37. [89] Ibid. pp. 823 & 832.

spirit of education, and a proper application of the constitution, giving each element in the population its due and so creating a national solidarity wider than that of race or language: a solidarity based on common interest and acceptance of the *Shari'a*, on equality between members of different races.[90]

From this moment he was active in attempts by the Ottoman Arabs to secure a recognized position for their nation within the Ottoman community. He was one of the founders of the Party of Decentralization in Cairo, and also started a semi-secret society (*Jam'iyyat al-jami'a al-'arabiyya*) with an oath of loyalty.[91] The Arab question from now on assumed in the pages of *al-Manar* an importance it was never to lose. Even at this time he was conscious of the danger of Zionist immigration to the Arabs of Palestine, and criticized the facilities given the Zionists, as he claimed, by the central government of the empire.[92]

During the First World War his thoughts on the subject moved farther, and for the first time the possibility of complete independence appeared. The pages of *al-Manar* bear witness to the struggle of conscience which it posed for him. The Arabs, he repeats, have always been faithful to the empire, out of loyalty to Islam; but the policy of turkization has changed everything, for the Arabic language is in danger, and it is the religious duty of Arabs to save it, even if this means that they are doing something which will weaken a Muslim State and involve the risk of European control. But characteristically, although Islam for him is the justification of Arab independence and must be the moral law of an Arab State, he emphasizes the full membership of non-Muslim Arabs in the national community; and adds that if there is an Arab region with a non-Muslim majority (no doubt he is thinking of Mount Lebanon) it can be independent, with a link with the Arab kingdom.[93]

Rida belonged to that wing of the nationalist movement which was willing to co-operate with England to secure independence, and he played a part in the negotiations of the war years; one of the British assurances was given to a group of seven Syrians in Cairo of whom he was a member. He quarrelled on this account with his friend Arslan, who, although not in sympathy with the Young Turk policy, believed that the dangers of breaking up the

[90] Ibid. p. 503.
[92] Ibid. xviii (1915–16), 538.
[91] Ibid. xxxi (1931–2), 719.
[93] Ibid. xx (1917–18), 36 ff.

union of Turks and Arabs were too great, and it would be best
to try to work for a change in Turkish policy. He himself seems
to have had growing doubts as the war went on, and is said to
have incurred the displeasure of the British authorities before it
ended.[94] The events of the years after the war increased these
doubts, and he took an active part in the new nationalist movement of resistance to French rule in Syria: as President of the
Syrian Congress which offered the crown of Syria to Faysal in
1920, as member of the 'Syro-Palestinian Congress' held at
Geneva in 1921, and as member of the executive committee set
up by this congress in Cairo, and which supported the cause of
Syrian and Palestinian independence actively, remained closely
in touch with the leading men of the country, and at times
negotiated with the French authorities. In this new age his
nationalist conviction led him into stronger opposition to the
European Powers. In France he had always seen the supporter
of the Christian missions, the systematic colonizer which had
destroyed the religious institutions and social system of North
Africa; but in England too he now recognized the enemy of
Islam: 'The British government has taken upon itself to destroy
the religion of Islam in the east after destroying its temporal
rule'.[95] In spite of the Turkish contempt for us, he confessed to
Shakib Arslan, I should prefer their rule to that of the Europeans[96] (although a few years later he changed his mind about
this, from disapproval of their atheism).[97] Significant of his
change is an article on Bolshevism, written just after the war.[98]
'Bolshevism', he says, is only another name for socialism, and
socialism means the liberation of the workers from capitalists and
oppressive governments. Muslims must hope for its success,
since they too are workers and suffer from the same oppression,
and if socialism succeeds the subjugation of peoples will end.
True, Communism is not in conformity with Islamic law, but
neither are the activities of the European governments.

It was partly this growing opposition to the European Powers
which made him the opponent of the Hashimite family, 'the
worst disaster that has befallen Islam in this age'.[99] Husayn and

[94] *al-Manar*, xxxi (1931–2), 719; Arslan, *Rashid Rida*, pp. 153–4.
[95] Rida, *al-Wahhabiyyun*, p. 47.
[96] Arslan, *Rashid Rida*, p. 315.
[97] Ibid. p. 435.
[98] *al-Manar*, xxiii (1920), 254.
[99] Rida, *al-Wahhabiyyun*, p. 9.

his sons, by relying too much on England, had opened the way to Britain to extend her control over the Arab and Muslim countries, and even in the holy province itself. They had cheated the Syrians with promises of full independence, while all the time they were in agreement with England, and were even willing to accept a French mandate; had betrayed the Arabs of Palestine; and were attacking their brother Arab rulers. They had administered the Hejaz badly—corruptly, inefficiently, greedily, without consultation. They like almost all the sharifs of Mecca were ignorant in religious matters, and were the enemies of 'all knowledge which could contribute to a spiritual and temporal reform'. Even their lineage was not half as noble as that of the Imam of Yemen; and on all these grounds Rida opposed Husayn's claim to the caliphate as well as his temporal ambitions.[100] (But when Husayn died he wrote of him in a way which was not unfair: the old king had been obstinate and ignorant, but intelligent, strong-willed, pure-minded, devout, and excellent company.)[101]

Dislike of the Hashimites, of their rule in the Hejaz as well as their general Arab policy, was one of the factors which led him to approve of the conquest of the Hejaz by 'Abd al-'Aziz ibn Sa'ud, although there was also a positive affinity between his own religious ideas and those of the Wahhabis. But he was not rigid in his political views, and his political convictions, particularly in regard to Syria, were more important than his feelings about one political leader or another. In the early 1930's he was involved in the secret Franco-Arab negotiations which aimed at a union of Syria and Iraq under Faysal, as a first step towards Arab unity. Although doubtful whether it was possible, he supported the plan in spite of his known sympathy for Ibn Sa'ud, but he did insist that the united State, if it came into existence, should make an alliance with Saudi Arabia and recognize the existing situation in the Hejaz; it should not be used as a base for a Hashimite reconquest of the Holy Places.[102]

Rida's political views changed considerably during his career, but the change was no more than one of emphasis, and his final aim was always what it had been, the welfare of Islam as he

[100] Rida, *al-Khilafa*, pp. 73 ff. (Fr. trs. pp. 123 ff.).
[101] *al-Manar*, xxxi. 718, 797.
[102] Arslan, *Rashid Rida*, pp. 600 ff.

conceived it. Justifying his attitude at the time of the Arab revolt, he asserted that the political interests of the Arabs were the same as those of the *umma* as a whole, for an independent Arab State would put new life both into the language of Islam and into its law; if the two had not been the same, he would have preferred his religious to his national duties, for they concerned the happiness of the next world as well as this.[103] Thus Islam takes priority over Arabism, and, by implication, the moral laws of Islam are binding on the national State; the nation is not a law to itself, it should act and can be judged by a law derived from something other than its own interest.

Such views continued to have their influence as long as Rida lived and wrote. He appealed to those who had had an Islamic education, or who had been brought up in the imperial days before 1908, and for whom the idea of the Islamic State as unified by common submission to divine law still had a meaning. His closest associate, Shakib Arslan, shared these views, and spread them in the course of a political career more active than his. A deputy in the Ottoman parliament from 1913 to 1918, Arslan supported the Young Turks during the war, as we have seen. From 1918 until his death in 1946 he lived mainly in Switzerland and elsewhere in Europe, voicing the claims of Syria and other Arab countries at the League of Nations, sometimes negotiating on their behalf with France and other Powers, and publishing a periodical, *La Nation arabe*, which had some influence at the time. He had close and friendly relations with North African political movements like the Association of Algerian 'Ulama', the Étoile Nord-africaine of Messali Hadj, the Destour in Tunis, and the first nationalist groups in Morocco, and he was indeed the link between them and the main stream of Arab national feeling in the east.

As a man of political conviction, as well as a master of Arab style, he continued to be honoured by nationalists until his death. But his influence declined in his last years. His support of Germany during the Second World War was not disliked among Arabs who had despaired of a settlement with England or France; but his defence of Italy, at a time when she was trying to build her own empire in Africa, met with much disapproval. Moreover, his Arabism was too close to the pan-Islamism of al-

[103] *al-Manar*, xx (1917–18), 34.

Afghani to win favour with a new generation. When he returned
to Syria for a brief visit after the signature of the treaty of 1936,
his speeches, in which he emphasized the Islamic nature of Arab
nationalism in a way which had become unfashionable and seemed
inopportune, met with much criticism. Long before he died he
and his like had been superseded as effective spokesmen of the
movement by men of a younger generation: those who had
grown up just before the war of 1914, in the secularist nationalist
atmosphere of Young Turk politics and Ottoman professional
schools; and those who came to maturity after the war, in the
government schools of the new Arab States, the American
University of Beirut, or the higher schools of England, France,
and the United States.

In the 1920's, and still more in the 1930's, there began to grow
up a new sort of nationalism, more thoroughgoing than that of
the older generation. It was not satisfied with the old methods of
organization and action: the loose and shifting associations of
local notables, knowing each other well, often related to each
other, accustomed to work together but each with his local
following and not prepared to subordinate himself to others; the
methods of patient negotiation, varied by occasional demonstrations or large congresses where aims were reaffirmed. Some of
these groups were, it is true, successful; for example, the
'National Bloc' in Syria, which secured the abortive treaty of
independence in 1936. But they had, in the eyes of the young,
certain defects: they were essentially alliances of independent
leaders, held together by precarious agreement; although in
principle concerned with Arab unity, in fact their horizon was
bounded by the problems of a specific Arab country; their aim
was not the seizure of independence, but the exertion of pressure
with a view to making an agreement with the dominant Powers;
they made no systematic attempt at national political education;
they had no clear idea of what should be done once independence
had been won. Side by side with them there gradually grew up
other parties, appealing mainly to a younger generation, hier-
archically organized, drawing their members in principle from
all Arab countries, and trying to evolve and spread a doctrine of
nationalism and programme of action. In Iraq the *Ahali* group,
formed in 1931, stood for parliamentary democracy, individual
rights, and sweeping social reform, while rejecting the doctrine

of class warfare and laying emphasis on the unity of the nation. In Syria the League of National Action, started in 1935, had a somewhat similar programme—national independence, Arab unity, secularism, social reform—although its interest was more in the struggle for independence than in the social problems which an Arab government would face. (This difference of emphasis is easy to explain: by this time Iraq was independent and Iraqis could hope to take part in ruling her; Syria was not, and the educated class was not in a position to take responsibility for policy, internal or external.)

Such new parties played a certain part in the politics of Syria and Iraq in the 1930's, but proved little more effective than those they wished to replace. They were mainly important because they tried to express a nationalist doctrine more systematic and uncompromising than that of their elders: a doctrine in which the change of emphasis we have noticed in the thought of Rashid Rida was carried to a conclusion from which he would have withdrawn. Put briefly, the centre of gravity was shifted from Islam as divine law to Islam as a culture; in other words, instead of Arab nationalism being regarded as an indispensable step towards the revival of Islam, Islam was regarded as the creator of the Arab nation, the content of its culture or the object of its collective pride.

For example, a young Iraqi teacher, 'Abd al-Rahman al-Bazzaz, in a lecture on 'Islam and Arab Nationalism',[104] denied that there was a contradiction between the two. The idea of a contradiction, he maintained, sprang from a western conception of Islam and of nationalism, and that so many Arabs had accepted it showed the intellectual domination of the west over them. In reality the content of Islam was the same as that of Arab nationalism; and this was true only of the Arabs, not of other Muslim nations. So far, Rashid Rida would have agreed, and we have come upon an argument like this in his own writings. But there is an essential difference. Rida would have defined Arab culture in terms of Islam; Bazzaz does rather the opposite. Islam is a national religion: the real Islam was Arab Islam, it was later destroyed by the other nations with their particularism. Islam indeed is a developed form of what was already present in the nature of the Arabs. Its moral ideals are the same as the natural

[104] Eng. trs. in *Welt des Islams*, iii (1954), 201.

morality of the Arabs, its political ideal of *shura* is identical with
the natural democracy of the beduin. The spread of Islam was the
medium through which the Arabs made their great contribution
to history.

The Arabic language, says Bazzaz, is the 'soul of the Arab
nation'. Those who speak Arabic are Arabs; but since Islamic
culture is the content of the Arabic language, it follows that all
who speak Arabic can appropriate Islamic culture and the
Islamic past as their own. Christian Arabs are as much a part of
the nation, and can take as intimate a pride in what it had done
in history, as Muslim Arabs. The conclusion is present by
implication in Bazzaz's warning against Muslim exclusiveness,
but it is drawn more explicitly, for obvious reasons, by two
Christian writers of the same generation. In them can be clearly
seen the process of appropriation by Christians of the Arab
Muslim heritage. One of them is Qustantin Zurayq, an Orthodox
Christian from Damascus, Professor at the American University
of Beirut, a distinguished medieval historian and consulting don
to a whole generation of nationalists. In 1939 he published a
volume of essays on national consciousness. Its starting-point is
a clear appreciation of the present position of the Arabs. Our
basic problem, he asserts, is that we have no convictions; having
no convictions, we cannot subordinate our individual desires and
passions to an organization rooted in a principle; therefore we
cannot act successfully as a group. Nationalism is the conviction
we need: that is to say, a sense of collective responsibility, the
will to create and maintain a community, but one of a specific
sort—a community which draws its inspiration and its principles
from a religion, and from our own religion. For Arabs, this
religion can only be Islam. This may seem surprising as coming
from a Christian, but it becomes clear when Zurayq goes on to
distinguish 'the religious spirit' (*al-ruh al-diniyya*) from 'sectarian
solidarity' (*al-'asabiyya al-ta'ifiyya*).[105] The assumptions underlying this distinction appear to be two: first, that all religions
contain the same core of truth, accessible alike to all men; and
secondly, that the moral principles of religion are those which are
necessary to build a stable and prosperous society. The 'symbols'
in which these principles are expressed differ from one religion
to another, but the difference is of cultural rather than intellectual

[105] Zurayq, *al-Wa'y al-qawmi*, pp. 112 & 207.

importance. It is in this sense that there is an essential connexion between the Arabs and Islam. Muhammad was the creator of Arab culture, the unifier of the Arab people, the man of conviction from whom they can draw their inspiration; but there is no suggestion that they should draw more than that from him, that they should be guided by Islamic law or the institutions of the caliphate. The Arabs of course must be a modern people, and to be modern means to adopt the institutions characteristic of the west.

A more extended and detailed exposition of what is fundamentally the same thesis was given by another Syrian, Edmond Rabbath, a Uniate from Aleppo, who played a leading part in the politics of the Nationalist Bloc and helped to negotiate the treaty of 1936. His book, *Unité syrienne et devenir arabe*, is an attempt to define the nature and limits of the Arab nation. 'There is no Syrian nation, there is an Arab nation',[106] he proclaims and defines the Arab nation in terms of several different factors: blood and origin, for the Arab nation, even outside the peninsula, has been formed by successive waves of immigration; language, the 'national factor *par excellence*';[107] and religion. His view of the political function of religion is that of the positivists: it plays a considerable part in the initial formation of nations, and religious solidarity is a forerunner of national solidarity, which prepares the way for political association and draws men together against a foreign invader. The religion which has played this role in Arab history is undoubtedly Islam, 'une religion d'essence nationale',[108] and the Islamic community was an embryonic Arab community.

What are the frontiers of the Arab nation? Rabbath's view is the same as that of the older generation. The Arab nation is to be found in the Arabic-speaking lands of Asia. It includes three geographical and human units: Iraq, the peninsula, above all Syria in the broader sense. Syria is a unity even if it is not a separate nation. Lebanon is part of it, but to some extent a distinct part: its consciousness is Arab like its language, but it has evolved 'a local form of Arab civilization',[109] a territorial consciousness like that of other Syrian districts but given permanence and stability by its tradition of religious freedom,

[106] Rabbath, p. 33.   [107] Ibid. p. 55.
[108] Ibid. p. 53.   [109] Ibid. p. 151 ff.

autonomy, Christian hegemony, and connexion with the west. For Arab nationalism to embody itself, there must be a union of the various fragments into which Syria has been split by the mandatory Powers (with a special position for Lebanon inside it); then a union of the Fertile Crescent, with Iraq as the 'pôle d'attraction autour duquel se cristalliseront pour s'organiser et agir, les espoirs du fédéralisme arabe';[110] later the Arabian Peninsula may join, but for the moment it must be left separate, given its difference in social and political development from the more advanced countries to the north. Egypt, in spite of her many affinities, has her own national sentiment; the countries of French North Africa are still in the pre-national stage, when religious has not yet been replaced by social solidarity, and Islam, not Arabism, is the only force capable of animating the masses.[111]

But religious solidarity is only a stage through which nations pass, and which by implication they outgrow. In Rabbath's work as in Zurayq's, Islam is the Arab past, not the future. They are both concerned to define and defend rather than prescribe, and we should not therefore look in their books for a programme of what the Arab State should do once united and independent. It is clear, however, where they would look for the bases of such a programme: Zurayq to the ideals of Anglo-Saxon liberalism, but with an emphasis on social reform and responsibility derived more perhaps from the European than the American tradition; Rabbath to the liberalism of the French Revolution. In spite of current difficulties with the French government, he looks beyond it to the 'true France', the France of the Revolution from whom, more than any other Power, the Arabs can expect help in reconstituting their national life.[112]

A member of a minority who identifies himself with the majority must pay for it, and the price is a certain wavering from one extreme to the other, from total acceptance to a remembrance of those things which prevent his being himself fully accepted. There remains a certain ambiguity in the Christian Arab's view of Islam; and it is not an accident that the clearest, most logical, most uncompromising doctrine of Arab nationalism, the clearest distinction between it and Islam, should have come from a Muslim—but from one who in another sense was himself marginal to the process he was describing, and saw it with the

---

[110] Ibid. p. 39.   [111] Ibid. pp. 320 ff.   [112] Rabbath, pp. 403–6.

uncomfortable clarity of the marginal man. Sati' al-Husri,
although of Syrian origin and related to the religious nobility of
Aleppo, was brought up in Constantinople and educated more
as a Turk than an Arab. His vernacular was Turkish, and he
acquired in youth the characteristic formation of the Young
Turk generation, based on the ideas of French positivism and
European nationalism. He held important posts in the Ottoman
Ministry of Education before the collapse of the empire compelled him like so many others to choose one or other side of his
complex tradition. He joined the Arab government in Damascus,
became Faysal's Minister of Education, and played an important
part in the final negotiations before the French occupation of
Damascus and the extinction of Faysal's kingdom; he has written
an important book of memoirs on the period. After the downfall
he followed Faysal to Iraq, held positions once more in the
Ministry of Education, and had much influence on the formation
of an Arab consciousness in Iraq. He was exiled from the
country after the failure of the coup d'état of Rashid 'Ali, and in
retirement in Beirut, then as an official of the Arab League in
Cairo, he began to write a series of essays having as their main
subject the theory of nationalism and the defence of Arab
nationalism. They belong strictly to the literature of the 1940's
and 1950's, but in a sense it is accidental that they were published
so late; an active career left little time for systematic writing, and
perhaps too the transition from one language to another delayed
the definitive crystallization of his thought. Essentially his ideas
belong to an earlier period, and they can be regarded as the final
articulation of that nationalist idea which became explicit in the
years after 1908 and dominated political life in Syria and Iraq
until 1945.

In his writings indeed one finds a 'pure' theory of nationalism
with all its assumptions clearly understood and accepted, all its
problems faced, a theory derived not only, as with other writers,
from English and French thought, but from its roots in German
philosophy; he has read Fichte, as no other Arab nationalist
seems to have done. Three sentiments, in his view, create political communities: nationalism, territorial patriotism, and loyalty
to the State. Since the beginning of the nineteenth century it is
the first which has been the most important and played the active
role in creating patriotism and establishing States: for modern

man, the fatherland is that in which his fellow nationals live, the claim of the State to his loyalty is based on its embodying the will of his nation.[113] It is possible for the object of all three sentiments to be identical: for all members of a single nation to live in a single *patrie*, no one else to live there, and the whole of the *patrie*, no more and no less, to be the territory of a single State. When this occurs, society is politically stable, and so are political thoughts and feelings. There is no dispute or ambiguity, no self-questioning, no division of loyalties. When it does not exist, then political ideas are complicated and ambiguous, and there is a division of political beliefs which may be dangerous.[114] In such circumstances, it is necessary to expound and defend the true concept of the nation: that is the main, one might almost say the only, aim of Husri's writings.

What then is the nation? Husri is entirely opposed to the idea of British and French thinkers that a nation is any group which wills to be a nation. A nation for him is something really existing: a man is, or is not, an Arab whether he wants to be or not. He criticizes Renan's famous definition of a nation:[115] 'Avoir des gloires communes dans le passé, une volonté commune dans le présent; avoir fait des grandes choses ensemble, vouloir en faire encore'. A nation has an objective basis, and in the last analysis this is first of all language. The Arab nation consists of all who speak Arabic as their mother-tongue, no more, no less.[116] (It may seem strange that Husri should adopt this view and so appear to go against his own experience. His own native language was Turkish, and he only set himself to master Arabic when the Ottoman Empire collapsed and he had to decide whether he was a Turk or an Arab. No doubt he would reply that what had made him an Arab was not his choice to be Arab rather than Turk but the fact that, having made this choice, he then set himself to acquire the Arabic language and make it the first language of his life and thought; and that the need to do this proved the fundamental importance of language in the life of a nation.) Second to language comes history. A common history is important but only secondary. It can strengthen, it cannot create, the national bond; and it can only strengthen if it is used

---

[113] Husri, *Ara' wa ahadith fi'l-wataniyya wa'l-qawmiyya*, pp. 3 ff.
[114] Husri, *Ara' wa ahadith fi'l-qawmiyya al-'arabiyya*, pp. 5 ff.
[115] Ibid. p. 46.
[116] Ibid. p. 44.

deliberately to do so. We are not the prisoners of our past unless we want to be; every nation must forget part of its history, and only remember what helps it.[117]

As for religion, Husri does not ignore its effect on human sentiments. It helps to create a kind of unity in the feelings of individuals: what that effect will be, and how it will be connected with national unity, varies from one religion to another. A national religion poses no problem, for it clearly reinforces national feeling; but with a universal religion like Christianity or Islam the matter is more complicated. It will have a tendency to create universalist and even anti-nationalist feelings; but this tendency is restrained by something else. Religions can only spread through the medium of national feeling. Every religion has an essential relationship with a specific language, through its preaching, its sacred books and rites; it can only spread through the medium of that language, and it will only spread so far as the nation which speaks the language has a national interest in spreading it. National feeling uses religion as a way of asserting itself:

When a religion is linked with a specific language it strengthens the roots of that language and preserves its structure more than any other social factor. The course of history shows us that when a religion splits up into a number of sects the fate of each sect is bound up in a special way with that of a particular language. The language concerned spreads with the spread of the faith which adopts it, and this extends the sway of the nation which was the original master of the language. . . . [For example] the Orthodox section of Christianity depends on the Greek text of the Gospels, and this has given a Greek colouring to the Orthodox Church; this is especially true of the Balkans, where the Greek Church had a strong moral domination over the Christian nations in Macedonia and Bulgaria, although it was itself under the political domination of the Ottoman Empire. . . . For this reason, the Bulgarian national revival began with a movement against the Greek Church and its Greek leaders, and . . . [led to] the creation of an autonomous national Church. . . . Thus the Bulgars put an end to the divisions which had appeared in their country between national and religious policy, and secured their national independence of the Greek Church before they had completed their political liberation from the Ottoman Empire.

These examples, I believe, suffice to show the force of national

[117] Husri, *Ara' wa ahadith fi'l-ta'rikh wa'l-ijtima'*, p. 185; *Ara' wa ahadith fi'l-wataniyya wa'l-qawmiyya*, p. 35.

differences as against religious ties, and to prove that even universal religions cannot efface national differences.[118]

There is here a clear reflection of Ibn Khaldun's theory of the relationship between religion and 'asabiyya: religion cannot by itself create a political community, it can only strengthen one already created by natural solidarity derived from a natural relationship. Such a view contains a certain implication, which Husri draws more clearly and consistently than other thinkers. Since the existence of a nation is logically prior to that of a religious community, it follows that it is not essentially connected with any one religion. Historically, the development of the Arab nation is closely bound up with Islam, but the Arabs are not essentially a Muslim nation: if they ceased to be Muslims they would still be Arabs. Thus the Arabic-speaking Christians are Arabs in precisely the same sense as the Muslims, and they can be Arabs without having to give up anything in their own religious tradition or accepting that of Islam. Indeed, it is precisely by way of their own religious tradition that they have become aware of their Arab nationality; their nationalism began with the struggle of the Arab Orthodox to throw off Greek control in the Patriarchate of Antioch, and that of the eastern Uniates to prevent the encroachment of Latin customs, rites, and ways of thought.[119]

Since a nation is to be defined first of all in terms of language, it includes all those who speak the language; its boundaries are those of the language, no more and no less. Thus Husri is equally opposed to the Islamic nationalists who claim that the Arabs have a political loyalty to the whole Islamic *umma*, whether Arabic-speaking or not, and to the regionalists who believe that there are distinct nations inside the Arabic-speaking world. He has spent much time trying to convince Egyptians that they are part of the Arab world. Even in the 1930's he was writing to this effect; and that is remarkable, both because the main current of Egyptian nationalism at that time was Pharaonic or Mediterranean, not Arab, and because the Arab nationalists of his generation, as we have seen, tended to look towards Baghdad rather than Cairo, and to think of the Arab nation as ending at Sinai (although among many of the younger generation there

---

[118] *Ara' wa ahadith fi'l-wataniyya wa'l-qawmiyya*, pp. 27–30.
[119] Husri, *Nushu' al-fikra al-qawmiyya*, pp. 158 ff.

already existed a romantic vision of a wider unity). As early as in 1936 we find him writing:

> Nature has provided Egypt with the qualities and distinctions which oblige her to take up the task of leadership in the awakening of Arab nationalism. She lies in the centre of the Arab countries; she forms the largest of those blocs into which the Arab world has been divided by policy or circumstance; this bloc has had a fuller share of the world civilization of modern times, and has become the main cultural centre of the Arab countries; she is the richest of all of them, and the most advanced in the institutions of the contemporary State, the most accomplished in eloquence and the literary arts.[120]

In later years he engaged in numerous polemics with Egyptian writers who at the time were advocating a purely Egyptian nationalism (among others, with Lutfi al-Sayyid[121] and Taha Husayn),[122] sustained by the conviction that history was on his side:

> The spread of [separatist] opinions does not render me afraid or pessimistic, because I believe they are the kind of 'clouds of despair' which normally take possession of souls when they meet with failure in the execution of a cherished plan, at some point in their work for it. But it is not long before [these clouds] disperse and disappear, when one thinks of matters with a certain calm and returns to work with something of resolution and hope.[123]

After 1945, when the League of Arab States was formed and Egypt became leader of it, history certainly seemed to justify his hope. He became director of the League's Institute of Arab Studies, the purpose of which he conceived as that of genuine national education; and his writings may well have been among the factors which gave to Egyptian nationalism its Arab colouring.

This extension of the concept of the Arab nation to include Egypt (and also North Africa) was a necessary consequence of defining it in terms of language alone. Among the Arabs, as almost everywhere in the Near East, linguistic or cultural nationalism proved stronger than territorial patriotism. Many reasons can be given for this: the example of German and Italian

---

[120] Husri, *Ara' wa ahadith fi'l-qawmiyya al-'arabiyya*, p. 75.
[121] Ibid. p. 81.
[122] Husri, *Ara' wa ahadith fi'l-wataniyya wa'l-qawmiyya*, pp. 96, 107.
[123] Husri, *Ara' wa ahadith fi'l-qawmiyya al-'arabiyya*, pp. 79–80.

nationalism, the influence of other nationalist movements in the Ottoman Empire, the hold of the Arabic language over those for whom it was a religious and a national language alike. But it was also perhaps due to the partition of geographical Syria after the First World War. Syria had always been the centre of Arab national feeling, but there had been growing up, in the generation before 1914, a certain patriotic feeling for 'Syria' as a geographical and historical entity. Had she become independent as an un-divided whole, Arab national feeling might have been focused upon that particular entity, and a certain balance between Arab and Syrian feeling achieved, as in Egypt and Iraq. The division into small States, of which only Lebanon was a natural unit, left national feeling with no existing State to focus upon, and turned it outwards. The Arab nationalists of the 'Syrian' States aimed indeed at a reunion of them in a greater Syria, but their ideal gradually expanded as it became clear that a union with other Arab countries might be easier than, and might indeed be the first step to, the reuniting of Syria. As a consequence, specifically 'Syrian' nationalism, such as we have come across before 1914, became weaker after 1918. In the 1930's, however, it had a certain revival with the creation of a party of which it was the first principle. This was the Parti Populaire Syrien (*al-hizb al-suri al-qawmi*, founded in 1932 by Antun Sa'ada. A Lebanese Christian brought up in Brazil, he may well have imbibed there the kind of Syrian patriotism which had been common among the educated class of Lebanon in the late nineteenth century, and which was preserved in the fossil communities of the Lebanese dispersion when it was tending to die out in the mother country itself. The party was rigidly organized on the lines of the fascist parties common in Europe in the 1930's, with a strict hierarchy and a sole and virtually all-powerful leader. It played intermittently an important part in the affairs of both Lebanon and Syria. In 1949 its leader, implicated in an attempt at in-surrection in Lebanon, took refuge in Syria and was handed over by the Syrian dictator, Husni al-Za'im, to the Lebanese govern-ment, which had him hastily tried and executed. The party had its revenge: the Lebanese Prime Minister responsible for the execution, Riyad al-Sulh, was assassinated by a party member in 1951, and Adib Shishakli, the Syrian dictator who succeeded Za'im at one remove, had once been a sympathizer. The wave of pro-Egyptian Arab feeling which was released in Syria after the fall of Shishakli was not favourable to the party, but in Lebanon it played an important part in the civil war of 1958, in support of President Sham'un and his pro-western policy.

Such influence and success as the party had it owed both to its cohesion and to its possession of a systematic nationalist doctrine, inculcated by a process of political education. This doctrine was expounded by Sa'ada himself in a general work of which the first volume only was published. The nation, he taught, is the fundamental unit of human history. It is created by interest and will, not by language or religion; it is autonomous, obeying no authority but that which emanates from itself.[124] By a detailed study of history he tried to show that there was in this sense a Syrian nation, with a common social consciousness developed over a long period of history. It included the inhabitants of the whole of geographical Syria, and had continued to exist as a separate entity even when incorporated in larger empires or broken up into smaller states. It had existed long before Islam; after the rise of Islam, its great days were those of the Umayyad caliphate, a Syrian State acting in conformity with the principles of Syrian civilization.[125] Politically, Sa'ada stood for the reunion of this unit and its complete political independence. Internally, he advocated the creation of a genuine and deep social unity, and for this there were two conditions. The first was the complete separation of religion and politics. So long as this did not exist, internal divisions would continue; for 'religious-political considerations', the separate existence of Lebanon was temporarily necessary. The second condition was far-reaching social and economic reform.

The party tended to be opposed to the idea of a general Arab union; it was impracticable, and also dangerous because it might divert men's minds and energies from what was possible. After 1945, however, it expressed its programme in a more 'Arab' fashion: it justified Syrian union as a first step towards a more general Arab grouping in which Syria, once united and independent, would take the lead; and it extended its definition of 'Syria' so as to include all the formerly Syriac-speaking countries—Iraq as well as geographical Syria.[126] Nothing could

[124] Sa'ada, *Nushu' al-umam*, pp. 137 ff.   [125] Ibid. p. 132.
[126] Sa'ada, *al-Nizam al-jadid*, pp. 67 ff.

illustrate more clearly than this the difficulty of maintaining a territorial concept of patriotism in an age and region where ethnic nationalism was dominant. As time passed and there grew up a new generation which accepted as natural frontiers which had been artificial, the idea of geographical Syria lost its force. But those factors which led to the decline of 'Syrian', strengthened 'Lebanese' nationalism. After the French occupation of 1918 Lebanese autonomy, which the Turks had abolished during the war, was restored. In 1920 Lebanon was proclaimed independent with enlarged frontiers; in 1922 her separate existence was recognized by implication in the mandate; in 1926 she became a republic with a parliamentary constitution. In this new and larger Lebanon the Maronites were not a majority, as they had been in the autonomous territory set up in 1861; they were simply the largest sect among several, but they still kept their political predominance, thanks partly to France's support for those who had been her clients during three centuries, partly to their own superior education and communal solidarity. But there was strong opposition both to their predominance and to the new Lebanon as such. The separate existence of a larger Lebanon was not recognized by most nationalists in Syria; nor by most of the Muslims incorporated in it by the change of frontiers in 1920; nor, at that time, by a large part of the non-Catholic Christians. Those who believed in the existence of independent Lebanon had to justify their belief more explicitly, and they tended to do so in one of two ways. They might maintain that Lebanon, although Arab, had—to use Rabbath's phrase—a local form of Arab civilization which was worth preserving, at least for the time; or they might define Lebanon as a refuge for Christians in the sea of Islam and of an Arab nationalism which was only another form of Muslim feeling, and the Lebanese people as a separate nation, Christian, Mediterranean, linked with the Latin Powers of Europe.

In the 1940's, as we shall see, the first type of Lebanese nationalism was to assume a new importance, because of changed circumstances; but in the twenty years between the wars it was the second which was predominant, and which was made articulate by a group of Lebanese writers whose formation and turn of thought, and often whose language, was European: in particular, the poets Charles Corm, Michel Chiha, and Sa'id 'Aql.

For these writers, there is a separate Lebanese nation. It first emerges into history in the time of the Phoenicians, and has gradually taken its present form. Two factors above all have moulded it: first its geographical position—the mountain which is its core serves as a land of refuge, but the great routes which pass on either side of them have always drawn the attention of the masters of the world—; and secondly the continuity of its population, unbroken since ancient times but swollen by an endless process of immigration, which has gone on until the present. (Writing in 1942, Chiha pointed out that one-tenth of the present population had come in during the last twenty-five years, and they included members of the Ottoman imperial family; it was fitting that the former sovereigns of the east 'should find their last refuge on our soil').[127]

In these ways there has been created a population which is unique, and cannot be described in terms other than its own:

> Dira-t-on après cela que le Liban d'aujourd'hui est sémitique? Dira-t-on qu'il est arabe? Chacun en jugera. Le Père Lammens, auquel on accorde je suppose quelque crédit, contestait que la Syrie elle-même fût arabe. Pour lui elle a un caractère original, elle est syrienne. Nous dirons pour notre part, avec des arguments plus décisifs encore, que la population du Liban est libanaise, tout simplement, et que réserve faite de naturalisations très récentes, elle n'est pas plus phénicienne qu'égyptienne, égéenne, assyrienne ou médique, grècque, romaine, byzantine, arabe, avec ou sans consanguinité, ou européenne par les alliances, ou turque par exemple.[128]

This nation, which has existed throughout history, has had since ancient times its own 'formes ataviques de la sensibilité nation-ale',[129] and has created its own society and civilization, on a small scale but not without importance for the rest of the world. One of the poets of the group indeed, with an enthusiasm common to national movements but here kept free from danger by its innocence, has claimed that Lebanon has played a unique part in forming the culture of the world. The idea of economic enter-prise, abstract thought, Christian love, the incarnation of truth in the Church, the art of politics perfected by the Umayyads —all these were contributed to the world by the Lebanese cities of Sidon, Jerusalem, Antioch, and Damascus, were passed on

[127] *Liban d'aujourd'hui*, p. 46.   [128] Ibid. p. 48.
[129] Corm, *L'Art phénicien*, p. xxxix.

from them to Egypt, Greece, Rome, and modern Europe, and transmitted from Europe back to Lebanon by way of Paris, 'the spiritual capital of the world and the one repository of its intellectual heritage'.[130] Poetic language has only an indirect relation to truth, and most writers in prose would have made less sweeping claims. They would have been content if Lebanon were recognized as an integral part of the world around the Mediterranean—'la mer élue; un élément providential et nécéssaire dans la marche de la création . . . les habitants de ses rivages se trouvent, ou qu'ils se rencontrent, un air de parenté'.[131] But even within this world it is, they claim, unique: it stands on the frontier with another world, that of the Arabian desert, the inland sea which stamps its mark no less on those who live around it.

Thus the civilization of Lebanon is not that of the surrounding countries, Mediterranean or Arab, because it bears the mark of both. It is not wholly Arab. The last thirteen centuries should not make us forget the forty which went before. It must be at least bilingual, and so bicultural; by interest and necessity it must lie open to ideas and goods from outside, free trade and travel must be the basis of its economic life as of its political security, but it must not lose itself and its nature in the process. It is profoundly united, but at the basis of its unity there lies a diversity no less profound. Since the Islamic conquest it has been divided into religious communities, each a closed society claiming the first loyalty of its members; hence a diversity not only religious but social and intellectual as well.[132]

It is from these facts that there springs the political problem of Lebanon. Itself a paradox, a blend of two worlds, it must try not to be untrue to either side of its nature or either of its two interests—to be itself, and to be part of something larger than itself. In internal policy, this means that the religious confessions must learn to live together. For this, there must be no revolutions or upsets which might bring communal loyalties and therefore communal divisions to the forefront of men's minds; there must be no domination of one community over another; only laws which can be applied equally to all parts of the nation should be adopted; there must above all be a free and sovereign Assembly,

[130] 'Aql, *Qadmus*, pp. 13 ff.   [131] Chiha, *Essais*, i. 17.
[132] Chiha, *Liban d'aujourd'hui*, pp. 39, 52, 60.

where religious communities can meet and unite for a common
control of political life—an assembly of which

le premier objet était de consolider chez nous le vouloir vivre en
commun, une assemblée nous permettant de faire délibérer ensemble
dans l'atmosphère de la chose publique, en les éloignant un moment de
l'intérêt confessionnel, le Maronite et le Sunnite, le Chiite, le Druze,
le Grec-Orthodoxe, le Melchite et les autres.[133]

While for other States political freedom is a condition of the good
life, for Lebanon it is a necessary condition of life itself.

Externally, Lebanon must try to maintain her own existence.
Her tragedy is that not only her existence but her structure
depend on forces beyond her control; in a small State, all
problems are problems of foreign policy. Lebanon must be
friendly with the masters of the world and the Near East whoever
they may be—with all who need to use her routes for armies or
for trade. But this does not mean that she does not have her
preferences. In the deepest sense she needs the west, the great
home of her culture, and can only be at ease, internally and
externally, if the west is strong, and its influence in the Eastern
Mediterranean paramount: 'Ici, au Liban, nous sommes, par
vocation et nécessité, les amis des maîtres du monde; mais, dans
l'intérêt de cet Orient auquel nous appartenons, nous ne sommes
pas disposés à nous résigner au déclin de l'Europe'.[134]

Implicit in such statements was the essential problem of
Lebanese nationalism. Chiha was careful to define Lebanon in
non-sectarian terms, as a country which could belong to Muslims
as well as to Christians, and on the same terms; and to define
'the west' in such a way as to include Islam as well as Christianity.
But his vision of Lebanon and Europe was one which, by its
nature, appealed far more to Lebanese Christians than to
Muslims. The Muslim communities might accept the existence
of Lebanon for political reasons, but they could not be so deeply
stirred as their Christian neighbours by the memory of church
bells ringing freely in the mountain villages, or the vision of
Athens, Rome, and Paris. Lebanon for them was not something
unique and separate; it could at best be an autonomous part of
the Arab world, and if forced to choose between the Arab world
and the west they would have no hesitation. How then to make

[133] Chiha, *Liban d'aujourd'hui*, p. 72.   [134] Chiha, *Essais*, i. 202.

acceptable to the Muslim half of the population a vision and a policy which only appealed to the Christian half? How to create an inter-confessional State based upon equality, while keeping final control of policy in Christian hands? How to avoid having to choose between the Arabs and the west? These were the inescapable dilemmas of the Lebanese Christian nationalist.

XII

TAHA HUSAYN

IN Egypt and Syria, as elsewhere in Asia, the nationalism of the years between the First and Second World Wars had two sides. It aimed at throwing off the political domination of Europe, at least to the extent of replacing foreign by indigenous administrators, even if it was willing to concede to England or France control of foreign policy and the maintenance of military bases. At the same time however it willingly, for the most part, accepted the supremacy of European civilization; a voice like that of Gandhi was rare, and not much listened to outside India, and in spite of the backward glance of national romanticism, and a certain defensive pride, it was generally accepted that European civilization was the highest in the world. The case for national independence was stated in terms of European ideas: only if Egypt were self-governing would it be possible for her to become a 'westernized' nation in the full sense—that is to say, to create a liberal, democratic political system and accept willingly the values of European culture. To secure independence and make proper use of it, help was looked for from Europe: Mustafa Kamil hoped that in its own interest the French government would check the growth of British power, Zaghlul appealed to the liberal conscience of England. In a sense too the moral judgement of Europe was accepted: the new nations must prove themselves, they must show Europe that they could rule themselves.

In general, a certain definition of European civilization was accepted: Europe was taken at the value it put upon itself—or more specifically, the value put upon it by the liberal thinkers of the nineteenth century. The bases of European civilization, the 'secret' of its strength and prosperity, were taken to be such factors as these: the existence of the national community, ruling itself in the light of its own interests; the separation of religion and politics; the democratic system of government, that is to say, the prevalence of the general will as expressed by freely elected parliaments and ministries responsible to them; the respect for individual rights, particularly the right to speak and write freely; the strength of the political virtues, of loyalty to the community and willingness to make sacrifices for it; above all, the organization of modern industry and the 'scientific spirit' which lay behind it.

The Wafd in Egypt gave formal adherence to these principles. Its first aim, that which held it together and gave it momentum, was to secure a reasonable arrangement with Great Britain, which would give Egypt internal autonomy and a recognized international status, while safeguarding legitimate British interests. Its vision of independent Egypt was conceived in terms of liberal thought: an Egypt where Muslims and Copts were united in the sacred bond of national loyalty, government was constitutional, individual rights respected, where women were free, national education was universal, and national industry raised the standard of living. In its brief periods of office, the Wafd, like other parties brought face to face with the need for decision, did not always respect its principles; and as successive quarrels gradually broke it up it lost some of its glamour as spokesman of the nation. But throughout these twenty years it remained the most powerful party in Egypt, and also the tarnished embodiment of a system of ideas which most educated men accepted.

Such ideas were expounded throughout the 1920's and 1930's by a number of gifted writers, not all of them adherents of the Wafd but all sharing to some extent a general attitude to politics and society: Ahmad Amin, 'Abbas Mahmud al-'Aqqad, Tawfiq al-Hakim, 'Abd al-Qadir al-Mazini, Taha Husayn. All masters of Arabic style, with a European education (English or French as the case might be) solidly grounded in a traditional culture, they were primarily men of letters. Their ideas were expounded for the most part in magazine articles, or by implication in novels and plays. They and others of their generation were the first group of novelists in modern Arabic, and some at least of them were interested in the possibility of the Arabic drama. (The classical literature had not known either of these forms, and their introduction from the west had been delayed by two difficulties: that of rendering conversation in a language where literary and colloquial forms were so far apart; and that of expressing the tension of personal feeling when writing of a society where women were secluded.) The most systematic thinker among them, as he is perhaps the most considerable artist, is Taha Husayn; he deserves study both for his own sake and because he can be regarded as the last great representative of a line of thought, the writer who has given the final statement of the system of ideas which underlay social thought and political action in the Arab countries for three generations.

Born in a small town of Upper Egypt in 1889, of a family poor but by no means among the poorest, Taha Husayn has been blind since an early age; and this perhaps explains both the quality of his imagination and something about his literary style—the thin line of development of narrative and argument, the endless repetitions of words, the long sentences formed of clauses linked by simple conjunction. In two volumes of auto-biography he has described the awakening of a blind boy's sensibility and mind. Educated first in an Islamic *kuttab*, he went to the Azhar at the age of thirteen. He did not like it much, but it played an essential part in his growth. He came into contact there with the ideas of 'Abduh, one or two of whose lectures he attended; and he acquired what could still be acquired there, a thorough knowledge of the Arabic language and its classical literature, taught well by a teacher of broader vision than most of his colleagues. Although he remained at the Azhar for ten years, before he finally left his thoughts had been drawn in another direction. He had read the Islamic modernists and the Lebanese journalists, had been drawn into the circle of Lutfi al-Sayyid and *al-Jarida*, had studied French and attended lectures at the new Egyptian University—lectures given by the great orientalists of Europe, Littmann, Nallino, Santillana, and which opened a new perspective on to his own inherited culture. Then in 1915 came four years in France, years which for him as for Tahtawi decided the destiny of his mind: he read Anatole France, attended Durkheim's classes, wrote a thesis on Ibn Khaldun, and married the wife who has been his eyes.

For thirty years or so after his return in 1919 he was at the very centre of literary and academic life in Egypt: as teacher and administrator in the universities of Cairo and Alexandria, an official in the Ministry of Education and, from 1950 to 1952, Minister of Education in the last Wafdist government. During this active period of his life he was involved in two great crises.

The first was in 1926, when a book of his on pre-Islamic poetry caused a scandal and had to be withdrawn. Applying the methods of modern critical scholarship to the ancient poetry of Arabia, he showed reason to doubt whether it had in fact been written before Islam. This aroused opposition both because it suggested a critical method which, if applied to the texts of religion, might cast doubt on their authenticity, and because it struck at the roots of the traditional structure of Arabic learning by which the faith was buttressed. Then in 1932 he was dismissed from his office as Dean of the Faculty of Arts at Cairo by the government of Sidqi Pasha because of his Wafdist sympathies; this won him much support, and in 1936 the next Wafdist government restored him.

These years of his greatest activity were also those of his richest production in a number of genres: novels, essays on literature, studies of Islamic history, the volumes of autobiography, and works on society and politics. His best was produced in the twenty years between 1919 and 1939, although since then he has written much and become the elder statesman of Egyptian letters, has received honorary doctorates and attended international seminars.

His most important work of social thought—one might almost say, his only work of systematic thought—is a book on the future of culture in Egypt, published in 1938. The date at which it was written explains its content. In 1936 there had been signed the Anglo-Egyptian treaty which officially ended the occupation and in 1937 the Montreux Convention which ended the Capitulations. There was a general feeling that a new period in the national life had begun. Egypt was independent: what did this really mean, and what should she try to do with her independence? The goal to which public life had been directed for a whole generation had been attained: what new goal now presented itself?

I felt, as other Egyptians did . . . that Egypt was beginning a new period of her life: she had obtained some of her rights, and must now set herself to important duties and heavy responsibilities. . . . We live in an age which can be defined as one in which freedom and independence are not an end to which peoples and nations strive, but a means to ends higher, more permanent, and more comprehensive in their benefits.[1]

[1] Husayn, *Mustaqbal al-thaqafa*, i, introd. p. 1 and 2.

Egypt should concern herself from now onwards with the quality of her national life. That quality he judges in the light of certain principles, of what may be called a 'philosophy' of society and history, derived to some extent from Ibn Khaldun, but more fundamentally from the French masters of his thought, Comte, Renan, Durkheim, and Anatole France. The aim of human life is civilization, and that means the control of nature and life by reason. The attainment of this is a gradual process, divided into several phases. In the early ones, religion and blind faith dominate the whole of man's life; later, reason asserts its independence of religion, and for a time there is a conflict between the two. In the end a balance is reached, and each rules supreme in its own sphere: it is the task of reason to direct human actions, of religion to fill man's heart, satisfy his emotions, inspire him to noble actions, console him in affliction.[2]

For Taha Husayn, the significance of modern Europe lies precisely in this, that it marks the highest stage yet reached in the process: the achievement of the ideal balance, leaving reason free to rule the social world, to subdue nature by the application of science, frame laws aiming at human happiness, and to create governments which will uphold law and reconcile interests. The Europe about which he first learned from the Lebanese journalists, and of which he was a part for four youthful years, possessed his imagination throughout his creative years. Europe for him means three things: humane culture, the civic virtues, democracy. Husayn is a writer before he is a thinker, with a response to beauty sharpened even if limited by his blindness. For him Europe is not only the repository of true ideas, it is the creator of beautiful images, above all those of poetry. When he writes of Greek poetry or drama there is no doubting his genuine personal feeling about the classical world, even if he sees it through the eyes of French secularist aesthetes, anxious to draw an anti-Christian moral—of his great exemplar Anatole France, or André Gide whom he knew and whose *Thésée* and *Oedipe* he translated into Arabic. He is no less whole-hearted in his praise for the civic virtues of Europe, the moral basis of the community. Europeans are willing to sacrifice everything for their convictions. It is not true that 'the west is materialistic', as orientals think; its material triumphs are the products of its

[2] Cf. Cachia, pp. 77 ff.

intellect and spirit, and even its atheists are willing to die for their beliefs.[3] For a European, the first political object of loyalty and sacrifice is the nation: to be modern and fully civilized means to belong to an independent nation. (If this now seems in one sense obvious and in another false, we should remember how few, in those days of the great empires, were the independent States of Asia and Africa.) But to be European also means to belong to a democratic nation; and to be democratic means to have a government responsible to a Chamber elected by universal suffrage. The date of the book, we have said, is 1938, but there is absolutely no sign of the different political ideas propagated at that time by Germany and Italy; and this is significant not of Husayn only but of Wafdist nationalism. Culturally it was deeply attached to France; in the euphoria produced by the treaty of 1936 it had no grievance against England; and it was afraid of Italy's ambitions to the west and south of Egypt.

Defined in this sense, Europe is the modern world; and Husayn believes that independent Egypt must become part of Europe, for that is the only way to become part of the modern world. This for him is the real meaning of the Anglo-Egyptian treaty and the Montreux agreement; they are an agreement between Egypt and Europe. Europe thereby has affirmed her faith in the civilization of Egypt, and Egypt has undertaken 'a clear and binding obligation before the civilized world that we shall tread the path of the Europeans in government, administration and legislation'.[4]

The next task before Egypt then is to show that the trust is not mistaken and the obligation can be fulfilled. We must make Egypt such, Husayn tells his fellow countrymen, that Europeans do not regard us as inferior, and we do not regard ourselves as inferior; and it is significant of the period in which he wrote that for him the way to do this is not to develop an Egyptian civilization which can compare with that of Europe, but to master that of Europe itself. We must convince ourselves that there is no difference between us and Europeans:

Believe me, dear reader, our real national duty, once we have obtained our independence and established democracy in Egypt, is to spend all

[3] Husayn, *Mustaqbal al-thaqafa*, i. 65.
[4] Ibid. p. 36.

we have and more, in the way of strength and effort, of time and money, to make Egyptians feel, individually and collectively, that God has created them for glory not ignominy, strength and not weakness, sovereignty and not submission, renown and not obscurity, and to remove from their hearts the hideous and criminal illusion that they are created from some other clay than Europeans, formed in some other way, and endowed with an intelligence other than theirs.

We must become European in every way, accepting both its good and its bad: 'We must follow the path of the Europeans so as to be their equals and partners in civilization, in its good and evil, its sweetness and bitterness, what can be loved or hated, what can be praised or blamed.'[5]

How can this be done? The first step, he believes, is for Egyptians to study their own history and understand that Egypt always has been part of Europe. He was writing in an age when the distinction between 'east' and 'west' was the commonplace of writers both eastern and western, and Egypt was usually placed in the eastern section. Typical of such thought is a book by a contemporary of his and roughly a member of the same group, Ahmad Amin. Entitled *The East and the West*, it was written a decade later but mirrors perfectly the received ideas of the time: the west believes in causality, cares only for the goods of the present world, is scientific in spirit, rational in economic life; the east needs to adopt the scientific spirit and economic organization of the west in order to revive and give the world its own 'spirituality and religion and contemplation'.[6] But Husayn, although he accepts the division of the world into two parts, believes firmly that Egypt belongs to the western not the eastern half. The essential distinction for him is one of spiritual not physical geography. There are two fundamentally different civilizations in the world, that which derives from Greek philosophy and art, Roman laws and political organization, and the moral values of Christianity, and that which derives from India; and Egypt is part of the first, not the second.

Why then is Egypt usually thought of as eastern? The false idea that she belongs to the eastern world springs, he suggests, from either of two causes: either from some common interest, political or economic, such as the interest of Asian and African countries in freeing themselves from European rule—but these

⁵ *Mustaqbal al-thaqafa*, pp. 41–42 & 45.   ⁶ A. Amin, *al-Sharq wa'l-gharb*, p. 18.

interests are superficial and transient and do not create the
lasting bond of a common civilization—or else from religious
unity—but this also cannot be the basis of a social and political
community. It is enough to consider the history of Egypt to
realize that the unity in which she participates, on these levels,
is that of the 'west'. She has not had continuous relations with
the countries of the genuine east; she has had such relations
with the countries where western civilization arose, those of the
Near East, the Aegean, and the Mediterranean. In these relations
she has not been passive only: she was herself one of the creators
of Mediterranean civilization, and throughout ancient times the
tide of influence flowed both ways between her and Greece. Her
own history within the western world has been continuous: even
when absorbed into the Islamic Empire she was one of the first
regions to 'restore her ancient personality' from the time of
Ibn Tulun onwards, and that personality still exists, firmly based
on geography, religion, language, and long history.[7]

Why then, it may be asked, have the present differences
arisen? Why have Egypt and the other countries of the Eastern
Mediterranean fallen behind those of Europe in civilization?
Taha Husayn gives the answer which, by his time, had become a
commonplace: it is the domination of the Turks which has
destroyed civilization. But he points out that this is only a passing
phase: Europe too had her dark ages, and the Muslim dark age
was less dark in Egypt than elsewhere; in spite of all that can be
said against the Azhar, it did protect Islamic civilization from the
Turks. The age of decline is ending in Egypt faster than elsewhere: in the last hundred years she has 're-europeanized' herself, has become European in her whole life, material and moral.
Even in her political life, her problem is the typical European
problem of democracy and autocracy; those who have ruled her
despotically (and no doubt he is thinking of Isma'il) have been
more like Louis XIV than Abdülhamid.[8] Her Islamic institutions themselves have been europeanized: for example, the
Shari'a courts are more like European law courts than like the
traditional Islamic courts. No doubt there are still differences
between Egypt and Europe, but they all spring from one fact:
Europe had her renaissance in the fifteenth century, Egypt had
hers in the nineteenth. But she is catching up fast, and this is an

[7] *Mustaqbal al-thaqafa*, i. 62 ff.   [8] Ibid. pp. 27 ff. & 32.

irreversible process, for even those who call themselves conservatives would not really want to go back to the past.

It is of course an obvious objection to Husayn's theory that the west, as ordinarily conceived, is Christian while Egypt is Muslim. It may seem that he is evading the problem of religious difference, and it has sometimes been suggested that the storm aroused by his book on pre-Islamic poetry shook him so deeply that since then he has avoided any discussion of Islam which might raise another storm. It is unnecessary, however, to adopt a hypothesis so unflattering: that he should not regard religious difference as important for his theme is perfectly consistent with his general views. For him, the distinguishing mark of the modern world is that it has brought about a virtual separation of religion and civilization, each in its own sphere. It is therefore quite possible to take the 'bases of civilization' from Europe without taking its religion.[9] This involves indeed one condition, which is that Egyptians too should be able to make the same separation. They can do so, and indeed it is easier for Muslims than for Christians, since Islam has no priesthood, and so there has grown up no vested interest in the control of religion over society. Islam assimilated Greek and Persian civilization easily, and can do the same with that of modern Europe. In a modern society, where the true role of religion is concerned with the emotions and not with reason, Islam can fill the part as well as Christianity. Taha Husayn would go even farther than this, and say that they are the same in essence. Islam came not to replace but to complete the Christian teaching.[10]

In the modern world, the focus of loyalty and the unit of society is the nation, and for Husayn the nation still means Egypt. The territorial unit is for him as for earlier thinkers the main object of social feeling. Like the others of his group, and like Lutfi al-Sayyid in the older generation, his national feeling is a warm romantic feeling focused on the country itself rather than on the community, and fed by a vivid evocation of Egyptian country life with its joys and sorrows. Such a feeling is very different from anything in earlier Egyptian thought or in the contemporary thought of other Arab countries (except perhaps for Lebanon). It may be regarded as the special contribution of this group to the modern Arabic consciousness: as novelists, they

---

[9] *Mustaqbal al-thaqafa*, pp. 54 ff.   [10] Ibid. p. 21.

wrote best when writing least pretentiously about the life of the countryside.

In principle, the Egyptian nation still includes all who live in the land of Egypt and think of it as their home; but it is rather less all-inclusive than in the thought of Tahtawi. Husayn like Zaghlul makes a certain distinction between real Egyptians and the European and Levantine colonies which control economic life. He does not however make any distinction between Muslim and Christian Egyptians. National sentiment for him is more important than any other. In the last analysis, he believes, the individual and his rights are higher than the nation; but among communities the nation is supreme. Even religion acquires its social value only as providing the content of the national idea and strengthening the unity of the nation: Islam is a factor in Egyptian nationalism,[11] and schools should teach the national religion just as they teach the national history. This also is quite consistent with his general beliefs. In his view, religion satisfies the emotions but is not something which can offer guidance in modern society or give principles by which acts can be judged. Islam happens to be the traditional religion of most Egyptians, that which satisfies their hearts, and so it should be taught. But for other nations other faiths would do just as well; and for Egyptian Christians, it is Coptic Christianity which satisfies them, and which therefore should be taught properly, for the sake of the nation's spiritual health.

It might be thought that in the last twenty years or so there has been a change in Taha Husayn's view of the relations between religion and nation. It has often been pointed out that in the 1930's and 1940's the religious element seems to become more important in his writing: together with such contemporaries as 'Aqqad and Haykal he began to write books about the Prophet, the early Muslim leaders, the heroic days of Islam. But if we inquire how Taha Husayn deals with religion in such books as *'Ala hamish al-sira* (1933–46) and *al-Wa'd al-haqq* (1950), it becomes clear that they do not mark a change in his view of Islam. Religion exists to give comfort to the hearts of men, by teaching certain general truths about the universe in powerful and moving symbols. These symbols must be judged by results, by whether they do in fact strengthen the individual or the

[11] Ibid. p. 81.

nation. But since men's minds change from age to age, the symbols must be expressed anew. Husayn's religious books must therefore be seen as attempts to re-tell the story of Islam in ways which will appeal to the modern Egyptian consciousness. The Prophet is presented as a hero in the modern sense, 'Uthman as the symbol of human weakness, 'Ali as the scrupulous Muslim ruler; the early history of the *umma* is described in terms of the struggle of truth and righteousness against the world, and the attempt to establish a reign of worldly justice. In each case, the symbol is not only restated in new terms, it is also subtly (and perhaps not quite consciously) re-cast in order to make an appeal to minds formed by western education. In *al-Wa'd al-haqq*, the accent is on the sufferings of the first Muslims, in a way which will appeal to those who live, whether they want to or not, in a moral world formed by Christianity: in *al-Fitna al-kubra* the orthodox caliphs are treated as early revolutionaries establishing a reign of social justice, a 'middle way' between socialism and capitalism, a system of social security 'rather like the Beveridge plan', a unique form of government uniting the advantages of all others, a daring and hazardous experiment which failed because it came too soon.[12]

Whatever its 'emotional' importance, religion cannot be the guide to political life or the touchstone of national policy: the idea of the nation must be defined in other than religious terms. Here Husayn differs somewhat from Tahtawi and Lutfi al-Sayyid. In spite of his formal evocation of the memory of the Pharaohs, the centre of his interest is in the Arabic period of Egyptian history. For him, the Arabic language is the common good of Egyptians, that which they have inherited from the past, and which gives them their duties and opportunities. Unlike the Islamic reformers, he does not emphasize the importance of language as a means to a religious awakening, but as the basis of a sound national life; and consistently, he regards it as no less important for Copts than for Muslims: 'the Arabic language is not the language of the Muslims only, but the language of all who speak it however much they differ in faith.'[13] He deplores the bad Arabic of the liturgies used in the eastern Churches, and is said to have offered to help in rewriting them, so that the Arab Christians could worship in good Arabic.

[12] *al-Fitna al-kubra*, i. 19.   [13] *Mustaqbal al-thaqafa*, ii. 486.

In his view, Egypt is not only the place where Arabic and its culture were preserved during the days of Turkish darkness; it is also the place where the language is being revived today. Thus Egypt is the centre of modern Arabic culture, and her mission in the Arab countries is to spread the modern sciences through the Arabic language: by the circulation of books and periodicals, the loan of teachers, the good reception of Arab students in Egypt, the unification of educational programmes and the establishment of Egyptian primary and secondary schools ('institutes of cultural co-operation') in other Arab countries.[14] This book, while being a final statement of a certain type of purely Egyptian nationalism, marks the first step towards the merging of Egyptian in Arab nationalism. As such, it is typical of the moment at which it was written: the signature of the Anglo-Egyptian Treaty had given Egypt the opportunity, for the first time in two generations, of following a foreign policy which was relatively independent, at least in Middle Eastern matters, and, as always, any Egyptian government would find its natural sphere of interest in the surrounding Arab countries. But, faithful to the line of thought which he closes, Taha Husayn intends no assertion of the superiority of the Arabic language and its traditional culture as against other languages and theirs. On the contrary, the purpose of reviving Arabic is to make it possible for a modern educated man to live in Arabic, and this involves absorbing into Arabic the whole of European thought. Much of his career has been given to this. He has, for example, both encouraged and himself made translations from the literature of ancient Greece, has tried the experiment of having Greek and Latin taught in the universities, and in later years has persuaded the government to set on foot a translation of the whole of Shakespeare.

Nations which achieved their unity and independence and created a deep cultural and social stability before the coming of popular independence, and among whom the virtues by which societies live are inculcated in the home, in literature, by the example of the past and of a flourishing public life, may find it difficult to understand how important the modern school has been and is in a country such as Egypt. This, no less than his own professional formation as a teacher and scholar, explains

[14] Ibid. pp. 519 ff.

the attention given by Taha Husayn to the reform of the system of schools. The first purpose of education, it is true, is culture and science; but it also plays a vital part in teaching the civic virtues and creating the conditions in which a democratic government can exist.

The greater part of the book is therefore a critique of Egyptian education and a programme for reform. Primary education, the basis of democratic life, should be universal and compulsory, secondary education poses more difficult problems. At the moment there are too many different kinds—religious, foreign, official. Thus they create cultural discord; and, while variety is not bad in itself,[15] there is a necessary minimum of harmony, which can only be brought about by a certain control from the government. The foreign schools are the best schools in the country, and so long as this is so they are a form of cultural capital. They should not be closed, but should be placed under some control in regard to the teaching of the national language, history and geography, and also the teaching of the national religion: Muslim children should be taught their own faith even in Christian mission schools. Even then, however, the foreign schools can never be quite satisfactory, for by their nature they cannot teach the young 'to love the Egyptian nation' or 'to protect Egyptian democracy'.[16] Egyptian religious schools—the primary and secondary schools attached to the Azhar—should be brought under government control;[17] as for the government schools, three important changes should be made. They should be expanded as quickly as possible. Husayn is aware of the objection to this: that it will create an educated class for which no posts can be found. This was a point made much earlier by Cromer, and used by him to justify his not having paid more attention to education; and by 1938 indeed the danger had become a real one, with the swift increase in the number of unemployed or underemployed graduates. But Husayn points out with some force that this is an argument which might well be used by a foreign government anxious above all to avoid political trouble; it is an ignoble argument for a national government to use, since its first aim must be to create a real democracy. To restrict education means to make ignorance the basis of national life; if expanding education leads to awkward social problems, the

---

[15] *Mustaqbal al-thaqafa*, i. 86.   [16] Ibid. p. 78.   [17] Ibid. p. 85.

only remedy is to change the social system so as to make new openings—in particular to put an end to oppression (in other words, carve up the big estates) and egyptianize economic life.[18]

The second change should be to make secondary education available to all who are willing to pay for it, and provide free places for poor and clever boys. Thirdly and most important, there should be a change in the content of education. In Egyptian schools at the time of which he was writing, that meant first of all a change in the teaching of languages. For this indeed is the basic problem of Arab schools today; how to teach Arabic, a difficult language with fixed and traditional methods of instruction; what foreign languages to teach, for they are the key not only to higher education but to a knowledge of the modern world; when and how to teach them. No foreign language, he suggests, should be taught before the fifth year; after that they should be taught intensively. There should be a choice of English, French, German, and Italian, and the classical languages too should be available for those who want to become real scholars: Greek and Latin for those who wish to specialize in the history and civilization of Europe, Hebrew and Persian for those who are concerned with the Arabic language and its literature. Apart from their intrinsic value, he points out, there is a whole section of Egypt's own history which Egyptians will not be able to make their own unless they know the classical languages: Egypt was Greek and then Roman for centuries, and so long as Egyptians do not know Latin and Greek they will have to see some part of their national heritage through the eyes of foreigners. Knowledge of the classics is a necessary implication of Egyptian nationalism.[19]

For higher education, Taha Husayn does not make such detailed suggestions, because in his view universities should not be controlled or directed by the government. They should have absolute freedom: financial freedom to do as they wish with grants made them by the government; academic freedom in all matters of teaching and learning. It is clear however that his conception of higher as of all education is a humane one: the university must be first of all an intellectual society based on 'love and friendship, co-operation and solidarity'.[20]

As a centre of higher education, the Azhar should enjoy the

[18] Ibid. pp. 142 ff.   [19] Ibid. ii. 258, 261, 275, 295, 301.   [20] Ibid. p. 442.

same freedom as the rest. It has an important part to play in forming the national culture of Egypt, because of the large number of its pupils, its close connexion with all classes of the people, and its own tradition. But its function is a specialized one: to be a centre of religious studies and therefore 'a source of spiritual life' for the nation. It should not take charge of general education: its traditional monopoly of producing Arabic teachers for schools should be ended, since it does not teach Arabic properly itself. (In the second volume of his autobiography, Husayn has made biting criticisms of the way in which he himself was taught there.) But even as a 'source of spiritual life' it must change: it should teach the real Islam, 'the religion of freedom, science and knowledge, . . . of development, progress and aspiration towards the ideal in material and spiritual life alike'; and it should teach also the proper concept of territorial patriotism, not the old idea of religious nationalism.[21] (He would say the same, *mutatis mutandis*, of Coptic religious education: that Coptic Christianity should be well taught is just as important for the strength and welfare of Egypt.)[22]

Some at least of these ideas Husayn was later able to put into practice. As adviser to the Ministry of Education in 1942–4 he played a large part in founding the University of Alexandria, and became its first Rector: his aim was to make it not a replica or overflow of the existing university in Cairo, but a real university free from the pressure of the ministry and the mob, setting its own standards and attracting the best among students and teachers, open to the Mediterranean, heir of the whole history of Alexandria and a centre of classical humanism. Later, as Minister of Education from 1950–2, he set on foot a vast expansion of State schools at all levels: new universities and higher colleges, new schools of every type, free secondary education, a curriculum revised on the lines he had himself suggested. The programme was much criticized, on the ground that he was changing and expanding the system too fast for its powers of growth. Whether the criticism was just or not, his programme like his book certainly showed how concerned he was with equality of opportunity. This indeed is a permanent element in his thought, and in later writings it has come further to the front. For example, in his *al-Mu'adhabun fi'l-ard* (1949) he expounds the doctrine

---

[21] *Mustaqbal al-thaqafa*, ii. 471 ff. & i. 92.   [22] Ibid. ii. 481.

of the two nations, the rich and poor between whom is no community of feeling; and expresses disappointment with that
independence which, ten years earlier, had stirred such hopes:
'This country which was made for freedom is still enslaved'.[23]

His criticism of the social and economic system is, however,
only sketched in lightly, and nowhere does he show a detailed
knowledge of social problems outside those of education. Such
knowledge and interest is more explicit in other writers of his
age. A contemporary of his, the Copt Salama Musa, preached
a sort of socialism, but derived less from Marx than from the
'advanced thought' of Edwardian England, from Shaw and
Wells and through them from Ibsen, Nietzche, and Tolstoy. A
nationalist, and a purely Egyptian one, he held that national
independence was of no value in itself, but must be combined
with internal change. Reform and independence go together, and
the enemies of the two have always been allies: European imperialists and Egyptian reactionaries have worked together.
Reform means, in essence, the creation of modern industry and
the adoption of a scientific culture: modern Egyptian culture is
not scientific, it is still literary, turned back towards the past and
based on contempt or ignorance of the peasant and worker.[24]
Here too the details are a little vague; and it was left to another
member of the same generation to fill them in. Hafiz 'Afifi, a
younger associate of Lutfi al-Sayyid and one of the founders of
the Liberal Constitutional Party in the 1920's, had turned his
attention to economic organization, and had helped to build up
the Misr group of companies, the first successful step taken by
Egyptians in modern industrial organization. In a book published
in 1938, and called *'Ala hamish al-siyasa* (On the Margin of
Politics), his starting-point is very much the same as that of
Taha Husayn. We have thought too exclusively about our relations with Great Britain, and the foreign communities; now we
have independence, we must ask what it is for. In answering this
question, his assumptions again are much the same as those of
Husayn: Egypt is a separate and homogeneous nation, her form
of government must be democratic, and that implies that she
should have a parliament, organized parties, and free elections. Free elections are essentially a rational choice between

[23] *al-Mu'adhabun fi'l-ard*, pp. 145 ff.
[24] Musa, *al-Adab wa'l-hayat*, pp. 12 ff. & 72.

programmes of action rationally thought out and presented, and which the parties really intend to carry out. His book is intended to help in the thinking out of a programme of positive social action, and deals with national health, education, public finance, and above all the organization of economic life. Just as Husayn sketched an ideal system of education which later governments have tried to a large extent to bring into being, 'Afifi's book suggests an economic policy which was later to become the generally accepted aim of all parties. In it there comes to the fore what is now the most pressing and least easily soluble problem of Egyptian life: to be a part of the modern world, Egypt must raise her standard of living; but the vast and ceaseless increase of her population is working in the opposite direction. If there is an answer to the problem it can only lie in rapid industrialization, and this involves a new tariff policy, new workers' legislation, better communications, industrial credit, and Egyptian participation in foreign companies.

XIII

EPILOGUE: PAST AND FUTURE

AN age passed away in 1939, and with it there went a certain type of political thought. In its most obvious expression, this thought was 'nationalist', whether Arab or Egyptian, Turkish or Persian, Kurdish or Jewish or Armenian: that is to say, it asserted that there existed between members of a certain group a link so strong and important that they should form a political community, and that a government possessed moral authority only if it expressed the will of that community and served its interests. There can be many different types of community, and in the Middle East of the period with which this book has dealt there were three main types of nationalism, each overlapping with the others but derived from a different principle. First in order of time there was 'religious' nationalism: the assertion that all who adhered to the same religion should form a single political community. In one sense this had been the fundamental political idea of the region since the Roman Empire became Christian and religious faith, whether personal or inherited, became the characteristic in terms of which a man was defined. But in another sense it was new, and a form of modern nationalism. The Muslim community as the pan-Islamic thinkers conceived it, or the Jewish community of the Zionists, was not held together by common profession of faith or the will to live in accordance with revealed law. It was held together by a common inheritance, not only of religious doctrine or wisdom but of the culture, the habits and the temperament which had grown up around it. The only religious demand such movements made was a negative one, that a Muslim or Christian or Jew should not formally abandon his ancestral faith and adopt another; positively, the links between the members of the community were affective and mundane—culture, the memory of things done in common, and secular interests. Except for Zionism, which built upon a particularly strong sense of solidarity and common interests, this type of 'religious' nationalism proved less stable than other types, although it continued to exist as an element in them: there was still a sense in which to be a Turk involved being a Sunni Muslim, and to be a Persian meant to be a Shi'i, and Arab consciousness was inextricably connected with Muslim consciousness. (When, after the Greco-Turkish War of 1920–2 the League of Nations tried to exchange Turks in Greece for Greeks in Turkey, the only criterion it could find was a religious one: members of the Orthodox Church were Greeks, whether they spoke Greek or Turkish, Muslims were Turks, whether they spoke Turkish or Greek.)

The second type of nationalism was that which was most familiar in the old and settled countries of western Europe: territorial patriotism, a sense of community with all who shared the same defined piece of land, rooted in love for that land itself. This was strongest in those parts of the Middle East where a settled community had lived for a long time in the same region, and where that region had relatively clear boundaries and an unbroken tradition of separate administrative or political existence: in Egypt, where the nationalism of the Wafd was purely Egyptian, in the mountains of Lebanon, in Tunisia. Wherever it existed, it tended to evoke memories of the land and those who had inhabited it in ancient times (Pharaohs, Phoenicians, or Hittites): both because to declare one's identity with an ancient past was a way of escaping from a more recent past, and because the more recent past, in most of the region, had been one of absorption into large supranational units—the caliphate and then the Ottoman Empire. In general, however, this kind of nationalism, even when it was strongest, tended to be weaker than in western Europe, both because frontiers were less stable and political forms more fragile, and because, except in favoured regions like the valleys of Lebanon or the Sahel of Tunisia, sedentary life was exposed to more enemies.

The third, and in the event the strongest, of the three kinds of nationalism was ethnic or linguistic, based on the idea that all who spoke the same language constituted a single nation and should form one independent political unit. For better or worse, this became the dominant political idea in the Middle East and superseded or absorbed others; thus in the Arabic-speaking countries the assertion that all who spoke Arabic formed a nation and should constitute one State or group of States proved to be the strongest political force, even if it had not yet embodied itself in a political form. But political ideas do not often exist in a pure state unmixed with others, even with their opposites: it was only rarely that the concept of Arab nationalism was stated with such force and logic as in the writings of Sati' al-Husri. In most thinkers, and in the formulations of most political parties and leaders, the Arab idea was blended with ideas drawn from other types of nationalism. It was closely linked with the idea of the Islamic community, and even for Arab nationalists who were Christians their nationalism implied a certain moral adherence to Islam, as a civilization if not as a religion. In the same way, for most of the thinkers with whom we have dealt Arab linguistic nationalism was blended with territorial patriotism. In this period, Arab nationalism was of prime importance in Syria (to use that term once more in its broadest sense), and the claim that all Arabs should be united was, by implication, a claim that the territorial unity of 'Syria' should be reconstituted, as it had existed (in all except the political sense) before the partition of the Ottoman countries after the First World War.

Nationalism is not a system of thought; it is a single idea which does not suffice by itself to order the whole life of society. But it is a potent idea, one of those which serve as centres of attraction to others. In the period with which we have dealt, there grew up within the framework of nationalism a whole content of ideas about the nature of man and his life in society. We have seen how this content was formed by a combination of elements drawn from two sources, which in the last resort could scarcely be distinguished from each other. One source was the liberal secularism of nineteenth-century England and France, directly assimilated and accepted: first expressed in Arabic by Bustani and his school, and passed on by them to Lutfi al-Sayyid and the school of Egyptian nationalists which he created. It was secularist in the sense that it believed that society and religion both prospered best when the civil authority was separate from the religious, and when the former acted in accordance with the needs of human welfare in this world; liberal in the sense that it thought the welfare of society to be constituted by that of individuals, and the duty of government to be the protection of freedom, above all the freedom of the individual to fulfil himself and so to create true civilization. The second source was the

M

Islamic 'reformism' which was formulated by Muhammad 'Abduh and Rashid Rida: Islamic because it stood for a re-assertion of the unique and perfect truth of Islam, but reformist in that it aimed at reviving what it conceived to be certain neglected elements in the Islamic tradition. But this revival took place under the stimulus of European liberal thought, and led to a gradual reinterpretation of Islamic concepts so as to make them equivalent to the guiding principles of European thought of the time: Ibn Khaldun's *'umran* gradually turned into Guizot's 'civilization', the *maslaha* of the Maliki jurists and Ibn Taymiyya into the 'utility' of John Stuart Mill, the *ijma'* of Islamic juris-prudence into the 'public opinion' of democratic theory, and 'those who bind and loose' into members of parliament. The effect of this, in what we have called the secularizing wing of 'Abduh's school, was to bring about a *de facto* separation of the sphere of civilization from that of religion and so to open another door to secular nationalism; but even in the other wing, that of Rida and the neo-Wahhabis, the distinction which they made between doctrine and worship, which were based on unchanging revelation, and the rules of social morality, which should be decided in the light of *maslaha*, led in the same direction, even if it was still maintained or at least asserted that those rules should be derived from the general principles of Islamic ethics.

In this system of ideas, whether drawn directly from Euro-pean liberal thought or indirectly by way of Islamic modernism, more emphasis was laid on national independence or individual freedom than on social justice. It can easily be seen from what has been said in this book, and indeed it was sometimes pointed out at the time, that the content of nationalism in this period included few precise ideas about social reform and economic develop-ment. This may have been a result of indifference, or of the fact that most of the leaders and spokesmen of the nationalist move-ments either belonged to families of standing and wealth or had raised themselves into that class by their own efforts. But it can also be explained by the liberal atmosphere of the time. The aim of nationalism was to release the national energy in economic as well as other spheres of life; in its economic aspect, independence was regarded as a process of liberating the economic life of the nation from foreign control and giving free scope to the forces of national enterprise which, it was generally believed, would bring about an increase of wealth and welfare. It was generally assumed that economic and social change, although desirable in themselves, could and should wait until after the attainment of independence and that independence could be attained without such change, by political means and by making use of the national strength which already existed. It was assumed also that, once independence was won, social progress would assuredly come about: few thinkers were aware of the problems of social policy in newly independent countries—the difficulties of maintaining standards of administration achieved under European control, of defining the frontiers between private enterprise and State control, and of obtaining the foreign capital necessary for rapid development without falling under foreign control of a new kind.

The essential aim of the nationalists was to win independence, but even this was conceived in a limited way. To be independent, in the language of the time, was to have internal autonomy and be a member of the League of Nations. But it did not exclude (in fact it almost implied) a permanent relationship with the former occupying Power: the maintenance of military bases and economic and cultural links, the subordination of policy in major matters of foreign relations. Indeed it could not have been otherwise: independent or not, the Middle Eastern States of the time could not escape the power of England and France. It lay all around them, embodied in armies, navies and air forces, in schools and banks and commercial economic enterprises. They had no choice between being dominated and being truly independent; they only had a choice between different degrees and kinds of domination.

Ibn Khaldun wrote of the attractive power which a ruling group exercises over the mind and imagination of the ruled, and Toynbee also has written of the force of mimesis by which a dominant minority can draw the majority after it. It was largely because of the inescapable presence of European power, resented but accepted, that the nationalism of this generation had an ambivalent attitude towards Europe. It desired to throw off the political domination of England or France, or at least their direct rule; but for help in doing so it appealed to the liberal conscience of the British and French, and its explicit aim in seeking independence was not to free itself completely from Europe so much as to have a new relationship with her—equal, trusting, based on spontaneous and complete acceptance of the values of the modern civilization which Europe had created. 'We must follow the path of the Europeans so as to be their equals and partners in civilization', said Taha Husayn, and for him, as for Bustani two generations earlier, it was true that this was the age of Europe, and to be modern was to be in communion with her.

Soon after Taha Husayn wrote these words the Second World War broke out, and in the next twenty years or so great changes took place, some more obvious than others. The most obvious was the change in the position of the European States, *vis-à-vis* each other and the rest of the world, brought about by the war. Europe lost her 'moral' ascendancy, that force of mimesis which she had exercised for so long, thanks both to her strength and to the superior virtues which lay or were thought to lie behind it. The spectacle of Europe tearing herself in pieces, and the sudden collapse of France, aroused doubts about both the strength and the virtues; perhaps Europe did not possess the 'secret' of stable happiness. Indeed these doubts were to some extent justified. Europe's position had in fact changed: it was not so much that her power had grown less *vis-à-vis* the countries of Asia and the Middle East, for if anything with the perfecting of modern armaments the balance of military force had shifted in favour of the highly industrialized countries. The change was on another level. There took place what has sometimes been called, perhaps unfairly, a 'failure of nerve': a growing reluctance to use strength in the same way as it had been used, to crush resistance. (This change came more quickly in England than in France, where the shock of the German occupation and the weaknesses of the body politic made it more difficult to with-draw willingly from what was left of France's imperial position.) Moreover the relations of the western Powers with one another had changed. Great Britain was no longer the strongest Power in the world or in the Middle East, although a combination of circumstances made it possible for her to act, in this one region of the world, as if she still were. The loss of her dominant position took place in the years between 1945 and 1954, when she first of all ceded responsibility for Greece, Turkey, and Persia to the United States, then suffered a major defeat in one of the main centres of her power, Palestine, and finally withdrew voluntarily from her position in Egypt and Iraq. This loss, however, did not become fully apparent until 1956, when she tried for the last time to act as the strongest Power, only to draw on herself the anger of those who were stronger. But although she had lost her hegemony, it was not assumed by any one Power: it was rather that the domination of one Power was replaced by the precarious balance of several, each able to insist that its interests should be taken into account but none of them able to establish its unchallenged domination.

One result of this new situation was that for the first time it became possible for the Middle Eastern States to be really independent. In some parts of the world national movements had to obtain independence by fighting the former imperial Power to a standstill (as happened in Indo-China and Algeria); but in others, and this was true of most Middle Eastern countries, they did it by taking advantage of the loss of strength, the change in political mood, and the new balance of forces in the region. By 1962 virtually the whole region was independent, and the first aim of nationalists was not to obtain but to preserve their independence. Hence the importance of the Afro-Asian bloc in the United Nations, which gave weak new States a collective power which, although fragile, was not illusory. Hence too the importance of the idea of neutralism, the theoretical basis of the bloc. For neutralism was not simply a desire to avoid being involved in the conflicts of the Great Powers, it was also the new form which the desire for independence had taken. As such its purpose was to use the rivalries of the Great Powers to create a zone in which none of them could impose its will, and it was almost universal as a political attitude in the countries of the region, although it might take various forms in different circumstances: Turkey and Persia had swung towards the western camp because of pressure from the other side, but if the pressure were relaxed they too would perhaps revert to a safer position in the middle.

What was perhaps less obvious was the emergence of another kind of independence. The old distinction between east and west, which dominated the thought of the period with which this book has dealt, had passed away. It was natural that the generation of 'Abduh and Rida, and even their successors in the

years between the wars, should look to the west as the repository
of modern civilization and teacher of the ways of thought and
techniques on which it depended. But the west by now had
carried out its historic mission of creating a new and unified
world. The world was one: first of all on the level of material
techniques, for while the great centres of creative science were
still where they had been a generation ago—in western Europe,
European Russia, and north America—there was an increasing
technical mastery everywhere, and general acceptance of the
fact that there existed only one kind of science and technique
which was valid—that there was one way only of making aero-
planes and curing diseases. Politically too the world had become
one: there was a single universe of political discourse. There
were of course different political systems, but the differences
could not be explained simply in terms of regional or national
character or tradition. The political problem of Asia and the
Middle East was not that of preserving a unique and traditional
system—the Muslim sultanate or the Chinese Empire—but that
of creating and maintaining one or other of the several types of
system which were possible in the conditions of modern society.
Everywhere, even in the most conservative societies, the traditional systems were being transformed into something more
modern: the ancient sultanate of Morocco, with its religious
sanction, had become a modern monarchy with a national
sanction, and even in the fastnesses of Arabia there were stirrings
of political change.

As a consequence of this, for the first time in modern history
it had become possible for eastern States, if they wished, completely to break their connexions with the west. It was no longer
necessary to have such a connexion if they wished to form part
of the modern world: they could reject it and still acquire all the
techniques and ideas on which modern civilization depended.
This had two opposing results. For a few politicians and thinkers,
acceptance of the west (whether out of interest or from conviction) became more deliberate and articulate, simply because
the choice had to be made and defended. But by others, since the
western connexion was no longer necessary, it was rejected as a
survival of the age of imperial control. This indeed was one of
the ways in which the Egyptian revolution of 1952 was significant: it brought to power men who, although fully alive to

the need for accepting the techniques of modern industry, and living in the universe of modern political discourse, yet refused to accept a privileged position for the west, and for whom the world of European culture meant little. For the first time in over a century Egypt was ruled by men who would not have echoed the words of Isma'il, 'Egypt is no longer a part of Africa', nor regarded Paris as the spiritual capital of the world.

This was not to say that they turned their eyes back from Paris to Mecca. The most important of all the changes which came to the surface in these twenty years was this: the past was abolished, whether it were the past of 'westernization' or the more distant past of the traditional societies. A new society was coming rapidly into existence, not only in what had been the most advanced of the Middle Eastern countries, but also—and in a more spectacular way—in the backward countries of the Arabian Peninsula. Economically this new society was marked by the growth of large-scale industry, the rational organization of agriculture, and the positive intervention of the government in both of them. As a result of these processes there emerged three new classes: an indigenous middle class of entrepreneurs, managers, and merchants; an 'intelligentsia' of technicians, officials, officers, and professional men and women; and an urban proletariat swollen by the surplus population of the countryside and beginning to organize itself in trade unions. As these grew, two other classes declined: the European and Levantine commercial bourgeoisie in the towns, the landowners in the countryside. The public life of the community ceased to be a matter for a small privileged group, and was enlarged by the emancipation of women, and by the development of new means of communication—the press, the cinema, radio and television—and the growth of a new literature adapted to them. The problems posed by the emergence of this new society were so new, complex, and strange that the past no longer had lessons. The minds and imaginations of men might still look to the past for inspiration, and draw from it the lesson (whether justified or not) that the Arabs had been great before and could be great again; and they might regard the culture inherited from the past as the basis of national solidarity. But they no longer believed, for the most part, that they had received from the past an unchanging norm of wisdom, a system of principles which had regulated and should always regulate the organization of society and the activities of the State, whether that norm were derived from the customs of the ancestors or the Sacred Law. The *Shari'a* indeed had been abandoned with astonishing speed and completeness. The process begun in the early nineteenth century with the adoption of codes on the European model was by now almost complete. In the realm of law, civil and criminal, commercial and constitutional, secular codes had replaced the religious, everywhere except in the most withdrawn parts of Arabia, and this had happened no less completely in a country such as Egypt, where it had taken place almost imperceptibly, than in Turkey, where it had been the product of revolution. In Turkey and Tunisia an attack had been made even on the last stronghold of the *Shari'a*, the law of personal status: polygamy had been abolished and civil marriage introduced, apparently without causing great scandal. It might indeed appear that the storm aroused in Tunisia in 1960 by the President's criticism of fasting during Ramadan was an example to the contrary; in fact it was not, for Ramadan had become in modern times the great manifestation of the unity of Islam, the month when Muslims believing or unbelieving became conscious of their past and affirmed their links with their ancestors, and the criticism was perhaps resented not because it ran counter to the *Shari'a* but rather because it threatened the solidarity of the Muslim community.

If thinkers and statesmen recognized a norm by which their acts could be judged, it was not to be found in the past but in the future. There had been formed an image of the future to direct and inspire action, and this was symbolized by the change in postage stamps, which no longer showed mosques or sphinxes or kings, but workers and peasants in heroic attitudes, shaking their fists at fate. Whether the régime was that of a nationalist republic or a constitutional monarchy, the image was much the same. Its emphasis was on the people (*al-qawm, al-sha'b*), where a generation earlier it would have been on the *watan*. The old nationalism called on men of good will to defend an oppressed *watan*, but in the new the people were active: holders of authority and masters of their own destiny, they pressed forward to remake the social world, and their own view of their own welfare was the final criterion of their actions. Welfare was no longer defined, at least in the first instance, in terms of individual freedom, but rather of economic development, a rise in general living standards and the provision of social services.

All these changes posed new problems for social and political thought. First of all, what was the nation? That is to say, what was the community which was and ought to be the source of political authority and the object of loyalty? Secondly, what was and should be the relationship between the welfare of the community and the inherited precepts and practices of religion? Thirdly, what was and should be the attitude of the nation, and of the State which embodied it, towards the outside world? Fourthly, which of several possible directions should the government follow in its attempts to further economic development and social welfare?

To some extent, the same answers were given to these questions by all the important trends of thought in the Middle East during the fifteen years after the war. But there were significant differences, not only in their programmes of action but in the principles from which they started. In the work of certain writers there could still be found the ideas which had inspired those of an earlier generation. Thus in some essays of the Lebanese philosopher Charles Malik there was an affirmation of the link with the west, the more impressive because grounded in a clearer insight into the meaning of western civilization. The west for him was no longer that of Rousseau or Comte or Mill. The roots of its culture went much farther back, into the Near East of ancient times:

The great moments of the Near East are the judges of the world . . . the one message deposited by the Near East in the whole of its history is . . . [that] there is an original transcendent order, full of meaning and power, open to the faithful and pure: an order creating, judging, disturbing, healing, forgiving.[1]

This civilization the west in its turn had offered back to the Near East, which should accept it, but could only do so if the west remained true to itself, that is to say to the ideas of reason, freedom, and transcendence which lay at its heart. In this process of offer and acceptance Lebanon had a special role to play: since the west was essentially Christian, the Near East needed a Christian intermediary which was also part of itself. Lebanon

[1] C. Malik, 'The Near East', *Foreign Affairs*, xxx (1951–2), 264.

alone could be such an intermediary; Israel could not, although she claimed to be, for she was not grounded in what was deepest in western civilization, and at the same time was radically estranged from the Near East in which she had established herself.[2]

In the same way, it was possible to find a prolongation into this later period of the modernizing Islamic thought which has formed the central theme of this book. An Iraqi thinker, 'Ali al-Wardi, wrote a series of books restating the history of Islam in terms of the revolutionary struggle to achieve justice; his thought was an attempt to interpret Islam in the light of what seemed most striking in the history of his own age, just as the school of 'Abduh had interpreted it in the light of the thought and achievement of theirs.[3] A similar purpose inspired a remarkable book by an Egyptian doctor, Muhammad Kamil Husayn: *Qarya zalima* (City of Wrong).[4] In form a meditation on the meaning of the Crucifixion, in effect it was a restatement of the teaching of Islam in the face of two dominant features of the age; the science of psychology, which challenged accepted thought as biology had done a hundred years earlier, and the threat of war. It started, as some of the followers of 'Abduh would have done, with a distinction between the spiritual and temporal orders: the latter 'is the work of man. It is imperfect, temporal, subject to change.... Thus the prohibitions that belong to the social realm must remain a wholly human sphere under safeguards for which man is responsible'.[5] But in regard to both realms, its teaching was not precisely that of 'Abduh's school. The temporal sphere, as they had taught, was ruled by reason, but reason spoke now with a different voice, preaching internationalism, pacifism, the wickedness of taking human life, the moral responsibility of each individual for the acts of his society; while in the sphere of religion the voice of God, which to an earlier generation spoke first of all in public, though the Quran, had become the voice of conscience speaking to the individual heart. It was conscience which set limits for human action, and laid down 'laws which the soul must not transgress unless it is to suffer disease'.[6]

Both these writers tried to show that the modern world could

[2] Malik, p. 242.   [3] Cf. al-Wardi, pp. 401 ff.
[4] References are to the Eng. trs.   [5] *City of Wrong*, p. 90.
[6] Ibid. p. 117.

be accommodated within Islam; a third, in a book which was banned, did so in a more radical way, by rejecting much that was usually regarded as Islamic. In 'Abd Allah al-Qasimi's *Hadhi hiya'l-aghlal* (These are the Chains), there is the familiar attack on religious stagnation, on passive other-worldliness, and on the dichotomy of spiritual and material. But an attempt is made to explain this false attitude of Muslims in terms of Islamic theology —of the belief of the orthodox theologians that God is the only real Agent, the direct cause of all events. The basis of strength and progress is the belief that man is a free agent and has power to perfect himself, and that the universe is governed by causal laws. The Arabs before Islam held this belief, and so did the early Muslims before their religion was corrupted from outside. But this does not mean that modern man should try to imitate the *salaf*, for there is progress in human nature as well as civilization, and perfection cannot be found in the past.[7]

Perhaps equally significant was the work of a writer who, although lacking originality of thought and distinction of manner, nevertheless succeeded in spreading a modernist interpretation of Islam among a large public. Khalid Muhammad Khalid drew once more the familiar distinction between true and false religion, between what was essential and what was not. But in his hands true religion virtually lost its meaning and became no more than 'a source of strength, fraternity, equality', a spiritual attitude rather than a creed. Moreover he drew the distinction more sharply, even crudely, than earlier thinkers would have done; religion which interfered in the secular realm was false, it was the tool of 'priesthood' in its attempts to obtain power and keep the people poor and ignorant. True religion indeed was only possible when social and economic justice existed; a full stomach was the necessary condition of spiritual life.[8] To achieve justice, society must remake itself; the changes needed were far-reaching and could be made only by revolutionary means. In one of his books Khalid sketched the outlines of a social revolution in Egypt: it would involve the division of large estates and fixing of agricultural rents, the nationalization of resources and protection of the rights of labour, the emancipation of women and birth-control. But it would also involve the creation of a real

---

[7] Qasimi, *passim*; cf. von Grunebaum, pp. 216–24.
[8] Khalid, *Min huna nabda'*, p. 43 (Eng. trs. p. 48).

parliamentary democracy and political parties; the revolution should be a democratic one.[9]

By such thinkers, Islam was restated and defended in terms appropriate to the age of psychology and revolution. A similar change took place in the idea of Arab nationalism, under the impact of a seminal disaster, the loss of Palestine. The creation of the State of Israel, the defeat of the Arab armies and expulsion of the Arab population had indeed a profound effect on Arab nationalist thought and started a far-reaching debate on the reasons for the Arab failure. Some of the younger Palestinian Arabs contributed to this debate,[10] but most light was shed on the subject by two thinkers who had come to maturity in the classical period of nationalism between the wars. Qustantin Zurayq, whose book on national consciousness we have already met, wrote another on 'the meaning of the disaster' (*Ma'na al-nakba*) in the critical days of 1948.[11] Nothing, he urged, was more important to the Arabs at the moment than the danger of Zionist expansion, which might in the end destroy them. It could be held back only if the Arabs were able to make use of all their strength in self-defence, and this would involve a transformation of their entire being. The basic cause of the disaster and the danger was that there did not exist an Arab nation in the real sense. 'A progressive, dynamic mentality will never be stopped by a primitive, static mentality';[12] it could be stopped only if there was a fundamental change in the Arab way of life. This involved the creation of a unified State, and economic and social development; but these in their turn involved an intellectual change: the Arabs must become 'in fact and in spirit . . . a part of the world in which we live',[13] accepting its material techniques, its secularism, its methods of scientific thought, and its moral values. This could only happen by means of an intellectual élite able to see itself and the Arabs with the clarity and humility that a true understanding of history alone could give. In a later work Zurayq defined the scope and nature of genuine historical thought.[14]

---

[9] Khalid, *Muwatinun*, pp. 109, 151.
[10] Sayigh (Sayegh), *Risala* and *Arab Unity*; H. Z. Nuseibeh.
[11] Eng. trs. *The Meaning of Disaster*.
[12] *Ma'na al-nakba*, p. 44 (Eng. trs. p. 36).
[13] Ibid. p. 47 (Eng. trs. p. 39).
[14] *Nahnu wa'l-ta'rikh*, chs. vi, viii, x.

A similar lesson was taught by the most intelligent and responsible of the Palestinian leaders, Musa al-'Alami, in a short book on the lesson of Palestine ('*Ibrat Filastin*).[15] It was partly concerned with specific mistakes made by the Arabs in dealing with the question of Palestine: the lack of preparation, of unity, of a clear conception of what the war would be like, and of seriousness in waging it. But behind these mistakes lay other, more general weaknesses: the lack of a permanent and effective unity, defects in the machinery of government, and above all the absence of political consciousness among the people and of contact between them and the government. If the Arabs were to resist the danger of Zionist expansion, there must be real unity, in the first instance between the countries of the Fertile Crescent (with a special position for Lebanon); and a reformed system of government, truly constitutional, rational in its policy and scientific in its administration, and concerned for the welfare of the people. The right to freedom, to work, to security and social services must be recognized; there could only be a nation in the real sense if the people had something of their own to defend.

In so far as Zurayq and 'Alami wrote of the means by which these reforms could be carried out, they placed their faith where the liberal nationalists had placed it: in the dedicated élite, working to create an enlightened national opinion and use it to bring about reform peacefully. But even among those who shared the same general outlook there were some who doubted whether such means were adequate. Thus Edmond Rabbath, in a lecture on the role of the élite, maintained that the nationalism of which he himself had been, twenty years earlier, so brilliant an exponent, had been an expression of a specific social process, the rise of the middle class; now that the process was over, the bourgeois nationalist élite could no longer give leadership to the nation, and power had slipped from its hands.[16] In similar terms a young Palestinian, Fayez Sayegh (Fa'iz Sayigh), maintained that a unified Arab nation could not be created by purely political methods; it involved a fundamental social change, for only the dynamic force created by such change would be able to bring unity about;[17] and a historian of nationalist convictions, 'Abd

[15] Eng. trs. 'The Lesson of Palestine', *Middle East J.*, iii (1949), 373–405.
[16] Rabbat (Rabbath), 'Muhimmat al-nukhba', *al-Abhath*, x (1957), 205–25.
[17] Sayegh, *Arab Unity*, pp. 161 ff.

al-'Aziz al-Duri, interpreted the whole of Arab history in terms of recurrent popular movements for liberation and unity.[18]

The tension between different types of nationalism came into the open at a congress of Arab writers held in Cairo in 1957, and at which there took place a discussion on pure and committed literature which raised by implication the question of individual freedom and national interest. Taha Husayn, by now the doyen of Arab writers and a champion of Arab rather than purely Egyptian nationalism, laid stress on the essentially free and tolerant spirit of Arab nationalism, while a Tunisian delegate spoke of intellectual liberty as necessary if literature were to be effective; but others laid more emphasis on the responsibility of the writer to his nation—we do not, said one of them, want a freedom which contradicts truth.[19] In another way, the tension between two types of nationalism came dramatically into the open in the Lebanese civil war of 1958. Since 1943 there had existed a 'national pact' between those (mainly Christians) who believed in an independent Lebanon linked with the west and those (mainly Muslims) who regarded Lebanon as a separate but integral part of the Arab world: the latter agreed to recognize Lebanese independence if the former would align its policy with that of the Arab States. After 1954 the agreement tended to break down, with the appearance of a new and more sweeping neutralist Arab nationalism, and the unwillingness of the western Powers to accept Middle Eastern neutralism. The fears of the Lebanese nationalists and the over-confidence of the Arab nationalists combined with Muslim grievances about the concentration of power in Christian hands and various personal factors to produce a civil war, which ended in a reassertion, however fragile, of the 'national pact'.[20]

Similar tensions could be seen in other Arab countries, but in general the tide of feeling, among the young, seemed to be flowing in favour of a more comprehensive Arab nationalism. It was given political form by the Ba'th party, founded in Damascus in the 1940's, and which played an important part in Lebanon, Jordan, and Iraq as well as Syria, and was largely responsible for the formation of the United Arab Republic in 1958. Being a

---

[18] al-Duri, *al-Judhur*, p. 55.
[19] Cf. 'Congrès des écrivains arabes', *MIDEO*, iv (1957), 326–57.
[20] Cf. Janbulat (Jumblat), *Fi majra al-siyasa*.

party striving for power, it could not afford to define its attitude as precisely as an isolated thinker, but a coherent doctrine was implied in its constitution and formulated by its founder, Michel 'Aflaq. This doctrine was, first of all, comprehensively Arab. It asserted the existence of 'one Arab nation with an eternal message'.[21] The national tie between an individual and his nation was the basis of political virtue, and for him 'whose language is Arabic and who lives in the Arab land ... and believes that he belongs to the Arab nation'[22] that tie could only be an Arab one. It excluded all national attachments to smaller units, local or religious, and included all Arab countries on the same footing.

One of the criticisms made by 'Aflaq of the older nationalism was that it had no content. In its first years, the Ba'th laid emphasis on the Islamic content of Arab nationalism. Islam was the 'national culture' of the Arabs; it was 'a veritable image and a perfect and eternal symbol of the nature of the Arab self'. Muhammad was 'all the Arabs', and it would be dangerous for Arabs to separate religion from nationality as the Europeans had done.[23] But for 'Aflaq the essence of Islam was its 'revolutionary' quality, and later, particularly after the Ba'th amalgamated with Akram Hawrani's Socialist party, it laid more emphasis on the need for social revolution. Its programme included the redistribution of wealth, the national ownership of public utilities and resources, the limitation of ownership of land, social insurance, labour legislation, the establishment of free trade unions, and the guarantee, of a minimum standard of living. It believed that Arab independence, Arab unity, and social justice could not be achieved apart from each other; socialism was an essential part of Arab nationalism.

The Ba'th was socialist and not Communist, and stood in principle for constitutional democracy. But in the years leading up to the creation of the United Arab Republic it linked itself closely with the military régime in Egypt. This was partly because its foreign policy was neutralist and its foreign links were primarily with the Afro-Asian bloc of which President Nasser was one of the leaders.[24] But there was also a positive reason: in

---

[21] *Dustur hizb al-ba'th al-'arabi al-ishtiraki*, p. 1.   [22] Ibid. p. 7.
[23] 'Aflaq, *Fi sabil al-ba'th*, pp. 43 ff.
[24] Cf. Maqsud, p. 100; Majdalani, 'Arab Socialist Movement', *in* Laqueur.

a region which was only half-conscious politically, those who
wished to bring about changes quickly tended to look for some
force which would do what had been done in other regions by the
pressure of informed and organized public opinion. 'The Arab
officer class', as an acute observer of Arab political life remarked,
'has become the repository of self-conscious political power at a
time when the traditional ruling class is bankrupt, the other
growing forces and trends have not crystallized, and the general
masses positively look to this class as a saviour'. [25] Of the various
military groups which took power in various countries, it was
the Egyptian which most succeeded in attracting to itself the
aspirations of Arab nationalism. But 'Nasserism', as the same
observer remarked, was an empirical radicalism, 'not an ideology
but an attitude of mind'. [26] Its first care was for the interests of
Egypt as it conceived them, and these interests it pursued in
flexible and changing ways. But this empirical and flexible policy
expressed two feelings which were widespread in Egypt and
other Arab countries. First of all there was a feeling for the
welfare of the peasant class, from which most of the military
leaders themselves came. Almost the first act of the régime was
to expropriate the large estates, and this was the beginning of a
policy described by President Nasser as 'socialist, democratic,
co-operative'; [27] it aimed at establishing agricultural co-opera-
tives, improving social conditions in the villages, and diverting
both foreign and Egyptian capital from investment in land and
buildings into investment in industry. But it is in the nature of
régimes which have been created through the overthrow of an
old order to keep up the revolutionary momentum; it was
because of this, because the land reforms of 1952 had not met the
needs of the poorer peasants, and also perhaps because of the
influence of other members of the Afro-Asian bloc, that, in
1961, the social and economic policy of Egypt took a sharp turn
towards the nationalization of industry and the imposition of
State control over the whole of economic life.

In foreign policy the overriding feeling which directed
Egyptian policy was one of solidarity with Asian and African
nations trying to free themselves from European control, and

[25] Khalidi, 'Political Trends in the Fertile Crescent', ibid. p. 123.
[26] Ibid. p. 125.
[27] Abdel-Nasser ('Abd al-Nasir), *Speeches and Press Interviews 1959*, p. 550.

the need for unity in face of the danger from the Great Powers. It was in this context that Egypt's Arab policy developed. It was natural that, once the British withdrawal made it possible for Egypt to follow a policy of her own, she should try to strengthen ties and cultivate friendships in the Arab region all around her; ever since the Anglo-Egyptian Treaty of 1936 Egypt's policy had increasingly become one of support for Arab union and independence. This process was carried farther by the military régime. President Nasser himself explained the two factors which led him into a pan-Arab policy—consideration of Egypt's own strategic interests, and feeling for other countries faced with British and French power.[28] But the long separate existence of Egypt, and the growth of a separate Egyptian nationalism in modern times, gave to her conception of Arab unity a special colour. It was clear from the speeches made by President Nasser after the union between Egypt and Syria that for him it was not primarily what it was for Syrians, the replacement of an artificial political order by a more natural one: it was rather that two peoples who had ties of history and culture would be stronger together than separately.[29] In the same way the link between Islamic countries was, in his view, one of political interest based on common sentiment; the Pilgrimage to Mecca was not a ticket to paradise, it should be a 'periodical political conference' at which co-operation between Islamic countries should be discussed.[30]

The guiding principle of such régimes and parties was that of national interest: of the right of a society to choose its own acts in the light of its own interests. But this principle, although dominant, did not go unchallenged. There were other trends of thought which, although claiming to be concerned with the national interest, would not have regarded it as the guiding principle of society. Such, for example, was the attitude of the *Ikhwan al-Muslimun* (the Muslim Brothers) and the writers connected with them, in Egypt and to a lesser extent in other Arab countries. The Brothers played an important part in Egyptian politics during the period of confusion between 1945 and 1954; after their suppression in 1954 they ceased to be openly active, but the type of thought which they embodied

---

[28] 'Abd al-Nasir, *Falsafat al-thawra*, p. 62 (Eng. trs. p. 49).
[29] Abdel-Nasser, *Speeches and Press Interviews*, passim.
[30] 'Abd al-Nasir, p. 79 (Eng. trs. p. 64).

continued to be important. For them nationalism was not enough, not simply in the sense that they looked beyond the nation to the larger community of Islam, but because they believed that the community, national or religious, should seek its welfare within the limits laid down by religious law. The founder of the movement, Hasan al-Banna', had frequented the circle of Rashid Rida in his youth, and tried to carry on *al-Manar* after Rida's death.[31] This is significant for, although Rida might have disapproved of the political methods of the Brothers, they accepted his general outlook. Like him, they condemned innovations in doctrine and worship, and accepted the rights of reason and public welfare in matters of social morality, but insisted that they should work within the limits imposed by the moral principles of Islam.[32] Yet it may be doubted whether they made clear how these principles should be applied in modern society. About the organization of the State indeed Hasan al-Banna' had definite ideas: political parties should be prohibited, the law should be reformed and brought within the bounds of the *Shari'a*, administrative posts should be given to those with a religious education. He made it clear too that the Islamic government should maintain a strict control over private morals and education: primary schools should be attached to mosques, religion should be the centre of education and Arabic its medium.[33] But ideas about the regulation of economic life were not so precise. The writers of this school of thought laid much emphasis on social justice, on the repudiation by Islam of inequality of wealth and class division, and on the social responsibilities of wealth.[34] But the programme they derived from these principles did not differ materially from that of the radical nationalists of the time, and it was difficult to discover in what precise way the economic organization of an Islamic society, as these thinkers viewed it, would have differed from that of other States in the modern world. As a political movement indeed the Brothers were more like a nationalist movement than like Mahdism or Wahhabism: their object was to generate popular energy in order to seize power rather than to restore the rule of Islamic virtue.

[31] al-Banna', *Mudhakkirat*, p. 49.
[32] M. al-Ghazali, *Laysa min al-Islam*, pp. 75 ff.
[33] al-Banna', *al-Rasa'il*, pp. 82 ff.
[34] Cf. Qutb, *al-'Adala*.

In the same way the Communist parties, while by no means denying the claims of nationalism, were offering another principle in terms of which it could be justified and by which its actions should be controlled. Writers of Communist tendency would insist indeed that they were the true nationalists and that nationalism became poisonous when not rooted in social justice,[35] and the programmes of Communist parties appealed to nationalist sentiment when they opposed colonialism and demanded that public utilities in foreign hands should be expropriated without compensation. But in other aspects of their programmes they appealed to other principles which ran counter to those accepted by most nationalists: their attempt to arouse the smaller peasants against the larger as well as against the big landowners ran counter to that idea of national unity which was a dogma of nationalism;[36] when they were neutralist, it was for reasons of tactics and not principle. During the years when Communists had great influence in Iraq the conflict came out into the open, and Communist policy in regard to land reform, to the minorities, and to Arab union was very different from that of the nationalists. Apart from a few Egyptian works there had not yet appeared in Arabic a sustained analysis of the problems of Arab society based on a mature knowledge of Marxist thought.

At this time ideas from the North African countries of Arabic speech began to flow into the main current of Arab thought. Tunisia, as we have seen, had had a movement of reform and modern thought in the middle of the nineteenth century, and one which had not been without influence in the eastern Arab world. But the French occupation of Algeria in 1830, of Tunisia in 1881, and of Morocco between 1912 and 1934 had confronted these countries with a special problem. It was not simply that they were under French rule while most of the Middle Eastern countries were under British, or that the French discouraged the spread of dangerous political ideas from the Arab east. The important factor was that the French occupation of North Africa was different in kind from either British or French control in the Middle East. The settlement of French farmers,

---

[35] Cf. Hanna, *Ma'na al-qawmiyya*.
[36] Cf. Bekdash, 'Report of Central Command of Communist Party', *Middle East J.*, vii (1953), 206–21.

business men, and professional men in Algeria first of all, and
then in Tunisia and Morocco, had certain important consequences. It threatened the population of North Africa with
permanent subjection and the gradual loss of their lands; it
made it more difficult for them to obtain or the French government to grant independence; and it led to the creation of a
French administration (whether direct as in Algeria or indirect
as in the other two) geared to the needs of the French communities more than of the indigenous population. This represented a
threat to the political institutions of Tunisia and Morocco, and
to the position of the Arabic language, and created difficulties for
a population obliged to conduct its business with a foreign
government in a foreign language, and itself deprived of the
opportunity to hold important posts in the administration. The
effort to meet these difficulties absorbed the energies of North
Africans for several decades. In Algeria the old bourgeoisie and
the class of artisans had largely disappeared during the period
of French occupation; it was only after 1860 that a new middle
class began to appear,[37] and only after the reform of the educational system in the late 1880's that there emerged, towards
the end of the century, a class of Algerians with a mastery of
French methods of thought. In Tunisia also a similar class
appeared only after a generation of French rule. The first new
movement of political thought came from these groups, and was
directed to convincing the French that Tunisians and Algerians
would be loyal to the existing régime only if they had a better
position within it. This was the point of view of the 'Young
Tunisians', a group of educated young men, mainly of Turkish
origin, who towards the end of the nineteenth century set themselves to help in the national education of their people. Their
ideas were eloquently expressed in *Le Tunisien*, a newspaper
edited by Ali Bach-Hamba in Tunis from 1907 to 1910, and in
the papers they presented to two congresses on North Africa,
held in Marseilles in 1906 and in Paris in 1908.[38] Their starting-
point was the existence of the French protectorate: they accepted
this without question, and their acceptance was not simply a
matter of political prudence, for like other nationalists of the age
their principles were drawn from those of the French revolution

---

[37] Cf. A. Berque, 'La Bourgeoisie algérienne', *Hespéris*, xxxv (1945), 131–9.
[38] *Questions tunisiennes*, p. 47; *Congrès de l'Afrique du Nord.*

and they believed in a French liberal conscience which would some day correct what was wrong with French policy. What they claimed was not full independence but a better position within the protectorate. The absolute power of the Bey should be curbed and a constitution established; European colonization was not repudiated in principle, but the Tunisians should be given their share of the State land which was being distributed to the *colons*; their industry and agriculture should be encouraged (about economic development this group had precise and mature ideas); Tunisians should be enabled to rise to the highest posts in the administration.[39] Above all, more modern schools should be opened. It may seem strange that these precursors of nationalism should have been asking for French education, while it was the spokesmen of the *colons* who were urging that the North Africans should be given an Arabic education, based on the Quran liberally interpreted and with notions of science and agriculture taught in Arabic. 'Il faut que les indigènes évoluent dans leur propre civilisation': this was the thesis of the *colons*, and the Young Tunisians replied to it that this was true of literature and the arts, but not of economic life, in which there was no path except that which had been trodden by Europe and America. While Arabic should be taught, and taught well, the sciences of the age should be taught through the medium of French, and in modern schools.[40] One of the activities of this group was to establish the Khalduniyya, an association for bringing modern knowledge to those who had had the traditional education of the Quranic schools and the Zaytuna mosque.

Much the same arguments were being put forward at this time by a few Algerians who had obtained a higher education in France. The French, they reasoned, must avoid the dangers of another Algerian rebellion like that of 1871. To do so they should give the Algerians a better position: they should be more fully represented in the local assemblies, have more opportunities to acquire a modern education and training for economic life, and administrative grievances should be removed.[41] Once more, the appeal was to those in France who wanted to make the idea of 'une France africaine qui soit . . . le prolongement de la Mère

[39] Cf. *Le Tunisien*, xvii (30 May 1907); xxxv (3 Oct. 1907); lxxviii (27 Aug. 1908).
[40] Cf. ibid. xi (18 Apr. 1907); xcvi (14 Jan. 1909), ff.
[41] Cf. articles by Ben Ali Fakar in ibid. xcii and xciv (17 & 31 Dec. 1908).

Patrie'[42] a reality; and once more, this was not mere prudence but the expression of a profound conviction on the part of those who, by studying in French schools, had become aware of a new world.

Even before the war of 1914 broke out, the thought of these groups was moving in the direction of nationalism. The emigration of Algerians from Tlemçen to the Ottoman Empire in 1911 was a sign that some at least of them had despaired of justice; it aroused much anxiety in France and led to an official inquiry.[43] In Tunisia at the same time relations between Young Tunisians and the French administration grew worse and, after a number of incidents, Ali Bach-Hamba and others were expelled. Bach-Hamba went to Constantinople where he was, during the war, a member of a North African committee which tried to organize risings against the French, not without success.[44] When the war ended nationalist feeling came more openly to the surface, here as elsewhere. In Algeria a movement led by a descendant of Amir 'Abd al-Qadir, the hero of the struggle against the French occupation, was short-lived; but in Tunisia nationalist feeling found expression in a party, the Destour (*Dustur*), and a programme. Embodied in a book published in French, *La Tunisie martyre* (1920), the programme still fell short of asking for independence: it demanded that the Bey and his ministers should be responsible to a Supreme Council of sixty, all of them Tunisian citizens and most of them elected on a wide suffrage; that the *colons* should no longer have privileges but be considered as Tunisian citizens after a residence of ten years; that the rights of individuals should be guaranteed, the judiciary be free, and Tunisians have the same right as Frenchmen to buy State domain. But the tone of the book was uncompromising, with a clear note of national pride and bitterness against France. The leader and spokesman of the Destour was 'Abd al-'Aziz al-Tha'alibi who, although he had worked with the Young Tunisians, was of traditional Islamic education and had come under the influence of Muhammad 'Abduh. But within a decade or so his leadership was being challenged by a younger group organized in the Neo-Destour, and with the aim of using the pressure of

---

[42] *Congrès de l'Afrique du Nord*, i. 69.
[43] Cf. Julien, p. 104.
[44] al-Fasi, *Muhadarat*, pp. 1 ff.

mass opinion and action to achieve complete independence. When, after years of exile, Tha'alibi returned to Tunis in 1937, he was soon defeated in a struggle for leadership by this group, and effective control of Tunisian nationalism passed into the hands of its founder and chief, Habib Bourguiba. From then until 1955 the struggle for independence was directed, and after 1955 the Tunisian State was constructed, by men for whom to be independent meant to enter the new world and the community of modern European culture.

In the writing and speeches of this group the profound mark of western culture was clearly to be seen. A journal kept in exile by one of the early members, Tahar Sfar, showed not only wide reading in French but the fruits of such reading, the habit of precise introspection and analysis of moral sentiments. When, for example, he reflected on the nature of sacrifice he struck a note unusual in Arabic political literature: 'Le sacrifice collectif s'accompagne très souvent d'une joie délirante; il est très gai. Le sacrifice individuel est triste. . . . Car on aime ce qu'on perd.'[45]

In their political methods too the western influence went deep. They were the only Arab political group which succeeded in organizing the workers into trade unions and using them in the political struggle. The beginnings of separate Tunisian trade unions went back to the 1920's; that movement was short-lived, but left its mark in a book by al-Tahir al-Haddad which showed the influence of French socialist ideas.[46] A later attempt was more successful and led to the creation of the powerful *Union générale des travailleurs tunisiens* which played an important part in the struggle for independence. Its political complement was the Neo-Destour party, with its cells throughout the country and its clear chain of command and communication.

The creation and control of this party was the achievement of Habib Bourguiba, whose writings and acts showed him to be both a political organizer and a political thinker of great distinction.[47] The starting-point of his thought was the primacy of reason, which 'doit s'appliquer à toutes choses en ce monde et commander toute activité humaine'.[48] This determined his political strategy: one should never allow oneself to be so moved

[45] Sfar, pp. 9–10.   [46] al-Haddad, *al-'Ummal al-tunisiyyun.*
[47] Cf. Lacouture, pp. 109–80.
[48] Bourguiba, *Bourguiba s'adresse aux cadres de la Nation*, p. 27.

by passion as to overplay one's hand, either by asking for more
than Tunisia, in her weakness, could hope to obtain or by rejecting what was offered because it was less than all one had asked
for. The correct strategy was to accept a partial offer and use it
as the *point d'appui* from which more could be asked for at an
opportune moment. But this involved a clear distinction between
what was inessential and those matters on which no compromise
was possible: when, in 1951, the French government put forward
the idea of a joint Franco-Tunisian sovereignty, this was rejected
out of hand, since a Tunisian State even with limited powers
was better than a mixed State with wider powers.[49]

It was in this way that Tunisian independence was obtained,
and Bourguiba believed that the same rational method should be
applied to building up a modern society. Two ideas underlay his
view of what should be done: those of the State, and of the
nation. The State must be strong, respected, standing above all
sectional or personal interests; only this could check the tendencies to individualism and disintegration which were strong
in Tunisia as in other Arab countries.[50] It should be primarily a
Tunisian State; for although Bourguiba believed in the unity of
Arab North Africa as a final goal, his nationalism was territorial
rather than ethnic. In his speeches there was a vivid sense of
place and history, and of the values of the settled life of the
countryside: 'Nous nous devons de conjurer la vie tribale qui
sévissait dans le pays et qui, propice au développement de
l'esprit du clan, s'oppose à l'instauration d'une véritable civilisation. Car il n'est pas de civilisation que dans un peuple séden-
taire.'[51] To restore the prosperous life of countryside and town,
to increase production and spread the fruits of it more evenly,
were the urgent goals of internal policy, here no less than in
Egypt; but he hoped to achieve them by the dynamic force and
cohesion of a party instead of a military group.

His general conception was of a Tunisia which should belong
to the west in its respect for liberty and reason and the organization of its social life; for his mind had been formed in the Paris
of the Third Republic, and his fundamental principles were
those of French revolutionary democracy. During the Second

---

[49] Bourguiba, *Discours de la victoire*, p. 36.
[50] Bourguiba, *Le Président Bourguiba dans le sud tunisien*, p. 53.
[51] Ibid. p. 19.

World War he always retained his belief in the final victory of England, France, and the United States, refused, when in the hands of the Italians, to commit himself to giving them support, and called on his followers to aid the Allies without conditions.[52] But this did not mean that he would prefer their interests to those of his country. In his writings there was an insistence on the personal humiliations of belonging to a colonized people, and a sharp criticism of the lack of generosity in France's attitude to colonial territories wishing for independence; his support for the Algerian cause troubled his relations with France even before the crisis of Bizerta came near to destroying them. Nor did his attachment to what was of value in the west mean that he was unaware of the links of Tunisia with the Afro-Asian world or with her own Islamic past. He had in fact an all-pervading sense of Islamic history, of the place of Tunisia in it, and the place of Islam in Tunisia. In his early years, the holding of a Eucharistic Congress in Tunis had seemed to him to be an insult to the Muslim population.[53] He did not think that there should be a sharp break with religion, as had happened in Turkey, for this would weaken the national unity. But no more did he believe that the laws of religion, too strictly applied, should be allowed to obstruct acts designed to further human welfare; in his criticism of the fast of Ramadan, he maintained that the principles of Islam should be interpreted flexibly, and that, just as in the past the hardships of travel had dispensed Muslims from the obligation of fasting, so too should the hard work of economic development in a backward country like Tunisia.[54]

If this Islamic element was present in the thought of the most consciously secular and modern of Tunisian politicians, it was still more so in that of others. The Zaytuna mosque in Tunis had for centuries been the home of Islamic learning in North Africa, and during the French occupation it became a centre of resistance to attempts to weaken the hold of the Arabic language. A new institution founded by Khayr al-Din played a similar part: the Sadiqiyya school, which aimed at giving a careful modern education with special attention to Arabic as well as European languages. The typical leader of the new régime, from Bourguiba

[52] Bourguiba, *La Tunisie et la France*, pp. 177 ff.
[53] *Bourguiba s'addresse aux cadres*, p. 41.
[54] Ibid. pp. 27 & 29.

downwards, had studied both at the Sadiqiyya and at the Lycée Carnot. In other North African countries also the religious element was important in the formation of nationalist movements. In Libya, the resistance to Italian rule was organized by the Sanusiyya, a reforming order which had obtained great influence in Cyrenaica before the Italians came, and was the only force solid enough to stand against them. In Morocco when the French protectorate was imposed in 1912 the traditional structure of society was still comparatively untouched by modernity. The Qarawiyyin mosque in Fez played a part similar to that of the Zaytuna and the Azhar as a rallying point of public sentiment, and the first tentative stirrings of national feeling, during the First World War, were inspired by religious shaykhs.[55] When conscious nationalism arose in the 1930's among the younger members of the great urban families, it did not reveal the same gulf between secular and religious elements, or the same domination of the secularized and westernized groups, as in some other countries. Because the French occupation had been shorter, Arabic culture was still strong in the leading bourgeois families, and there were not yet two separate educated classes. The storm aroused in 1930 by the French attempt to create customary tribunals among the Berbers, which would judge matters of personal status in accordance with custom, not the *Shari'a*, united both those who feared for the unity of Morocco and those who resented the attack on the revealed law. Later, during and after the Second World War, the support given by the sultan to the nationalist cause made it possible to rally a wide section of public opinion. For all these reasons, it was possible for religious and secular to work together in framing the first plan of reforms in 1934 and founding the Istiqlal party in 1945.

It might seem that Algerian nationalism was an exception to this. It is true, that when it became an effective political force, with the outbreak of the revolt in 1954 and the organization of an army and a government in exile, its leaders were men, mostly young, who had received their training in the French army or professional schools, whose language of culture and political action was French, whose conceptions of political method and the organization of government were derived from France, and whose ideas of social and economic organization were those of

[55] Cf. al-Fasi, *al-Harakat*, pp. 94 ff.

European radicalism. It was clear that they hoped, when victorious, radically to remould Algerian society and to make Algeria the most modern of Arab States.

But it is one of the functions of national revolts to form nations, to blend into a whole elements which had previously been separate and even opposed,[56] and not the least of the elements which the F.L.N. incorporated into its own movement was a tradition of religious nationalism. The first strong movement of resistance to the French invasion, in the 1830's and 1840's, had been led by Amir 'Abd al-Qadir, the basis of whose authority was religious, and who won support by a characteristically Muslim blend of piety and political skill; the second, in 1871, had been inspired by men from families with a tradition of learning and authority. As a modern educated class emerged, in the early decades of the present century, not all its members followed the path of the Young Tunisians towards integral nationalism; on the contrary, many of the *évolués*, even when bitterly critical of French policy, would have been willing to accept their incorporation into France in return for the removal of practical grievances and the grant of equal rights without loss of their personal status as Muslims.[57] When opposition to the whole conception of a French Algeria began to appear again, it was among two groups whose thought was Islamic or contained an Islamic element. One was the Association of Algerian 'Ulama', founded in 1931; inspired by Ben Badis, a member of one of those religious families of Constantine which, almost alone in Algeria, had preserved their local standing since the Middle Ages, its first purpose was to spread knowledge of the true Islam and to extend Islamic education by founding schools and in other ways. But its activities had political implications. It believed that a true national renaissance could only come about on the basis of a sound religious life, and thus was opposed to assimilation; by stressing Islamic unity it also stressed the national unity of Algerians; it stood for the separate Islamic personality of Algeria and its ultimate independence with the aid of France.[58] The other was the movement initiated by Messali Hadj among the Algerian workers in Paris and which took

---

[56] Cf. Lacheraf, 'Le Nationalisme algérien en marche vers l'unité', *Temps modernes*, xi (1956), 1827.
[57] Julien, pp. 128 ff.
[58] Ibid., pp. 111 ff.

different forms from 1926 onwards: a movement strongly nationalist from the beginning, with a radical social policy influenced by the Communists even when opposed to them, but standing also for the adoption of Arabic as an official language and for a strengthening of the Islamic basis of society.[59]

Even those nationalists whose culture was entirely French were conscious of their own Arab Muslim tradition. That tradition had always been weaker in Algeria, which had no great centres of urban culture, than in Tunisia, and the long wars of the occupation had almost destroyed it; once having become conscious of themselves as Algerians, the nationalists felt the need to reassert their link with the past before it was too late. Thus Mostefa Lacheraf, in a thoughtful essay on Algerian nationalism, laid stress on its links with the Algeria of the days before the French came;[60] and Ferhat Abbas was conscious and proud of his heritage before he drew the political implications from it. His conversion to full nationalism was a slow one: it was only gradually and under pressure of events that he moved from being a supporter of the French connexion to belief in federation without assimilation, then (with the Manifesto of 1943) to the demand for an autonomous republic associated with France, and finally, after long disillusionment, to full support for the F.L.N.[61] But in a book of essays published as early as 1931 he was already evoking the happiness of Algeria before the occupation, a country of prosperous peasants even if badly governed,[62] and denouncing the horrors of the French conquest, of those 'cinquante ans qui furent pour nous "les années terribles", où nous fûmes traqués sans merci, comme des bêtes fauves'.[63] The arrival of the French had indeed given Algeria good administration and territorial unity, but it had deprived the Algerians of rights. There had been no real assimilation, which could only be based on equality. If the edifice built by France was to last, Algerians must be treated as equals but allowed to remain Muslims: 'Que les gens de *l'Afrique latin* le veuillent ou non, nous sommes Musulmans et nous sommes Français. Nous sommes indigènes et nous sommes Français'.[64]

[59] Julien pp. 117 ff.
[60] Lacheraf, 'Nationalisme algérien', *Temps modernes*, xii (1956), 214–55.
[61] *De la Colonie vers la province*, p. 112.
[62] Lacouture, p. 265–324.
[63] Ibid. p. 97.　　　　　　　　　　[64] Ibid. p. 24.

He defends Islam with no less fervour for having studied it through the medium of French. The true Islam was a simple faith, teaching the family virtues, pure democracy, the use of reason, and true equality. It had faced with success the challenge now faced by France, of giving equality to those it had absorbed. After a long decline it was now reviving; he mentions the names of Ibn Sa'ud, Mustafa Kemal, and 'Abduh.[65]

It is not surprising that he mentions 'Abduh for, apart from Libya where special conditions existed, the type of Islam to which the nationalists of North Africa appealed was the reformism of the school of 'Abduh. The Young Tunisians and the Destour in Tunis were linked with the reforming party in the Zaytuna;[66] the true Islam which the Algerian 'Ulama' preached was that which 'Abduh had taught; and in Morocco one of the links between the nationalists and the sultan was their common opposition to the kind of mysticism which 'Abduh had criticized. This was partly thanks to the personal influence of 'Abduh himself, for he had twice visited Tunis and had associates there; and partly, in a later generation, to Shakib Arslan, who preached from Geneva a blend of Islamic reformism and Arab nationalism which had a strong appeal to young North Africans. But there were other reasons for the influence of this type of thought: the members of the orders of mystics, the marabouts, had for centuries played a particularly large part in North African Islam. They were doubly suspect to the nationalists: because the French were accused of making use of them to keep the population quiet and ignorant; and because they preached an other-worldliness and passivity which were incompatible with the desire of the nationalists to arouse the energy of their people and use it to obtain independence and remake society.

Under the impulse of 'Abduh, a number of North Africans had written books expounding a similar view of Islam. Tha'alibi had written, in French and with help, a defence of the liberal spirit of the Quran;[67] and, in the 1920's al-Tahir al-Haddad had studied the position of women in Islamic law and society in a book reminiscent of those of Qasim Amin.[68] Now, after the Second World War, a number of writers raised once more the

[65] Ibid. pp. 59, 67, 94.   [66] Cf. *Le Tunisien*, lxxvii (13 Aug. 1908).
[67] See Benattar &c, *Esprit*.   [68] al-Haddad, *Imra'atuna*.

question what was the true Islam and what was its place in modern society. The Tunisian Mahjub Bin Milad (Ibn Milad) suggested that the true Islamic tradition was the rationalist tradition of the Mu'tazilites and the philosophers;[69] and the leader of the Moroccan Istiqlal party, 'Allal al-Fasi, gave a critique of Muslim thought and society and a plan of reform in a book suggestively called *Self-Criticism*. The book begins with a critique of false ways of thought about religious and social problems and a definition of the correct way. In particular, it explains the way in which the concept of the nation should be understood. The nation is created by a link between a specific land and its people; and in this sense there is a separate Maghribi (North African) nation, formed by the nature of its own land and past. Its national life cannot be divorced from the teachings of Islam. The separation of religion and society and the idea of the secular State are products of Christianity and the experience of Europe; they cannot and need not exist in Islamic society. An Islamic State can only be based on religion, but on religion rightly interpreted. By and large, Fasi's version of Islam is that of the school of 'Abduh: Islam exalts reason and freedom, encourages progress, and rejects all intermediaries between man and God. It should be the basis of a truly national education, and of a modern legal system: instead of the present multiplicity of jurisdictions, there should be an 'Islamic Maghribi law' derived primarily from the *Shari'a* and the practices of the Maghrib. Islam could also be the basis of economic life; for there is a specifically Islamic teaching about the use of property, and if accepted it will ensure social justice and liberate men from 'economic servitude'.[70]

An Algerian thinker of French culture and some originality, Malek Bennabi, posed the question in a different way. If Islamic thought and society were decadent, it was because Muslim man was decadent. Religion in its period of growth is a 'catalyst of human virtues'; in its period of decline it becomes individualist and encourages believers to turn their backs on human society. In Islam the sign of this decay was the domination of the marabouts, and the emergence of a type of mind incapable of thought and afflicted with moral paralysis. The coming of Europe had enabled Muslims to escape from their decadence, by breaking up their rigid social order and freeing them from belief in

[69] Ibn Milad, *Tahrik*.   [70] *al-Naqd al-dhati*, pp. 100 ff., 152, 197, 336.

occult forces and fantasies. But western civilization, being itself in decline, could not give Muslims what they needed, a basis for the social virtues. This could come only from a restoration of the true Islamic doctrine of man.[71]

Bennabi inclined to think that the Muslim Brothers could offer Islam what it needed; but another writer, while emphasizing with equal force the need for a doctrine of man, left it as a problem in his readers' minds. Mahmoud Messadi was the Tunisian writer whom we have met defending intellectual freedom at the Writers' Congress in Cairo.[72] Much of what he heard there shocked him, and he later wrote a series of articles on the dangerous tendency of modern Arabic thought. The communal consciousness of the Arabs had passed through three stages in modern times: from pan-Islam through pan-Arabism to the new nationalism (*qawmiyya*). This last differed from the others in that it was based on language and not religion; while concerned for social justice, it rejected or ignored the doctrine of man which lay at the basis of Islam. In consequence, it showed a tendency to 'la "socialisation" hâtive et systématique de l'homme . . . Il s'agit que dans sa mentalité, son comportement, sa pensée et même ses moeurs, l'homme soit désormais déterminé par la société.'[73] Against this the writer set his own profession of faith: in 'un humanisme arabo-musulman, parfaitement viable, à une conception de l'homme en Islam parfaitement valable', and in the liberty of man beyond all social and economic determination. It was difficult, however, to say whether such words marked the beginning of a new attempt to struggle with the most intimate problems of Islam, or were signs of an Arab Muslim's respect for a faith which he still held in affection, and which reminded him of the greatness of his past, even if it could no longer shape his laws.

[71] *Vocation de l'Islam.*   [72] Cf. p. 356 above.
[73] 'Islam, nationalisme et communisme', *Études méditerranéennes*, v (1958), 1–14.

SELECT BIBLIOGRAPHY

Note: The list of periodicals excludes European and American periodicals which are well known to specialists.

When two dates are given (e.g. 1366 [1946–7]) the first refers to the year of the Muslim era and the second to that of the Christian.

1. PERIODICALS

Al-Abhāth. Beirut, 1948–.
Al-Hilāl. Cairo, 1892–.
IBLA. Tunis, 1938–.
L'Indépendance arabe. Paris, 1907–8.
Al-Jinān. Beirut, 1870–85.
Al-Manār. Cairo, 1898–1936.
MIDEO: Institut Dominicain d'Études Orientales,
  Mélanges. Cairo, 1954–.
Al-Muqtaṭaf. Beirut–Cairo, 1876–1950.
Nafīr Sūriyya. Beirut, 1860–1.
Al-Naḥla. London, 1877–80.
Le Tunisien. Tunis, 1907–10.
Al-'Urwa al-wuthqā. Paris, 1884. (*See also* al-Afghānī, Jamāl al-Dīn.)

2. WORKS IN ARABIC

'Abd Allāh, King. *Mudhakkirāt.* Amman, 1947.
'Abd al-Karīm, 'Izzat. *Ta'rīkh al-ta'līm fī 'aṣr Muḥammad 'Alī.* Cairo, 1938.
'Abd al-Nāṣir, Jamāl. *Falsafat al-thawra.* Cairo, n.d. (Eng. trs.: Abdel-Nasser, Gamal. *The Philosophy of the Revolution.* Cairo, n.d.).
'Abd al-Rāziq, 'Alī. *al-Ijmā' fi'l-sharī'a al-islāmiyya.* Cairo, 1947.
—— *al-Islām wa uṣūl al-ḥukm.* Cairo, 1925. (Fr. trs.: L'Islam

et les bases du pouvoir, by L. Bercher. *R. des études islamiques*, vii (1933), 353–91; viii (1934), 163–222.)

—— ed. *Min āthār Muṣṭafā 'Abd al-Rāziq*. Cairo, 1957.

'Abd al-Rāziq, Muṣṭafā. *Muḥammad 'Abduh*. Cairo, 1946.

—— *Tamhīd li ta'rīkh al-falsafa al-islāmiyya*. Cairo, 1944.

'Abduh, Ibrāhīm. *Ta'rīkh al-waqa'i' al-miṣriyya*, 1828–1942, Cairo, 1942.

—— *Taṭawwur al-ṣaḥāfa al-misriyya*. Cairo, 1951.

'Abduh, Muḥammad. *al-Islām wa'l-Naṣrāniyya*. Cairo, 1367 [1947–8].

—— *al-Islām wa'l-radd 'alā muntaqidīhi*. Cairo, 1327 [1909–10].

—— *Risālat al-tawḥīd*. Cairo, 1361 [1942–3]. (Fr. trs.: *Rissalat al-Tawhid*, by B. Michel and Moustapha Abdel Razik. Paris, 1925.)

—— *Tafsīr al-fātiḥa*. Cairo, 1901.

—— *Tafsīr juz' 'amma*. Cairo, 1341 [1922–3].

—— *Tafsīr sūrat al-'aṣr*. Cairo, 1321 [1903–4].

—— *Taqrīr muftī al-diyār al-miṣriyya fī iṣlāḥ al-maḥākim al-shar'iyya*. Cairo, 1900.

—— and Riḍā, Muḥammad Rashīd. *Tafsīr al-Qur'ān al-ḥakīm*. Cairo, 1346–54 [1927–36]. 12 pts.

al-Afghāni, Jamāl al-Dīn. al-Ḥūkuma al-istibdādiyya. *Al-Manār*, iii (1900–1), 573–601.

—— *al-Radd 'ala'l-dhahriyyīn*. Cairo, 1903. (Fr. trs.: *La Réfutation des matérialistes*, by A. M. Goichon. Paris, 1942.)

—— and 'Abduh, Muḥammad. *al-'Urwa al-wuthqā*. Beirut, 1328 [1910]. 2 vols.

'Afīfī, Ḥāfiz. *'Ala hamish al-siyasa*. Cairo, 1938.

'Aflaq, Michel. *Fī sabīl al-ba'th*. Damascus, 1959.

—— *Ma'rakat al-maṣīr al-wāḥid*. Beirut, 1958.

al-'Alamī, Mūsā. *'Ibrat Filasṭin*. Beirut, 1949. (Eng. trs.: The Lesson of Palestine. *Middle East J.*, iii (1949), 373–405.)

al-Alūsī, Maḥmūd Shihāb al-Dīn. *Rūḥ al-ma'ānī*, I/i. Cairo, n.d.

al-Alūsī, Nu'mān. *Jalā' al-'aynayn*. Cairo, 1298 [1880–1].

Amīn, Aḥmad. *Ḥayāti*. Cairo, 1950.

—— *al-Sharq wa'l-gharb*. Cairo, 1955.

—— *Zu'amā' al-iṣlāḥ*. Cairo, 1948.

Amīn, Qāsim. *al-Mar'a al-jadīda*. Cairo, 1901.

—— *Taḥrīr al-mar'a*. Cairo, 1899.

Anṭūn, Faraḥ. *Ibn Rushd wa falsafatuhu*. Cairo, 1903.

'Aql, Sa'īd. *Qadmūs.* Beirut, 1947.

al-'Aqqād, 'Abbās Maḥmūd. *Sa'd Zaghlūl.* Cairo, 1936.

Arslān, Shakīb. *Ḥāḏhir al-'ālam al-islāmi.* Cairo, 1925. 2 vols.

—— *Limāḏhā ta'akhkhar al-muslimūn?* Cairo, 1358 [1939–40].

—— *Rashīd Riḍā aw ikha' arbā'in sana.* Cairo, 1937.

Badawī, Aḥmad. *Rifā'a al-Ṭahṭāwi Bey.* Cairo, 1950.

Bakhīt al-Muṭi'ī, Muḥammad. *Ḥaqīqat al-Islām wa uṣūl al-ḥukm.* Cairo, 1926.

al-Bannā', Ḥasan. *Muḏhakkirāt al-da'wa wa'l-dā'iyya.* Cairo, n.d.

—— *al-Rasā'il al-thalāth.* Cairo, n.d. (Fr. trs. of pt. iii: Vers la lumière, by J. Marel. *Orient,* iv (1957), 37–62.)

Bayram, Muḥammad. *Safwat al-i'tibār.* Cairo, 1302–11 [1884/5–1893/4]. 5 vols.

al-Bazzāz, 'Abd al-Raḥmān. *al-Islām wa'l-qawmiyya al-'arabiyya.* Baghdad, 1952. (Eng. trs.: Islam and Arab Nationalism, by S. G. Haim. *Welt des Islams,* iii (1954), 201–18.)

al-Bustānī, Buṭrus. *Khiṭāb fi'l-hay'a al-ijtimā'iyya.* Beirut, 1869.

—— *Khuṭba fi ādāb al-'arab.* Beirut, 1859.

—— Ta'līm al-nisā'. *In* Fu'ād Afrām al-Bustānī, ed., *al-Mu'allim Buṭrus al-Bustānī.* Beirut, 1929.

—— and others, ed. *Dā'irat al-ma'ārif.* Beirut, 1876–1900. 11 vols.

al-Bustānī, Sulaymān. *'Ibra wa ḏhikrā.* Cairo, 1908.

Dāghir, Yūsuf. *Maṣādir al-dirāsa al-adabiyya,* ii, Beirut, 1955.

Dasātir al-bilād al-'arabiyya. Cairo, Arab League, 1955.

Dasūqī, 'Umar. *Fi'l-adab al-ḥadīth.* Cairo, 1951. 2 vols.

Dibs, Yūsuf. *Ta'rīkh Sūriyya.* Beirut, 1893–1905. 8 vols.

al-Dūrī, 'Abd al-'Azīz. *al-Juḏhūr al-ta'rīkhiyya li'l-qawmiyya al-'arabiyya.* Beirut, 1960.

—— and others. *Dirāsāt fi'l-qawmiyya al-'arabiyya.* Beirut, 1960.

Dustūr ḥizb al-ba'th al-'arabi al-ishtirākī. n.p., n.d.

al-Duwayhī, Isṭifānūs. *Ta'rīkh al-azmina.* Beirut, 1951.

al-Fārābī, Abū Naṣr. *Arā' ahl al-madina al-fāḍila,* ed. A. Nādir. Beirut, 1959. (Fr. trs.: Idées des habitants de la cité vertueuse, by R. P. Jaussen, Karam, and J. Chlala. Cairo, 1949.)

al-Fāsī, 'Allāl. *al-Ḥarakāt al-istiqlāliyya fi'l-Maghrib al-'arabi.* Cairo, 1948. (Eng. trs.: The Independence Movements in Arab North Africa, by H. Z. Nuseibeh. Washington, 1954.)

—— *Muḥāḍarāt fi'l-Maghrib al-'arabi.* Cairo, 1955.

—— *al-Naqd al-dhātī*. Cairo, 1952.

Ghālī, Mirīt Buṭrus. *Siyāsat al-ghad*. Cairo, 1951. (Eng. trs.: *The Policy of to-morrow*, by I. al-Faruqi. Washington, 1953.)

al-Ghazālī, Abū Ḥāmid. *Ihyāʾ ʿulūm al-dīn*. Cairo, 1296 [1878–1879]. 4 vols.

—— *al-Iqtiṣād fiʾl-iʿtiqād*, ed. M. al-Qabbānī. Cairo, n.d.

al-Ghazālī, Muḥammad. *al-Islām waʾl-awḍāʿ al-iqtiṣādiyya*. Cairo, 1952.

—— *Laysa min al-Islām*. Cairo, n.d.

al-Ḥaddād, al-Ṭāhir. *Imraʾatunā fiʾl-sharīʿa waʾl-mujtamaʿ*. Tunis, 1930.

—— *al-ʿUmmāl al-tūnisiyyūn wa zuhūr al-ḥaraka al-niqābiyya*. Tunis, 1346 [1927–8].

Ḥāfiẓ, Aḥmad Fatḥī. *Saʿd Zaghlūl Bāshā fī ḥayātihi al-niyābiyya*, i. Cairo, n.d.

Ḥamza, ʿAbd al-Laṭīf. *Adab al-maqāla al-ṣuḥufiyya fī Miṣr*. Cairo, n.d. 5 vols.

Ḥannā, George. *Maʿnā al-qawmiyya al-ʿarabiyya*. Beirut, 1959.

Haykal, Muḥammad Ḥusayn. *Mudhakkirāt fiʾl-siyāsa al-miṣriyya*. Cairo, 1951–3. 2 vols.

—— *Tarājim miṣriyya wa gharbiyya*. Cairo, n.d.

Ḥukm hayʾat kibār al-ʿulamāʾ fī kitāb al-Islām wa uṣūl al-ḥukm. Cairo, 1925. (Fr. trs.: *R. du monde musulman*, lix (1925), 302–5; cf. *R. des études islamiques*, ix (1935), 75–86.)

Ḥusayn, Muḥammad Kāmil. *Qarya ẓālima*. Cairo, 1954. (Eng. trs.: Hussein, M. K. *City of Wrong*, tr. K. Cragg. Amsterdam, 1959.)

Ḥusayn, Ṭāhā. *ʿAlā hāmish al-sīra*. Cairo, 1958. 3 vols.

—— *al-Ayyām*, Cairo, 1958. 2 vols.

—— *Fiʾl-adab al-jāhilī*. Cairo, 1958.

—— *al-Fiṭna al-kubrā*, i. Cairo, 1947.

—— *al-Muʿadhdhabūn fiʾl-arḍ*. Cairo, 1958.

—— *Mustaqbal al-thaqāfa fī Miṣr*. Cairo, 1938. 2 vols. (Eng. trs.: *The Future of Culture in Egypt*, by S. Glazer.)

—— *al-Waʿd al-ḥaqq*. Cairo, 1950.

al-Ḥuṣrī, Sāṭiʿ. *Ārāʾ wa aḥādīth fiʾl-ʿilm waʾl-akhlāq waʾl-thaqāfa*. Cairo, 1951.

—— *Ārāʾ wa aḥādīth fiʾl-qawmiyya al-ʿarabiyya*. Cairo. 1951.

—— *Ārāʾ wa aḥādīth fiʾl-taʾrīkh waʾl-ijtimāʿ*. Cairo, 1951.

—— *Ārāʾ wa aḥādīth fiʾl-waṭaniyya waʾl-qawmiyya*. Cairo, 1954.

—— *al-Bilād al-ʿarabiyya waʾl-dawla al-ʿuthmāniyya*. Beirut, 1960.

—— *Muḥāḍarāt fī nushū' al-fikra al-qawmiyya*. Cairo, 1955.

—— *al-ʿUrūba bayn duʿātihā wa muʿāriḍihā*. Beirut, 1957.

Ibn ʿĀshūr, Muḥammad al-Fāḍil. *al-Ḥaraka al-adabiyya waʾl-fikriyya fī Tūnis*. Cairo, 1956.

Ibn Jamāʿa, Badr al-Dīn. *Taḥrīr al-aḥkam fī tadbīr ahl al-Islām*, ed. H. Kofler. *Islamica*, vi (1934), 349–414; vii (1935), 1–34. (German trs.: *Islamica*, vii (1935), 34–64; terminal vol. (1938), 18–129.)

Ibn Khaldūn, ʿAbd al-Raḥmān. *Muqaddima (Prolégomènes)*, ed. E. M. Quatremère. Paris, 1858. 3 vols. (Eng. trs.: *The Muqaddimah*, by F. Rosenthal. New York, 1958. 3 vols.)

Ibn Mīlād, Maḥjūb (Bin Mīlād). *Taḥrīk al-sawākin*. Tunis, 1956.

Ibn Taymiyya, Taqī al-Dīn. *al-Siyāsa al-sharʿiyya*, ed. A. S. Nashshār and A. Z. ʿAṭiyya. 2nd ed. Cairo, 1951. (Fr. trs.: *Le Traité de droit public d'Ibn Taimiya*, by H. Laoust. Beirut, 1948.)

Isḥāq, Adīb. *al-Durar*. Beirut, 1909.

al-Jabartī, ʿAbd al-Raḥmān. *ʿAjāʾib al-āthār fiʾl-tarājim waʾl-akhbār*. Cairo, 1322 [1904–5]. 4 vols.

Janbulāṭ, Kamāl (Jumblat, K.). *Fī majrā al-siyāsa al-lubnāniyya*. Beirut, n.d.

al-Jisr, Ḥusayn. *al-Risāla al-ḥamīdiyya*. Cairo, 1322 [1904–5].

Kāmil, ʿAlī Fahmī. *Muṣṭafā Kāmil fī arbaʿa wa thalāthīn rabīʿan*. Cairo, 1908–11. 9 pts.

Kāmil, Muṣṭafā. *al-Masʾala al-sharqiyya*. Cairo, 1898.

al-Kawākibī, ʿAbd al-Raḥmān. *Ṭabāʾiʿ al-istibdād*. Cairo, n.d.

—— *Umm al-qurā*. Cairo, 1931.

Khālid, Khālid Muḥammad. *Min hunā nabdaʾ*. Cairo, 1950. (Eng. trs.: *From Here We Start*, by I. al-Faruqi. Washington, 1953.)

—— *Muwāṭinūn . . . lā raʿāyā*. Cairo, 1951.

Khayr al-Dīn Pāshā. *Aqwam al-masālik fī maʿrifat aḥwāl al-mamālik*. Tunis, 1284–5 [1867–8]. (Fr. trs.: Général Kheredine, *Réformes nécessaires aux états musulmans*. Paris, 1868.)

Khāzin, Philippe & Farīd. *al-Muḥarrarāt al-siyāsiyya waʾl-mufāwaḍāt al-duwaliyya ʿan Suriyya wa Lubnān*. Jūniya, 1910–1911. 3 vols.

al-Kitāb al-dhahabī li yūbīl al-Muqtaṭaf al-khamsīnī. Cairo, 1926.

Kurd 'Alī, Muḥammad. _Gharāʾib al-gharb_. Cairo, 1923. 2 vols.

—— _al-Islām waʾl-ḥadāra al-ʿarabiyya_. Cairo, 1934–6. 2 vols.

—— _Kunūz al-ajdād_. Damascus, 1950.

—— _Maṣādir al-thaqāfa al-ʿarabiyya_. Cairo, n.d.

—— _Mudhakkirāt_. Damascus, 1948–51. 4 vols.

Luṭfallāh Khān, Mīrzā. _Jamāl al-Dīn al-Asadabādī_. Ar. trs. by S. Nashʾat & A. Ḥasanayn. Cairo, 1957.

Luṭfī al-Sayyid, Aḥmad. _Mushkilat al-ḥurriyāt fiʾl-ʿālam al-ʿarabī_. Beirut, n.d.

—— _al-Muntakhabāt_. Cairo, 1937–45. 2 vols.

—— _Ṣafaḥāt maṭwiyya_. Cairo, 1946.

—— _Taʾammulāt_. Cairo, 1946.

al-Maghribī, 'Abd al-Qādir. _al-Bayyināt_. Cairo, 1344 [1925–6]. 2 vols.

—— _Jamāl al-Dīn al-Afghānī_. Cairo, 1948.

Majdī, Ṣāliḥ. _Ḥilyat al-zaman bi manāqib khādim al-waṭan_. Cairo, 1958.

Majmūʿat al-rasāʾil waʾl-masāʾil al-najdiyya. Cairo, 1344–9 [1925/6–1930/1]. 4 vols.

Majmūʿat al-tawḥīd al-najdiyya, ed. Muḥammad Rashīd Riḍā. Cairo, 1346 [1927–8].

al-Makhzūmī, Muḥammad. _Khāṭirāt Jamāl al-Dīn_. Beirut, 1931.

al-Maqdisī, Anīs. _al-Ittijāhāt al-adabiyya fiʾl-ʿālam al-ʿarabī al-ḥadīth_. Beirut, 1960.

Maqsūd, Clovis. _Maʿnā al-ḥiyād al-ijābī_. Beirut, 1960.

Marrāsh, Fransīs. _Ghābat al-ḥaqq_. Cairo, 1298 [1880–1].

al-Marṣafī, Ḥusayn. _Risālat al-kalim al-thamān_. Cairo, 1298 [1880–1].

al-Mawardī, 'Alī ibn Muḥammad. _al-Aḥkām al-sulṭāniyya_. Cairo, 1298 [1880–1]. (Fr. trs.: _Les Statuts gouvernementaux_, by P. Sagnan. Algiers, 1915.)

Mishāqa, Mīkhāʾīl. _al-Jawāb ʿālā iqtirāḥ al-aḥbāb_. Beirut, 1955.

Mūsā, Salāma. _al-Adab waʾl-ḥayāt_. Cairo, n.d.

—— _Ḥurriyat al-fikr_. Cairo,

—— _Tarbiyat Salāma Mūsā_. Cairo, 1947.

al-Muʾtamar al-ʿarabī al-awwal. Cairo, 1933.

al-Nadīm, 'Abd Allāh. _Sulāfat al-Nadīm_. Cairo, 1897–1901. 2 vols.

Qabādū, Maḥmūd. *Dīwān.* Tunis, 1294-5 [1877-8]. 2 pts.

Qalʿajī, Qadrī. *Saʿd Zaghlūl.* Beirut, 1948.

al-Qasīmī, ʿAbd Allāh. *Hādhī hiya'l-aghlāl.* Cairo, 1946.

Quṭb, Sayyid. *al-ʿAdāla al-ijtimāʿiyya fi'l-Islām.* Cairo, 1954. (Eng. trs.: Sayed Kotb, *Social Justice in Islam,* by J. B. Hardie. Washington, 1953.)

Rabbāṭ, Edmond. Muhimmat al-nukhba fī khalq al-muwāṭin al-sāliḥ. *al-Abḥāth,* x (1957), 205-25.

al-Rāfiʿī, ʿAbd al-Raḥmān. *ʿAṣr Ismāʿīl.* Cairo, 1948. 2 vols.

—— *ʿAṣr Muḥammad ʿAlī.* Cairo, 1947.

—— *Fī aʿqāb al-thawra al-miṣriyya.* Cairo, 1947-51. 3 vols.

—— *Miṣr wa'l-Sūdān.* Cairo, 1948.

—— *Muḥammad Farīd.* Cairo, 1948.

—— *Muṣṭafā Kāmil.* Cairo, 1950.

—— *Ta'rīkh al-ḥaraka al-qawmiyya.* Cairo, 1938. 2 vols.

—— *al-Thawra al-ʿurābiyya wa'l-iḥtilāl al-injilīzī.* Cairo, 1949.

—— *Thawrat sanat 1919.* Cairo, 1946. 2 vols.

al-Razzāz, Munīf. *Maʿālim al-ḥayāt al-ʿarabiyya al-jadīda.* Beirut, 1960.

Riḍā, Muḥammad Rashīd. *al-Khilāfa.* Cairo, 1341 [1922-3]. (Fr. trs.: *Le Califat dans la doctrine de Rashid Rida,* by H. Laoust. Beirut, 1938.)

—— *al-Manār wa'l-Azhar.* Cairo, 1353 [1934-5].

—— *Muḥāwarāt al-muṣliḥ wa'l-muqallid.* Cairo, 1324 [1906-7].

—— *Nidāʾ ila'l-jins al-laṭīf.* Cairo, 1351 [1932-3].

—— *al-Sunna wa'l-shīʿa.* Cairo, 1947. 2 vols.

—— *Ta'rīkh al-ustādh al-imām al-shaykh Muḥammad ʿAbduh.* i, Cairo, 1st ed. 1931; ii, Cairo, 2nd ed. 1344 [1925-6]; iii, 2nd ed. 1367 [1947-8].

—— *al-Wahhābiyyūn wa'l-Ḥijāz.* Cairo, 1344 [1925-6].

—— *al-Waḥy al-muḥammadī.* Cairo, 1947.

—— *Yusr al-Islām wa uṣūl al-tashrīʿ al-ʿāmm.* Cairo, 1928.

—— and Muḥammad ʿAbduh. *Tafsīr al-Qurʾān al-ḥakim.* Cairo, 1346-54 [1927-36]. 12 pts.

Rustum, Asad. *al-Maḥfūzāt al-malikiyya al-miṣriyya (A Calendar of State Papers).* Beirut, 1940-3. 4 vols.

Saʿāda, Anṭūn. *al-Niẓām al-jadīd.* n.p. 1950.

—— *Nushūʾ al-umam.* Vol. i. Damascus, 1951.

Saʿīd, Amīn. *al-Thawra al-ʿarabiyya al-kubrā.* Cairo, 1934. 3 vols.

al-Ṣaʿīdī, ʿAbd al-Mutaʿāl. *Taʾrīkh al-iṣlāḥ fiʾl-Azhar*. Cairo, 1943.

al-Sammān, Muḥammad ʿAbd Allāh. *Usus al-ḥukm fiʾl-Islām*. Cairo, 1953. (Eng. trs.: The Principles of Islamic Government, by S. G. Haim. *Welt des Islams*, v (1958), 245–53.)

Sarkīs, Yūsuf. *Muʿjam al-maṭbūʿāt al-ʿarabiyya waʾl-muʿarraba*. Cairo, 1928–31. 2 vols.

Ṣawāyā, Mikhāʾīl. *Sulaymān al-Bustānī wa Ilyādhat Hūmirūs*. Beirut, n.d.

Sāyigh, Fāʾiz. *Risālat al-mufakkir al-ʿarabī*. Beirut, 1955.

al-Ṣayyādī, Muḥammad Abuʾl-Hudā. *Dāʿī al-rashād li sabīl al-ittiḥād waʾl-inqiyād*. Constantinople, n.d.

—— *Tanwīr al-abṣār*. Cairo, 1306 [1888–9].

Shafīq, Aḥmad. *Ḥawliyyāt Miṣr al-siyāsiyya*. Cairo, 1926–8. 4 vols.

Shaykhū, Louis. *al-Ādāb al-ʿarabiyya fiʾl-qarn al-tāsiʿ ʿashar*. Beirut, 1924–6. 2 vols.

al-Shayyāl, Jamāl al-Dīn. *Rifāʿa Rāfiʿ al-Tahṭāwī*. Cairo, 1958.

al-Shidyāq, Aḥmad Fāris. *Kanz al-raghāʾib fī muntakhabāt al-Jawāʾib*. Constantinople, 1288–9 [1871/2–1880/1]. 7 pts.

—— *Kashf al-mukhabbaʾ ʿan funūn Urubbā*. Constantinople, 1299 [1881–2].

—— *al-Sāq ʿalaʾl-sāq fī mā huwaʾl-Fāryāq*. Cairo, n.d. 2 vols.

al-Shidyāq, Ṭannūs. *Akhbār al-aʿyān fī Jabal Lubnān*. Beirut, 1859.

Shihāb, Ḥaydar. *Lubnān fī ʿahd al-ʿumarāʾ al-shihābiyyīn*. Beirut, 1933. 3 vols.

Shumayyil, Shiblī. *Falsafat al-nushūʾ waʾl-irtiqāʾ*. Cairo, 1910.

—— *Majmūʿa*. Cairo, n.d.

al-Tahṭāwī, Rifāʿa Rāfiʿ. *Anwār Tawfīq al-jalīl fī akhbār Miṣr wa tawthīq Banī Ismāʿīl*. Cairo, 1285 [1868–9].

—— *Manāhij al-albāb al-miṣriyya fī mabāhij al-ādāb al-ʿaṣriyya*. Cairo, 1912.

—— *al-Murshid al-amīn liʾl-banāt waʾl-banīn*. Cairo, 1289 [1872–1873].

—— *Nihāyat al-ījāz fī sīrat sākin al-Ḥijāz*. Cairo, 1291 [1874–5].

—— *Takhlīṣ al-ibrīz ilā talkhīṣ Bārīz*. Cairo, 1905.

Tājir, Jacques. *Ḥarakat al-tarjama fī Miṣr*. Cairo, 1945.

Ṭarāzī, Philippe de. *Taʾrīkh al-ṣaḥāfa al-ʿarabiyya*. Beirut, 1913–1933. 4 vols.

Wajdī, Muḥammad Farīd. *al-Madaniyya wa'l-Islām*. Cairo, 1933.

al-Wardī, ʿAlī. *Wuʿāz al-salāṭīn*. Baghdad, 1954.

Yakan, Walī al-Dīn. *al-Maʿlūm wa'l-majhūl*. Cairo, 1909–11. 2 vols.

Yazbak, Yūsuf. *Thawra wa fitna fī Lubnān*. Beirut, 1938. (Eng. trs.: *Lebanon in the last years of feudalism, 1840–1868*, by M. Kerr. Beirut, 1959.)

al-Zabīdī, Murtaḍā. *Ithāf al-sāda*. Cairo, 1311 [1893–4]. 10 vols.

Zaghlūl, Aḥmad Fatḥī. *Sirr taqaddum al-Inkilīz al-saksūniyyin* (tr. from E. Demolins, q.v.). Cairo, 1329 [1911–12].

Zaghlūl, Saʿd. *Āthār al-zaʿim*, ed. Muḥammad Ibrāhīm al-Jazīrī, i. Cairo, 1927.

—— *Majmūʿat khuṭab*. Cairo, 1924.

Zaydān, Jurjī. *Mashāhīr al-sharq*. Cairo, 1910–11. 2 vols.

—— *Ta'rīkh ādāb al-lugha al-ʿarabiyya*, iv. Cairo, 1937.

al-Zayyāt, ʿAbduh Ḥasan. *Saʿd Zaghlūl min aqḍiyatihi*. Cairo, 1932.

Zurayq, Qusṭanṭīn. *Maʿnā al-nakba*. Beirut, 1948. (Eng. trs.: *The Meaning of the Disaster*. Beirut, 1956.)

—— *Naḥnu wa'l-ta'rīkh*. Beirut, 1959.

—— *al-Waʿy al-qawmī*. Beirut, 1939.

3. WORKS IN OTHER LANGUAGES

Abbas, F. *De la Colonie vers la province: le jeune Algérien*. Paris, 1931.

Abdel Nasser, G. (ʿAbd al-Nāṣir, Jamāl). The Egyptian Revolution. *Foreign Affairs*, xxxiii (1955–6), 199–211.

—— *Speeches and Press Interviews 1958*. Cairo, n.d.

—— *Speeches and Press Interviews 1959*. Cairo, n.d.

Adams, C.C. *Islam and Modernism in Egypt*. London, 1933.

Adnan (Adivar), A. *La Science chez les Turcs ottomans*. Paris, 1939.

al-Afghani, Jamal al-Din. L'Islamisme et la science. *J. des Débats*, 18 & 19 May 1883 (reprinted in Fr. trs. of *al-Radd ʿala'l-Dhahriyyin*).

—— Philosophie de l'Union Nationale, tr. M. Hendessi. *Orient*, vi (1958), 123–8.

Ahmed, J. M. *The Intellectual Origins of Egyptian Nationalism*. London, 1960.

Alexander, J. *The Truth about Egypt*. London, 1911.

Amin, Osman. *Muhammad Abduh, essai sur ses idées philosophiques et religieuses*. Cairo, 1944.

Anderson, J. N. D. Recent Developments in Shari'a Law. *Muslim World*, xl (1950), 244–56; xli (1951), 34–48, 113–26, 186–198, 271–88; xlii (1952), 33–47, 124–40, 190–206, 257–76.

Antonius, G. *The Arab Awakening*. London, 1938.

Ataturk, Kemal. *Nutuk*. Istanbul, 1934. 3 vols. (Fr. trs.: *Discours du Ghazi Moustafa Kemal*. Leipzig, 1929. Eng. trs.: *A Speech delivered by Ghazi Mustapha Kemal*. Leipzig, 1929.)

Azoury, N. *Le Réveil de la nation arabe*. Paris, 1905.

al-Banna, Hasan. La Nouvelle Renaissance du Monde Arabe et son Orientation, tr. A. Miquel. *Orient*, vi (1958), 139–44.

Bekdash, K., tr. H. Glidden. Report of the Central Command of the Communist Party in Syria and Lebanon in January 1951. *Middle East J.*, vii (1953), 206–21.

Benattar, C., Sebaï, E., and Ettéalbi, A. *L'Esprit libéral du Coran*. Paris, 1905.

Bennabi, M. *Vocation de l'Islam*. Paris, 1954.

Berkes, N. The Historical Background of Turkish Secularism. *In* R. Frye, ed., *Islam and the West*. The Hague, 1957, 41–68.

Berque, A. La Bourgeoisie algérienne. *Hespéris*, xxxv (1948), 131–9.

Berque, J. L'Afrique du Nord entre les deux guerres mondiales. *Cahiers Internationaux de Sociologie*, xxx (1960), 3–22.

—— *Les Arabes d'hier à demain*. Paris, 1960.

Binder, L. Radical Reform Nationalism in Syria and Egypt. *Muslim World*. xlix (1959), 96–110, 213–31.

Blunt, W. S. *Diaries*. London, 1932.

—— *The Future of Islam*. London, 1882.

—— *Gordon at Khartoum*. London, 1911.

—— *The Secret History of the British Occupation of Egypt*. London [1923].

Bourguiba, H. *La Bataille de l'évacuation*. Tunis, 1959.

—— *Bourguiba s'adresse aux cadres de la nation*. Tunis, 1961.

—— *Les Congrès du Neo-Destour*. Tunis, 1959.

—— *Discours de la victoire*. Tunis, 1959.

—— Nationalism: Antidote to Communism. *Foreign Affairs*, xxxv (1957–8), 646–53.

—— *Le Président Bourguiba dans le sud tunisien*. Tunis, 1959.

—— *La Tunisie et la France.* Paris, 1954.

Bowman, H. *Middle East Window.* London, 1942.

Broadley, A. M. *How We Defended Arabi.* London, 1884.

Brockelmann, C. *Geschichte der arabischen Literatur.* Leiden, 1937–49. 5 vols.

Browne, E. G. *The Persian Revolution.* Cambridge, 1910.

Cachia, P. *Ṭāhā Ḥusayn.* London, 1956.

Califat et Souveraineté Nationale. *R. du monde musulman*, lix (1925), 3–81.

Caspar, R. Le Renouveau moʻtazilite. *MIDEO*, iv (1957), 141–202.

Chevallier, D. Aux Origines des troubles agraires libanais en 1858. *Annales*, li (1959), 35–64.

Chiha, M. *Essais.* Beirut, 1950–2. 2 vols.

—— *Liban d'aujourd'hui.* Beirut, 1949.

Colombe, M. *L'Évolution de l'Egypte, 1924–50.* Paris, 1951.

Congrès de l'Afrique du Nord, Paris 1908. Paris, 1909. 2 vols.

Le Congrès des Ecrivains Arabes. *MIDEO*, iv (1957), 326–57.

Corm, C. *L'Art phénicien.* Beirut, n.d.

Cromer, Lord. *Modern Egypt.* London, 1908. 2 vols.

Demeerseman, A. Au Berceau des premières réformes démocratiques en Tunisie. *IBLA*, xx (1957), 1–12.

—— Un grand témoin des premières idées modernistes en Tunisie. *IBLA*, xix (1956), 349–73.

—— Indépendance de la Tunisie et politique extérieure de Khereddine. *IBLA*, xxi (1958), 229–78.

Demolins, E. *À Quoi tient la supériorité des Anglo-Saxons?* Paris, 1897. (Ar. trs.: *see* Zaghlūl, Ahmad Fathī.)

Douin, G. *La Mission du Baron de Boislecomte.* Cairo, 1927.

Doughty, C. M. *Travels in Arabia Deserta.* London, 1923. 2 vols.

Düstur. Constantinople, 1289–96, [1872–9]. 4 vols.

Encyclopaedia of Islam. 1st ed. Leiden, 1913–38. 4 vols. and suppl. 2nd ed., 1954–.

Fénélon, [F. de la Mothe-] *Aventures de Télémaque.* Paris, 1828. 2 vols.

Fesch, P. *Constantinople aux derniers jours d'Abdul-Hamid.* Paris, 1907.

Finn, J. *Stirring Times.* London, 1878. 2 vols.

Fitoussi, E. and Benazet, A. *L'Etat tunisien et le protectorat français.* Paris, 1931. 2 vols.

Fremantle, A. *Loyal Enemy*. London, 1938.

Gardet, L. *La Cité musulmane*. Paris, 1954.

—— *La Pensée religieuse d'Avicenne*. Paris, 1951.

Ganem, H. *Les Sultans ottomans*. Paris, 1901–2. 2 vols.

Gendzier, I. L. James Sanua and Egyptian Nationalism. *Middle East J.*, xv (1961), 16–28.

Gibb, H. A. R. 'Arabiyya. *Encyclopaedia of Islam*. 2nd ed., vol. i.

—— An Interpretation of Islamic History. *J. of World History*, i (1953), 39–62.

—— Al-Mawardi's Theory of the Khilafah. *Islamic Culture*, xi (1937), 291–302.

—— *Modern Trends in Islam*. Chicago, 1947.

—— Some Considerations on the Sunni Theory of the Caliphate. *Arch. d'histoire du droit oriental*, iii (1948), 401–10.

—— Studies in Contemporary Arabic Literature. *Bull. School of Oriental Studies*, iv (1926–8), 745–60; v (1928–30), 311–322 & 445–66; vii (1933–5), 1–22.

—— ed. *Whither Islam?* London, 1932.

—— and Bowen, H. *Islamic Society and the West*. London, 1950–1957. 2 vols.

Gökalp, Z., tr. and ed. N. Berkes. *Turkish Nationalism and Western Civilization*. London, 1959.

Goldziher, I. *Die Richtungen der islamischen Koranauslegung*. Leiden, 1920.

Graf, G. *Geschichte der christlichen arabischen Literatur*, iii. Rome, 1949; iv. Rome, 1951.

Grunebaum, G. E. von. *Islam: Essays in the Nature and Growth of a Cultural Tradition*. London, 1955.

Guizot, F. *Histoire de la civilisation en Europe*. Paris, 1838.

Haim, S. G. Alfieri and al-Kawākibī. *Oriente moderno*, xxxiv (1954), 321–34.

—— Blunt and al-Kawākibī. *Oriente moderno*, xxxv (1955), 133–143.

—— Intorno alle origini della teoria del Panarabismo. *Oriente moderno*, xxxvi (1956), 409–21.

—— Islam and the Theory of Arab Nationalism. *Welt des Islams*, iv (1955), 124–49.

Heyd, U. *Foundations of Turkish Nationalism*. London, 1950.

Heyworth-Dunne, J. *Introduction to the History of Education in Modern Egypt*. London, 1938.

Horten, M. Muhammad Abduh: sein Leben und sein theo-
logische-philosophische Gedankenwelt. *Beitrage zur Kenntnis
des Orients*, xiii (1915), 85–114; xiv (1916), 74–128.

Hourani, A. H. The Changing Face of the Fertile Crescent in the
Eighteenth Century. *Studia Islamica*, viii (1957), 89–122.

—— Historians of Lebanon. *In* B. Lewis and P. M. Holt,
Historians of the Middle East. London, 1962.

—— *A Vision of History*. Beirut, 1961.

Hurewitz, J. C. *Diplomacy in the Near and Middle East*. London,
1956. 2 vols.

Hurgronje, C. Snouck. *Verspreide Geschriften*, iii. Bonn–Leipzig–
Hague, 1923.

al-Husri, S. Qu'est-ce que le nationalisme, tr. R. Costi. *Orient*,
xii (1959), 215–26.

Inal, M. K. *Osmanlı Devrinde Son Sadrıazamlar*. Istanbul, 1940–
1953. 14 pts.

Ismail, A. *Histoire du Liban*. i, Paris, 1955; iv, Beirut, 1958.

Jomier, J. *Le Commentaire coranique du Manâr*. Paris, 1954.

Jouplain, M. *La Question du Liban*. Paris, 1908.

Julian, C.-A. *L'Afrique du Nord en marche*. Paris, 1952.

Jung, E. *La Révolte arabe*. Paris, 1924–5. 2 vols.

Kamel, M. (Kamil, Muṣṭafā). *Lettres égyptiennes françaises
adressées à Mme Juliette Adam, 1895–1908*. Cairo, 1909. (Eng.
and Ar. trs.: *Egyptian French Letters*. Cairo, 1909.)

—— *Égyptiens et Anglais*. Paris, 1906.

Kedourie, E. *England and the Middle East*. London, 1956.

—— *Nationalism*. London, 1960.

—— Sa'ad Zaghlul and the British. *In* A. Hourani, ed. *St
Antony's Papers xi, Middle Eastern Affairs ii*. London, 1961,
139–60.

Kerr, M. *Muhammad Abduh and Rashid Rida*. Ph.D. thesis.
School of Advanced International Studies, Johns Hopkins
Univ., Washington, 1958.

—— Rashīd Riḍā and Islamic Legal Reform. *Muslim World*, l
(1960), 99–108, 170–81.

Khairallah, K. T. *Les Régions arabes libérées*. Paris, 1919.

—— La Syrie. *R. du monde musulman*, xix (1912), 1–143.

Khalidi, W. Political Trends in the Fertile Crescent. *In* W. Z.
Laqueur, ed., *The Middle East in Transition*. London, 1958,
121–8.

Khayr al-Din Pasha. A mes enfants; Mémoires de ma vie privée et politique. *In* M. S. Mzali and J. Pignon, Documents sur Khéredin. *R. tunisienne*, xviii (1934), 177–225; xix–xx (1934), 347–96.

—— Mon programme. *In* M. S. Mzali and J. Pignon, Documents sur Khéredin. *R. tunisienne*, xxi (1935), 51–80.

—— Le Problème tunisien vu à travers la question d'Orient. *In* M. S. Mzali and J: Pignon, Documents sur Khéredin. *R. tunisienne*, xxii (1935), 209–33; xxiii–iv (1935), 289–307; xxvi (1936), 223–54.

—— Réponse à la calomnie. *In* M. S. Mzali and J. Pignon, Documents sur Khéredin. *R. tunisienne*, xxx (1937), 209–52; xxi–ii (1937), 409–31.

Lacheraf, M. Constantes politiques et militaires dans les guerres coloniales d'Algérie, 1830–1960. *Temps modernes*, xvi (1960–1), 727–800.

—— Le nationalisme algérien en marche vers l'unité. *Temps modernes*, xi (1956), 1822–45.

—— Nationalisme algérien: le sens d'une révolution. *Temps modernes*, xii (1956), 214–55.

Lacouture, J. *Cinq hommes et la France.* Paris, 1961.

Lammens, H. *La Syrie.* Beirut, 1921. 2 vols.

Lambton, A. K. S. Quis Custodiet Custodes: some reflections on the Persian theory of government. *Studia Islamica*, v (1956), 125–48; vi (1956), 125–46.

—— The Theory of Kingship in the *Naṣīḥat ul-Mulūk* of Ghazālī. *Islamic Q.*, i (1954), 47–55.

Landau, J. M. *Parliaments and Parties in Egypt.* Tel Aviv, 1953.

Laoust, H. *Essai sur les doctrines sociales et politiques de Takī-d-Din Aḥmad B. Taimīya.* Cairo, 1939.

—— Le Réformisme musulman dans la littérature arabe contemporaine. *Orient*, x (1959), 81–107.

—— Le Réformisme orthodoxe des 'Salafiya'. *R. des études islamiques*, vi (1932), 175–224.

Layard, Sir H. A. Memoirs, viii. B.M., Add. MSS. 38938.

—— *Autobiography.* London, 1903. 2 vols.

Le Bon, G. *Les Lois psychologiques de l'évolution des peuples.* Paris, 1894.

Lecerf, Jean. Šibli Šumayyil, métaphysicien et moraliste contemporain. *Bull. d'études orientales*, i (1931), 153–86.

Lewis, B. *The Emergence of Modern Turkey*. London, 1961.

—— The Impact of the French Revolution on Turkey. *J. World History*, i (1953), 105–25.

—— Some observations on the Significance of Heresy in the History of Islam. *Studia Islamica*, i (1953), 43–63.

Lloyd of Dolobran, Viscount. *Egypt since Cromer*. London, 1933–4. 2 vols.

Longrigg, S. H. *Syria and Lebanon under French Mandate*. London, 1958.

Mahdi, M. *Ibn Khaldûn's Philosophy of History*. London, 1957.

Majdalani, G. The Arab Socialist Movement. *In* W. Z. Laqueur, ed., *The Middle East in Transition*. London, 1958, 337–50.

Malik, C. Call to Action in the Near East. *Foreign Affairs*, xxxiv (1955–6), 637–54.

—— The Near East: the Search for Truth. *Foreign Affairs*, xxx (1951–2), 231–64.

Martineau, H. *The Positive Philosophy of Auguste Comte*. London, 1875. 2 vols.

Memmi, A. *Portrait du colonisé précédé du portrait du colonisateur*. Paris, 1957.

Messadi, M. Islam, nationalisme et communisme. *Études méditerranéennes*, v (1958), 1–14.

Midhat Pasha. *La Turquie, son passé, son avenir*. Paris, 1878. (Eng. trs.: *Nineteenth Century*, iii (1878), 981–1000.)

Monchicourt, C. *Documents historiques sur la Tunisie: relations inédites de Nyssen, Filippi et Calligaris*. Paris, 1929.

Montagne, R. Réactions arabes contre le Sionisme: Congrès de Bloudane. *Entretiens sur l'évolution des pays de civilisation arabe*, ii. Paris, 1938.

Montesquieu, C. de. *Considérations sur les causes de la grandeur des Romains et de leur décadence*, ed. C. Jullien. Paris, 1918.

—— *De l'Esprit des lois*. Paris.

Nuseibeh, H. Z. *The Ideas of Arab Nationalism*. Ithaca, N.Y., 1956.

Penrose, S. *That They May Have Life*. New York, 1941.

Public Record Office. F.O. 78/2955, No. 649 (22 July 1879), Layard to Salisbury; No. 654 (23 July 1879), Layard to Salisbury.

Qubain, F. I. *Inside the Arab Mind*. Arlington, Virginia, 1960.

Questions tunisiennes: *communications présentées au Congrès Colonial de Marseille (5–9 September 1906) par MM. Lasram et De Dianous.* Paris, 1907.

Rabbath, E. [Rabbāṭ, Edmond]. *Unité syrienne et devenir arabe.* Paris, 1937.

Ramsaur, E. E. *The Young Turks.* Princeton, 1957.

Raymond, A. *British Policy towards Tunis, 1830–1881.* D.Phil. thesis. Oxford, 1953.

Renan, E. *L'Avenir de la science.* Paris, 1890.

—— *Averroès et l'Averroïsme.* 3rd ed. Paris, 1866.

—— *Histoire des origines du Christianisme.* Paris, 1863–83. 8 vols.

—— *L'Islamisme et la science.* Paris, 1883.

—— *Nouvelles études d'histoire religieuse.* Paris, 1884.

—— *Qu'est-ce qu'une nation?* Paris, 1882.

Rosenthal, E. I. J. *Political Thought in Medieval Islam.* Cambridge, 1958.

Rossi, E. *Documenti sull'origine e gli sviluppi della questione araba, 1875–1944.* Rome, 1944.

—— Una Traduzione turca dell'opera 'Della Tirannide' di V. Alfieri . . . *Oriente moderno,* xxxiv (1954), 335–7.

Saab, H. *The Arab Federalists of the Ottoman Empire.* Amsterdam, 1958.

Sahli, M.-S. De l' 'assimilation' a l' 'intégration': une mystification politique. *Temps modernes,* xi (1955), 591–615.

as-Sa'id, Nuri. *Arab Independence and Unity.* Baghdad, 1943.

Salibi, K. *Maronite Historians of the Mediaeval Lebanon.* Beirut, 1959.

Samné, G. *La Syrie.* Paris, 1920.

Sayegh, F. A. [Ṣāyigh, Fā'iz]. *Arab Unity.* New York, 1958.

Schacht, J. *Esquisse d'une histoire du droit musulman.* Paris, n.d.

—— Islamic Law in Contemporary States. *Am. J. Comp. Law,* viii (1959), 133–47.

—— L'Évolution moderne du droit musulman en Égypte. *In Mélanges Maspéro,* iii. Cairo, 1935–40, 323–34.

Sékaly, A. Les deux Congrès musulmans de 1926. *R. du monde musulman,* lxiv (1926), 3–219.

Senior, N. W. *Conversations and Journals in Egypt and Malta.* London, 1882. 2 vols.

Sfar, T. *Journal d'un exilé.* Tunis, 1960.

Spencer, H. *First Principles.* London, 1911.

Steppat, F. Nationalismus und Islam bei Mustafa Kamil. *Welt des Islams*, iv (1956), 241–341.

Storrs, Sir R. *Orientations*. London, 1937.

Tapiero, N. *Les Idées réformistes d'al-Kawakîbî*. Paris, 1956.

Testa, Baron I. de. *Recueil des traités de la Porte ottomane avec les puissances étrangères*, iii. Paris, 1866.

Toderini, G. *Letteratura turchesca*. Venice, 1787. 3 vols. (Fr. trs.: *Littérature des Turcs*. Paris, 1789. 3 vols.)

La Tunisie martyre: ses revendications. Paris, 1920.

Ubicini, A. *Lettres sur la Turquie*. Paris, 1853–4. 2 vols. (Eng. trs.: *Letters on Turkey*, tr. Lady Easthope. London, 1856. 2 vols.)

La Vérité sur la Question Syrienne. Constantinople, 1916.

Walzer, R. *Greek into Arabic*. Oxford, 1962.

Young, G. *Egypt*. London, 1927.

Zeine, Z. N. *Arab-Turkish Relations and the Emergence of Arab Nationalism*. Beirut, 1958.

—— *The Struggle for Arab Independence*. Beirut, 1960.

SUPPLEMENT

This is not a full list of the numerous books and articles on the subject of the book which have appeared since it was published. It includes some of the most important of them, particularly those which have persuaded me to revise some of the ideas expressed in the book, as well as a few earlier books which I failed to notice when I wrote it. I do not mention new editions of Arabic works, but I draw attention to a few translations of them. I have also taken the opportunity to correct a few mis-statements.

For a full bibliography: J. Berque *et al.*, *Bibliographie de la culture arabe contemporaine* (Paris, 1981).

For translated extracts from Arab writers of the period dealt with: A. Abdel-Malek, *Anthologie de la littérature arabe contemporaine: II Les essais* (Paris, 1965) and *La pensée politique arabe contemporaine* (Paris, 1970).

CHAPTER I. THE ISLAMIC STATE

Much new work is being done on the development of Islam as a religious system and of Islamic political thought, mainly in the form of articles and monographs. For a survey of the central tradition of political thought, that of the jurists: A. K. S. Lambton, *State and Government in Medieval Islam* (Oxford, 1971).

The reinterpretation of Ibn Khaldun has been carried further: A. al-Azmeh, *Ibn Khaldun: an Essay in Reinterpretation* (London, 1982), 'bibliographical orientations' at the end.

I have used the expression *ahl al-sunna wa'l-jama'a* in a broad and loose way, defined on p. 8, of which scholars might not approve. See H. Laoust, *Les schismes dans l'islam* (Paris, 1965).

CHAPTER II. THE OTTOMAN EMPIRE

The older syntheses on which I relied have now been largely superseded. See: H. Inalcik, *The Ottoman Empire: the Classical Age 1300–1600* (London, 1973); N. Itzkowitz, *Ottoman Empire and Islamic Tradition* (New York, 1972).

The statements about the communal nature of Ottoman and other Muslim societies, pp. 29–30, need to be modified: A. H. Hourani and S. M. Stern, ed., *The Islamic City* (Oxford, 1970).

The formal recognition of empire-wide Christian and Jewish communities came much later than is implied on p. 30 (also on p. 273): B. Braude, 'Foundation Myths of the Millet System' and K. B. Bardakjian, 'The Rise of the Armenian Patriarchate of Constantinople', both in B. Braude and B. Lewis, ed., *Christians and Jews in the Ottoman Empire* vol. 1 (New York, 1982), pp. 69–88 and 89–100 respectively.

CHAPTER III. FIRST VIEWS OF EUROPE

For general surveys of the changes in Islamic thought in the eighteenth century: J. Voll, *Islam: Continuity and Change in the Modern World* (Harlow, Essex, 1982): F. Rahman, *Islam*, 2nd ed. (Chicago, 1979).

Our views of the Ottoman Empire in the eighteenth century, and in particular of the Ottoman hold over society, need to be revised: T. Naff and R. Owen, ed., *Studies in Eighteenth Century Islamic History* (Carbondale, Ill., 1977); N. Itzkowitz, 'Eighteenth Century Ottoman Realities', *Studia Islamica*, 16 (1962), 73–94; A. Hourani, 'The Ottoman Background of the Modern Middle East' in Hourani, *The Emergence of the Modern Middle East* (London, 1981), pp. 1–18—to be referred to as *Emergence*; K. Barbir, *Ottoman Rule in Damascus 1708–1758* (Princeton, 1980); A. Raymond, *Artisans et commerçants au Caire au XVIIIe siècle*, 2 vols. (Damascus, 1973–4).

Statements on Ottoman reform, in this and later chapters, also need to be modified: N. Berkes, *The Development of Secularism in Turkey* (Montreal, 1964); S. Mardin, *The Genesis of Young Ottoman Thought* (Princeton, 1962); R. H. Davison, *Reform in the Ottoman Empire 1856–1876* (Princeton, 1963); U. Heyd, 'The Ottoman 'Ulema and Westernization in the Time of Selim III and Mahmud II' in Heyd, ed., *Studies in Islamic History* (Jerusalem, 1961), pp. 63–96; W. R. Polk and R. L. Chambers, ed., *Beginnings of Modernization in the Middle East: the Nineteenth Century* (Chicago, 1968).

On the impact of the reforms in Syria: M. Ma'oz, *Ottoman Reform in Syria and Palestine 1840–1861* (Oxford, 1968); D. Chevallier, *La société du Mont Liban a l'époque de la révolution industrielle en Europe* (Paris, 1971); K. Salibi, *The Modern History of Lebanon* (London, 1965).

On Muhammad 'Ali: A. Lutfi al-Sayyid Marsot, *Egypt in the Reign of Muhammad Ali* (Cambridge, 1983); Groupe de Recherches et d'Etudes sur le Proche Orient, *L'Egypte au XIXe siècle* (Paris, 1982).

On Tunisia: L. C. Brown, *The Tunisia of Ahmad Bey 1837–1851* (Princeton, 1974); A. Abdesselem, *Les historiens tunisiens des XVIIe, XVIIIe et XIXe siècles* (Paris, 1973).

For another analysis of the Arab encounter with the West: I. Abu Lughod, *Arab Rediscovery of Europe* (Princeton, 1963). B. Lewis, *The Muslim Discovery of Europe* (London, 1981) explains the context within which this process can be understood.

There are now two translations of relevant parts of the chronicles of al-Jabarti: Abd al-Rahman al-Jabarti, *Journal d'un notable du Caire durant l'expedition francaise*, trs. J. Cuoq (Paris, 1979); *Al-Jabarti's Chronicle of the First Seven Months of the French occupation of Egypt*, trs. from another version of the chronicle, S. Moreh (Leiden, 1975).

I should have said more about the expansion of European trade and the process by which the Middle East was drawn into the world-economy: R. Owen, *The Middle East in the World 1800–1914* (London, 1981); C. Issawi, *An Economic History of the Middle East and North Africa* (London, 1982).

On the growth of the two main centres of intellectual life: J. Abu Lughod, *Cairo: 1001 Years of the City Victorious* (Princeton, 1971); L. Fawaz, *Merchants and Migrants in Nineteenth Century Beirut* (Cambridge, Mass., 1983).

CHAPTER IV. THE FIRST GENERATION: TAHTAWI, KHAYR AL-DIN AND BUSTANI

On the Ottoman contemporaries: Berkes and Mardin, *supra*.

On al-'Attar, a precursor of Tahtawi: P. Gran, *Islamic Roots of Capitalism 1760–1840* (Austin, Texas, 1979); G. Delanoue, *Moralistes et politiques musulmans dans l'Egypte du XIXe siècle*, 2 vols. (Cairo, 1982).

On Tahtawi; Delanoue, *supra*; K. Husry, *Three Reformers* (Beirut, 1966); J. R. Cole, 'Rifa'a al-Tahtāwī and the Revival of Practical Philosophy', *The Muslim World*, 70 (1980), 29–46.

On Khayr al-Din: Abdesselem, *supra*; translation of *Aqwam al-Masālik*, L. C. Brown, *The Surest Path* (Cambridge, Mass., 1967).

On Bustani: A. L. Tibawi, 'The American Missionaries in Beirut and Butrus al-Bustani' in A. Hourani, ed., *Saint Antony's Papers 16: Middle Eastern Affairs*, 3 (London, 1963), pp. 137–82; B. Abu Manneh, 'The Christians between Ottomanism and Syrian Nationalism: the Ideas of Butrus al-Bustani', *International Journal of Middle East Studies*, 9 (1980), 287–304.

Unaccountably there is no reference in the book to another important figure of this generation, the Egyptian 'Ali Mubarak (1823–93); in particular, his *'Alam al-dīn*, 4 vols. (Alexandria, 1882). See Muhammad Amara, introduction to a new edition of Mubarak's work, *al-A'māl al-kāmila lī 'Alī Mubārak*, vol. 1 (Beirut, 1979), pp. 9–308; B. F. Musallam, 'The Modern Vision of 'Ali Mubarak' in R. B. Serjeant, ed., *The Islamic City* (Paris, 1980); W. al-Qadi, 'East and West in 'Ali Mubarak's

'Alamuddin' in M. Buheiry, ed., *Intellectual Life in the Arab East 1890–1939* (Beirut, 1981), pp. 21–37.

CHAPTER V. JAMAL AL-DIN AL-AFGHANI

All previous work has been superseded by N. R. Keddie, *Sayyid Jamāl ad-Dīn "al-Afghānī": a Political Biography* (Berkeley, 1972). Appendix I contains irrefutable evidence that Jamal al-Din was of Persian birth and Shi'i education. For another view of his beliefs and activities: E. Kedourie, *Afghani and 'Abduh: an Essay on Religious Unbelief and Political Activism in modern Islam* (London, 1966).

On the period of the Ottoman constitution and Sultan Abdülhamid, Berkes and Mardin, *supra*; R. E. Devereux, *The First Ottoman Constitutional Period* (Baltimore, 1963); B. Abu Manneh, 'Sultan Abdul-Hamid II and Shaikh Abulhuda al-Sayyadi', *Middle Eastern Studies*, 15 (1979), 131–53.

I can no longer maintain that there was so much difference between the ideas of Jamal al-Din and those of Sayyid Ahmad Khan, on whom see C. W. Troll, *Sayyid Ahmad Khan: a Reinterpretation of Muslim Theology* (New Delhi, 1978).

CHAPTER VI. MUHAMMAD 'ABDUH

There is now an English translation of *Risalat al-tawhīd*: *The Theology of Unity*, trs. I. Musa'ad and K. Cragg (London, 1966).

On 'Abduh's juridical thought: M. Kerr, *Islamic Reform: the Political and Legal Theories of Muhammad Abduh and Rashid Rida* (Berkeley, 1966).

CHAPTER VII. 'ABDUH'S EGYPTIAN DISCIPLES: ISLAM AND MODERN CIVILIZATION.

For the Egyptian background: A. Schölch, *Ägypten den Ägyptern!* (Zurich, 1972), Eng. trs. *Egypt for the Egyptians* (London, 1981): Afaf Lutfi al-Sayyid, *Egypt and Cromer* (London, 1968); J. Berque, *L'Egypte, impérialisme et révolution* (Paris, 1967), Eng. trs. by J. Stewart, *Egypt, Imperialism and Revolution* (London, 1972).

On Ahmad Lutfi al-Sayyid: C. Wendell, *The Evolution of the Egyptian National Image: from its Origins to Ahmad Lutfi al-Sayyid* (Berkeley, 1972).

On 'Abd al-Raziq: H. Enayat, *Modern Islamic Political Thought* (London, 1982).

CHAPTER VIII. EGYPTIAN NATIONALISM

For the background of political history: Berque, *supra*; A. Lutfi al-Sayyid-Marsot, *Egypt's Liberal Experiment 1922–1936* (Berkeley, 1977).

On 'Abd Allah Nadim: G. Delanoue, '*Abd Allah Nadim (1845–1896). Les idées politiques et morales d'un journaliste égyptien*', *Bulletin d'Etudes Orientales*, 17 (1961–2), 75–119.

On Sanu': I. L. Gendzier, *The Practical Visions of Ya'qub Sanu'* (Cambridge, Mass., 1966).

On Zaghlul and the Wafd: M. Anis, *Dirāsāt fī thawrat sanat 1919* (Cairo, 1963).

CHAPTER IX. RASHID RIDA

On Kurd 'Ali: S. Seikaly, 'Damascene Intellectual Life in the Opening Years of the Twentieth Century: Muhammad Kurd 'Ali and *al-Muqtabas*', in M. Buheiry, *supra*, pp. 125–53.

On Rida: Enayat, *supra*; Kerr, *supra*; A. Hourani, 'Sufism and Modern Islam: Rashid Rida' in *Emergence*, pp. 90–102.

CHAPTER X. CHRISTIAN SECULARISTS: SHUMAYYIL AND ANTUN

For the background: A. Hourani, 'The Middleman in a Changing Society: Syrians in Egypt in the Eighteenth and Nineteenth Centuries' in *Emergence*, pp. 103–23; H. Sharabi, *Arab Intellectuals and the West: the Formative Years 1875–1914* (Baltimore, 1970).

On Antun: D. M. Reid, *The Odyssey of Farah Antun: a Syrian Christian's Quest for Secularism* (Minneapolis, 1975).

On Zaydan: T. Philipp, *Gurgi Zaidan: His Life and Thought* (Beirut, (1979).

CHAPTER XI. ARAB NATIONALISM

For a reassessment of the basic historical work on the subject, that of George Antonius: A. Hourani, 'The Arab Awakening Forty Years After' in *Emergence*, pp. 193–215.

On the Islamic basis: Enayat, *supra*.

On Kawakibi: Husry, *supra*.

On the formative period, 1900–1920: C. E. Dawn, *From Ottomanism to Arabism: Essays on the Origins of Arab Nationalism* (Urbana, Ill., 1973); R. I. Khalidi, *British Policy towards Syria and Palestine 1906–1914* (London, 1980) and 'Arab Nationalism in Syria: the Formative Years' in W. W. Haddad and W. Ochsenwald, ed., *Nationalism in a Non-national State: the Dissolution of the Ottoman Empire* (Columbus, Ohio, 1977), pp. 207–37; F. Ahmad, *The Young Turks* (Oxford, 1969); P. Khoury, *Urban Notables and Arab Nationalism* (Cambridge, 1983); M. Khadduri, ''Aziz 'Ali al-Misri and the Arab Nationalist Movement' in A. Hourani, ed., *Saint Antony's Papers 17: Middle Eastern Affairs*, 4 (London, 1965), pp. 140–63.

On the Christian background: D. Hopwood, *The Russian Presence in Syria and Palestine 1843–1914: Church and Politics in the Near East* (Oxford, 1969).

On the development of Lebanon: J. P. Spagnolo, *France and Ottoman Lebanon 1861–1914* (London, 1977); M. Buheiry, 'Bulus Nujaym and the Grand Liban Idea 1908–1919' in Buheiry, *supra*, pp. 62–83.

On Azoury: S. Wild, 'Negib Azoury and his book *Le reveil de la nation arabe*' in Buheiry, *supra*, pp. 92–104; E. Kedourie, 'The Politics of Political Literature, Kawakibi, Azoury and Jung' in *Arabic Political Memoirs and Other Studies* (London, 1974), pp. 107–23.

On al-Husri: W. L. Cleveland, *The Making of an Arab Nationalist: Ottomanism and Arabism in the Life and Thought of Sati' al-Husri* (Princeton, 1971); W. Kazziha, 'Another Reading into al-Husari's Concept of Arab Nationalism' in Buheiry, *supra*, pp. 154–64. Al-Husri died in 1968; this chapter was written while he was still alive, hence certain uses of tenses.

CHAPTER XII: TAHA HUSAYN.

On Husayn Haykal: B. Johansen, *Muhammad Husain Haikal: Europe und der Orient im Weltbild eines ägyptischen Liberalen* (Wiesbaden, 1967).

On Salama Musa: I. I. Ibrahim, 'Salama Musa: an Essay on Cultural Alienation', *Middle Eastern Studies*, 15 (1979), 346–57; G. Contu, *Gli aspetti positivi e i limiti del laicismo in Salamah Musa 1887–1958* (Naples, 1980). English translation of his autobiography: *The Education of Salama Musa* (Leiden, 1961).

Taha Husayn died in 1973. This chapter was written while he was still alive, hence certain uses of tenses.

CHAPTER XIII. EPILOGUE: PAST AND FUTURE

No attempt is made here to deal with movements of thought after 1962 for their own sake, but some books published since then, or not noticed by me previously, give new interpretations of the period with which this book deals: A. Abdel-Malek, *Idéologie et renaissance nationale: l'Egypte moderne* (Paris, 1969); M. A. al-'Ālim and A. Anīs, *Fi'l-thaqāfa al-miṣriyya* (Beirut, 1955); L. 'Awaḍ, *Ta'rīkh al-fikr al-miṣri al-hadīth*, 2 vols. (Cairo, 1967–9), and *al-Mu'aththirāt al-ajnabiyya fi'l-adab al-'arabī al-ḥadīth*, 2 vols. (Cairo, 1963). J. Berque, *Les arabes d'hier a demain* (Paris, 1960), Eng. trs. by J. Stewart, *The Arabs, their History and Future* (London, 1964); H. Djait, *La Personnalité et le devenir arabo-islamiques* (Paris, 1974); A. Laroui, *L'Idéologie arabe contemporaine* (Paris, 1967), and *La Crise des intellectuels arabes* (Paris, 1974), Eng. trs. *The Crisis of the Arab Intellectual* (Berkeley, 1976); Z. N. Maḥmūd, *Tajdīd al-fikr al-'arabī* (Beirut, 1971).

On the Muslim Brothers: R. P. Mitchell, *The Society of the Muslim Brothers* (Oxford, 1969).

On the Ba'th Party: K. S. Abu Jabir, *The Arab Ba'th Socialist Party: History, Ideology and Organization* (Syracuse, N.Y., 1966).

I was mistaken to say nothing about the Egyptian works re-interpreting modern Egyptian history from a broadly Marxist point of view, p. 361; for example, R. Sa'īd, *Ta'rīkh al-ḥaraka al-ishtirākiyya fī miṣr 1900–1925* (Beirut, 1972) and *al-Asās al-ijtimā'ī li'l-thawra al-'urābiyya* (Cairo, 1966); S. A. al-Shāfi'ī, *Taṭawwur al-ḥaraka al-waṭaniyya al-miṣriyya 1882–1956* (Cairo, 1957). See also M. Rodinson, *Marxisme et monde musulman* (Paris, 1967).

On North Africa: J. Berque, *Le Maghreb entre deux guerres* (Paris, 1962), Eng. trs. by J. Stewart, *French North Africa: the Maghrib between Two World Wars* (London, 1967); A. Laroui, *Les origines sociales et culturelles du nationalisme marocain 1830–1912* (Paris, 1980); J. Abun-Nasr, 'The Salafiyya Movement in Morocco: the Religious Bases of the Moroccan Nationalist Movement' in A. Hourani, ed., *Saint Antony's Papers 16: Middle Eastern Affairs* 3 (London, 1963), pp. 90–105; A. Merad, *Le réformisme musulman en Algerie de 1925 à 1940* (Paris, 1967); J. C. Vatin, *L'Algérie politique: histoire et société* (Paris, 1974).

M. Lacheraf's essays are now collected in *L'Algérie, nation et société* (Paris, 1965).

I was wrong to say that most Tunisian leaders had been to the Lycée Carnot.

INDEX

Note.—As a general rule, persons are indexed under their last name, but it is impossible to be consistent in this. Cross-references are given where a doubt might arise.